INTERCULTURAL EUROPE

INTERCULTURAL EUROPE

Diversity and social policy

Edited by

Jagdish Gundara
Institute of Education, University of London

and

Sidney Jacobs
University of Plymouth

Aldershot • Burlington USA • Singapore • Sydney

Published by
Ashgate Publishing Ltd
Gower House
Croft Road
Aldershot
Hants GU11 3HR
England

Ashgate Publishing Company
131 Main Street
Burlington
Vermont 05401
USA

Ashgate website: http://www.ashgate.com

British Library Cataloguing in Publication Data
Intercultural Europe : diversity and social policy
1. Social work with minorities 2. Minorities – Europe – Social conditions 3. Europe – Social policy
I. Gundara, Jagdish II. Jacobs, Sidney
361.9'4

Library of Congress Cataloging-in-Publication Data
Intercultural Europe : diversity and social policy / edited by Jagdish Gundara and Sidney Jacobs.
p. cm.
Includes bibliographical references and index.
ISBN 1–85742–346–1
1. Europe–Social policy. 2. Pluralism (Social sciences)–Europe.
3. Ethnicity–Europe. 4. Intercultural communication–Europe.
5. Multicultural education–Europe. I. Gundara, Jagdish S.
II. Jacobs, Sidney, 1942–
HN373.5.I49 2000
305.8'0094–dc21 99–41123
CIP

ISBN 1 85742 346 1

Typeset by Manton Typesetters, Louth, Lincolnshire, UK.

Printed in Great Britain by
Antony Rowe Ltd, Chippenham, Wiltshire

Contents

List of Contributors

Giovanna Campani, Professor of Intercultural Education, University of Florence.

Roy Carr-Hill, Research Professor, Institute of Education, University of London, and Reader in Medical Statistics, University of York.

Mary Coussey, Senior Associate, Judge Institute of Management Studies, University of Cambridge.

Thalia Dragonas, Professor, Department of Pre-school Education, University of Athens.

Phillip Drummond, Lecturer in Education, Institute of Education, University of London.

Mari Fitzduff, Professor, University of Ulster and Director, Initiative on Conflict Resolution and Ethnicity.

Anna Frangoudaki, Professor of the Sociology of Education, Department of Pre-school Education, University of Athens.

Beth Ginsburg was a research associate attached to the Migrant Policy Group, Brussels, Belgium (when the article was written).

Jagdish Gundara, Reader in Education and Head, International Centre for Intercultural Studies, Institute of Education, University of London.

Peo Hansen, Research Fellow, Department of Political Science, University of Umeä, Sweden.

Roger Hewitt, Senior Research Fellow, Centre for Urban and Community Research, Goldsmiths' College, University of London.

Paul Iganski, Senior Lecturer in Social Policy, University of Sussex.

Sidney Jacobs, Senior Lecturer in Social Policy, University of Plymouth.

Crispin Jones, Senior Lecturer in Education, Institute of Education, University of London.

John Rex, Professor Emeritus, University of Warwick.

Carl-Ulrik Schierup, Professor of Ethnic Studies and Director of The Centre for Studies on Migration, Ethnic Relations and Globalisation (MERGE), University of Umeä, Sweden.

Ranjit Sondhi, Senior Lecturer, Community and Youth Work, Westhill College of Higher Education, Birmingham.

John Wrench, Senior Researcher, Danish Centre for Migration and Ethnic Studies, Esbjerg, The University of Southern Denmark.

Acknowledgements

We are most grateful to the editors at Ashgate Publishing for their continuous support and encouragement. The Institute of Education, University of London and the Department of Social Policy and Social Work, University of Plymouth, generously provided us with the opportunity, space and resources to undertake this work. Also, we wish to thank our colleagues at both institutions, too numerous to mention, whose interest and intellectual stimulation was a continuous source of inspiration. Sidney Jacobs also records his thanks to Mary Reeves for her continued support and love throughout the editing of this book.

It is of course the effort, energy and scholarship of our contributors who made it all possible and to all of them our most heartfelt thanks.

List of Tables

1 Introduction: Cultural Diversity and Social Policy

Sidney Jacobs and Jagdish Gundara

Cultural diversity

The politico-ethnic map of Europe was drastically altered after 1918 following the defeat of Imperial Germany, the dismantling of the Hapsburg and Ottoman Empires, and the fall of Czarist Russia to the Bolsheviks. Informed by the Wilsonian vision of national self-determination for the people of Europe, the peace settlements reached after the First World War succeeded in reducing numbers within national minorities to roughly 30 million compared to about 60 million in 1914. In the process, the proportion of minority nationalities in the total population of the countries of eastern and central Europe declined from 50 to 25 per cent (Sharp 1996:25). While the political restructuring of Europe was imposed upon the defeated nations, 'even the victors were not immune to the pace of change'; for example, 'Britain had to concede virtual independence to Ireland and to a partition of the island which rested to a considerable extent on the notion of "self-determination"' (Dunn and Fraser 1996:2–3). Nevertheless, despite the efforts of the politicians and the determination of minorities to free themselves, very substantial populations still found themselves part of national minorities in the new Europe after the peace settlements had been signed and President Wilson and the others had returned home. The 'national question' was, in other words, only partially resolved with consequences that have reverberated through Europe ever since.

While Woodrow Wilson proclaimed that 'every people should be left free to determine its own polity, its own way of development, unhindered, unthreatened, unafraid, the little along with the great and powerful' (in Sharp 1996:11), in practice self-determination proved extremely complex and difficult to implement. It was a victors' peace and abstract principles of freedom were certainly not allowed to overshadow their perceived self-interests. Steadfastly clinging to their own empires, the victorious powers proceeded to divide Germany's overseas possessions and Turkey's Middle Eastern provinces, the spoils of war, among themselves. The principles of self-determination were, of course, never intended to apply to Europe's colonies overseas. Britain, for instance, made that abundantly clear when deciding 'not to allow any black troops to take part in London's victory celebrations: the much trumpeted Peace march of 19 July 1919' (Fryer 1984:315). Indeed, it was only announced in February 1999 that commemorative gates were to be erected for 'the millions of soldiers from the Indian sub-continent, Africa and the Caribbean who fought for the British Empire in two world wars'. Apart from a Gurkha statue, there is no other memorial in London to these troops (*The Daily Telegraph*, 25 February 1999).

Among Europe's national minorities, an estimated 13 million Germans were left outside the borders of Germany after the First World War. Their exclusion provided the sparks that were once again to set the fires of war alight in Europe. The incorporation of all ethnic Germans within the borders of an enlarged Third Reich was a central plank of the Nazi project. German expansionism proved enormously popular both within the country and among the minority German populations outside, creating momentum for the invasion of Poland and war in Europe. The Nazis 'through their murder of six million Jewish men, women and children ... brought to a tragic end the immensely creative, millennial Ashkenazic culture of Central and East European Jewry' (Wistrich 1992:78). As that mostly Yiddish-speaking culture has been destroyed forever, the exact ethnic composition of pre-war Europe, in which Jews were an integral part, can never be recreated. The German occupation of Europe, particularly in the east, decimated, terrorized and dislocated entire civilian populations. In response to the brutality of that occupation, policies adopted in the aftermath of war, including the expulsion of the German-speaking communities of Sudetenland, Poland and elsewhere, ushered in the start of the Cold War. Thus, the Second World War produced far greater ethnic homogeneity in Europe than was achieved after 1918. It was to prove a relatively temporary state of affairs. While 'mass murder and mass expulsion ('repatriation') did indeed drastically simplify the ethnic map of Europe', as Hobsbawm (1993:157) observes, 'the movement of peoples has since restored the ethnic complexity which barbarism sought to eliminate.' Thus, since 1945, European ethnicity has been recast and is now more complex and diverse than ever before. It is estimated that no fewer than 30 million people migrated to western Europe between 1945 and the early 1970s, making it 'one of the greatest migratory movements in human history' (Castles et al. 1984:1).

They entered a Europe that was, and largely remains, obsessed by questions of 'race', religion and cultural diversity.

There are in the world 'several thousand cultural and ethnic groups' (Dunn and Fraser 1996:6). Most therefore occupy minority group status in their own countries. Further, as Hobsbawm points out:

> In a world in which probably not much more than a dozen states out of some 180 can plausibly claim that their citizens coincide in any real sense with a single ethnic or linguistic group, nationalism based on the establishment of such homogeneity is not only undesirable, but also largely self-destructive. (1993:186)

Nevertheless, extreme nationalism, in its various modern guises, is seemingly still intent on creating racially and ethnically 'pure' states, apparently oblivious to both the lessons of history and the impracticalities of the arithmetic, let alone the moral repugnance of their exclusivist agendas. While ethnic nationalism is now no longer the force it once was, it still retains some of its political appeal. Its undiminished capacity to generate hate and violence in Europe was all too clearly demonstrated in the mass killings, rape, torture and expulsion of ethnic minority populations which marked the disintegration of the former Yugoslavia.

Beth Ginsburg and Ranjit Sondhi in their contribution to this book (Chapter 16), offer an idealistic conception of social and cultural diversity which demands:

> ... recognition that everyone speaks from a particular place, out of a particular history, out of a particular experience, and a particular culture, without being strait-jacketed by the binary oppositions of black and white, male and female, gay and straight. We are all ethnically located, but exist in the knowledge that our boundaries are being constantly crossed and recrossed by the categories of race, gender, sexuality and class.

In reality, however, diversity is still far more likely to evoke rejection, intolerance and exclusion than, in any positive sense of the word, recognition. For example, Mari Fitzduff (Chapter 7), pointing to the extreme world of Northern Ireland, suggests that a 'pyramid-segmentary' structure was created 'in which different categories of a social, political, cultural and theological nature rarely cut across one another, and segregation in the North of Ireland became the norm'. In the wider European context, Jagdish Gundara (Chapter 3) observes, even the basic question of where Europe begins and ends is still contested. The question 'who is and who is not to be counted as European?' still arouses intense passions. At issue, it appears, are the European credentials of ethnic minority communities. It is not only those who have settled relatively recently in the postwar period whose rights to belong in Europe are constantly challenged. Long-established populations, like the Roma, who have lived in Europe for over five centuries or the Balkan Muslims, whether of Turkish origin or European converts to Islam, are still widely regarded as outsiders. The complexity of social diversity, Gundara argues, needs to be recognized but that 'ought not to start and end with immigrant groups and refugees'. Peo Hansen (Chapter 6), in his analysis of the identity politics pursued by the EU, suggests that it has adopted a 'highly selective version of European culture' which largely excludes ethnic minorities, identified as not belonging to the national community.

In his searching examination of the underlying theoretical and methodological assumption employed by both political sociology and cultural studies in the study of migrant communities in Europe, John Rex (Chapter 4) argues that these 'have to be understood in terms of three points of reference': 'orientation to the homeland', 'orientation towards the land of settlement' and 'orientation to onward migration'. The cultures of ethnic minority groups in Europe are clearly both complex and dynamic and need to be understood within the global context of changing economic, political and social processes. As Fulbrook and Cesarani write: 'the construction and politicization of boundaries between people, of inclusion or exclusion, are socially constructed, historically changing phenomena, rather than enduring, immutable entities' (1996:217). These points are well illustrated by Roger Hewitt (Chapter 12) in his discussion of youth culture in Europe. On the one hand, he identifies an 'inclusive movement' in which, for instance, 'new contexts have been provided for youth cultural activities in the realms of musical production and consumption, sports, art and video projects etc.' On the other hand, throughout Europe, young males are often heavily involved in racist incidents. 'Youth culture', he argues, 'is itself a politically malleable instrument' and therefore, 'struggles at the cultural level are particularly pertinent for the role of youth in the development of interculturalism in Europe'.

Phillip Drummond (Chapter 19) in his wide-ranging analysis of British cinema, captures the multi-layered complexities of interculturalism as represented on film. He concludes that intercultural relations are 'a pervasive and routine component of the cinema's everyday reworking of the social world'. Drummond brilliantly illustrates that 'the intercultural' within cinema, and that to be found in literature, theatre, popular culture and the arts in general, provides cultural studies with a richness and subtlety of analysis which brings the topic to life, attributes sometimes missing in the abstract theorizing and dry empiricism of the social sciences. On the other hand, John Rex (Chapter 4) feels that, as yet, cultural studies does not provide 'an adequate basis in itself for political sociology'.

Social policy

In his introduction, Sidney Jacobs (Chapter 2) stresses that racism in Europe needs to be analysed within its historical context, dating back, at least, to the Atlantic slave trade and the ages of imperialism and colonialism. Cognizance also needs to be taken of the rise of 'scientific racism' and racial anti-semitism in the late nineteenth century through to Nazism and its aftermath in the twentieth. Social Darwinists, increasingly politically important in Britain and elsewhere during the early period of the twentieth century, urged the state to abandon its commitment to *laissez-faire*, especially with regard to social policies. State welfare provision, it was argued, was necessary to ensure the survival of the existing social order. Social Darwinism was especially influential in legislation involving children and the family. There was growing anxiety within ruling political circles about declining birth-rates among their own class, combined with alarm at the prospect of population growth among the 'unfit', including most immigrants and ethnic minorities. Unless checked, the swelling numbers of those at the bottom of society, it was widely believed, threatened to overwhelm the nation. Women of all classes were blamed – the poor for failing as mothers and the rich for placing their own careers above motherhood. Middle-class women were 'castigated for entering careers or higher education rather than motherhood ... they were "shirking" their "racial" duty to breed, "sinning against nature". The invidious effects of feminism were often cited' (Bland 1995: 226). Almost a century later, in the 1970s, widely held beliefs about the supposed criminality of Afro-Caribbean youth in Britain were derived from assumptions about the inherent pathology of the black family, perceived as being largely matriarchal. In other words, black women, thought to perform poorly as mothers , were essentially blamed for the alleged misbehaviour of their sons (see CCCS 1982).

Europe's obvious reluctance to admit Turkey to full membership of the EU would appear to have less to do with concern about human rights abuses than with the politics of population, intertwined with general antipathy towards Islam. In other words, Europe seems rather more preoccupied with the fact that Turkish membership would add over 50 million Muslims to the EU's population than with either the shortcomings of Turkish democracy or the oppression of the Kurds. As Freedman writes, 'one of the factors keeping Turkey out of the European Community is the anxiety among existing members that Turkey's high birthrate would lead it to export its surplus population throughout the Community' (1991:288). Concern about Turkish population growth must be viewed within the contexts of both declining fertility in all EU countries and the fact that during the postwar period, as Mary Coussey (Chapter 5) observes, immigration has 'been essential to maintain the growth of population of the EU'. The fear of population growth among 'undesirable' ethnic groups apparently still haunts Europe in the late twentieth century. Eugenics, with the rest of scientific racism, was discredited after 1945 by its association with Nazism. Nevertheless, many of its ideas, even if now largely expressed in terms of 'cultural' differences rather than 'race', have clearly survived. It is within this context that Anna Frangoudaki and Thalia Dragonas (Chapter 10), argue that 'intercultural education can be a means of change if pupils understand that the notion of cultural purity, intrinsic in all discriminatory ideas, is based on an indirect claim for the elimination of differences.'

Although the modern welfare states created in Europe after 1945 were 'colour-blind' in that entitlement was not made conditional on either 'race', religion or ethnicity, the traditional link between nationality and eligibility for welfare benefits remained largely intact. In particular, during the early postwar years, when the rotation of migrant labour was (with the exception mainly of Britain) widely in use throughout western Europe, so-called 'guestworkers' were largely denied civil, political and social rights. Marxist analyses of the benefits derived by capitalism from the large-scale use of migrant labour tend to concentrate on both economic and political advantages. For example, savings in social costs derived from the importation of 'ready-made' workers who, without rights of settlement, were also effectively excluded from welfare state benefits, including social security, pensions, health, education and housing. Further, migrant workers were continually exposed to the threat of deportation for even relatively minor breaches of their conditions of entry, such as unemployment, temporary destitution and/or political activism disapproved of by the state. It meant that migrants, constituting a substantial proportion of the labour force, because of their vulnerability to deportation and state harassment, were essentially excluded from active participation in political and trade union organizations. That significantly weakened the collective strength of European labour movements (see, for example, Gorz 1970; Castells 1975). This situation has altered considerably since the late 1960s, particularly in the countries of northern Europe. Thus, John Wrench (Chapter 18) observes that within the EU, with the exceptions of Austria and Greece, trade unions 'are now generally happy to see migrants extended full rights of citizenship and to regard them as workers to be organized'.

An ever-increasing proportion of ethnic minority populations are now European-born and citizens of the countries in which they live and work. Even where the 'guestworker' system previously dominated and where, even now in the late 1990s, most third-country nationals are still denied citizenship, as in Germany, immigrant workers and their offspring have generally been granted full rights of residency and work. However, as Wrench notes, ethnic minority workers, even when in possession of citizenship rights, are still 'likely to suffer disadvantage' as a consequence of racial discrimination. He points out that ethnic minority workers who enjoy formal rights are likely to be 'in competition in the labour market with white workers'. On the other hand, temporary migrant workers with minimal rights together with undocumented or illegal workers 'are unlikely to be competing with white nationals in the same labour market'. Under these circumstances, Wrench writes that 'it is difficult to separate out the effects of "racism" from the straightforward exploitation of a relatively powerless group of workers'. It is in the countries of southern Europe where the problems associated with illegal migrant labour markets are now mostly located. In Italy, Giovanna Campani (Chapter 9) observes that the segmentation of the labour market 'explains the apparent contradiction existing between the active presence of immigrants and high unemployment in Italy'. The native unemployed, she suggests, are not interested in working in peripheral labour markets where the workforce is predominantly migrant.

Carl-Ulrik Schierup, in his discussion of the poverty debate in Europe and the United States (Chapter 8), observes that an essential difference between left and right-wing analyses of poverty is that whereas the former identifies ethnic minority exclusion from the welfare state as the key problem, New Right discourse tends to assume the opposite. As Schierup notes, Charles Murray, in the application of his 'underclass' thesis to the British situation, singles out the 'excessive use of the welfare services' as the problem, leading to 'a pathological "culture of dependency"'. Murray identifies illegitimacy as a defining characteristic of the 'underclass', seen by him as a 'mainly a black problem' in the United States (1990:9). In Britain, while quoting data showing that 48 per cent of live births among West Indians are illegitimate, he is unable to pin the blame for the 'underclass' on the black community because of its relatively small size. Clearly, Murray blames, in traditional fashion, the poor, especially the women among them, for their own poverty.

Schierup's perceptive analysis raises the question of whether or not the 'Americanization' of poverty in Europe is likely to occur in the near future. In particular, he poses the possibility of urban areas, with high ethnic minority concentrations, being transformed into ghettos on the American model. He suggests not, concluding that '"underclass" as applied within the American context ... does not directly apply to the conditions prevailing among disadvantaged urban populations in Europe'. However, it is primarily the survival of its welfare states, he argues, which stands between Europe and the importation of American-type ghettos from across the Atlantic. It appears that Schierup, rightly in our view, places social policy at the centre of the intercultural debate in the context of a multicultural Europe.

Sidney Jacobs (Chapter 15) argues that racism is clearly identifiable as a cause of poor housing among ethnic minorities. Housing authorities throughout Europe, whether in the private or public sectors, tend to define 'race', rather than either racism or poor housing, as the problem. Jacobs, confirming Schierup's conclusions, suggests that ethnic minority concentrations, invariably found in areas of poor-quality housing in virtually all the major towns and cities of western Europe, do not as yet resemble American-type black ghettos, neither in terms of scale, nor ethnic homogeneity nor degree of deprivation. The use of 'ghetto' within a modern European context thus appears highly misleading, serving merely to stigmatize ethnic minorities. Moreover, as Coussey (Chapter 5) notes, 'immigrants brought much of value; they rehabilitated declining areas, imported new energies and businesses and invigorated cultural and social life.' In other words, ethnic minorities have often acted as a catalyst, revitalizing previously impoverished slum areas, particularly within inner cities. But as Coussey argues, 'one has to search for information which shows the positive contribution of immigrants and ethnic minorities.'

Roy Carr-Hill (Chapter 17), in his wide-ranging examination of health care, concludes that 'there are clear inescapable inequalities in both achieved health and access to health care' between indigenous and ethnic minority populations in Europe. However, in the health field, problems of definition and measurement are, he suggests, 'daunting'. There is not even agreement about 'what health is'. In any event, 'most of the epidemiological evidence presented is based on doubtful samples'. Nevertheless, 'the obvious culprit' causing differences between groups in society, Carr-Hill observes, is 'poverty and – in the New Europe – social exclusion'. The centrality of poverty to the study of interculturalism in Europe is also stressed by a number of the other contributors to this book. For example, Jagdish Gundara and Crispin Jones (Chapter 11) suggest that poverty is 'the greatest impediment to learning the minority communities face'. In their discussion of issues involved in education and older migrants, both racism and ageism are examined. The authors observe that, compared to men, there are 'even graver problems confronting older, isolated women and/or illiterate women because they are triply jeopardized, due to the gender discrimination that is endemic in society'. Giovanna Campani (Chapter 14) points out that by the early 1990s, of the almost 13 million migrant workers in Europe, roughly half were women. She suggests that women migrants increasingly 'find themselves confined in traditional female jobs, particularly domestic work and the sex industry, where super-exploitation is normal'. In the process, migrant women workers are frequently rendered invisible. For example, as John Wrench (Chapter 18) notes, among trade unions even those 'with good records of organizing migrant workers have been guilty of neglecting the issues of migrant women'. In educational terms, Frangoudaki and Dragonas (Chapter 10) argue that 'gender discrimination has a particular importance for intercultural education', noting that it 'is closely related to the traditional conception of nations, since all national ideologies are fundamentally sexist'. Hansen (Chapter 6) suggests that educational policies developed within the EU, take 'on the role of passing on an official and highly selective version of European culture'. He adds that:

> ... an education policy promoting an identity defined in such frozen and narrow cultural terms, therefore, excludes the great number of EU inhabitants who do not meet these implied ethno-cultural requirements, and risks giving further credence to the exclusionary processes already in place in the member states.

Expansion of the European Union

The fall of the Berlin Wall in 1989 and the subsequent collapse of communism reopened borders closed for four decades by the Cold War. With the disintegration of the Iron Curtain the traditional movement of peoples from East to West resumed on a massive scale. Although previously urging flight from communism, western European governments, alarmed by the numbers flooding in, almost immediately tried to stem the tide by reintroducing border controls. Indeed, the flow of 'east Europeans attempting to escape the economic rubble of communism' has been described as 'the modern version of the Mongol hordes' (Cesarani and Fulbrook 1996:3). However, border controls are soon to be dismantled again and moved eastwards in 2002/3 when the Czech Republic, Estonia, Hungary, Poland and Slovenia, together with Cyprus, are expected to join the EU. A second wave, including Turkey, Malta, Russia and the rest of eastern Europe, will have their applications for membership considered after 2010. This would leave Iceland, Norway and Switzerland, unless these reconsider, together with Albania and the remaining states of the former Yugoslavia, as the only European countries outside of the EU.

As the West draws her impoverished eastern cousins into the embrace of her very ample bosom, the gross economic inequalities existing between the old and new member states is bound to become increasingly problematic. Even now, as the 15 member states move towards ever greater monetary and political union, the EU already appears endlessly diverse and immensely complex. Uneven development between and within its existing regions is clearly apparent, in terms of wealth, poverty, levels of investment, industrialization, technology, taxation, employment rates, welfare and social policies, and, not least of all, equal opportunities for women, ethnic minorities and others. Citizenship rights within the EU are still to be harmonized, leading to policy anomalies and contradictions between member states. When the EU rapidly expands eastwards, the poverty and relative economic backwardness of the former communist states will contrast sharply with the affluence of the West, even compared to its poorer regions. As the *Guardian* newspaper reports, in terms of GDP, the average EU citizen's annual wage is £13,000. In comparison, in Poland the average is barely a third of that amount while the Romanians and Bulgarians, in the second wave of applicants, are less than half as well off as the Poles. It is estimated that enlargement in 2002/3 will 'increase the EU's population by 17 per cent but add only 3 per cent to the club's GDP' (*Guardian*, 25 November 1998). The implications are likely to be as much social and political as economic and the EU needs to give priority to all three aspects rather than, as hitherto, to the economic alone. This book attempts to address some of these issues.

As the citizens of the new member states acquire freedom of movement throughout the EU as a right of membership, there is every reason to anticipate that large-scale migration westwards will resume. The traditional regional role occupied by much of middle Europe, of being both a melting pot and continental crossroads, interrupted during the Nazi and Communist years, is already beginning to re-emerge. But the flow of immigrants from the former Warsaw Pact countries will carry with them ideological baggage, the contents of which include sexism and intolerance of minorities combined with little direct experience of democratic institutions. Despite claims to egalitarianism and internationalism, the old communist regimes were essentially closed, dogmatic and totalitarian, presiding over highly elitist, patriarchal, xenophobic and racist societies. Their collapse appears to have revived ethnic nationalism and, with it, the old hatreds of the past which although previously present had been largely kept under control by the communists. Their reappearance has led, for example, to the breakup of Czechoslovakia, growing discrimination against Russians in Latvia and elsewhere, and anti-Semitism which has seemingly re-emerged everywhere even though, with the exception of Hungary, no Jewish community of any significant size survived the German occupation of central and eastern Europe. In Russia, despite the virulent anti-Semitism of extreme right-wing groups like Pamiat, Klier argues that it is not the Jews but 'the diasporas of Caucasian peoples ... targeted as the "exploiters of the Russian people"', who appear most vulnerable to 'ethnic murders or pogroms' (1993:137).

Mary Coussey (Chapter 5) suggests that, for aspirant members of the EU, 'their human rights record is one relevant criterion for acceptance.' In this respect she detects some signs of progress, pointing to the examples of Hungary and Bulgaria where measures have been variously taken to improve the living conditions and employment prospects of the Roma. However, there appear to be alarming increases in violence and racist hostility towards the Roma and Sinti who, invariably occupying the very bottom segments of society, are massively discriminated against throughout Europe, East and West. Evans, for instance, reports that neo-Nazis in Germany liken Romani refugees 'to a "dirty plague" contaminating German society' (1996:44). In the Czech Republic, Romanies discriminated against in employment, also suffer social segregation'. As a consequence, Jarabov'a (1998:92) suggests that 'the outlook for the future is not very promising'. Similarly, in Romania, Aluas and Matei note that:

> Gypsies' access to education, the labour market, social services and other facilities is sometimes more difficult than for the average citizen because of the rejection they suffer. Town hall officials, medical nurses or school masters might refuse to deal with Gypsies simply because of their ethnic membership. (1998:107)

As these authors further report, Gypsy villages were burnt down while 'local police officers looked on passively and did not intervene to protect them' (p.107). Indeed, Reemtsma notes that when the houses of Roma were burned down in one village, 'the mayor and the priest were actively involved in the attacks' (1993:196).

Given the very serious persecution and poverty suffered by the Roma throughout eastern Europe, it is likely that large numbers are poised to move westwards as the EU expands. They are very unlikely to be welcomed in the West where intense political agitation, aimed at reducing the numbers of refugees and asylum seekers allowed in, is already focused on the Roma, among other 'undesirables'. For instance, the German-Romanian Agreement of 1992, largely targeted on Roma, allows for the easy deportation of illegal immigrants by denying them the right to claim political asylum. It has led, Reemstra suggests, 'to the creation of a category "Gypsy" perceived as below the general category of asylum seekers who so far had been at the bottom of the "ethnic hierarchy"' (1993:202).

Paul Iganski (Chapter 13) notes that in the study of racist violence research tends largely to focus on postwar immigrant communities while neglecting 'historically victimized groups'. In particular, he singles out the plight of the Gypsies, enmity against whom has resurfaced 'with a new virulence'. Roger Hewitt (Chapter 12), observes that, when tolerated by society, even relatively minor expressions of racism could potentially have serious consequences. Thus, vandalism, graffiti and name-calling establish 'a pattern of intimidation' which, he argues, is 'linked through fear to the more dramatic acts of violence and assault'. It creates the conditions, he suggests, 'for the daily misery and anxiety that many thousands of black and minority ethnic families endure ... all across Europe'. The difficulties faced by society in legally confronting racism are examined by Iganski in his closely argued chapter. He extends his analysis beyond the usual description of racist violence to analyse some of the key legal and philosophical issues involved in legislating against racist violence. In exploring the debate surrounding proposals to outlaw 'racially motivated' violence, incitement to racial hatred and Holocaust denial, he identifies 'a fundamental conflict between the right to freedom from hatred on the basis of "racial", ethnic, or religious identity and the right to freedom of expression'.

Many of the contributors to this book look to the EU to promote interculturalism actively, both at the level of individual member states and through its own institutions. Thus, for example, Gundara and Jones (Chapter 11) call upon both the EU and the Council of Europe to 'work towards a Charter of Rights for Older People in a European intercultural context'. However, the message emanating from the EU is at best contradictory, varying from the positive, through the politics of procrastination and omission, to the actually negative. Thus, Coussey (Chapter 5) points to both the 1997 European Year against Racism and the inclusion of a general non-discrimination clause in Article 13 of the Treaty of Amsterdam as two examples of measures adopted 'to improve the position of immigrants and people from ethnic minorities'. On the other hand, in terms of its identity politics, Hansen (Chapter 6) argues that the EU, 'instead of creating legitimacy and popular support for the EU project, ... runs the risk of widening even further the several roads to ethnic, political and social exclusion already paved in the member states'. It would seem mistaken to rely entirely on 'reform from above' rather than also building on the organizational strengths, both actual and potential, of ethnic minorities themselves. Thus, Campani (Chapter 9) stresses the significance of their 'local networks of protection and solidarity'. Similarly, Rex (Chapter 4) points to the example of Punjabi communities in Britain who 'are in part organized by political parties such as the Communist Parties of India which have already been engaged in class struggle at home and which now must adapt their tactics to the fight for justice in the land of settlement'. However, the onus must primarily be on the EU, together with member states, to act decisively. As Fitzduff (Chapter 7) concludes, 'the salient lesson' to be learnt from the years of bitter conflict in Northern Ireland is that 'there is a need for those responsible for public policy to be much more aware of the murmurings of those who are feeling left out on the sidelines of society, and to be much braver in addressing issues of equality, pluralism and inclusion'. She goes on to add that 'it appears particularly important that such responses should happen long before the murmurings turn into hostility and alienation that may eventually take many years to control, and be very costly for both people and government alike.'

References

Aluas, I. and Matei, F. (1998), 'Discrimination and Prejudice: Minorities in Romania', in Jolly, D. (ed.), *Scapegoats and Social Actors: The Exclusion and Integration of Minorities in Western and Eastern Europe*, London: Macmillan.

Bland, L. (1995), *Banishing the Beast: English Feminism & Sexual Morality 1885–1914*, Harmondsworth: Penguin.

Castells, M. (1975), 'Immigrant Workers and Class Struggle in Advanced Capitalist Societies: The Western European Experience', *Politics & Society*, 5(1).

Castles, S. with Booth, H. and Wallace, T. (1984), *Here for Good: Western Europe's New Ethnic Minorities*, London: Pluto.

CCCS Race and Politics Group (1982), *The Empire Strikes Back: Race and Racism in 70s Britain*, London: Hutchinson.

Cesarani, D. and Fulbrook, M. (1996), 'Introduction', in Cesarani, D. and Fulbrook, M. (eds), *Citizenship, Nationality and Migration in Europe*, London: Routledge.

Dunn, S. and Fraser, T.G. (1996), 'Introduction', in Dunn, S. and Fraser, T.G. (eds), *Europe and Ethnicity*, London: Routledge.

Evans, M. (1996), 'Languages of Racism within Contemporary Europe', in Jenkins, B. and Sofos, S.A. (eds), *Nation & Identity in Contemporary Europe*, London: Routledge.

Fryer, P. (1984), *Staying Power: The History of Black People in Britain*, London: Pluto.

Freedman, L. (1991), 'Conclusion', in Freedman, C. and Saunders, J. (eds), *Population Change and European Security*, London: Brassey's.

Fulbrook, M. and Cesarani, D. (1996), 'Conclusion', in Cesarani, D. and Fulbrook, M. (eds), *Citizenship, Nationality and Migration in Europe*, London: Routledge.

Gorz, A. (1970), 'Immigrant Labour', *New Left Review*, 61.

Hobsbawm, E.J. (1993), *Nations and Nationalism since 1780*, Cambridge: Cambridge University Press.

Jarabov'a, Z. (1998), 'The Romany Minority in the Czech Lands', in Jolly, D. (ed.), *Scapegoats and Social Actors: The Exclusion and Integration of Minorities in Western and Eastern Europe*, London: Macmillan.

Klier, J.D. (1993), 'The Pogrom Tradition in Eastern Europe', in Bjorgo, T. and Witte, R. (eds), *Racist Violence in Europe*, London: Macmillan.

Murray, C. (1990), 'Underclass', in Murray, C. et al. (eds), *The Emerging British Underclass*, London: IEA Health & Welfare Unit.

Reemstra, K. (1993), 'Between Freedom and Persecution: Roma in Romania', in Bjorgo, T. and Witte, R. (eds), *Racist Violence in Europe*, London: Macmillan.

Sharp, A. (1996), 'The Genie that would not go back into the Bottle: National Self-Determination and the Legacy of the First World War and the Peace Settlement', in Dunn, S. and Fraser, T.G. (eds), *Europe and Ethnicity*, London: Routledge.

Wistrich, R.S. (1992), *Anti-Semitism: The Longest Hatred*, London: Thames Mandarin.

2 Race, Racism and Social Policy in Europe: An Historical Introduction

Sidney Jacobs

Introduction

By the end of the nineteenth century, the European powers had carved up most of the world between them. Through conquest and the subjugation of native peoples, and the expropriation of their lands,wealth and labour, vast empires were created. Imperialism, Europeans felt, involved them in a civilizing mission to the rest of humanity. Its purpose was to bestow trade and commerce, law and order and Christianity on a world which they saw as essentially chaotic, primitive and barbarous. It was inhabited, they firmly believed, by persons of inferior racial stock. Europe's growing obsession with questions of race marked virtually all aspects of nineteenth-century life and culture. In the process, white men became convinced of their superiority, not only in relation to colonial populations outside but also to Europe's indigenous religious, linguistic and ethnic minorities. They also held very similar views about women and their own working classes. Indeed, race, gender and class became intertwined within racial theories designed to sustain existing power relations between capital and labour, men and women and the 'races' hierarchically ordered. These ideas, found at the very heart of high politics, crucially influenced the development of the social policy of the period.

In a profusion of widely influential treatises published during the late nineteenth and early twentieth centuries, race and racism were assumed to be scientific concepts. These works tended to extol the virtues of racial purity while warning of the dire consequences that awaited even powerful nations careless or misguided enough to tolerate miscegenation. Non-Europeans were generally thought to belong to inferior races, among whom black Africans were usually regarded as the most inferior, even sub-human. These ideas were reflected, at times with the utmost brutality, in the administration of empire. Similarly, minorities within Europe were variously thought to be inferior, troublesome and threatening: Czarist Russia's 'Asiatic hordes', 'the Turk', the Irish, the Roma, a miscellany of Slavs and, above all, Jews.

The racism derived from Europe's overseas ventures could not but interact with long-established, home-grown traditions of intolerance and persecution. As Kiernan writes, the treatment of 'subject minorities was not always gentler than in colonies outside, and must have been roughened by the habits formed by Europe's ruling classes in dictating to other continents' (1969:28). The historic roots of internal and externally derived racism, although distinct with clearly differing ideological, political and economic determinants, also frequently intersect and overlap. However, studies of anti-Black racism and anti-Semitism, for example, tend barely to acknowledge the existence of the other, let alone their commonalities. Miles notes that both the colonial and the labour migration paradigms of racism explain neither 'certain contemporary expressions of racism in Europe' nor all their 'historical modalities' (1993:44). This is demonstrated, he suggests, 'by the silence' within these analyses on the issue of anti-Semitism. And yet, virulent anti-Semitism, endemic to most of pre-war Europe, persisted long after 1945 and has since re-emerged in various forms. For example, 'anti-Semitism without Jews', found in nineteenth-century Basque nationalism, reappeared throughout postwar Europe, particularly in Poland, Germany and Austria. While racism is, of course, always historically specific, its modern development during the late nineteenth century, as variously manifested in antipathy towards both colonial peoples and Jews, among others, was commonly nurtured by that exclusive 'one race, one nation' nationalism which characterized right-wing politics of the day. During the nineteenth century, Hobsbawm observes, it was fashionable to use both race and nation 'as virtual synonyms, generalizing equally wildly about "racial"/ "national" character' (1993:108). In the same period, with the rise of racial anti-Semitism in Germany, Goldhagen argues, 'it became impossible to discuss the German *Volk* without conjuring up notions of race, and hence of Jewish exclusion from Germany' (1996:68). The Right has ever since tended to identify nation with race. In contrast to the Left's traditional commitment, rhetorically at least, to internationalism, narrow right-wing nationalism is both emotive and uncomplicated and apparently timeless in its appeal to wide cross-sections of the population, particularly in times of crisis and upheaval.

The essential point argued in this chapter is the simple one that racism in contemporary Europe needs to be analysed within its full historical context dating back, at least, to the Atlantic slave trade, through the ages of imperialism and colonialism, to Nazism and the Holocaust. It also needs to be stressed that while it is possible to arrive at broad generalizations about racism in Europe, it is highly unlikely that a 'European racism' exists distinct from that which is historically specific to each nation state. Furthermore, the discussion here largely focuses on Britain, France and Germany rather than on Europe as a whole. The primary purpose is to attempt to link historically race to class and gender, and all three to the development of social policy during the nineteenth century through to the creation of the modern welfare state in Europe after 1945. The underlying principles of social welfare, it is suggested, incorporate many traditional assumptions about race which originated in earlier periods. In these terms, postwar immigrants to Europe entered an intensely hostile white world in which 'it was their labour that was wanted not their presence' (Sivanandan 1981/2:112). The supposed universalism of welfare state provision was never meant to include the welfare needs of immigrant/migrant workers and their families and in practice, particularly during the early postwar years, rarely ever did.

Slavery, imperialism and colonialism

Industrialization and the rise of capitalism in Britain during the late eighteenth and early nineteenth centuries owes a considerable debt to British involvement and subsequent domination of the Atlantic slave trade. 'By the early 1780s', Hobsbawm notes, 'more than half of all slaves exported from Africa made profits for British slavers' (1969:54). Figures cited by Fryer show that as a result of the slave trade, between 1445 and 1870, 'Africa lost altogether 40–50 million of its population' (1989:9). The number of slaves imported to the Americas from Africa from the late fifteenth century to the 1870s is generally estimated to total between 11 and 13 million. (see, for example, Thomas 1997:805.) This proved catastrophic for Africa but so very lucrative for Europe, particularly Britain and, to a lesser extent, France and the other slave trading nations. (While the diverse consequences for Africa of the Atlantic slave trade are hotly disputed by historians, a discussion of the issues raised in this debate is beyond the scope of this chapter.) The triangular trade in slaves, raw materials and manufactured goods between Europe, Africa and the Americas generated much of the commerce and capital necessary for industrial 'take-off'. As Williams observes, 'the West Indian islands became the hub of the British Empire, of immense importance to the grandeur and prosperity of England' (1967:52). Slavery, if not the actual or only midwife, was certainly most prominently present at the birth of capitalism. In terms of racism, the enormity of the enterprise, built on seemingly insatiable greed and sustained for so long by remorseless brutality, necessarily required that Europeans humiliate, demonize and dehumanize Africans. It is psychologically impossible to enslave people, Fanon observes, 'without logically making them inferior through and through' (1967:40). Together with the Caribbean, British rule in India proved extremely profitable. Between 1757 and 1815, 'Britain's loot from India was worth between £500 million and £1,000 million' and it was this, Fryer suggests, that 'furnished the second of those "special forced draughts" which were needed to ignite Britain's industrial revolution' (1989:20). The consequences for India were also catastrophic. As Fryer concludes, 'under British imperial rule the ordinary people of India grew steadily poorer' (1989:23). For instance, he quotes official figures which show that between 1854 and 1901 almost 29 million Indians starved to death.

During the nineteenth century, living and work conditions for Europe's peasantry and emerging working classes, whether in the slums of London, Glasgow, Paris or Berlin, were appalling, often little better than that existing in the colonies. In addition, until 1918, a large proportion of Europeans, as Kiernan notes, 'occupied a more or less colonial status' (1969:28). Both the Czarist and Hapsburg Empires were, of course, multinational and multicultural. Kiernan writes that 'Czechs, Serbs, and so on' were regarded, by both Austrians and Hungarians, as 'barbarians' (1969:28). Burleigh and Wippermann suggest that 'the alleged cultural superiority of the Germans was used to legitimise German rule over former West Slav and Polish territories' (1991:25). As these authors further add, 'the "German drive to the east" ... gradually assumed quasi-biological aspects' (p.26). In Ireland almost a million people starved to death in the Famine of 1846–47 which, relative to size of population, Hobsbawm points out, was 'the greatest human catastrophe of the nineteenth century anywhere in the world' (1969:93). Lord Salisbury, the Conservative leader 'supporting coercion in Ireland, said that Irishmen were as unfit for self-government as Hottentots' (Kiernan 1969:28). The 'ugliest features' of colonial rule, Kaye writes, 'were not restricted to Europeans' overseas endeavours. The racism and violence of imperialism and colonialism "recoiled" and "barbarized" European life as well' (1995:18). Thus, for example, Clayton reports that, in 1845, the French Army under Marshall Bugeaud in Algeria corralled almost a thousand people in caves of whom over half were asphyxiated (1988:21). In Paris in 1848, after the defeat of the insurrection,

> ... the bloody three-day repression that followed was a replica of the Algerian campaigns of Bugeaud ... the insurgents were coralled into eastern Paris, their

> barricades broken down by troops with North African experience and North African brutality ... little quarter was given and several thousand prisoners perished. (Clayton 1988:22).

Again in May 1871, the repression of the Paris Commune by Marshal MacMahon who was 'quintessentially an *Armée d'Afrique* general' largely repeated the events of 1848: 'the fighting was marked by especial ferocity and brutality, at least 20,000 being killed' (p.23).

Within all the European empires, rebellions were commonly suppressed with exemplary ferocity lest other subject peoples should be tempted to question imperial authority. Thus, Wilson suggests that British Conservatives opposed Home Rule for Ireland because, it was believed that it 'would lead to the break-up of empire, encouraging nationalist revolts elsewhere in more prized possessions, most especially India' (1985:155). Following the Indian Mutiny of 1857–58, the British, Fryer writes, 'took a ferocious and terrible revenge. Many thousands of unarmed Indians, including faithful domestic servants, were indiscriminately butchered, regardless of sex or age' (1989:109). Similarly, Jamaica's 1865 rebellion was 'bloodily repressed' by Governor Eyre (pp.99–100). Within the French Empire, the crushing of the Kanak rebellion in New Caledonia in 1878 left 1,200 of them dead compared to 200 whites (McPhee 1992:270). In the 1920s, the Druze uprising in Syria was 'put down with considerable severity' which included, 'a cash bounty for each Druze head brought in to French headquarters' (Clayton 1988:112). In Namibia in 1904, the Herero people took up arms against German occupation and were savagely suppressed. As Davidson comments:

> ... few colonial wars have deserved the name genocide: this one does. General von Trotha drove the surviving Herero regiments and their women and children, the remnants of a whole people, deliberately into the waterless sands of the Omaheke. Only a tiny number survived. (1973:277–8)

In the Congo, the atrocities committed by the forces assembled by King Leopold were, Kiernan writes, 'of a sort and on a scale not seen again in the world until the Nazi epoch' (1969:226). The Belgium Government assumed responsibility for the Congo in 1908 but continued to treat Africans 'as a race of juvenile criminals' (p.208).

In Tasmania the entire black population was wiped out: 'men and boys were castrated and otherwise mutilated; women were raped, flogged and burnt with brands; children's brains were dashed out' (Fryer 1989:38). After visiting Tasmania in 1836, the Revd Thomas Atkins concluded that 'savage tribes disappear before the progress of civilized races', in accordance with 'a universal law in the Divine government' (Kiernan 1995:110). By the late nineteenth century, mass murder was no longer explained and justified by appeals to Divine intervention but by the 'laws' of Nature. Thus, Kiernan writes, 'tacit agreement was spreading in Europe ... that primitive races were bound to be displaced, even to die out' (1969:268). Whatever Europe achieved during the 'age of imperialism', and clearly much was done that was to prove of lasting benefit, most subject people paid a terrible price. Within Europe's overseas empires, largely imposed by force of arms and built upon assumptions of their own racial superiority, Europeans were able to justify, to themselves at least, the most savage and relentless oppression, exploitation, and mass murder even, of supposed 'lesser breeds'. It produced a cultural climate of racial arrogance which inexorably devalued human life, not only in the colonies but in Europe as well. Fuelled by plunder, blood and conquest, it was to reverberate, with devastating consequences, through the twentieth century. In 1935, responding to criticisms of Italian atrocities committed in Ethiopia, Mussolini claimed that 'Ethiopians were a barbaric, inferior race ... [who] remained "unworthy to stand side by side with civilized nations"' (Lauren 1988:119).

In Britain, Tory radicals like Joseph Chamberlain argued that the profits of empire, rather than increased domestic taxation, should finance state welfare provision, thus buying social peace and stability at no extra cost to the rich. Similarly, the rise of imperialism in Germany, Hobsbawm suggests, 'has been explained primarily in terms of "the primacy of domestic politics"' (1989:69). Cecil Rhodes, quoted at length by Lenin, called for imperial expansion to settle surplus European populations, declaring that 'if you want to avoid civil war, you must become imperialists' (1969 ed.:225). Rhodes believed that 'impatience, irritation, and hatred are accumulating in all the countries of the old civilisation and are becoming a menace to public order' (p.230). Emigration to the colonies was variously proposed as a solution to Britain's domestic social problems. It was assumed, Constantine suggests, that 'emigration would remove the perceived excess supply of labour from Britain which was causing low wages, unemployment and overcrowding' (1991:64). In addition, as women in Britain outnumbered men, only migration would enable surplus females to fulfil their 'natural destinies' – 'it appeared evidently necessary to find the "spare" women either employment or husbands' (p.65). It was also envisaged that urban working-class migrants would, in the process, be transformed into rural producers. In these terms, the dumping of surplus populations abroad, it was thought, would simultaneously solve problems of urban poverty and congestion at home, while providing additional British 'stock' in the colonies, to produce and consume in the interests of the British market. Thus, in addition to economic advantages, Constantine notes, 'physical, military and moral aspects' were also usually stressed (1991:66). However, the claimed economic and social benefits of Empire migration never fully materialized.

'There is no good evidence', Hobsbawm concludes, 'that colonial conquest as such had much bearing on the employment or real incomes of most workers in the metropolitan countries, and the idea that emigration to colonies would provide a safety-valve for overpopulated countries was little more than a demagogic fantasy' (1989:69). Still, the political gains derived by the ruling classes from Empire proved to be of considerable importance. 'Empire', as Hobsbawm observes, 'made good ideological cement' (1989:70).

During the Boer War, following the relief of Mafeking in 1900, Feldman writes, 'boisterous street celebrations erupted the length and breadth of Britain. The jubilant crowds lent credence to Conservatives who believed that the cause of empire offered them one way of appealing to the working class electorate' (1994:131). The Conservatives won a landslide victory in the 1900 elections. In virtually every British election since, the Tories have, with considerable success, endeavoured to play the 'patriotic card', most spectacularly, in recent times, in 1983 following the Falklands conflict. The German Social Democratic Party increased its share of the votes and seats won in every Reichstag Election between 1890 and 1912 with the exception of 1907, the so-called 'Hottentot Election', when it lost 38 seats for 'unpatriotically' opposing German policy in south-west Africa (Tegel 1987:24). That policy, it is worth recalling, included the massacre of the Herero people in 1904. Its seems that 'imperialism encouraged the masses ... to identify themselves with the imperial state and nation, and thus unconsciously to endow the social and political system represented by the state with justification and legitimacy' (Hobsbawm 1987:70). The working-class leadership, it seems, were also variously seduced by patriotic flag-waving. Thus, Eduard Bernstein, 'the father of democratic socialism', endorsed colonialism, as distinct from imperialism, 'almost without reservation' (Fletcher 1987:1). According to Fletcher, 'he frequently defended colonialism in the brutal terminology of Social Darwinism ... [and] strongly urged German Social Democrats to support the colonizing activities of even the Kaiser's government' (p.49). In Italy, following defeat in Ethiopia in 1896, Prime Minister Francesco Crispi, 'who harshly suppressed disturbances at home, turned to jingoism to provide a synthetic unity and national purpose' (Kiernan 1995:177). McPhee notes that most of the 4,000 Communards exiled to New Caledonia enrolled in military units to suppress the Kanak rebellion of 1871 (1992:248). The French Socialist Party participated in government in the early twentieth century without making 'abandonment of colonies a condition of such participation' (Davis 1967:103). In Britain, the 1899–1902 Boer War split the Fabian Society. The Social Democratic Federation, while opposing the war, blamed it on Jewish mine-owners, thus contributing to an 'anti-semitic hysteria' (p.108). The British trade union and labour movements, Cohen notes, campaigned for immigration control, particularly aimed at restricting Jewish immigration, leading to the 1905 Aliens Act (1985:75). Stedman Jones comments that at its birth in 1900, the British Labour Party '*de facto*, accepted not only capitalism, but monarchy, Empire, aristocracy and established religion as well' (1982:118). Despite the anti-war rhetoric of the Second International prior to the outbreak of hostilities in 1914, 'it seems very odd, in retrospect, that anyone should have seriously believed, ... that most Labour leaders, whether in Britain, France, Germany or Austria, would refuse to support their governments in case of war' (Miliband 1973:39). Overwhelmingly in 1914, the working classes on both sides opted for national as against international solidarity.

Eugenics and racial anti-Semitism

Count de Gobineau, in his *Essay on the Inequality of Human Races*, published in the early 1850s but little read until the 1880s, argued that 'the motor of history was the struggle between the White, Yellow and Black races' (Eatwell 1995:7). He believed that 'the white race originally possessed the monopoly of beauty, intelligence and strength. By its union with other varieties, hybrids were created' and thus, was 'threatened by a bastardized proletariat' (Banton 1967:32). His ideas exercised 'a pervasive influence over Western (especially German and French) politics, literature, history and intellectual culture' (p.33). Mosse (1978:55) considers that de Gobineau was not anti-Semitic but it was others, popularizing his ideas, who later directed them against Jews. Richard Wagner, for example, held that 'the Jews represented all that was opposed to the good and beautiful' (p.102). Houston Stewart Chamberlain regarded Jews as the 'Devil incarnate' who posed a 'demonic threat to the chosen German race' (Burleigh and Wippermann 1991:36). Similarly, for Hitler, the motor of history had become the struggle for survival between Aryans and 'the Jew'. In *Mein Kampf*, 'the Jew' is depicted as 'the embodiment of absolute evil: the "struggle" against "him" was both righteous and good' (p.40).

Darwin's *On the Origin of the Species by Means of Natural Selection*, published in 1859, fired Europe's intellectual imagination. Darwinian theory was applied to race and, variously also to nation, class and gender. These notions were disseminated throughout Europe by the social Darwinists. Thus, for example, in 1894, Kidd's *Social Evolution*, 'a work of slender merit, sold a quarter of a million copies' (Banton 1967:37). Natural selection was used to explain away the gross inequalities existing in society. It was simply a matter, in Spencer's phrase, of 'the survival of the fittest'. There was little room for sentiment in a world where nature, as described by Tennyson, was 'red in tooth and claw'. Thus, justification was found for the early results of industrial capitalism whereby a few made fortunes while most of the rest laboured long hours, in hazardous conditions, for near-starvation wages. The ruling classes had always understood this to be the natural order of things; social Darwinism merely provided the 'scientific' explanation. Similarly, the morality of even the worst aspects of imperialism and colonialism was defended in social Darwinist terms. The victims of European excesses were seen to belong to biologically weak races, believed, anyway, to be historically destined for extinction. The 'inferior races', it was felt, should not be allowed to hamper progress and concern for their plight was dismissed as mere sentimentalism.

Banton (1967:37) considers that the key element within social Darwinism 'was the idea of variations transmitted by heredity, which were subject to a process of selection', ultimately ensuring 'the continuance of the best-adapted types' (1967:37–38). In these terms, miscegenation was seen as unnatural, a threat to the purity of the 'race', undermining the very foundations of the nation itself. Thus, the mere presence of 'inferior aliens' within Europe, especially Jews, came to be viewed as a danger to national survival. Similarly, the very poorest in society, the casual labouring class, it was feared, would contaminate the rest of the population. Eugenics, founded by Sir Francis Galton in 1883, grew out of social Darwinism as the means of ensuring the survival of the 'race'. It was defined by him as ' "the science of selective breeding": those deemed "fit" or "desirable" were to be encouraged to propagate, while those deemed "unfit" or "undesirable" were to be discouraged, even prevented' (Bland 1995:223). Hobsbawm describes it as 'a programme for applying the selective breeding technology familiar in agriculture and livestock-raising to people' (1989:253). Eugenics became linked with growing anxieties felt by the ruling classes of Europe about the declining birth-rate among their own kind, combined with fears about the alleged profligacy of the lower orders. It produced, Quine observes, 'a proliferation in many different nations of a vast range of alarmist literature on the immanent threat of demographic extinction' (1996:8).

During the late nineteenth century, anti-Semitism, long endemic to most of Europe, changed its primary focus from religious to racial bigotry. This development occurred in parallel to social Darwinism but also could not but reflect the eugenics debate, then fashionable within intellectual circles throughout Europe. A deep current of intellectual anti-Semitism has long existed within European thought. Thus, for example, Pois writes that Alfred Rosenberg, the chief Nazi ideologue, was indebted to German Romanticism from which 'he derived concepts of national individuality, collective national consciousness, anti-Semitism, racial supremacy and a general anti-urban bias' (1970:20). He adds that 'it was a tragedy of German history that Rosenberg could well consider himself to be a *Kulturmensch* while being a racist. In German intellectual history, the two terms were not mutually exclusive.' During Weimar, Goldhagen notes, university student organizations were already 'captured by nationalist, *volkisch*, and antisemitic forces, often by electoral majorities of two-thirds to three-quarters' (1996:83). He quotes Max Weber who, in 1920, commented that the 'academic atmosphere' had become 'extremely reactionary' and 'radically anti-Semitic', expressing 'a relatively new kind of nationalist, populist and anticapitalist anti-Semitism'. After 1893, it was according to Lukacs, 'a phenomenon observed in many countries' (1993:132). It achieved political success when Karl Lueger was elected Mayor of Vienna in 1897, to become 'the first democratic politician to triumph anywhere in Europe on an explicitly anti-Jewish platform' (Wistrich 1992:63). The new anti-Semitism was also 'the common denominator of the Dreyfus case, of anticapitalist anti-Semitism in England during the Boer War and later in the Marconi affair, of the rise of Cuza's Anti-Semitic Party in Rumania etc.' (Lukacs 1993:132). Whereas previously, in theory if not always in practice, Jews could avoid persecution by converting to Christianity, there was no cure from the affliction of being seen as a genetic threat to the racial purity of the nation, not even baptism. However, it must be noted that anti-Semitism has traditionally been expressed in racist as well as religious terms. Thus, for example, the Spanish Inquisition continued to persecute Jewish converts to Catholicism 'since Jewish blood was assumed to be irrevocably polluted ... "New Christians", for centuries after the expulsion, were seen as a foreign body in Spanish society which threatened its integrity' (Wistrich 1992:37). It appears though that the new 'race science' of eugenics, whose initial ideas were mostly derived from European experiences of imperialism, blended with age-old anti-Semitism. It produced an explosive mixture that eventually led to Auschwitz.

Despite anxieties periodically raised during the nineteenth century about the 'yellow' or 'black peril', the 'menace' of Islam and other imaginary invading forces, the Chinese, Arabs, Africans, Indians, and even the Turks, were essentially seen as an outside threat, unlike the Jews who were perceived as the 'enemy within'. In France, McPhee notes, colonial policies even assumed 'the potential of colonized people to become full French citizens' (1992:270). But relatively few ever succeeded: for example, in 1939 only 0.5 per cent of the inhabitants of French West Africa had full citizenship (Kiernan 1969:239). Davidson argues that, compared to the British, 'the French were just as systematic in their racism while camouflaging its reality behind Jacobin verbiage that promised much and meant, in practice, remarkably little' (1992:47). The *assimilado* policy within the Portuguese Empire proved equally marginal. Thus, in 1950, in Mozambique, with a population of over six million, there were only 4,555 *assimilados* (Mondlane 1969:50). Within their empires,the Portuguese, Italians and Spanish 'generally retired behind a miasmic fog of Christian beatitude which none of them intended to honour, or even thought they should honour' (Davidson 1992:48). Citizenship once granted can of course be withdrawn, as after 1933 German Jews discovered to their cost. In practice, in the nineteenth century, 'real' Europeans were, for most people, decidedly both white and Christian although, in some places, Protestants and Catholics still tried to deny the other citizenship rights, Thus, for example, in France there developed 'a more virulent anti-semitism and anti-Protestantism after 1871: both minorities were seen as "foreign", "anti-Christian", disproportionately powerful and revolutionary. The Protestant population also stood condemned as "German"' (McPhee 1992:261).

In 1916, statistics about Jewish participation in the German armed forces were collected – the so-called 'Jew-count' – to ascertain whether or not Jews were evading frontline service. As Mosse points out, 'the Jews were made highly visible in the midst of the war, singled out from the rest of the population. Their patriotism alone was questioned' (1978:172). Despite some 12,000 German Jews having been killed and a further 35,000 decorated for bravery during the First World War (Burleigh and Wippermann 1991:78), the myth widely persisted throughout the Weimar years that Jews, together with the Left, were responsible for both Germany's military defeat and the harsh terms of the peace treaty that followed – that is, both were blamed for the 'stab in the back'. Of course, 'Nazi propaganda maintained that Jews had left the fighting to others' (p.78). It seems that no sacrifice, not even dying in battle, can ever be enough to dispel racist stereotypes. Jews in Germany, as in the rest of Europe, essentially remained outsiders. Jews, Muslims, Gypsies, assorted colonials and other 'foreigners' deemed to be non-white and/or non-Christian – that is, 'non-European' – have always been, in a variety of ways, excluded from belonging to the nation proper. In essence, the same message is still being beamed to Europe's postwar migrant labourers and their European-born offspring. It labels them as 'outsiders' because, either in part or in combination, their 'race', religion and culture are all essentially regarded as both 'alien' and immutable, disqualifying them, now and for all time, from being 'proper' Europeans. Even when formal citizenship rights have generally been granted, as in Britain, acceptance, in the sense of fully belonging as an integral part of the nation, is still largely withheld. Thus, Gilroy, in observing that 'there ain't no black in the Union Jack', suggests that 'blacks are systematically excluded', despite their citizenship, from the 'celebration of England and Englishness' (1987:12).

With the defeat of Nazi Germany in 1945, racist theories based on ideas of biological superiority were discredited. Instead, what is fashionably termed the 'new' or 'cultural' racism, variously focusing on cultural rather than racial differences, has come to dominate racial discourse in late twentieth-century Europe. Barker suggests that at the core of this racism 'is a theory of human nature ... such that it is natural to form a bounded community, a nation, aware of its differences from other nations. They are not better or worse. But feelings of antagonism will be aroused if outsiders are admitted' (1981:21). In a sense, the 'new' racism appears to be a restatement of the rationale, dating from the 1950s, used to justify apartheid in the old South Africa. Indeed, within that context, Tobias writes that there is an underlying assumption that 'cultural differences are unchangeable, are part of man's [*sic*] nature, his heredity' (1961:14). The 'new' racism is not even new to Europe as a fundamental corollary of nineteenth-century racist theories was the conviction that superior races produce superior cultures. Thus, Africa was generally viewed as a continent with neither history nor culture. Davidson notes that in 1909, with 'no effective evidence save racist prejudice', African doctors, even though possessing qualifications from British medical schools, were excluded from the West African Medical Service (1992:45). It derived from the 'notion that Europeans should never be obliged to serve under Africans ... [which] became the touchstone of all imperialist culture' (p.47). Europeans felt that, in order to become 'civilized', educated Africans 'must cease to be Africans' while, on the other hand, 'they should never be allowed to become Europeans' (p.47). Thus, uneducated, rural Africans, 'the "uncorrupted child of nature"' came to be preferred to 'Europeanized Negroes' (p.45). Similarly, in India, 'the least objectionable inhabitants of British India, in British eyes, were those least touched by the white man's learning' (Kiernan 1969:312). The moral purpose of nineteenth-century imperialist expansion, Christians and liberals at home liked to believe, was its purported 'civilizing mission' to the world. But, by the close of the century, 'doubt crept in about whether European civilization really was good for those exposed to it' (p.312). Even the highly educated among subject people were thought incapable of acquiring, at best, more than a veneer of Western culture. Increasingly, it came to be seen as a corrupting rather than a beneficial influence. The internalization of Western culture was simply regarded as beyond the moral and mental capacities of most, if not all, non-whites. These ideas inextricably linked culture with race and nation and were applied equally to overseas populations and to minorities within Europe, particularly, with the rise of racial anti-Semitism, to Jews. Already, in late nineteenth-century Germany, there was a sense 'of Jews intruding into, subverting and ultimately controlling German intellectual and cultural life' (Wistrich 1992:60). Thus, assimilated Jews were seen to pose a threat to German culture from the inside.

At the close of the twentieth century, eugenics still exerts an influence on political life, for example, in the genocidal conflicts that erupted in Rwanda in 1994, as Prunier (1995) illustrates. He links these directly to the pseudo-scientific racist ideas projected on to that country by nineteenth-century European colonialism. While 'the Tutsi and Hutu categories' were 'integral' to traditional society and thus were not invented by the Belgians, what was invented by them were 'forms under which they were supposed to relate to each other in order to fit in with the ideological fantasies and practical needs of the Europeans' (p.347). The Tutsis, whom the Europeans 'saw as definitely too fine to be "negroes"' (p.6), were regarded as physically, mentally and socially superior to the Hutu. These ideas, reflecting 'the almost obsessive preoccupation with "race" in late nineteenth century anthropological thinking' (p.5), redefined the population in racist terms, labelling the Tutsi as superior and the Hutu and Twa as inferior races. This categorization which favoured the Tutsi over the others 'actually governed the decisions made by the German and even more so later by the Belgian colonial authorities'. Over a period of sixty years of colonial rule, it created 'a very dangerous social bomb' (p.9). Almost certainly, other explosive racist relics of colonial rule are elsewhere still dangerously ticking away.

'Race', class and social policy

During the nineteenth century, Kiernan observes, 'inferior Europeans and non-Europeans were thought of in not very different terms' (1969:28). Certainly, the working class, particularly the bottom strata, were mostly assumed to be innately inferior. Miles writes that, on the one hand, the working class were excluded from the nation, being regarded as 'urban savages, and hence as a "race apart", in need of civilization' while, on the other, they were included as members of a 'racialized' nation: 'each nation was seen to have a "racial" character, composition and history' (1993:47). This apparent contradiction would have, in practice, been resolved by the distinction made during the last decades of the nineteenth century between the 'deserving' and 'undeserving' poor. Previously, in ruling-class minds, the urban poor were seen as an undifferentiated mass whose revolutionary potential needed to be suppressed. As described by Hobsbawm, 'the city was a volcano to whose rumblings the rich and powerful listened with fear and whose eruptions they dreaded' (1969:87). In 1850, Bismarck is reported to have 'thundered against big towns "as hotbeds of revolution", which should be raised to the ground' (Bebel 1971:83). Similarly, Stedman Jones observes, 'the rookeries of central London were considered to be hot-beds of the "dangerous classes", the foci of cholera, crime and chartism' (1971:167). In other words, the ruling classes, fearing the city, attributed to it and its denizens, all the ills of society – disease, criminality and insurrection. In *Mein Kampf*, Hitler held 'the Jew' responsible for 'prostitution, syphilis, and the "spiritual prostitution" of the German people' (Burleigh and Wippermann 1991:41).

The eighteenth-century 'Romantic movement and the growth of a holistic nationalism have most frequently been cited as laying the intellectual foundations of fascism' (Eatwell 1995:5). He goes on to add that 'the Jew was pilloried as the epitome of capitalist materialism – a view particularly prevalent in the German *volkisch* movement, which railed against the evils of urban, industrial society' (p.6). Indeed, during the twentieth century, anti-urbanism characterizes the far Right. For instance, 'Pétain's government promised to "deindustrialize" France and make it a peasant country once more' (Quine 1996:84).

By the 1880s, the bottom stratum of the British working class, 'the casual residuum', Stedman Jones suggests, 'was no longer a political threat – only a social problem' (1971:321). Their mere presence in cities was seen to pose a serious eugenic danger to the survival of the nation. It meant that the poor in Victorian Britain, 'did not emerge as objects of compassion. They were generally pictured as coarse, brutish, drunken, and immoral ... an ominous threat to civilization' (p.285). Thus, drastic solutions were called for. Charles Booth, for example, described the poorest in society as 'a savage, semi-criminal class of people' to be 'harried out of existence' (Yeo 1973:108). The next lowest group, he recommended, should 'be removed from the labour market and placed in industrial colonies' (p.106). Their confinement, Stedman Jones (1971:307) notes, was to be in conditions of 'semi-servitude'. Samuel Smith proposed technical education for the poor, to 'de-odorize, so to speak, this foul humanity', to be followed by emigration to the colonies (p.310). Fabians, among them H.G. Wells and G.B. Shaw, advocated 'sterilisation of the failures' (p.333). The changing approach 'to the problems of the casual poor ... was both more social darwinist in style and more punitive in intent' (p.328).

Although now no longer seen as politically threatening, the casual poor were regarded as no less dangerous than before. The bourgeoisie were particularly alarmed at what they imagined to be the irresponsible procreation, profligacy and degeneracy of the lower orders, leading to the moral contamination of the 'respectable' working class and, ultimately, to the nation itself being overwhelmed. Much of the social policy of the period was aimed at containing rather than helping the poorest in society. As such, social reform from the standpoint of the casual labourer was not so much progress as misfortune. When not entirely excluded from benefits, the very poor tended to be treated by the state even more harshly than before. The distinction between 'deserving' and 'undeserving' poor was, and largely still remains, deeply embedded at the centre of social policy.

Governments throughout Europe, during the late nineteenth and early twentieth centuries, became increasingly obsessed with the threat of socialism. In order to pre-empt its perceived menace and counter its attractions, the state, most notably in Germany and Britain, intervened in social welfare provision. As A.J. Balfour famously concluded in 1895: 'social legislation ... is not merely to be distinguished from Socialist legislation but it is ... its most effective antidote' (Fraser 1975:129). Of German policy, Moses writes, 'the purpose of the sickness, accident and old-age insurance legislation of the mid 1880s was to persuade the working class that the paternalistic state would take care of their welfare'. He adds: 'Bismarck's much vaunted social-service legislation was merely a tactical move to preserve the monarchical-capitalist system from the looming threat of socialist trade-union militancy' (1987:29). Similarly, Hay attributes the primary motivation behind the 1906–14 Liberal welfare reforms in Britain to 'the desire to retain as much as possible of the existing capitalist economic system, at a time when it was under increasing pressure from within and without' (1975:62). It was organized labour, mostly comprising relatively well-paid, skilled men, which emerged as the main beneficiaries of welfare reform. It was precisely among these workers that the growing socialist threat was seen to reside. Having become 'an increasingly crucial sector of the workforce both economically and politically' (Thane 1982:87), the state offered them social welfare reform, more or less as a 'bribe' in an attempt to buy social peace and stability. Thus, Bismarck's social insurance schemes, Thane notes, 'covered most regularly employed workers but excluded the lowest-paid irregularly employed ... the great majority of women were also excluded' (p.109). Similarly, the British 1911 National Insurance Act targeted skilled working-class men in secure employment. As Thane concludes, 'the lowest paid, the irregularly employed and women – gained least of all' (p.98). Aliens too tended to be excluded from welfare benefits. In other words, the poorest and most vulnerable in society, who were most in need but economically weak and politically harmless, were offered little or no state help. Thus, for example, a 1913 British report, directed at 'schools for mothers' or, as later called, infant welfare centres, 'maintained that the schools should be trying to educate the upper working class ... not the very poor and destitute ...whose ways were too idle and vicious to be reformed' (Lewis 1980:480).

Both the opponents and advocates of social welfare reform looked to social Darwinism for support. Those in favour of maintaining traditional *laissez-faire* policies argued that the degeneracy of the residuum 'was the result of the violation, even reversal, of natural selection'. This, it was believed, was due to 'the distortions of philanthropy, state aid and modern medicine, facilitating an artificial lifespan of the "unfit" and undesirable' (Bland 1995:224). However, the closing decades of the nineteenth century were marked by mounting pressures for social reform. These were years of rapid social, cultural and technological change. Periodic economic crises, coupled with growing working-class militancy, created an atmosphere of fear which pervaded the capitals of Europe, concentrating ruling-class minds on the 'dangers' of socialism. Further, rivalry amongst the European powers for imperial, political and economic hegemony intensified, erupting in conflagration in 1914. Pressure for state intervention in social policy increasingly came from within sections of the ruling classes determined to create a strong state in order to preserve their existing power, wealth and privilege. Social Darwinism, just as it had previously sustained *laissez-faire*, now provided the intellectual rationale favouring state welfare provision. The survival of nation, 'race' and empire was seen to be at stake and, thus, far too important to be left to market forces alone. On behalf of capital, the guiding hand of the state was urgently required to safeguard vital national interests. In Britain, 'social imperialism', with adherents across the entire political spectrum, achieved prominence as a result of anxiety felt about the fitness of British recruits for the 1899–1902 Boer War. Espousing notions of racial purity and the superiority of British 'stock', the social imperialists linked social reform with national efficiency and imperial expansion. Their influence is apparent in the 1906–14 Liberal welfare reforms, particularly in child welfare legislation which largely aimed to ensure, as Fraser explains, 'that the new generation of children, tomorrow's Imperial Army, was properly nourished' (1975:137).

After 1918, an increasingly shrill campaign to tighten British immigration control was conducted by the press, particularly *The Times* and the *Morning Post*. The latter newspaper, Cesarani notes, had previously published the English version of *The Protocols of the Elders Of Zion* (1987:3). The agitation led to the 1919 Aliens Act which contained within it three main objectives: 'a vindictive desire to punish former enemies', 'Government's intention to arm itself against radicalism and labour unrest' and 'an atavistic anti-alienism directed at East End Jews'. As a result, over 30,000 'enemy aliens' – mainly Germans, Austrians, Hungarians and Turks, together with 7,000 Russians, 'probably all Jews'– were deported, 'often in distressing circumstances'. As Cesarani further notes, 'since the press ... were making popular the notion that Jews were synonymous with Bolsheviks and that the Bolsheviks were financed by the Germans, "anti-alienism" conveniently subsumed all three' (p.7). In addition, following race riots in British ports in 1919, 600 black men were repatriated. As the weekly paper *John Bull* commented, 'these coloured Britons had all done first-class war work, yet they were treated worse than repatriated enemy aliens' (Fryer 1984:309).

In Germany, the mass unemployment of the interwar years meant that the numbers of foreign workers were reduced from almost a million in 1907 to about 100,000 in 1932. Nevertheless, measures to protect German workers were introduced by the Weimar Republic which included: 'strict state control of labour recruitment, employment preference for nationals, sanctions against employers of illegal migrants and unrestricted police power to deport unwanted foreigners' (Castles and Miller 1993:61). Jews were blamed for unemployment and economic crises – capitalism, the stock exchange, international finance, democracy, the media, decadence in the arts and, especially Marxism, were all portrayed as being part and parcel of the 'Jewish conspiracy' for world domination. The 1917 Revolution, Wistrich stresses, 'was depicted as a prelude to the future "Bolshevisation" of Germany and the beginning of the last stage in world Jewry's coming bid for global hegemony'. As Wistrich explains, 'this organic linkage of anti-Communism with antisemitism ensured in the long run the support of the traditional elites in German society for Hitler's political programme' (1992:70). Similarly, Kolb writes that the Nazis were 'only victorious in the end because the old elites of the industrial and landowning classes, the military aristocracy and the upper middle class, were determined to replace Weimar by an authoritarian system' (1988:125–6). He goes on to suggest that the Nazis were regarded by them 'as an acceptable ally in the fight against democracy, against the parliamentary system and the organized working class' (p.126). Clearly, whatever reservations the German ruling classes might have had about Nazi barbarism, including its openly murderous anti-Semitism, their overriding concern was the 'threat of communism'.

In France, with about 1.4 million soldiers killed during the 1914–18 War, population levels were only maintained by relatively large-scale immigration. Antagonism towards immigrants was closely related to the economic situation, for example, during the 1930s slump, 'the French authorities organized the forcible repatriation of trainloads of Poles' (Hargreaves 1995:7). In 1932, maximum quotas for foreign workers in firms was fixed, followed by laws permitting dismissal of foreigners in sectors where there was unemployment. It seems that in France as in Germany, 'the right to work' was made dependent on nationality. In other words, immigrants 'provided a scapegoat for the economic crisis' (Castles and Miller 1993:61). With the rise of fascism, over 100,000 Jewish refugees entered France during the 1930s. The election of Leon Blum's Popular Front Government in 1936 reinforced the establishment's already deeply embedded anti-Semitism, xenophobia and anti-left paranoia. The extreme right-wing newspaper, *Action Française*, for example, referred to Blum as the 'circumcized hermaphrodite', at the head of a 'cretinistic-talmudist cabinet' (Jackson 1990:250–1). The attacks concentrated on Blum 'as Socialist, Jew/Alien, ... traitor to his class and head of the first government supported by Communists' (p.250). As Jackson further explains:

> The anti-semitic theme allowed the right to contrast its Frenchness with the foreignness of its opponents ... The arrival of refugees from Germany, Spain and central Europe provided further ammunition: "All the scum of Europe has settled here". ... The theme of the alien was linked to the fear of public disorder. (p.250)

The celebrated phrase 'rather Hitler than Blum' (though as Jackson (p.256) points out, it 'may never have been uttered'), encapsulates the prevailing political climate of Popular Front France, virtually on the eve of the Second World War. It seems that the fear of communism, inextricably linked to anti-Semitism, rather than Nazism, dominated the politics of the period.

Cohen notes that the 1906–14 Liberal welfare reforms which laid the foundations of the future British welfare state, 'made eligibility for benefit dependent on immigration status' (1985:74). For instance, the 1908 Old Age Pensions Act excluded both aliens and the wives of aliens. It also required both a twenty-year naturalization period and twenty years' residence in the UK which, in effect, prevented most naturalized Jews from receiving pensions. Health insurance, under the 1911 Act, which provided for sickness, disablement and maternity benefits, also discriminated against aliens on the grounds of both nationality and residential criteria. Unemployed aliens, who had been engaged in war-work, were refused payment under the 1919 'out of work donation' scheme. Subsequently, most unemployment insurance legislation during the interwar period discriminated against aliens. The London County Council refused to grant scholarships to foreign-born children even when naturalized British subjects. It also precluded aliens from employment by the authority and proposed that aliens be excluded from all municipal housing (Cohen 1985:80–6). In short, 'aliens suffered discrimination in areas of social welfare, housing, employment and education provided by the state and local authorities' (Cesarani 1987:14). During this period, the acquisition of British nationality assumed increasing importance as protection against 'the mounting wave of deportations' (Cohen 1985:88). However, the naturalization process was expensive and excessively slow, containing obstacles designed specifically to frustrate and delay applications, particularly from Jews who were extremely vulnerable to deportation (Cesarani 1987; Cohen 1985). While the foreign-born, even when naturalized, were often excluded from a wide range of welfare benefits, in practice even British-born Jews, 'naturally' regarded as 'undeserving', were frequently denied their rightful claim to benefit. Thus, for example, Max Cohen, in his autobiography, *I was One of the Unemployed,* writes that when destitute during the 1930s he was refused poor relief when it became apparent that he was Jewish (1945:45). He was told to apply instead to the Jewish Board of Guardians where he was in turn refused help on the grounds of being British. He was also informed that as a single person he was ineligible for relief, reflecting the family bias of contemporary welfare provision. Cohen's response was to ask, 'doesn't a single man have to eat – pay rent?' (p.48).

The 1919 race riots that took place in British ports shook the black community, then mostly of seafaring origin. The wartime demand for black labour, Fryer writes, 'fizzled out' with the peace in 1918 and 'once again shipping companies chose to sign on white foreign seamen rather than Black British seamen' (1984:298). With reference to the 1919 'out of work donation', Fryer reports that the Ministry of Labour 'sent secret instructions to labour exchange managers that unemployed black seamen of British nationality should be left in ignorance of their rights' (p.299). After the slump began in 1929, Government paid a subsidy to shipowners on condition that only British labour was employed on subsidized ships. It essentially deprived black seamen of the chance to work. In 1935, there were an estimated 3,000 non-European seamen in Cardiff and the local police assumed that all were alien 'regardless of any documentary evidence a man might produce to prove that he was British' (p.356). In the period 1918–45, 'the racism that poisoned the everyday lives of black people in Britain ... characteristically did so in the form of what was called the "colour bar"'. In industry it was 'virtually total'. The colour bar also meant 'the refusal of lodgings, refusal of service in cafes, refusal of admittance to dance halls ...' (p.356). Black people, like Jews, were regarded as racially inferior and hence as "undeserving" in social welfare terms. Consequently, the almost complete economic, residential and social segregation of the black community that resulted, apparently regarded as normal, was rapidly taken for granted by the rest of society. Thus, for example, Janet Hitchman in her autobiography, describes how black children in Dr Barnado's Homes were as a matter of course segregated from other children. On being shown around, as a newly arrived thirteen year-old orphan, she was told, 'that cottage mother has all black children. If you were black you'd go there' (1966:147). Thus even voluntary welfare agencies such as Barnado's practised racial segregation.

'Race', gender and family policy

During the late nineteenth and early twentieth centuries, the eugenics debate, increasingly linked to social policy, was largely preoccupied with child welfare and consequently with women and the family. In so far as these concerns were translated into policies, the implications for the welfare of women, other than as mothers, were almost entirely detrimental. In the years before 1914, as the prospect of war grew ever closer, the need to stem population decline became increasingly urgent. Informed by eugenics, the politics of the period combined anxiety about the decline in the birth-rate among the 'better stocks' with alarm at the prospect of population growth among less 'desirable' elements, particularly the poor and immigrants. In 1907 Sidney Webb famously warned that, unless stopped, Britain would be filled by 'freely-breeding alien immigrants' with the country as a consequence 'gradually falling to the Irish and the Jews' (Davin 1978:23). Women, essentially white, Christian and respectable, as a matter of national duty, were expected to sacrifice career and well-being by producing and caring for large numbers of children. Their primary role was to be 'mothers of the race'. It seems the survival of Empire, no less, depended upon the reproductive capacity of the finest of British womanhood.

The patriarchal family was seen to be under threat and in need of protection. Thus, for example, in her study of Dutch family law between 1870 and 1910, Sevenhuijsen notes that, within the sociological debate of the period, 'social-Darwinism, sociobiology and eugenics were combined in a discourse that took sexual difference and the sexual division of labour as its point of departure' (1992:182). In social policy terms, 'unmarried mothers were denied automatic parental rights and rights to social services such as child allowances and pregnancy benefits, out of fear that this would contaminate womanhood'. She goes on to add that 'the argument that the state should not encourage extra-matrimonial reproduction and licentiousness remained dominant until far into the twentieth century' (p.186). Throughout Europe, the state increasingly intervened in the private lives of citizens, attempting to encourage marriage and fecundity. Thus, as Quine notes, in 1920 the French required single men and women and married couples without children to pay additional income tax (1996:40). Similarly, Italy in 1926 imposed a bachelor tax on unmarried men: 'While Italian fascist ideology elevated the status of mothers and sought to edify maternity in propaganda and policies aimed at women, French pronatalism exalted paternity and determined to favour fathers with privilege and reward' (p.54). With a clear emphasis on paternity rights, welfare reforms were mostly focused on male *chefs de famille*. According to Quine, it 'conveyed the message that procreation was a political duty, much like military service, which men had to perform for the sake of the grandeur and prosperity of the *patrie*' (p.55).

Quine observes that 'pronatalist and familist credos contributed to the consolidation of many authoritarian regimes', even becoming, she suggests, their 'defining feature' (1996:86). Thus, the Salazar dictatorship in 1932 'launched a patriotic crusade for national regeneration and the restoration of the family as the pillar of Portuguese society ... an integral nationalism extolling *Deus, Patria, e Familia* became the basis for ... [the] regime which survived until 1974' (pp.86–7). Under Franco, Spain also implemented 'a population policy which used Catholicism, pronatalism and nationalism as the ideological trappings for dictatorship' (p.88). Mussolini, in his overriding quest for an empire, made population growth, expressed in terms of Italy's expanding military and colonial needs, a major political priority: 'The demographic campaign was central to fascist rule in Italy. The "battle for the birthrate" was tied to the larger foreign policy and political aims of fascism' (p.35). As Mussolini proclaimed, within this scheme of things, women's 'natural role was caring for a new generation of warriors' (Eatwell 1995:64). 'Fascism ... accentuate[d] the discrimination Italian women already faced in politics, education, the law, the economy and the family' and it was all justified 'by repeated mention of the so-called "natural hierarchy" between the sexes' (Quine 1996:49). Throughout Europe, women's role in society was increasingly defined as that of mother, with the state taking little or no interest in her other capacities as citizen and worker. After the First World War, women who had entered the labour market tended to be pushed back into the home to make way for returning soldiers. Through the slumps and depressions of the interwar years, women were variously excluded from the workforce so as to ease male unemployment. In Britain, the increasingly stringent measures introduced during the 1920s to restrict entitlement to unemployment insurance was primarily directed at 'scroungers' and married women.

Governments throughout Europe, seemingly convinced of the racial superiority of their own people, contemplated policies to encourage population growth among the 'strong' while weeding out the 'weak'. The primary purpose, it appears, was to build armies and to ensure the survival of both 'race' and nation. In Scandinavia, for example, over 100,000 people, 90 per cent of them women, were forcibly sterilized between 1929 and 1976 (*The Observer*, 24 August 1997). However, eugenics was most enthusiastically supported by the right-wing totalitarian regimes that took root in interwar Europe, particularly in Germany where the position of women in society was drastically eroded after 1933. As Burleigh and Wippermann (1991:242) write, 'the attitudes of leading Nazis towards women were profoundly reactionary.' Thus, for example, in 1933 the admission of women to universities was limited to 10 per cent of total annual intake (p.258). While the essential demand placed on women was to produce children for the Third Reich, 'the Nazis attached no absolute value to fecundity in itself. They were also hostile to women who burdened the welfare services and the "racial community" with an excess of biologically "undesirable" progeny' (p.258). It led in 1933 to the compulsory sterilization of those deemed by the regime to be suffering from an hereditary illness. This was defined to include: congenital feeble-mindedness, schizophrenia, manic depression, hereditary epilepsy, Huntington's chorea, hereditary blindness, hereditary deafness, serious physical deformities and chronic alcoholism (p.137). Later, the list was extended to include vagrants, Sinti and Roma and the so-called 'Rhineland Bastards', the offspring of French colonial troops and German mothers. Described as the 'black rape of Germany' (Mosse 1978:176), the presence of these troops exercised 'German politicians of all shades', including the Social Democratic President, Friedrich Ebert (Burleigh and Wippermann 1991:128). In 1927, Bavarian Government officials recommended sterilization but that was rejected because of 'the demoralising effects upon the children's German mothers' (p.129). In 1937, public health authorities and academic experts helped the Gestapo locate the children who were then compulsorily sterilized (p.130).

Almost immediately after their seizure of power, the Nazis began translating their plans for selective 'breeding' into reality. The 'euthanasia' programme, the 'destruction of worthless life', was already under discussion in the 1920s, suggesting to Burleigh and Wippermann 'how widespread subscription to selective breeding and extermination, albeit in the guise of "eugenics" ... had become in the Weimar Republic' (1991:141). They also report 'the apparent lack of public reaction to Hitler's espousal of the most extreme elements in the "eugenic" case' – for instance, when he declared to the 1929 Nuremberg Party rally, 'if Germany was to get a million children a year and was to remove 700,000–800,000 of the weakest people, then the final result might even be an increase in strength' (p.142). In the event, an estimated 200,000 children were abducted for purposes of 'germanization' in occupied eastern Europe with only 15–20 per cent being reunited with their parents and relatives after the war (p.72). In 1939, Hitler authorized an 'euthanasia' programme and by the time it was officially halted in 1941, in response to public pressure, it is generally estimated that over 90,000 mental patients and others regarded as 'undesirable', including the 'asocial' and homosexual, were gassed. It appears that 'the regime's policies had come into serious conflict with ingrained moral precepts and compassion towards the weak. Of course, these seem to have subsequently gone into limbo in the case of the extermination of the Jews' (p.151).

The aim of encouraging the procreation of those regarded as ethnically valuable to enable the conquest of *Lebensraum*, while preventing the birth of the ill, the asocial and racially 'worthless' was at the heart of the Nazi project. It was all directed, as Burleigh and Wippermann note, towards 'the realisation of a particular barbarous utopia' (p.42). These authors are highly critical of historians who distinguish between Nazi racial and social policies, wrongly regarding the latter as 'modern or even socially revolutionary'. They point out that all the social policy measures were 'motivated by racial considerations, firstly because both "alien races" and the "less valuable elements" of the German population were excluded from the benefits of Nazi "social policy", and secondly, because all these social improvements were designed to encourage the reproduction of certain types of people' (p.39). As Goebbels declared in 1938: 'We must have a healthy people in order to prevail in the world.' In other words, Nazi welfare objectives were 'designed to strengthen the collective biologically and politically and not to assist needy individuals' (p.69). Thus, in 1933, a marriage loan was provided with repayment cancelled on the birth of the fourth child but was conditional on the women giving up employment and, after 1935, was explicitly denied to Jews and other 'undesirables'. From then on, 'social policy was indivisible from the "selection" of "alien" races and those of "lesser racial value"' (p.48). Under the 1935 Law for the Protection of German Blood and Honour, Jews were forbidden to marry or have extramarital sexual relations with 'Aryan' partners (p.45). Later that year, 'Gypsies, negroes and their bastards' were also forbidden to marry Germans (p.49). Also in 1935 the Law for the Protection of the Hereditary Health of the German People made possession of a 'certificate of fitness to marry' mandatory for all prospective marriage partners. In this way, the whole German population was gradually registered (p.49). As a consequence, it became possible to make 'marriage loans, tax rebates and family allowances ... conditional upon racial criteria. Inevitably, this meant that it became dangerous even to apply for these benefits' (p.252). An enormous bureaucracy was created to investigate the 'racial' origins and the mental and physical health of the German people. It required considerable ingenuity, energy and resources to devise, administer and monitor and there appears to have been no shortage of willing helpers from among all classes of Germans. As Quine observes, 'medicine, science and the state colluded in the implementation of a population and race policy whose ultimate aim was genocide' (1996:128). Similarly, Burleigh and Wippermann conclude that 'there were few areas of Nazi racial policy which did not involve academics in its formulation and legitimisation and many of the latter were culpably involved in its implementation' (1991:56).

Postwar Europe: the racist legacy

The Atlantic Charter, the first statement of war aims issued in 1941 by Roosevelt and Churchill, offered the people of occupied Europe freedom and democracy coupled with a vague promise of 'social security'. Thus, the Allied vision of the Europe that would emerge following the defeat of the Third Reich included the prospect of future social policy reform. The right to 'social security' was subsequently adopted by the ILO in 1944 and incorporated within the UN's 1948 Universal Declaration of Human Rights (Baldwin 1990:108). The Atlantic Charter also affirmed American and British respect for 'the right of all peoples to choose the form of government under which they will live', and expressed the desire 'to see sovereign rights and self-government restored to those who have been forcibly deprived of them' (Cole 1947:1061). Although addressed to 'all peoples', it was clearly occupied Europe, rather than either the colonies or the American South, that the Western leaders had in mind. Indeed, Churchill 'quickly made it clear that these principles did not apply to British colonial territories' (Lauren 1988:139). Germany was opposed by segregated armies, most notably the American and South African – the US armed forces were only desegregated after 1948. Clearly, the war was not an anti-racist crusade. While the world was horrified by the extent of Nazi barbarity, there was, and largely remains, a reluctance to focus on racism as the defining feature of Nazi Germany. But, as expressed by Burleigh and Wippermann, 'the millions of victims are a reminder of the purposiveness with which the regime went about the most crucial part of its desolate agenda, namely the creation of a functioning racial state' (1991:4).

Barkan suggests that 'the Nazi regime has compelled us all to recognize the lethal potential of the concept of race and the horrendous consequences of its misuse' (1992:1). Within intellectual discourse, he observes, the defeat of Nazism led to the 'retreat of scientific racism'. Yet, while Europe repudiated Nazism and has, for the moment at least, turned its back on fascism, racism still festers at all levels of society throughout the continent. In social policy, after 1945 when Europe's welfare states were in 'the making', many of the underlying principles remained saturated by nineteenth-century assumptions abour 'race', nation, gender and class. That these ideas were informed by a combination of social Darwinism, social imperialism, racial anti-Semitism and eugenics, all later adopted and refashioned by the Nazis, appears to have passed largely unnoticed. Thus, while eugenics and other manifestations of 'scientific racism' were thoroughly discredited, notions about 'inferior races', patriarchy and the 'lower orders', albeit now mostly expressed in cultural terms, still remain politically influential. Thus, for example, West German policy towards women was couched 'in the language of pronatalism, motherhood, the sanctity of family relations, and in the state's attempt to shape these private relationships, there were striking continuities across the divide of 1945' (Moeller 1989:164).

In Britain, Cohen argues that the racism intrinsic to the postwar welfare state has its origins in the 'hidden history of anti-semitism in turn of the century Britain' (1985:73). He further notes that 'the ideological concepts of efficiency, eugenics, nation and empire', so clearly linked to social policy during the early 1900s, 'have been a constant in the debate about welfare throughout this century' (p.73). The 1905 Aliens Act, largely designed to restrict Jewish entry to Britain, was the beginning of a legislative process making eligibility for a wide range of social benefits 'dependent on immigration status' (p.74). This link between immigraton control and state welfare provision remains at the centre of the modern welfare state and cannot be understood, Cohen concludes, 'other than as a construct of the basest nationalism' (p.92). The British, resolutely anti-Nazi during the war, managed to avoid reflecting upon their own anti-Semitism. Thus, for example, while about a quarter of all refugees in Europe's displaced persons camps after 1945 were Jewish survivors of the Holocaust, of those recruited by Britain as migrant workers less than 1 per cent were Jewish. As a senior Foreign Office official, quoted by Kushner, explained, the recruitment of Jews would lead to 'opposition from public opinion at home' (1994:420). Ernest Bevin, the Foreign Secretary, Kushner writes, 'was particularly hostile to Jewish immigrants' (p.421). He adds that 'Jews, like blacks, were seen as undesirable immigrants because they would not assimilate and were of inferior stock'. While Belsen entered the English language as signifying starvation and emaciation, anti-Semitism retained its pre-war legitimacy in Britain, apparently even at the highest levels of government.

Postwar migrants to Europe encountered racism on a massive scale. But Europeans somehow managed to distance that racism from that which had informed Nazism. For example, during the war, 'nearly ten million forced labourers, a third of them women, were abducted from all over Europe' (Enzensberger 1994:128). As Burleigh and Wippermann observe, 'the arduous and dirty work was to be performed by a racially-categorised foreign workforce, which became incorporeal during non-working hours' (1991:262). Then as now they were euphemistically referred to as 'guests', in a situation where:

> ... most German workers seem to have been largely indifferent to the fact that they were working alongside an undernourished army which emerged spectrally from freezing camps but was excluded from public air-raid shelters and swimming baths, and which could be strung up for doing things which the rest of the

> population took for granted. ... the principal reason for this response was that Nazi racial policy towards foreign workers interacted with the arrogant self-regard, chauvinism, and racism of some sections of the German working class. This suggests that the Nazis' novel efforts to replace class with racial society found a ready response in significant sections of the population. Judging by studies of how many 'German workers' treat their Turkish colleagues in present-day factories or service industries, these attitudes seem to have survived the Nazi period. (Burleigh and Wippermann 1991:303)

Schonwalder suggests that the nearly eight million foreign workers in Germany in 1944 must have 'habituated Germans to the presence and the subordination of non-German[s]' (1996:163). Among these were about 600,000 former Italian soldiers who after 1943 had refused to fight for Germany and as a consequence 'had received awful treatment' (p.162). Barely a decade later, the Federal Republic once again recruited Italian migrant workers. And yet, as Schonwalder notes, 'forced labour was not an issue of public debate after 1945 and was not perceived as part of Nazi crimes' (p.163). West German politicians, she observes, 'were eager to suppress any parallels with the past' (p.162). The postwar silence on the issue of foreign workers, she argues, allowed 'a return to the utilization of migrant labour without a public debate about its traditions as well as to allow the unnoticed reconstruction of the pre-1945 legal framework for foreign labour and the control of aliens' (p.163). In addition, the German constitution, as Wilpert reminds us, is based on an historic belief that the modern German state 'is legitimately founded on one culture, one nation ... and a biological principle of descent' (1993:70). Thus, Germany retains a *volkisch* national identity, firmly based on notions of blood which, although rooted in a much earlier age, were central to Nazi ideology. It means that Swabian Germans, for instance, who first settled in Romania in the twelfth century, have an automatic right to enter Germany and be granted citizenship while the German-born children of migrant workers are denied these rights. In the process, an increasing number of German-born people have acquired the anomalous status of being 'second or third generation immigrants'. On the other hand, establishing proof of German ethnicity, Wilpert notes, involves 'the use of criteria similar to those employed within the Nazi system' (p.73). Very often the proof provided is their father's or grandfather's membership of a Nazi organization. Indeed, it appears that membership of the SS is the most common proof required for recognition as an *Aussiedler* which, of course, excludes Jewish applicants. As Wilpert concludes, 'Here we see how the racist rationale, central to the system Hitler exploited, remains a major principle for determiming access to privileged rights within German society' (p.74).

From the West's ideological perspective, there was little to be gained after 1945 from dwelling on the essential racist nature of Nazism and even less from attempting to place it within an historical context that encompasses slavery, imperialism and colonialism and, not least of all, their own anti-Semitism. Reluctant to admit that much more could have been done to save European Jewry, the West could not afford to draw even distant parallels between its own racism, both at home and in the colonies, and that of the Nazis. After all, following Germany's defeat, the European powers soon became embroiled in a series of essentially racist, colonial wars. Better to portray Nazism as an inexplicable evil without historic parallel for which Hitler and his immediate henchmen were entirely to blame. Thus, with the onset of the Cold War, West Germany, now needed to stand as a bulwark against communism, was absolved of blame and responsibility. The essential abandonment of the Allied de-Nazification programme in Germany after 1946 and the subsequent political failure to draw significant lessons from the rise and fall of Nazism, constitutes, it is suggested, an opportunity lost to begin seriously the process of rooting out racism from Western society. In Germany, Rathzel argues, 'no connection can be made between ... the rise of racism today and the past; all meaningful continuities and connections have been deliberately blanked out' (1990:45). The price, in Europe, has largely been paid by the new ethnic minority communities formed since 1945. This is not to say that the claimed retreat from racism is false – in social policy as in other areas of life real progress has been made since 1945. Rather, that reform has been exceedingly slow and uneven and, given the scale of the problem, quite insufficient. It has also, largely by design, bypassed the Roma who continue to suffer appalling poverty and racism everywhere in Europe.

References

Baldwin, P. (1990), *The Politics of Social Solidarity*, Cambridge: Cambridge University Press.

Banton, M. (1967), *Race Relations*, London: Tavistock Publications.

Barkan, E. (1992), *The Retreat of Scientific Racism*, Cambridge: Cambridge University Press.

Barker, M. (1981), *The New Racism*, London: Junction Books.

Bebel, A. (ed.)(1971), *Society of the Future*, Moscow: Progress Publishers.

Bland, L. (1995), *Banishing the Beast: English Feminism & Sexual Morality 1885–1914*, London: Penguin Books.

Burleigh, M. and Wippermann, W. (1991), *The Racial State: Germany 1933–1945*, Cambridge: Cambridge University Press.

Castles, S. and Miller, M.J. (1993), *The Age of Migration*, London: Macmillan.

Cesarani, D. (1987), 'Anti-alienism in England after the First World War', *Immigrants & Minorities*, 6(1).

Clayton, A. (1988), *France, Soldiers and Africa*, London: Brassey's.

Cohen, M. (1945), *I was One of the Unemployed*, London: Gollancz.

Cohen, S. (1985), 'Anti-semitism, Immigration Controls and the Welfare State', *Critical Social Policy*, 5 (1), Summer.

Cole, G.D.H. (1947), *The Intelligent Man's Guide to the Post-War World*, London: Gollancz.

Constantine, S. (1991), 'Empire Migration and Social Reform 1880–1950', in Pooley, C.G. and Whyte, I.D. (eds), *Migrants, Emigrants and Immigrants*, London: Routledge.

Davidson, B. (1973), *The Africans: An Entry to Cultural History*, Harmondsworth: Penguin Books.

Davidson, B. (1992), *The Black Man's Burden: Africa and the Curse of the Nation-State*, London: James Curry.

Davin, A (1978), 'Imperialism and Motherhood', *History Workshop Journal*, 5.

Davis, H.B. (1967), *Nationalism & Socialism*, New York: Monthly Review Press.

Eatwell, R. (1995), *Fascism: A History*, London: Chatto & Windus.

Enzensbeger, H.M. (1994), *Civil War*, London: Granta Books.

Fanon, F. (1967), *The Wretched of the Earth*, Harmondsworth: Penguin Books.

Feldman, D. (1994), 'Nationality and Ethnicity', in Johnson, P. (ed.), *Twentieth-Century Britain: Economic, Social and Cultural Change*, London: Longman.

Fletcher, R. (1987), 'The Life and Work of Eduard Bernstein', in Fletcher, R. (ed.), *Bernstein to Brandt: A Short History of German Social Democracy*, London: Edward Arnold.

Fraser, D. (1975), *The Evolution of the British Welfare State*, London: Macmillan.

Fryer, P. (1984), *Staying Power: The History of Black People in Britain*, London: Pluto.

Fryer, P. (1989), *Black People in the British Empire*, London: Pluto.

Gilroy, P. (1987), *There Ain't No Black in the Union Jack: The Cultural Politics of Race and Nation*, London: Hutchinson.

Goldhagen, D.J. (1996), *Hitler's Willing Executioners: Ordinary Germans and The Holocaust*, London: Little, Brown & Company.

Hargreaves, A.G. (1995), *Immigration, 'Race' and Ethnicity in Contemporary France*, London: Routledge.

Hay, J.R. (1975), *The Origins of the Liberal Welfare Reforms 1906–1914*, London: Macmillan.

Hitchman, J. (1966), *The King of the Barbareens*, Harmondsworth: Penguin Books.

Hobsbawm, E.J. (1969), *Industry and Empire*, Harmondsworth: Penguin Books.

Hobsbawm, E.J. (1988), *The Age of Capital 1848–1875*, London: Cardinal.

Hobsbawm, E.J. (1989), *The Age of Empire 1875–1914*, London: Cardinal.

Hobsbawm, E.J. (1993), *Nations and Nationalism since 1780*, Cambridge: Canto.

Hobsbawm, E.J. (1994), *Age of Extremes: The Short Twentieth Century 1914–1991*, London: Michael Joseph.

Jackson, J. (1990), *The Popular Front in France: Defending Democracy, 1934–38*, Cambridge: Cambridge University Press.

Kaye, H.J. (1995), 'Introduction: Imperialism and its Legacies', in Kiernan, V.G. (ed.), *Imperialism and its Contradictions*, New York and London: Routledge.

Kiernan, V.G. (1969), *The Lords of Human Kind*, London: Weidenfeld and Nicolson.

Kiernan, V.G. (1995), *Imperialism and its Contradictions*, (ed. Kaye, H.J.), New York and London: Routledge.

Kolb, E. (1988), *The Weimar Republic*, London: Unwin Hyman.

Kushner, T (1994), 'Immigration and "Race Relations" in Postwar British Society', in Johnson, P. (ed.), *Twentieth-Century Britain: Economic, Social and Cultural Change*, London: Longman.

Lauren, P.G. (1988), *Power & Prejudice*, Boulder: Westview Press.

Lewis, J. (1980), 'The Social History of Social Policy: Infant Welfare in Edwardian England', *Journal of Social Policy*, 9(4), October.

Lenin, V.I. (1969), 'Imperialism, The Highest Stage of Capitalism', in Lenin, V.I., *Selected Works*, London: Lawrence & Wishart.

Lukacs, J. (1993), *Budapest 1900: A Historical Portrait of a City and its Culture*, London: Weidenfeld.

McPhee, P. (1992), *A Social History of France 1780–1880*, London: Routledge.

Miles, R. (1993), 'The Articulation of Racism and Nationalism: Reflections on European History' in Wrench, J. and Solomos, J. (eds), *Racism and Migration in Western Europe*, Oxford: Berg.

Miliband, R. (1973), *Parliamentary Socialism*, London: Merlin Press.

Moeller, R.G. (1989), 'Reconstructing the Family in Reconstruction Germany: Women and Social Policy in the Federal Republic, 1949–1955, *Feminist Studies*, 15(1).

Mondlane, E. (1969), *The Struggle for Mozambique*, Harmondsworth: Penguin Books.

Moses, J. (1987), 'Socialist Trade Unionism in Imperial Germany, 1871–1914', in Fletcher, R. (ed.), *Bernstein to Brandt: A Short History of German Social Democracy*, London: Edward Arnold.

Mosse, G.L. (1978), *Toward the Final Solution: A History of European Racism*, London: J.M. Dent & Sons.

Pois, R. (1970), 'Introduction', in Pois, R. (ed.), *Alfred Rosenberg: Selected Writings*, London: Jonathan Cape.

Prunier, G. (1995), *The Rwanda Crisis 1959–1994: History of a Genocide*, London: Hurst & Co.

Quine, M.S. (1996), *Population Politics in Twentieth Century Europe*, London: Routledge.

Rathzel, N. (1990), 'Germany: One Race, One Nation?', *Race & Class*, 32(3).

Schonwalder, K (1996), 'Migration, Refugees and Ethnic Plurality as Issues of Public and Political Debates in (West) Germany', in Cesarani, D. and Fulbrook, M. (eds), *Citizenship, Nationality and Migration in Europe*, London: Routledge.

Sevenhuijsen, S. (1992), 'Mothers as Citizens: Feminism, Evolutionary Theory and the Reform of Dutch Family Law 1870–1910', in Smart, C. (ed.), *Regulating Women: Historical Essays on Marriage, Motherhood and Sexuality*, London: Routledge.

Sivanandan, A. (1981/2), 'From Resistance to Rebellion: Asian and Afro-Caribbean Struggles in Britain', *Race & Class*, XXIII, 2/3.

Stedman Jones, G.S. (1971), *Outcast London*, Harmondsworth, Penguin Books.

Stedman Jones, G.S. (1982), 'Working-class Culture and Working-class Politics in London, 1870–1900: Notes on the Remaking of a Working Class', in Waites, B., Bennett, T. and Martin, G. (eds), *Popular Culture: Past and Present*, Beckenham: Croom Helm.

Tegel, S. (1987), 'The SPD in Imperial Germany, 1871–1914', in Fletcher, R. (ed.), *Bernstein to Brandt: A Short History of German Social Democracy*, London: Edward Arnold.

Thane, P. (1982), *The Foundations of the Welfare State*, London: Longman.

Thomas, H. (1997), *The Slave Trade: The History of the Atlantic Slave Trade 1440–1870*, London: Picador.

Tobias, P.V. (1961), *The Meaning of Race*, Johannesburg: South African Institute of Race Relations.

Williams, E. (1967), *Capitalism and Slavery*, London: Andre Deutsch
Wilpert, C. (1993), 'The Ideological and Institutional Foundations of Racism in the Federal Republic of Germany', in Wrench, J. and Solomos, J. (eds), *Racism and Migration in Western Europe*, Oxford: Berg.
Wilson, R. (1985), 'Imperialism in Crisis: the Irish Dimension', in Langan, M. and Schwarz, B. (eds), *Crises in the British State 1880–1930*, London: Hutchinson.
Wistrich, R.S. (1992), *Anti-Semitism: The Longest Hatred*, London: Thames Mandarin.
Yeo, E. (1973), 'Mayhew as a Social Investigator', in Thompson, E.P. and Yeo, E. (eds), *The Unknown Mayhew*, Harmondsworth: Penguin Books.

3 The Political Context of Intercultural Public and Social Policy in Europe

Jagdish Gundara

The basic assumption of this chapter is that single initiatives on their own cannot solve all societal problems. Political action and economic measures are fundamental for ensuring adequate social provision in a diverse Europe.

Social welfare as a process does take place within the context of the political system and is all the more critical because, as we enter the twenty-first century, many of the gains of the modern state in the nineteenth century, including political, civil and cultural rights, are being reversed. How, one might ask, have these hard-won rights and developments been overridden by the recent rise of racism, narrow ethnicism and narrow nationalism? In many parts of Europe, seemingly normal national communities, organized groups and forces have unleashed violence at various levels: neighbourhoods, localities, regions and nations. Civilized and educated polities have turned into Hobbesian jungles. The rise of ethnicized violence raises questions about why such violence has arisen from within what were considered stable, educated and civilized states. Conflict and violence in the past few decades has not been between states, but within nation states. Public policy systems have a role in either inhibiting or exacerbating inter-ethnic conflict.

When a political state loses its capability to cope as groups or populations become either superfluous to its needs or is unable to provide for them, this has led to extreme situations. While state systems have tended to impose controls, populations have either resisted, migrated or been reduced to refugees through civil strife and/or economic dislocation. Hence, all sections of the population but particularly young people, whether wealthy or poor, are subject to uncertainty and change. For a variety of different reasons young people act in irrational, erratic and violent ways. There are, for instance, numerous examples of wealthy communities and young people becoming involved, for example, in ethnic and/or football violence. As Hans Magnus Enzensberger writes about young people:

> Youth is the vanguard of civil war. The reasons for this lie not only in the normal pent-up physical and emotional energies of adolescence, but in the incomprehensible legacy young people inherit: the irreconcilable problem of wealth that brings no joy. But everything they get up to has its origins, albeit in latent form, in their parents, a destructive mania that dares not express itself in socially tolerated forms – an obsession with cars, with work and with gluttony, alcoholism, greed, litigiousness, racism and violence at home. (1994:42–3)

Where communities are poor and have little hope for the future, resistance to the status quo arises out of despair and despondency. Such developments illustrate the importance of balanced public and social policies to enable young people to feel included in European societies. The inability of any civil authority to govern, and to adequately educate and provide for all sections of all communities – adults, parents and young people – adds to conflictual situations.

At one level, the education systems have failed to develop critical faculties, as well as analytical powers, which can obviate the slide into ethnic strife and chaos. Nations use symbols legitimated by political systems of their invented identities which construct 'us' and 'them', 'belongers' and 'strangers'. When some 'strangers' are poor, they become even more estranged because rich 'strangers' can be constructed to be one of 'us' by national authorities. Public policy systems play a role in either exacerbating or resolving these dilemmas.

It seems that national authorities are still able, with apparent impunity, to violate the human rights of their own citizens. International interventions rarely, if ever, seem able to stop these violations. When UN forces have been deployed in 15 or so conflict situations, they have largely been ineffective. There are over 50 conflicts tabulated by Stevenhagen (1996) in the recent period.

Action to alleviate problems of ethnic conflict can be initiated at supranational, national, regional level and local levels. Supranational agencies like NATO, the Organization of Security and Cooperation in Europe (OSCE), and the Council of Europe can play a role in stabilizing ethnic conflicts at the European regional level, and regional bodies like the European Union can initiate positive action. The European context presents particular regional prospects and problems for resolving racism and inter-ethnic relations.

Intercultural Parliamentary action in Europe

Issues of xenophobia and racism in Europe, as in other parts of the world, have relevance for public and social policy and it is for parliamentarians to consider these matters, refine them and to develop their own agenda. A second major concern of parliamentarians within Europe ought to be to establish a European-wide intercultural parliamentary group which cuts across all political parties. The assumption here is that intercultural relations are not the prerogative of any particular political perspective or any one political party, since issues of racism and xenophobia are widespread. The millennium as a historic moment might provide such an opportunity. This would require parliamentarians across the party political divides to work together to enhance notions of multicultural Europe into the twenty-first century. It is to be hoped that the 1997 European Year against Racism has initiated a process to deal with these issues and to establish a more systematic institutional framework to counter racism and xenophobia. However, a 'Year Against Racism' is not sufficient: only long-term strategies can deal with this malaise.

The setting up of the European Monitoring Centre for Racism and Xenophobia in Vienna also provides a regional institutional focus. National Round Tables will provide a network and linkage with the Vienna Centre. The Vienna Centre ought to consider the implications of high levels of narrow nationalism, xenophobia and racism in prospective member states from eastern and central Europe who propose to join the European Union. The urgent need for this arises because reactionary, xenophobic, racist and fascist groups are already mobilized in Europe. Unless there is a serious consideration to develop prophylactic intercultural policies, the threat to multicultural democratic polities could undermine stability in Europe.

The definition of Europe itself is problematic. Where does Europe begin, where does it end and who are the Europeans? Does it begin at the Atlantic Ocean and end at the other side on the Pacific Ocean, or are the Urals the dividing line? Who belongs and who is excluded from being a European?

All states must engage in developing strategies for dealing with a range of issues in relation to the national question, national minorities and immigrant communities. The need to form coherent political principles to legitimize societal diversity arises not least of all because the abominable phenomenon of 'ethnic cleansing' has reared its ugly head again in Europe only fifty years after the defeat of Nazism in 1945 (Mazower 1998). Racism in Europe has a long pedigree and history.

At the European Union level, it is essential that racism is monitored and effectively dealt with. Further, negotiations at the intergovernmental level should continually ensure that racism, interculturalism and issues of equity are effectively dealt with. The member states of the European Union ought to provide treaty competence when renegotiating treaties, to ensure that prophylactic measures are devised, which can effectively negate racism and xenophobia. Article 13 of the Maastricht Treaty has already started this process, authorizing the Community to take action on issues of racial, ethnic or religious belief. The amendment of the Treaty and the addition of Article 29 allows member states to take common action to prevent racism and xenophobia by allowing different national police forces to cooperate.

For the first time since the establishment of the European Community in 1957, new Articles 13 and 29 establish legal competence and protection against racism, xenophobia, anti-Semitism, religious hatred and intolerance. After ratification a Community directive will establish a common standard which protects all citizens within the Union, and require member states to pass their own legislation to enforce this standard.

More than 150 non-government organizations (NGOs) have established the Starting-Line Group as a lobbying network to issue a Directive on the rights of third-country nationals. It is understood that during successive presidencies of the EU there will be a strengthening of anti-discrimination legislation within the Union.

In Britain, the Commission for Racial Equality has requested reform of the Race Relations Act. The proposals urge the government to place responsibility for racial equality on the leaders of public and private institutions. The right not to be discriminated against, as well as extending the scope of anti-discriminatory law within the mainstream of British institutions, is being urged (CRE 1998).

Definitions and terminology

Terms like 'multiculturalism' and 'social diversity' are used descriptively, in contemporary discourse, to highlight the 'non-European Other'. If issues of intercultural relations and an equitable intercultural public and social policy are to become a reality, then different groups have to be treated as being central, rather than marginal, to European society. Part of the problem which needs to be addressed is institutionalized exclusion and racism within public and social systems. Interculturalism as a dynamic of intergroup relations in multicultural European societies can either be positive and inclusive, or racist or exclusive.

The first issue is how to define 'culturally diverse' and 'multicultural societies'. A taxonomic framework of states which include linguistic, religious, social class, nationalities and ethnic groups means that most European societies have been historically, and largely remain, very diverse. Hence, EU member states need to develop inclusive intercultural policies to ensure that, in legal and legislative terms, all groups who reside in a polity have citizenship rights.

It is however exceedingly important that such constitutional instruments negate 'the internal decomposition of the community, created by racism' (Balibar and Wallerstein 1991). Development of intercultural measures have to start by negating racism, xenophobia, narrow nationalism and ethnicism. Such intercultural learning can only be meaningful if it helps resolve the practice of 'exclusionary power and powers of exclusionary institutions' (Goldberg 1993:235–6). Hence, the task is one of developing a critical interculturalism which is based on sound intellectual foundations and is firmly grounded in the core functioning of institutions.

Historical facts are subject to distortion whether by the dominant nationality, or by racial, linguistic or religious dominance. Teaching history as a 'story' has various pitfalls and one way of ensuring that young people acquire a critical understanding of the past is to allow them skills to interpret and analyse historical evidence, narratives or documents. At this level there is a need for an intervention of historians and social scientists to provide a taxonomy of what constitutes a multicultural society, for example, the Council of Europe's Tbilisi Project's attempts to write a non-triumphalist history of the Caucasus region (*Independent on Sunday*, 4 October 1998). If societies are considered to have become multicultural because of the presence of immigrants, then parliamentarians and policy makers confront a totally different set of questions and issues than if societies are seen as historically diverse or multicultural. In Europe, as 'borders go down, walls go up' (*Guardian*, 15 February 1995). A contemporary discourse has become structured by creating a relationship between crime, drugs, terrorism and immigrants which are seen as part of a chain of equivalence. If social diversity and migration are subjected to historical analysis, then immigrants can be seen as merely highlighting what are the underlying, existing features of diversities, based on linguistic, religious, territorial and social class. Hence, terms like 'ethnic' 'national minorities' or 'ethnic majorities' require further analysis. Who defines these groups? How are these terms used and by whom? Social diversity is complex and its recognition ought not to start and end with immigrant groups and refugees, normally referred to as 'ethnic groups', especially as dominant groups are seldom recognized as having an 'ethnicity' or ethnic identity. A historical and contemporaneous analytical framework which integrates social diversity with its analysis may make it less likely that such issues are marginalized by society. However, even when a society is seen as being multicultural, this is not always reflected in its social policies.

Terminological issues also revolve around the Janus-headed nature of the nation which may have 'ethnic' features as well as constructions based on modern constitutions. The latter should ensure equality, liberty and fraternity in legal terms and relate to questions of citizenship. Citizens, particularly young people, need to learn that the nation and a society are complex entities that are not subject to singular or simplistic readings. The failure of many public institutions to do this is a major cause of exclusion and ethnically-based violence.

Public policies

Exclusion in socially and culturally diverse societies and nations breeds mentalities of exclusivity. These have led to an ethnic Armageddon in many parts of the world, and European states need to guard against such developments encroaching within the European Union. States, therefore, ought to safeguard the citizenship rights of all groups to ensure not only an equitable resolution of conflicts but to establish prophylactic public and social policies which strengthen democratic ideas. Such national policies ought to bridge ethnic, religious, linguistic and racial differences. Civil and political rights need to be validated in all socially diverse environments to ensure that the civil state is strengthened. In socially diverse local and national contexts, increased tensions can lead to tribalization and fragmentation of communities, particularly if economically weak groups are not reskilled for new jobs. This, as Castells has written, would lead to the 'globalisation of power flows and the tribalisation of local communities' (1989: 350).

The development of intercultural public and social policies ought to ensure that no group loses jobs due to rapid technological change in society and rising levels of deskilling which have accompanied these changes. The clear danger, faced by groups of immigrants, as well as by women and the unskilled among exposed indigenous groups, refugees, travellers and Roma, is that all are being made increasingly vulnerable. The rise of intergroup tensions in this context is likely to be very serious.

Intercultural democratic processes are far from being actualized (Dunn 1993). A number of problematic issues, about ensuring equity and quality in our democracies for all citizens, remain unresolved. Provision of equal access, equal opportunity and equality of outcomes is still not a feature of European societies. The harshness and inequalities of the market economy are more manifest than equality and quality of public and social policy provision.

It is also important that in representative democracies all groups have a 'voice' – without a powerfully secular and inclusive demos, a reversion to narrow identities and fragmentation of the polity could become a reality within Europe. Political systems have so far been ineffective in providing this 'voice' to all citizens, particularly to young people within marginalized communities.

More importantly, at the Council of Europe, expansion into eastern and central Europe draws in new member states whose traditions of democratic politics and recognition of diversity are very limited. Hence, the Council of Europe and increasingly the European Union ought to ensure that inclusive democratic politics are seen to be a condition of belonging to these regional organizations. The denial of citizenship rights to third-country nationals is not only a violation of human rights but of international standards. Yet, the centre-right opposition in Germany to the grant of citizenship rights to the foreign and especially the Turkish community raises spectres of populist racism. The campaign by Christian Democratic Party and the Christian Social Union is not only unChristian by violation of international standards. If the law is enacted, only three million of the eight million immigrants would acquire citizenship (*Guardian*, 5 January 1999).

Unless major interventions to protect human and citizenship rights are undertaken, the likely rise of exclusivist polities will have negative and destabilizing consequences across Europe, empowering neo-Nazis, raising levels of street and political violence and strengthening the hand of extra-parliamentary and undemocratic groups.

Belongingness

The other issue which should be raised is that of 'belongingness' of all groups in European societies. Dominant nationalities tend to see Europe as 'theirs'; 'others' are regarded as aliens who do not belong and are seen to encroach upon it. There are obviously specificities of different localities, communities, families and groups which provide a different colour, texture and hue to different parts of many European countries. Differences of local politics, economies and histories also exist and these intersect and interact differently within national, European and global contexts.

The sharing of space by the dominant and subordinate, the colonizer and the colonized, the rich and poor, comes together in polities, making the functioning of modern democratic societies complex. This complexity includes the way in which material and social goods are produced and distributed, including the political, economic, literary, cultural and the media. The 'other' is no longer out there, but here, and as Chambers' states, there is an intersection of 'histories, memories and experiences' (Chambers 1994:6). It is important to develop an agenda for public and social policy and create spaces where we can negotiate the complexity of our societies, both in rural areas and cities. Such an analysis should be inclusive of all groups who live in them. In establishing such a context, past and current exclusions need to be put to rights, making it possible to initiate a dialogue between all those living in Europe. The interaction and intersection of the histories of cultures and languages enables the construction of a more realistic understanding of the past, and better informs us of the present which may, in turn, have implications for constructing a less biased and a more meaningful future. For instance, in Spain, the teaching of history should include the contributions Islam, Judaism and the regional nationalities like the Basques, Galicians or Catalans have made to Spanish culture, civilization and history, raising issues of antipathy, conflicts and cooperation and undermining triumphalism.

Communities are not only situated within their localities but have other identities, both at national and supranational levels which lends an enormous range of heterogeneity to the society and its life. The complexity of all this defies simplistic definition by either the dominant or subordinate cultures. Political systems, in most parts of the world, have not come to terms with the public policy implications of this reality.

Societies as such embody notions of 'belongingness' as well as of alienation. They have both features of a universalistic nature as well as particularisms and local differences. Yet, non-confederal localisms can become parochial, racist, insular, stagnant and authoritarian. Thick and textured layers of political, social and economic contexts intersect with history, culture and language. European societies therefore provide possibilities and prospects of an infinite nature and yet can also be lonely and confining. The confederal nature of society requires that integrative thinking and structures should link individual groups and localities. The challenge for the political and educational system is to develop a shared and common value system in which inclusive rights and responsibilities will be developed as an outcome of the work of schools, social and political institutions.

Such a political initiative needs to establish broad-based social policies, measures, strategies, actions and institutional changes. It will require monitoring to ensure that international standards are being met. Without the development of these strategies, combined with the analysis of the negative aspects of exclusion there will be further proliferation of racial and ethnic conflict.

There is an urgent need for the formation of a network of institutions and structures to initiate further work: the collation of good public and social policy practices at European level, the development of the Internet and other informational networks, the dissemination of findings and the establishment of educational, social policy and political strategies for different contexts.

Political education and human nature

The role of politics in society is predicated on the fact that political education itself is necessary for all sections of society. Politically under-educated or ill-educated and inactive members of societies are bad citizens because they can misrepresent the complexity of humanity and society, and opt for simplistic solutions based on populist politics, often encouraging authoritarian and undemocratic solutions to complex societal issues (Advisory Group on Citizenship, Final Report 1998). The Minister of Education David Blunkett and the Qualifications and Assessment Authority are consulting people nationally on the nature of citizenship education within the National Curriculum in Britain (QCA 1999).

The Macpherson (1999) Report into the Stephen Lawrence murder highlighted the existence of institutional racism and the need to tackle it within education. Academic learning of politics and active citizenship can both help to negate aspects of institutional racism within British as well as other European societies. A politically literate and competent citizenry are an important aspect of democratic societies so that groups cannot be construed in stereotypical terms.

Hitherto, however, the rationale for not providing political education is the claim that ordinary people are not capable of understanding complex issues and are susceptible to narrow party political propaganda. Elites sometimes suggest that, because human nature is largely negative, it is better not to inculcate interest in political issues amongst the masses. Citizenship education has the potential of making young people understand the legitimation role of constitutional arrangements in modern democracies.

The assumptions being made in this chapter are twofold. First, political awareness, knowledge and understanding is necessary for the masses to grasp both the inherent complexity of society and their rights and responsibilities within it. Secondly, the assumptions about the negativity of human nature also require scrutiny and comment. Thus, if human nature is considered to be negative then selfishness, conflict and violence will be seen to be deeply embedded in human consciousness and educational and other socializing influences will have no role to play in changing patterns of behaviour and social relations. It is commonly argued that human nature is basically selfish and to expect human beings to be social is an uphill task.

The contention of this chapter is that there is as yet insufficient evidence to allow definitive statements about human nature to be made. In other words, human nature needs to be seen as neither good nor bad. The human capacity to be social or selfish is still an open issue and the potential for both exists among people. Human nature as such may neither be Hobbesian nor Rousseauic but has the potential, the proclivity and the capacity to be both.

Individuals may hold not only selfish but also social instincts and the interaction between nature and nurture can result in social contracts based on equality for both individuals and groups. This, however, is not a simple matter because the mind is not a *tabula rasa*: it encodes both personal and larger historical legacies which make the issue of equitable socialization very complex.

The role of political education and involvement is to enable the establishment of a healthier balance between the selfish and the social by accepting the sanctity and autonomy of the learner. The development of such autonomous learners would enable them to negotiate some of the complexities of societies. Education systems with a political education syllabus would enable the emergence of thinking citizens who would be less likely to seek solutions to conflicts through violence. The education of the young also ought to involve the unpacking of the underpinnings of 'evil' in society. However, this is also a broader task of public and social policy and requires an interagency approach, necessary because inasmuch as truth and veracity are inherently human values so are lying and deception. Broader social and public policy measures are necessary to deny the roots of evil, lying and deception, and such policies include the curbing of the cruel treatment of children.

In educational terms, the common manifestation of children's ill treatment and violence against them leads to a lowering of their academic performance, higher levels of truancy and the drift into criminal and violent behaviours.

Intercultural social policies need to take cognizance of the diverse contributions and needs of women. Women from different communities and in different national contexts are represented in a range of positions in socioeconomic terms. Their position has been impacted upon and they have been involved in changing the private and public domains with different capacities, especially in relation to their patriarchal and socioeconomic positions They have also contributed to resistance against racism and essentialized notions of their complex and multiple identities (Rattansi and Westwood 1994:15–31).

Such general social involvement and political educational issues raise problems about the level of academic autonomy allowed by the state within its education system. If the state is insecure it will tend to control directly the education system for dominative or nationalistic purposes. Regional European and other international organizations have a role to ensure that these tendencies are curbed and that states are held responsible for the international legal instruments to which they are signatory.

Political and education systems also have a responsibility to determine the ways and directions in which technology will be developed and used. If it is allowed to be rationalized and instrumentalized to perpetuate violence, then technology reinforces the inherent evil forces in societies. The role of education and public policies to channel technological developments into peaceful and positive directions is essential to obviating conflict and violence.

Racism and diversity

In this section interpretations of what has been called, interchangeably, 'multicultural initiatives', 'multi-ethnic' and 'multiracial society' are discussed. For instance, in educational terms, while most schools have not changed to take account of immigrant children, some have changed. Some of these changes were linked to deficit and disadvantage models of immigrant children. In the 1980s, the discourse among educationalists was fragmented between those who advocated 'multicultural' policies and those who called themselves anti-racist.

Some social policy makers maintain that the issue of 'race' tends to be blurred by the term 'multiculturalism', while others hold that it is not even a relevant category. This chapter assumes that racism is an important variable in many societies, that there is sufficient evidence of the pervasiveness of xenophobia and racism and that the term 'multicultural' provides an appropriate description of institutions, communities and society. In Britain, the 1976 Race Relations Act (however weak) and the Commission for Racial Equality (however ineffectual), both aimed at eliminating racism, are in themselves indicators of its existence at both individual and institutional levels in British society.

One assumption underlying racism is that some cultures are superior to others, and that assimilation is desirable. In the United States, a study of majority–minority groups relations was undertaken to explore this assumption. Acceptance of diversity without assumptions of cultural hierarchies was based on three propositions:

1 Since individuals have no choice as to their ancestry it is undemocratic to penalize them for an aspect of their permanent identity over which they have no control.

2 Each minority group culture has within itself valuable and positive attributes.
3 The proposition that all men and women are created equal does not mean that there are no differences between people but that all merit equal respect and treatment.

These assertions were made by Kallen and other liberal philosophers early in the twentieth century at a time when European immigrants were expected to reject totally their national backgrounds and assimilate into an Anglocentric American society.

In the 1960s an American scholar, Gordon, postulated that the United States was a plural society. He stated that there exists both structural pluralism and cultural pluralism in US society (Kallen 1924). Structural pluralism can be demonstrated by the existence of diversity among minority groups who are separated on linguistic, religious and racial lines. At the minority-group level, structural pluralism exists in the form of institutions which are relevant to specific communities. The existence of a minority-group press, religious organizations – for example, temples and synagogues – and educational institutions, such as Jewish schools, is an indicator of this recognition.

In the context of the state, cultural pluralism exists and focuses on the ideologies and institutions of society with the 'structurally assimilated' schools in the public institutional framework. In the British context this is exemplified by the comprehensive state school system. At the wider social level, cultural pluralism is complicated by the autonomy of groups which either demand or already posses a high degree of equality, or segmentation and dominance.

A society which continues to represent aspects of segmentation and dominance is South Africa where the politically dominant white minority until recently autocratically governed the majority black population. The new South African political institutions have attempted to transform radically the context of these hierarchal relations but socioeconomic divisions continue to exist. In other countries like France and Britain, the trend ranges from segmentation and dominance to a situation of group autonomy within a context of equality. In other words, distinct cultural groups within this institutional setting maintain their distinction over time. If, for instance, the majority or minority groups are not allowed certain levels of autonomy, they may then make demands for separate institutions, be those on racial, linguistic or religious grounds.

A major theory of cultural pluralism views integration as racial assimilation – that is, the socialization of minority children with children from the dominant community. If and when some elements of majority or minority communities accept this postulation, they might do so on the grounds that if their culture resembles that of the dominant group they may become more acceptable. Conversely, such groups may fear that failure to accept the dominant value system would leave them open to oppression and persecution in the future. Those of the minority group who experience self-hatred might also adopt the dominant norm and reject those of their own culture. Unless the political, social and education systems deal with these issues of dominance, integration as racial assimilation is merely 'token desegregation' (Gordon 1964). If there are no changes in the social structure, in institutional frameworks and the substance of provision, then the larger patterns of inequality and exclusion are likely to continue. A major proportion of minority communities consequently reject this form of assimilation and integration. British models of the 1960s and 1970s, including Roy Jenkins' ideas of cultural pluralism, were basically integrationist. In education and housing, the policy of 'dispersal' of immigrant students within the school system and families within particular estates was based on assumptions of integration.

While the dominant group might support assimilation, those from racial minority communities typically favour the cause of diversity. This perspective on the part of the latter allows for the affirmation of values which are other than Euro-conformist or Euro-centric. One justification for this perspective amongst minorities and long-settled immigrants might be that they are often bicultural and bilingual and possess traits of the dominant group as well as their own distinctive culture. Social institutions which accept diversity in racial terms presuppose that pupils, parents and teachers have equal status based on equal power. However, this is not always the case as, in both institutional and structural terms, the dominant group does not allow power to slip from its hands. Yet, paradoxically, unless institutional barriers to participation are removed, groups remain excluded and, in fact, often demand separate provision. In terms of schools, factors such as social class and diverse languages complicate pedagogic issues particularly if the schools are controlled by local communities or religious groups, yet face national examinations to legitimize their knowledge. Furthermore, immigrant groups do not control either the institutions, economic resources or political power which would allow them to become independent of the dominant group (Rist 1978). Thus, separate institutions do not necessarily further intercultural links or relations with other socially segregated groups. Yet the five million or so Muslims in France still feel that the secular school does not accommodate difference, for example the controversy over the head scarf emerged again in 1999 (*Guardian*, 11 January 1999). This issue is symptomatic of deeper cleavages in society which require resolution through substantive and inclusive public and social policies.

Deprivation and disadvantage models

The reality of social classes means the existence of assimilation on a class basis, raising issues for those who are poor or 'disadvantaged'. Conservatives in this debate tend to postulate an inferiority based on genetic factors while liberals tend to stress that the disadvantage is the result of past discrimination based on sex, race, class, ethnic or territorial grounds, resulting in the existence of disadvantaged sections of the community. A combination of these forms of discrimination, so the argument runs, may contribute to family breakdown, which may have led to the inadequate socialization of individuals, accumulated social deficit and a resistance to schooling. In educational terms, such explanations form the basis of various remedial or compensatory programmes. In the United States, such thinking determined the initiation of programmes like Head Start. In other words, what children from poor classes needed was an initial dose of socialization to acquaint them with the values, behaviour and ideas of the middle-class white population (Carby 1980). The critics argued that Head Start was unsuccessful in the long term, assuming, it seems, that such programmes were on the scale of the Marshall Plan and thus were to alleviate centuries of economic, cultural and social exploitation. Purely educational responses to disadvantage based on economic, social and cultural grounds are inadequate. Only broader social and public policy initiatives can reverse the situation.

Knowledge and inclusiveness

Issues of knowledge and curriculum are critical to the way in which European states construct themselves. Inclusions and exclusions of knowledge have implications for ethnic conflict, peace and stability in a state. The assumption here is that Eurocentric curricula are inimical to the strengthening of European polities. These can in fact weaken nation states by privileging dominant discourses, especially since the histories, languages and knowledge of European national minorities and new Europeans will remain excluded.

Knowledge systems confront dual challenges as European integration takes shape. On the one hand Europe confronts a Eurocentric tradition in many domains of knowledge. These hegemonic understandings are informed by the imperialism of Europe. As Edward Said writes:

> Without significant exception the universalising discourses of modern Europe and the United States assume the silence, willing or otherwise, of the non-

> European world. There is incorporation; there is inclusion; there is direct rule; there is coercion. But there is only infrequently an acknowledgement that the colonised people should be heard from, their ideas known. (Said 1993)

As a result of the imperial enterprise, not only is Europe in the world but the world is in Europe. This interpenetration of cultures and civilizations have universal implications and need to be analysed at the broadest possible level. Ostensibly, this has profound implications for the transfer of knowledge within and outside Europe in planning public and social policies. Yet, discourses from the colonized peripheries and subordinated nationalities are still treated as being marginal in most contexts.

Martin Bernal indicates how, in the eighteenth and nineteenth centuries, Europeans developed a historiography which denied the earlier understanding that the Greeks in the Classical and Hellenistic periods had learnt as a result of colonization and interaction between Egyptians, Phoenicians and Greeks (Bernal 1987). Part of the reason for this new historiography has been that with the rise of racism and anti-Semitism in Europe, the European Romantics and racists wanted to distance Greece from the Egyptians and Phoenicians and construct it as the pure childhood of Europe. It was unacceptable from their perspective that the Europeans would have developed any learning and understandings from the Africans or the Semites.

The notion of a northern European culture, separated from the world south of the Mediterranean, is largely a mythical construction. The contributions to knowledge in the ancient period from this immediate region include Mesopotamian astronomy, the Egyptian calendar and Greek mathematics, enriched by the Arabs. As Samir Amin states:

> The opposition Greece = the West/Egypt, Mesopotamia, Persia = the East is itself a later artificial construct of Eurocentrism. For the boundary in the region separates the backward North African and European West from the advanced East; and the geographic unities constituting Europe, Africa, and Asia have no importance on the level of the history of civilization, even if Eurocentrism in its reading of the past has projected onto the past the modern North–South line of demarcation passing through the Mediterranean. (Amin 1989:24)

The debate about how and where 'civilization' arose is important for the development of public and social policies. It is also a part of a wider concern with the intellectual strait-jacket that Eurocentric political and education systems can impose. In this sense it is always necessary to consider ways in which both formal and informal understandings of the European polity can be modified or changed. As long as European societies are considered from one or another narrowly nationalist perspective, public and social policy will remain trapped in the tramlines of nationalist tautology. And within this approach questions of racism, xenophobia and ethnicisms will remain unchallenged within the mainstream discourses and policies in European societies.

A fundamental issue that this book raises is how these alternative definitions of knowledge and understandings of Europe ought to be built into mainstream public policies so that inclusive and democratic measures can strengthen the fabric of societies through equity and social justice. Such measures would enhance stability and the quality of life of all those who live in Europe.

References

This chapter is based on a Report commissioned by UNICEF International Child Development Centre, Florence.

Advisory Group on Citizenship, Final Report (Chair: Professor Bernard Crick) (1998), *Education for Citizenship and Teaching of Democracy in Schools*, London: Qualifications and Curriculum Authority.

Amin, S. (1989), *Eurocentrism*, London: Zed Books.

Balibar, E. and Wallerstein, I. (1991), *Race, National, Class: Ambiguous Identities*, London: Virgo.

Bernal, M. (1987), *Black Athena: The Afro-Asiatic Roots of Classical Civilisation*, Vol. 1, New Brunswick: Rutgers University Press.

Carby, H. (1980), 'Multiculture', *Screen Education*, 34, 64–5.

Castells, M. (1989), *The Informational City*, Oxford: Blackwells.

Chambers, I. (1994), *Migrancy, Culture, Identity*, London: Routledge.

CRC (Commission for Racial Equality) (1998), *Reform of Race Relations Act 1976*, London: CRE.

Dunn, J. (1993), *Democracy: The Unfinished Journey 508 BC to 1993*, Oxford: Oxford University Press.

Enzensberger, H.M. (1994), *Civil War*, London: Granta Books.

Goldberg, D.T. (1993), *Racist Culture*, Cambridge, MA: Blackwells.

Gordon, M. (1964), *Assimilation in American Life*, New York: Oxford University Press.

Guardian, London, 15.2.1995, 5.1.1999, 11.1.1999.

Independent on Sunday, 4.10.1998.

Kallen, H.M. (1924), (reprinted 1970), *Culture and Democracy in the United States*, New York: Arno Press.

Macpherson, Sir W. (1999), *The Stephen Lawrence Inquiry*, London: The Stationary Office Ltd, CM 4262.

Mazower, M. (1998), *Dark Continent: Europe Twentieth Century*, London: Allen Lane.

QCA (Qualifications and Curriculum Authority) (1999), *Review of the National Curriculum in England: The Secretary of State's Proposals*, London: QCA.

Rattansi, A., and Westwood, S. (1994), *Racism, Modernity and Identity on the Western Front*, Cambridge: Polity.

Rist, R. (1978), *The Invisible Children: School Integration in American Society*, Cambridge, MA: Harvard University Press.

Said, E. (1993), *Culture and Imperialism*, London: Chatto & Windus.
Stevenhagen, R. (1996), *Ethnic Conflicts and the Nation-State*, London: Macmillan Press Ltd.

4 Political Sociology and Cultural Studies in the Study of Migrant Communities in Europe

John Rex

A gap has opened up between the study of the political sociology of the relations between immigrant communities and their societies of settlement in Europe and that of the study of cultural relations, focused particularly on the concept of cultural hybridity. This chapter will attempt to set out some of the underlying theoretical and methodological assumptions of these two types of study and to problematize the question of the relations between them before going on to suggest a more complex notion of 'cultural hybridity'.

It is important to note that this chapter deals with a limited subject matter, namely that of communities and individuals migrating from dependent societies to metropolitan centres. It does not deal with earlier migrations of administrators, missionaries, entrepreneurs and settlers from the imperial centre to colonies in the heyday of imperialism. The attempt to treat all such migrations as similar in terms of the concept of transnational communities or diasporas is regarded here as mischievous and misleading. The difference between the two types of migration lies essentially in the power which migrants can deploy.

So far as the use of the terms 'diaspora' and 'transnational communities' is concerned, the term 'diaspora' is used in either a narrow or a much looser sense. In its narrower sense, it derives from the experience of Jews dispersed after a traumatic experience and seeking to return to 'Zion', an experience which is seen as being paralleled by that of Africans transported as slaves to the New World, whose descendants seek to return to Africa. In a broader sense it refers to all populations who have migrated to other countries and retain some connection with their homeland (Cohen 1997). In this looser sense of the term it is sometimes replaced by the term 'transnational communities'. The distinction which is being made here, however, is a different one, discriminating between transnational communities in terms of the power of the migrants.

Major points of political and cultural reference amongst migrant communities and individuals

Recent migrations to Europe should not be understood in essentialist terms. They are driven by shifts in the political challenges which are presented in various changes of the migration process and the responses which the migrant communities make to them, and the 'cultures' which such communities exhibit must be understood in relation to this essentially political and economic process.

An important attempt has been made by Massey and his colleagues to consider the way in which the study of these communities has been dealt with in terms of a number of different though possibly overlapping theories of migration and settlement (Massey et al. 1993). I have sought to place my own theorizations within the context of their work (Rex forthcoming). In my view migrant communities and their 'cultures' in Europe must be understood in terms of three points of reference. First there is the reference to the changing society, politics and culture of the homeland. Second, they refer to the adjustment of the community and its culture to the politics and culture of the land of settlement (commonly referred to as the 'host society'). Finally, they are oriented to the business of possible onward migration.

Spanning these three situations, the key actors will be some sort of extended kinship group seeking to improve its estate. Such kinship groups have some members in the homeland, some in the land of present settlement and some in the countries of possible onward migration.

Orientation to the homeland

The migrant community's connections with the homeland will in the first place involve some kinship connections. Those who have migrated will seek to improve the position of their kin in the homeland through remittances, through recruiting spouses from the homeland and through visits and the sending of some of their children there for part of their socialization and education.

In this relationship with the homeland, the migrant community will necessarily be involved in its class and status order and its politics. There its relatives will seek to acquire land and other economic resources, to build houses, to improve their status and to participate in political conflicts. Such a relationship will be dialectical: the class, status and political system of the homeland will place limits on the options available to kin groups, while this class, status and political system will itself be modified by the actions of migrants and their relatives.

Orientation to the land of settlement

Turning to relations with the land of settlement or the host society, it should not be thought that what we face is the confrontation of a modern and usually industrial society with immigrants with traditional cultures. What the immigrants are seeking to do is to enter the social system of the land of settlement and to win equal treatment within it. Another way of understanding this is to see the migrant communities and their kin groups as seeking to move within a total imperial social system. In their homeland, their position had been defined by their degree of access to and control of the economic and political system, but all such positions would appear to be unfavourable in the total imperial order to major class positions in the political order of the host society. It is advantageous to make a move from most colonial class positions even to what are thought as inferior positions in the host society's political and class system. They will have to fight, not merely against ordinary exploitation, but against their exclusion from the benefits which the inferior working classes have won for themselves. This means that the migrant community will itself have a 'modern' orientation. Its politics and 'culture' will be changed by the challenges which the host society presents and it may well be that the political culture of the homeland itself involves modernizing elements. By way of illustration one may consider the case of the Punjabi communities in Britain. They are in part organized by political parties such as the Communist Parties of India which have already been engaged in class struggle at home and which now must adapt their tactics to the fight for justice in the land of settlement.

This fight for justice is pursued in the first place by kin groups but, in pursuing it, they will need allies. They will therefore act together with other kin groups who share their language, culture and religion; as a result the collective actors in the land of settlement will be more than merely kin-based groups. Their action is affected by these relationships, while, on the other hand, the various linguistic, cultural and religious groupings themselves come to have a new political significance. Some of the efforts of the migrant community are therefore likely to be devoted to sustaining such groupings, and it therefore seems that, along with their instrumental orientations, the migrants are concerned with preserving their cultural identity. Not surprisingly even the most modernized of migrant families deal with the life events of birth, marriage and death in their temples, mosques and churches.

Pulling against this orientation to the maintenance of what appear to be traditional identities will be the formation of alliances with class-based groups in the host society. The migrants will join trades unions and political parties of the host society, even though they may have to fight within these organizations for their own special interests. Thus the Indian Workers Association in Britain encourages its members to join British trades unions, while at the same time operating as a union within the unions to defend Indian workers' interests (see Rex and Tomlinson 1979: Chapter 4).

One should add here that the problem is complicated by the fact that some migrants are not entering working-class jobs but actually taking up opportunities in business. These opportunities may at first occur through servicing the migrant community itself or with filling otherwise unfilled niches in the host economy. However, once such businesses are established, they may also enter the economic mainstream. Migrant businesspeople will then face similar dilemmas to those facing migrant workers and their organizations.

Further problems face migrant communities because of the involvement of their children and grandchildren in the economy, politics and culture of the host society. Some of them may defect from their communities altogether, a price which must be paid as one of the costs of migration. At any moment, however, the descendants of migrants may find themselves in alternative positions. They may find advantages in reaffirming their commitment to their parents' culture; they may, as Schierup and Alund (1990) have pointed out in dealing with Yugoslav migrants in Sweden, form alliances with disaffected elements in the host society, or they may renounce any connection with traditional culture and simply join in the mainstream.

Complex as this situation is, we should also note that collective action by clearly defined migrant communities is not the only option available. Some kin groups and even some individuals may be expected to produce their own individual strategies for seeking justice or adapting to the process of settlement.

A further special problem is that of gender differentiation. Within migrant communities, women may face different problems from men and some migration will involve, in the first place, the migration of women as domestic servants, cleaners, nurses, brides or sex workers. The various special challenges of these roles mean that any traditional subordination of women is likely to be challenged in the migration process. Here again, however, the defence of special women's interests does not mean that there will not be occasions on which women fight for justice collectively with men.

Orientation to onward migration

All of these factors point to a complex politics of the land of settlement. One should note, however, what has been said above about orientation to onward migration. This is a factor which will prevent any tendency towards total assimilation. While it is true that disadvantaged elements in the host society may, particularly in the imperial countries, sometimes seek better opportunities in the colonies or elsewhere, the option of onward migration may be even more accumulation of wealth and education as a means to an end and be mainly concerned to moving on to other countries. Thus Indian, Pakistani and other immigrants in Britain may have in mind eventual more economically successful migration to North America. There they will face further challenges of settlement not structurally dissimilar to those which they have faced in Britain.

The study of community and culture amongst migrants

So far I have dealt with the politics and the culture of migrant communities, seeing their culture as intertwined with their responses to political challenges in the process of survival or of improving their economic condition. Mostly in my own writing, however, I have been inclined to use the more inclusive term 'ethnic mobilization', which requires further explication. The term 'ethnicity' is one which is much disputed between those who, following an early formulation of Geertz (1963), regard ethnicity as primordial and those who, following Frederick Barth (1969), see it as essentially instrumental or situational. The concept of ethnic mobilization inclines towards the latter view of ethnicity, but recognizes that in mobilizing for action the group or community calls upon given cultural resources.

This, however, involves a distinct use of the term 'culture'. It refers not to some specialized activity, but to all the forms of organization, the ideas, values and goals to be found within a particular population. It is close to the common anthropological usage of the term deriving from E.B. Tylor (1994) who defines culture as consisting of all those forms of 'knowledge, art, beliefs, morals, law and any other set of capabilities acquired by man as a member of society'. When many sociologists refer to minority culture or ethnicity, they are simply referring to all the forms of organization and ideas which control the population in the course of collective action.

A quite different conception of 'culture' is that which regards it as the product of the activity of specialized groups producing ideas concerned with interpreting human experience, which go beyond the mere process of survival. It is concerned with the production of new meanings and expresses itself in the various arts, including high or elite art as well as popular artistic expressions.

I have further complicated, some might say confused, this issue in a separate discussion of the nature of an egalitarian multicultural society in contemporary Europe. Arguing for this ideal I have suggested that such societies would have a shared public political 'culture', centring on the idea of equality for all individuals, and more private communal 'cultures' of separate groups based upon different languages, religions and customary family practices (Rex 1996; Guibernau and Rex 1997). Some of those who have criticized this conception would argue that the term 'culture' should not be applied to the shared body of political ideas but that it should be reserved for the body of ideas and practices which serve to bond the members of separate communities. The former would then be seen as constituting the realm of politics and the latter as being concerned with culture.

In any case the notion of two domains of ideas, one shared and public involving political ideas, the other cultural and belonging to separate communities, is difficult to sustain. There do seem to be certain areas in which more is shared between groups than political ideas, the simplest example being of these is that of a new cuisine which comes to be shared between different groups and becomes part of the culture of the whole society. Another is that of the arts: poetry, drama, literature may also develop in this way, coming to be, not simply related to, and the possession of, particular groups, but belonging to the total society. Even the artistic culture of the dominant indigenous group is affected in this way. The Booker Prize for literature has recently been most commonly awarded to immigrant writers or indigenous writers dealing with problems of intergroup relations. Such writing also forms a predominant part of the literature reviewed in prestigious journals such as the *New York Review of Books*. At a more mundane level, the Indian dish called 'Chicken Tikka Masala' has become the most popular *English* dish.

Thus, along with the concept of culture which we use in discussing ethnic mobilization, and with the concept of the private communal cultures of migrant ethnic minority groups, we must recognize the emergence of new shared cultural expressions produced by specialized groups, both within the different minority groups and transcending them in the interrelationship between the minority groups and the host society.

The study of these new cultural expressions has become a discipline in itself, divorced from the sort of political sociology of ethnic mobilization which has been discussed here. This study has appealed particularly to those whose training is in the study of literature – important amongst these is Stuart Hall, whose qualifications were in literature as a Rhodes scholar in Oxford. He was one of the main advocates of a cultural studies approach when he became Professor of Sociology in the Open University. In this case, however, cultural studies combined with the study of the institutional complex of what most sociologists called 'modernity', which was contrasted with the institutional complex of pre-modern society. (See Hall and Gieben 1992; Allen, Braham and Lewis 1992; Bocock and Thompson 1992; Hall, Held and McGrew 1992). This interest in modernity was based upon reflections on European history rather than on empirical studies.

In its more specific concern with 'culture', the new cultural studies approach drew *inter alia* on the work of Homi Bhabha (1994), but as Friedman has pointed out Bhabha refers exclusively to literary works as the source material for the author's depiction or 'theory' of social reality in the contemporary world (Friedman 1997).

Still within the sphere of cultural studies, it should be noted that Hall's approach went beyond the study of literary works to include popular culture. This had been the concern of the Centre for Contemporary Cultural Studies which Hall had taken over from Richard Hoggart, who in his *Uses of Literacy* (1957) had been particularly concerned with the modern media. One of the most important writers to emerge from the Centre in its later form was Gilroy. Not trained as a sociologist, Gilroy addressed himself to the study, not of the elite culture of literature, but to all forms of popular cultural expression, focusing particularly on popular music and its lyrics (Gilroy 1987, 1993).

The empirical material used by Gilroy dealt purely with these cultural products and did not involve a political sociology, although he seems to assume that these cultural expressions reflected an underlying political reality. A similar assumption appears to have underlain the work of the Council of Europe which, in preparing for a study of culture and urban neighbourhoods, defined culture as 'encompassing both amateur and professional activities in the fields of literature, the visual and performing arts, the crafts, design, fashion, film and video, photography, radio, television, the press and electronic music' (Bianchini 1994).

We may now ask what the relation was between the studies of culture in this sense and the political sociology which has underlain my own studies of ethnic mobilization. In my belief, it cannot be assumed that the culture which Gilroy or the Council of Europe urges us to focus on completely reflects an underlying political reality. Nor can it be assumed without question that such culture controls political reality as the poet, Shelley, once suggested when he said that poets were the unacknowledged legislators of the world. Here I find myself in sympathy with the work of Margaret Archer who criticizes much sociology of either 'upward conflationism' (in which the social is reflected in the cultural), or downward conflationism (in which culture determines the structure of society) (Archer 1988). Archer's own approach is to insist upon an analytic dualism in which cultures and societies have their own separate dialectic and trajectory, although they are also seen as interacting with one another.

It would seem to me that the relationship of cultural expressions to society might in principle be regarded in a number of alternative ways – as reflecting underlying social reality, or as ordering that reality – but it may also be seen as cathartic, giving expression precisely to those ideas and goals which are *not* realized in politics. Thus when popular West Indian poets in Britain seem to refer to a war against the police in which blacks have won some kind of victory, the political reality is that they did not win, or at most achieved some kinds of compromise. Similarly it could be said that while the so-called 'kitchen sink' dramatists of the early 1960s commanded the superstructure of ideas, the political infrastructure remained in the same hands. I do not wish to assert dogmatically that culture reflects or controls political reality or that it involves catharsis. What I do wish to assert is that the relationship between culture and politics, between superstructure and infrastructure should be problematized before cultural studies is regarded as providing an adequate basis in itself for political sociology.

Cultural hybridity

For Bhabha (1994), migrants exist in a double cultural space and produce a new culture which is necessarily 'hybrid'. He opposes this new hybrid culture to the unitary culture of the modernizing state. Gilroy's position in his later work, *The Black Atlantic* (1993), is similar: he criticizes the notion of a black culture drawing wholly on the anti-colonial liberation struggle or on some kind of Africanism, and suggests instead that this culture meets with and is hybridized by the experience of struggle in societies of settlement like Britain.

Gilroy's position comes closer to that which we have discussed above in looking at the social organization and ideas of migrant groups. We suggested that the 'culture' of such groups had three points of orientation and was a complex reality. We are, however, saying something more than that this culture is hybrid – a term which is fairly vacuous. Instead, we have sought to show how this culture is related to essentially political action. We did not refer simply to cultural products produced by cultural specialists (whether elite or popular) but to ideas and forms of organization and action which arose in the course of political action. The relation between culture in this sense and the specialized culture exhibited in cultural products and expressions is then problematic.

The notion of hybridity used in cultural studies remains largely unexplained. It has to be asked whether hybridity simply involves juxtaposed elements or whether the new 'hybrid' culture does not contain within itself some kind of functional unity of meaning, apart from any function it may be seen as having in terms of a political sociology. Some critics have also asked whether hybrids consisting simply of juxtaposed elements would not be sterile.

Culture and diaspora

It should now be noted that because of his interest in cultural hybridity, Gilroy transforms the notion of diaspora in a peculiar and distinctive way. For him one of the things which emerges in diaspora is not merely the preservation of a traditional culture or the creation of a new culture based upon the notion of a return to Africa, but a culture which is necessarily hybrid. The diasporic community is then seen as one which adheres to this new developing hybrid culture. This is quite clearly a different conception of diaspora from those which we have discussed above.

Other types of migration and settlement

As a matter of convenience I have developed a model of migration and settlement based upon economic migration from colonies and dependent territories to metropolises both during the phase of imperialism or in its aftermath. Using this as a base, however, we should also note that Europe has also received other kinds of migrants.

Many migrants are in fact much closer geographically and culturally to their host societies. Southern Europeans from Italy, Portugal, Spain, Greece and Yugoslavia were essentially cross-border migrants whose institutions were not dissimilar to those of the north-western European societies and who were easily able to maintain links with their homelands. They could continue to maintain a dual loyalty to their homeland societies and to the land of settlement. A number of authors who contributed to the volume *Immigrant Associations in Europe* (Rex, Joly and Wilpert (eds) 1987) have discussed this problem. They show how homeland governments, the Catholic Church and left-wing parties such as the Communist Party played a continuing, transnational role in the organization of immigrant communities.

A further set of problems occurs for immigrants who may have a loyalty, not simply to a single homeland but to political and cultural communities which are themselves international – for example, many Muslim immigrants who identify with the resurgence of Islam in a variety of countries and of immigrants from the Caribbean who identify with black politics and culture in the United States.

Migrants from the Caribbean also have another set of problems. Their ancestral African cultures and forms of social organization were largely destroyed in the process of enslavement and they were forced to adopt, albeit as inferiors, their masters' language, religion and cultures. To some extent therefore they saw themselves, even before migration, as belonging to what they thought of as the 'Mother Country', but their inferior position as well as their identification with the black experience meant that they developed their own versions of the Mother Country's institutions and culture. On the one hand, this culture was creolized; on the other, it was a culture of resistance.

A quite different set of problems appeared to face refugees and political migrants, particularly those coming from eastern Europe after the collapse of communism. Only a few of these were refugees in a narrow sense of being in personal danger, but the reason for their migration was none the less flight from intolerable political conditions, often involving civil war. They might in many cases have been concerned about their kin and identified with those who had not been able to escape; some of these would seek only temporary refuge while waiting to return when conditions changed. But some faced the fact that their kin and their homeland communities had actually been destroyed and that they would have to construct new communities where they were settled. No single account can be given of the political and cultural situation of all the political migrants, even from individual countries. They faced a wide range of differing situations and produced a variety of different responses.

However, some overlap does exist between political and economic migrants. Their homelands were affected not only by the breakdown of law and order, sometimes involving civil war, but by the breakdown of their homeland economies. To some extent therefore they can be seen as coming from dependent economies and societies to modern and relatively successful capitalist and welfare state economies in the West.

Apart from the differentiations which can be made between different types of migrant communities, others might be made between different host societies in the kinds of mix of immigrant groups which they receive. Britain, for instance, has been mainly concerned with immigrants from the Indian sub-continent and from the Caribbean although it now must deal also with new populations of political migrants and asylum seekers. France has had to deal with Muslim immigrants from the Mahgreb. Germany has, through its guestworker policy, dealt with workers deliberately recruited from Turkey. The Netherlands has had to receive immigrants of varying kinds of descent from its former colonies, but has also had to deal with Moroccan and Turkish migrants. Italy has its own particular mix of communities and problems.

Emigration and immigration in the case of Italy

The case of Italy may be considered as exemplifying the complexity of the problem of emigration and immigration in contemporary Europe. Earlier studies of migration in Europe often referred to Italy as a 'sending society'. Now, however, Italy receives immigrants from other parts of the European Union, from America and from the South. Their numbers are difficult to estimate for a variety of reasons, as the study by ISMU in Milan indicates (Angeli 1995). There is also a large number of illegal immigrants, some of whom are known to some of the authorities, but others may not be registered by anyone. A reasonable guess seems to be that, taking legal and illegal immigrants together, there are just under a million in an Italian population of 57 million.

As to the national origins of non-EU immigrants, there are a variety of different estimates from the Ministry of the Interior and the Italian Statistical Office. According to these, the largest groups in order are from Morocco, the former Yugoslavia, the United States, the Philippines, Tunisia, Albania, Senegal, Egypt, Sri Lanka, China, Brazil, Poland and India. Immigrants other than those from the US are concentrated in certain regions and cities. Lombardy has some 74,000, the Lazio region 60,000 and Romagna 28,000. Social scientists from a number of Italian cities were subsequently asked by the UNESCO MOST Programme to prepare so-called 'templates' for a conference in Amsterdam which would provide comparative material on the mix of immigrants in these cities. In fact the categories employed in these studies varied from one city and region to another and the data were still incomplete. None the less they do provide us with some information on the present situation. According to these papers, two-thirds of the immigrants to Milan (Zanfrini 1997) were from the less developed countries and, in Rome, there were 158,000 foreigners from non-EU countries, including some from the Americas (both the USA and Latin America) (Collicelli 1997). According to the Milan study, 'The Mahgreb immigrants from Morocco, Algeria and Tunisia are the largest communities and the ones that generate the greatest concern among the local autochthonous population. More recently such concern has focussed on Albanian and former-Yugoslav migrants.' The study also records that 'As for sub-Saharan Africa one of the largest and most studied communities is the Senegalese community: most belonging to the Murid brotherhood which is known to have a peculiar pattern of integration which acts upon a marked sense of belonging and community solidarity.' In the case of Tome, Filipinos are the largest community in terms of numbers, followed by those from the US, the former Yugoslavia, Poland and Spain, according to a 'Caritas-Rome processing of statistics based on Ministry of the Interior data' (Collicelli 1997). Surprisingly no figures are recorded for Senegalese.

Different communities of foreigners are in any case integrated to differing degrees. Those from the US present few problems and are not noticed as immigrants; the Egyptian community is said to be well integrated. The immigrants from the South are thought of as giving most 'cause for concern'. Compared with north-western European countries, Italy and its various cities and regions are dealing with a relatively new set of problems that involve a variety of different types of immigrant.

Caritas-Rome also provides a breakdown of resident foreigners by religious belief. This shows that of 194,000 resident foreigners 79,000 are Catholics, 47,000 other Christian, 40,000 Muslims, 7,000 Jews, 7,000 Shintoist-Buddhists, 6,000 Hindus, 1,300 Tao-Confucianists, 2,600 Animists and 10,000 others (Collicelli 1997). Such figures (which I have rounded from those provided by Caritas-Rome) give a rough guide to the kinds of problem of integration for the non-Catholic communities.

It seems that Italy is now experiencing a new set of problems, which north-west Europe experienced in the 1960s and 1970s. The communities involved are relatively small and differ very much amongst themselves. Some are regarded as more problematic than others. Possibly a concern about immigrant problems means a concern about communities from the less developed world, especially in Africa, Muslim communities, Filipinos and political migrants particularly from Albania. Each of these has its own special problems and, as a result, there can be no single policy for dealing with all of them. So far as their culture is concerned, the degree of cultural integration, hybridity or segregation and marginalization will differ from case to case. In terms of the theoretical ideas developed earlier in this chapter, therefore, there is not a single Italian case but a variety of different problems.

Finally, given the peculiar geography of Italy and its proximity to Africa, it will be the 'soft underbelly' of Europe for migration to other parts of the European Union under the Schengen Agreement. Thus, whatever, the special problems of integrating immigrants in particular cities and regions, the other countries of Europe will be concerned about Italian immigration policy.

The study of cultural relations between immigrant communities and their host societies in Europe

We must now return to the question of what is involved in the studies of culture and cultural hybridity. As I have said above we need to construct more complex concept and need to deal with more complex data than that suggested by contemporary cultural studies.

In the first place we need to take account of culture in the wider sense in which the term is used by those who study immigrant minority groups and what I have often called their 'ethnic mobilization'. Here we have to look at all the forms of organization and ideas which control or influence the behaviour of different populations. Such cultures could be thought of as 'hybrid' but it might be more useful to say that any hybridity derives from the fact that members of these populations have simultaneously held different points of orientation. All of this has to be described in any account of migrant cultures. It involves more than the study of culture produced by cultural specialists and more than the study of cultural products.

Another important focus of study would be the changing culture of host societies. These societies have their own political ideas and ideals as well as ways of life which have developed over centuries. It must be asked to what extent they change as a result of their encounter with incoming groups of migrants. They may themselves become 'hybrid'. It should also be noted, however, that in the imperial countries the ideas, ideal and ways of life of the host nation have always been affected by imperial and colonial relationships. In a recent article, Back (1997), has shown how the local culture and the very architecture of the buildings of Deptford in London was shaped by this experience.

When all these kinds of culture and cultural hybridity have been studied, there is, however, a more specialized set of problems which concern the activities of cultural specialists whose work is to produce cultural products. Even if we suppose that migrant communities have fixed forms of social organization and traditional ideas which influence and govern the experience of their members, a distinction can be made between the culture which forms part of the day-to-day life of ordinary people and the culture which is produced by cultural specialists and involves the creation of cultural products. Such specialists also operate in the more complex forms of ethnic mobilization which we have discussed. A slightly different perception of the problem of the cultures which come into existence in societies of settlement is obtained, however, if the focus of our interest is not on the separate communities but on their relationship with the land of settlement. This relationship produces its own culture, cultural specialists and cultural products.

My plea would be for a study of culture and cultural hybridity which takes account both of the day-to-day culture of ordinary people and the culture of specialists. When these have both been analytically distinguished and described, the final task would be to go on to analyse and describe their relationship. This is what I would see as the more complex and necessary approach to cultural hybridity which combines the insights of political sociology and the study of culture in the more specialized sense.

Finally, however, I would point out that the study of cultural hybridity is not the only problem thrown up by the coming of migrants to established European societies. Another set of questions concerns the political justice of the relationship between migrants and their hosts. That is a separate question and the one which I have sought to emphasize in talking about the shared political culture of egalitarian multicultural societies. An interest in cultural hybridity provides no excuse for avoiding this problem.

References

Allen, J. et al. (1992), *Political and Economic Forms of Modernity*, Cambridge: Polity Press and Oxford: Blackwells.

Angeli, F. (1995), *Migrations in Italy, the First Report*, Cariplo Foundation for Information and Studies of Ethnicity, Milan: ISMU.

Archer, M. (1988), *Culture and Agency*, Cambridge: Cambridge University Press.

Back, L. (1997), 'Globalisation, Culture and Locality', *Sociology Review*, 7(2), Deddington, Oxfordshire: Phillip Allan.

Barth, F. (1969), *Ethnic Groups and Boundaries*, London: George Allen and Unwin.

Bhabha, H. (1994), *The Location of Culture*, London: Routledge.

Bianchini, F. (1994), *Working Paper for Cultural Neighbourhoods Project, Towards a Methodology for the Project*, Strasbourg: Council of Europe.

Bocock, R. and Thompson, K. (1992), *Social and Cultural Forms of Modernity*, Cambridge: Polity Press and Oxford: Blackwells.

Cohen, R. (1997), *Global Diasporas*, London: UCL Press.

Collicelli, C. (1997), *Rome*, a 'Template' submitted to the UNESCO MOST Project on Multiculturalism and Modes of Citizenship in Europe, Amsterdam.

Friedman, J. (1997), 'Global Crises, the Struggle for Cultural Identity and Intellectual Porkbarrelling: Cosmopolitans versus Locals, Ethnics and Nationals in an Era of De-hegemonisation' in Werbner, P. and Modood, T. (eds), *Debating Cultural Hybridity*, London and New Jersey: Zed Books.

Geertz, C. (1963), *Old Societies and New States*, New York: Free Press.

Gilroy, P. (1987), *There ain't no Black in the Union Jack*, London: Hutchinson.

Gilroy, P. (1993), *The Black Atlantic*, London: Verso Press.

Guibernau, M. and Rex, J. (1997), *The Ethnicity Reader*, Cambridge: Polity Press.

Hall, S., and Gieben, B. (1992), *Formations of Modernity*, Cambridge: Polity Press and Oxford: Blackwells.

Hall, S. et al. (1992), *Modernity and its Futures*, Cambridge: Polity Press and Oxford: Blackwells.

Hoggart, R. (1957), *The Uses of Literacy*, London: Chatto and Windus.

Massey, D. et al. (1993), 'Theories of International Migration. A Review and Appraisal', *Population and Development Review*, 19 (3), September, New York.

Rex, J. (1996), *Ethnic Minorities in the Modern Nation State*, London and New York: Macmillan.

Rex, J. (forthcoming), 'Migration in the Study of Transnational Communities', in Taylor, E. et al. (eds), *Migration Theories*, Madrid: Ortega Y Gasset Foundation.

Rex, J. et al. (1987), *Immigrant Associations in Europe*, Aldershot: Gower.

Rex, J. and Tomlinson, S. (1979), *Colonial Immigrants in a British City*, London: Routledge and Kegan Paul.

Schierup, C-U., and Alund, A., (1990), *Paradoxes of Multiculturalism*, Aldershot: Gower.

Tylor, E.B. (1994), *Collected Works*, London: Routledge.

Werbner, P. and Modood, T. (1997), *Debating Cultural Modernity*, London and New Jersey: Zed Books.

Zanfrini, L. (1997), *Milan*, a 'Template' submitted to the UNESCO MOST Project on Multiculturalism and Modes of Citizenship in Europe, Amsterdam.

5 Ethnic Diversity in the European Union: Policies for New Europeans

Mary Coussey

Introduction

The 1997 European Year against Racism and the inclusion of a general non-discrimination clause in Article 13 of the Treaty of Amsterdam, have stimulated interest at European level in measures to improve the position of immigrants and people from the ethnic minorities. The Council of Europe has also been concerned about the position of immigrants, and for some years has been working to improve community relations and equality of opportunity for immigrants and national and ethnic minorities. This chapter considers the continuing demographic and economic significance of ethnic minorities in the EU, and analyses some key conditions and measures which are needed to ensure that they progress in participation and access. Two primary requirements are political recognition of the need for action, and for public authorities to take a lead in implementing measures.

The Council of Europe, founded in 1949, to achieve greater unity between European parliamentary democracies, is the oldest European intergovernmental institution, with forty members. Its statutory principles are pluralist democracy, respect for human rights and fundamental freedoms and the rule of law. It carries out a range of intergovernmental activities concerned with human rights and social justice, and has been centrally concerned with the position of immigrants. The 1991 report was an analysis of the experience of the 'old' countries of immigration of their efforts to integrate different immigrant communities and to improve relations between these communities and the original populations (Council of Europe 1991). Crucially this report identified the need for equal opportunities as the basis of a good community relations policy. It was followed in

1992 by a project which produced practical guidelines for member states on the implementation of community relations policies, and on the measures needed to provide equal opportunities (Council of Europe 1992). The guidelines were based on analysis of first-hand experience of a wide cross-section of officials, project managers, immigrants and people from the ethnic minorities, from a wide variety of backgrounds, circumstances and perspectives.

Although there are wide differences between western Europe and the new member states in political context, historical background and the language used to describe the problems, in reality many European states are experiencing similar problems in coming to terms with cultural and ethnic diversity. Immigrants and ethnic minorities tend to be marginalized, to suffer from discrimination, and to have weaker legal status and problems of access in many areas of society. In framing social policies, the focus has been on tackling these problems. But it is important to put them into perspective and focus on some key demographic and economic facts which are usually overlooked.

The forgotten demographic and economic contribution of ethnic minorities in Europe

The best estimate of the overall non-EU immigrant population is about 4.5 per cent, of which the largest group originates from Turkey, followed by those who originate from former Yugoslavia, Morocco and Algeria (CEC 1995). These statistics are, however, based on nationality, and exclude naturalized immigrants and the descendants of immigrants, that is to say, ethnic minorities. The EU's ethnic minority population, is much larger; about 5 per cent, rising to a possible 8 per cent depending on definitions.

Countries with the largest immigrant and ethnic minority populations are Belgium, Germany, France, the UK, Austria and the Netherlands. It is estimated that about 20 per cent of the French-born population now has one parent or grandparent of immigrant origin (Tribalat 1991). Luxembourg also has a large population of immigrants, but mainly from other EU countries, especially Portugal and Italy.

In the twelve EU countries, the proportion of women immigrants has increased from 30 per cent of the immigrant population in 1980, to about 45 per cent in 1992. This is partly because of structural change: more women are finding work. They are in demand in domestic and health care employment, in hotels and restaurants, entertainment and tourism. Examples include Philippine women in northern Italy, and Polish women in Germany.

In all EU countries, there has been a fall in fertility, and this has become most pronounced in the last twenty years. Since 1975, in the UK, the Netherlands, Belgium, France and Luxembourg, fertility has been at or lower than levels needed to maintain the same size population, and in Germany and Austria, fertility rates are even lower. Italy and Spain have the lowest fertility rates in the world, although the fall began later than in the northern countries. Immigration has therefore been essential to maintain the growth of the population of the EU. France in particular has had a lower fertility rate than needed to meet demand for labour, and it is estimated that, by 1986, 40 per cent of the growth of the French population since the Second World War was contributed by the descendants of immigrants arriving from the turn of the century, from Italy, Spain, Portugal and, later, from Algeria and Morocco.

In the next 25 years, the number of young people, that is, those aged under 20, in the EU will fall by 11 per cent; the number of working-age adults will decline by about 6.4 per cent, and the numbers of retired adults will increase by 50 per cent.

The reverse is true for the ethnic minority and immigrant populations of the EU. The age structure of the immigrant population is younger than the population as a whole. They also have higher fertility, partly because there are more in the childbearing ages, and also because it takes a generation for

Table 5.1 The most 'aged' countries in the European Union, 1992

Percentage of population of 65 years and over.	
Sweden	17.9
UK	15.7
Belgium	15.4
Denmark	15.4
Austria	15.3
Italy	15.2
France	15.0
Germany	15.0
Greece	14.8
Spain	14.1
Finland	13.9
Luxembourg	13.8
Portugal	13.6
The Netherlands	13.2

Source: Stalker 1995.

immigrants' fertility to fall to that of the host population. This younger age structure also continues into the next generation, and thus the ethnic minority population is younger, and will continue to grow. For example, it has been estimated that ethnic minority people will contribute 30 per cent of population growth in the Netherlands (Bureau voor Economische Argumentatie 1994).

Overall, there will be fewer young people leaving education and entering the labour market. In contrast, there will be a 'boom' in the numbers of young people from the ethnic minorities, because of the younger age structure of these groups. They will have a rejuvenating effect on the overall demographic profile, and reduce the effect of the 'ageing' of the population. For example, in the UK, the average age of people from all ethnic minority groups in 1995 was 27, compared with 38 for the white population.

These demographic differences between the majority and immigrant/ethnic minority populations of the Union have important economic and social consequences. As there will be fewer economically active people, and an increase in the proportion of inactive older people (over 65 years), immigrants and ethnic minorities will play a significant part in compensating for population ageing, and will also be helping to support the dependent generation. However, the demographic contribution of the existing ethnic minority and immigrant populations of the EU countries will not be sufficient to make up for the overall decline in population numbers.

It has been estimated that in order to compensate for the 'demographic ageing', net immigration to the European Union would have to rise by five to seven million (CEC 1995). Other estimates suggest that Belgium would need to attract immigrants at the annual rate of 40,000, Austria at the rate of 10,000 and Spain the rate of 100,000 in order to have numerically stable populations. In Germany, there will continue to be a need for immigrants, and their proportion in the workforce in western Germany will need to rise to 18 or 19 per cent by the year 2010 to compensate for labour shortages. A recent study in Italy has estimated that 50,000 immigrants per year will be needed to counter-balance the effects of the drop in population, and the ageing demographic profile. Greece has also experienced a drop in the fertility rate and has a pool of hard to fill jobs. There is no doubt that there will continue to be a demand for new immigrants in the labour markets of Europe, particularly in service industries and for seasonal labour in agriculture.

Although there has been little systematic analysis of the value of immigration to the EU, there have been a few national studies which show that immigrants bring economic benefits. The younger age structure of the immigrant and ethnic minority population means that, in many countries, they are a net contributor to the social welfare 'balance sheet'. For example, a study in Austria has shown that immigrants make a net economic contribution to the Austrian state (*Migration News Sheet*, March 1997). The country received some 32.5 billion ASch from income tax, VAT and social security payments from immigrants. It paid out 22.2 billion ASch in health care and social allowances to immigrants. The same is true in Germany. It has been calculated that immigrants contribute about 25 billion DM more into the public purse than they receive in benefits. In 1989, employed immigrants paid 7.8 per cent of all old-age insurance contributions, and received only 1.9 per cent of all social security benefits in the same year (Bundesministerium für Wirtschaft 1994).

Immigrants are significant creators of new small and medium-sized enterprises. In general, a higher proportion of immigrants is self-employed, often because of the barriers which they meet in achieving a career in established enterprises. In the UK, the Netherlands and France, immigrants and ethnic minorities have a higher than average self-employment rate, but it varies according to the ethnic group concerned.

For example, in Germany, the number of small and medium-sized firms owned by people of Turkish origin is growing, and there are now over 40,500 Turkish-owned enterprises employing over 135,000 people (*Ausländer in Deutschland*: 1995). In Dusseldorf, a Turkish Employers' Association formed to represent Turkish-owned companies has become a link for Turkish investment in Germany, and for German investment in Turkey, and a collaborator for business links in the new republics in Central Asia. It is estimated that immigrants generate earnings of 200 billion DM annually, or 10 per cent of Germany's total domestic earnings (Bundesministerium für Wirtschaft 1994).

Similarly in the Netherlands, immigrants and ethnic minorities are involved in running almost 8,000 small enterprises in catering, retail and service industries. A study of the trade connections of the ethnic minority population in the Netherlands identified several ways in which they contributed to strengthening Dutch overseas trade (Bureau voor Economische Argumentatir 1994). Ethnic minority entrepreneurs formed trading links with their countries of origin, and this made trading easier for Dutch enterprises, as they could exploit and develop existing networks, and also could involve Dutch ethnic minority people in the import–export functions, using their knowledge and language skills. Ethnic minority entrepreneurs also created alternative lower-priced import channels for existing products, which had a beneficial effect on competition. Although it has not been fully investigated, it is calculated that ethnic minority entrepreneurs' trade with their countries of origin amounts to 10 per cent of the total exports of the Netherlands. In future, the Netherlands' ethnically diverse population will make the country an attractive trading partner. For example, it is recognized, as it is in Germany, that there are opportunities for significant growth in trade with Turkish-speaking areas in the new republics of Central Asia.

A study in Finland shows that immigrant-owned small businesses are growing, especially in consulting and import/export enterprises, taking the opportunity offered by Finnish companies to expand in international markets (Hyrsky 1996). This could be an important indication of a future potential growth area for immigrant enterprises, linked with the awareness by big businesses of the need to expand to new markets.

Ethnic minority businesses are also developing in new areas, servicing the corporate headquarters, financial institutions and export centres of big cities such as Paris, London and Amsterdam. These tend to be started by young well-educated ethnic minorities, and show potential for growth. Some of these are economic investors, forming financial networks with their countries of origin, such as Singapore and Malaysia. This type of immigration of the highly skilled and educated is increasing, and is economically and socially important.

Although many ethnic minority businesses are small, nevertheless, they are creating employment. It has been estimated that in the Netherlands, ethnic minority businesses have created an additional 50,000 jobs (Bureau voor Economische Argumentatir 1994). The study also estimated that ethnic minorities in the Netherlands are also consuming the equivalent of 11 billion guilder, which has the effect of increasing employment by 70,000 persons.

Political recognition and leadership needed

Immigrants brought much of value: they rehabilitated declining areas, imported new energies and businesses, and invigorated cultural and social life. Yet one must search for information which shows the positive contribution of immigrants and ethnic minorities. Because of the emphasis on the fears of the receiving population, fostered by some politicians, the focus is on the problems and on the perceived 'threat' to European society, and immigrants are portrayed as marginalized and excluded. There are of course negative aspects, and it is important to know the extent of racial and ethnic discrimination and disadvantage, so that policies and solutions can be devised. But it is easier to tackle these problems in a socially fair and tolerant way if the questions of immigration and multi-ethnic societies are put in context and the benefits are fully acknowledged and publicized. This requires a new political recognition of the benefits of diverse societies in Europe, and proactive policies to remove discriminatory practices and legal barriers to full political and economic participation for settled immigrants.

Assertions of ethnic or cultural identity are presenting challenges to the nation state, at the same time as the nation state is facing challenges from increasing cooperation at European level. Recognition of cultural diversity has been easier in countries such as the Netherlands, the UK, Belgium and the Nordic countries than in France and Germany. Spain too seems willing to adopt a positive approach to diversity, perhaps having accepted the principle in relation to her national minorities.

Analysis of different approaches in a wide variety of circumstances in different countries makes it possible to identify some key conditions which are essential for managing ethnically diverse societies. The causes of ethnic discrimination, of economic and social marginalization and the exclusion of immigrants, and ethnic minorities, are complex and cumulative. Barriers to access are evident in employment, housing, education and health care provision.

Governments, national and state, and local and public authorities, have the key role. This role embraces exercising leadership, taking and stimulating positive action, allocating funds, and giving tangible support to work to reduce ethnic inequalities, and to promote the values of equality and active tolerance.

Those in public life have a particular responsibility when it comes to reducing racism and xenophobia, stopping ethnically motivated violence, and practising active tolerance. Politicians in particular, must exercise positive leadership in what they say in public. They must openly support efforts to create a more tolerant climate. There is clear evidence that racist and xenophobic attitudes are reinforced above all by negative public debates which focus on the undesirability of immigrants or minorities. That is why it is important that immigration and tolerance towards minorities are not linked in public discourse and policy development.

Those in public life also have responsibility in what they do. It means that leading institutions must set the standard in having effective equal opportunities programmes, and actively recruit and train immigrants or people from ethnic and national minorities for all positions and levels. This is particularly important in public service employment.

Educational provisions should be adapted to promote values of tolerance, and to raise awareness of the benefits of culturally diverse societies. If there are minorities from disadvantaged backgrounds, it is essential for remedial action to begin as early as possible, at least before the age of seven.

The media have an important responsibility as they can influence the climate of opinion and help counter negative stereotypes. The dominant media can report on minorities in a balanced way. For example, they can show how cultural diversity contributes to and enriches society, and avoid constant focus on problems or conflicts. They can recruit minorities especially in visible media, for example as journalists in mainstream programmes. This helps present multi-ethnic or cultural images as the norm. Examples include the BBC and some independent television companies in the UK, who implement training schemes designed to encourage ethnic minority people to enter as journalists and production staff. The BBC has set itself the goal of ensuring that their workforce reflects the nation it serves. BRTN, the public radio and television network of the Flemish community in Belgium, has also had a training scheme to encourage ethnic minority reporters. The training projects 'More Colour in the Media' in Germany, Sweden, Greece, the UK and the Netherlands, are encouraging ethnic minority people to enter the media.

Campaigns against racism and xenophobia can influence public opinion. Information needs to be disseminated on the contribution of minorities, to help dispel myths and negative stereotypes. For example, the UK, the Netherlands, Germany and the Nordic countries regularly publish information about the position of immigrants and ethnic minorities. Germany has been particularly active in disseminating information about the positive contribution of immigrants. The federal government publishes data to counter stereotypes about immigrants, and a monthly newsletter on immigrants with data and positive images and articles.

Measures to reduce barriers

Protection against racial or ethnic discrimination, against threatening racist behaviour and violence are vital elements of a national strategy. This requires not only effective legal instruments, but also effective enforcement and support for the victims. Countries such as Belgium, Britain, the Netherlands, Sweden and Denmark have an independent agency to help people bring cases of discrimination (Council of Europe 1995). This helps even the odds against an unrepresented or disadvantaged minority, who would find it difficult to bring an action unaided against a powerful institution. There is a need to ensure that existing legislation is adequate and, more important, that the victims can have easy access to enforcement machinery, conciliation and support for bringing cases. These agencies soon built up expertise in assessing the evidence of the more subtle acts of discrimination. Other countries, for example, Germany, Italy and France, relied on clauses in articles of the constitution or the criminal code to give protection. In general, these are ineffective because of the higher threshold of evidence needed to bring successful prosecutions.

The police and judiciary also need to vigorously enforce the sanctions against threatening racist behaviour, displays and violence; police and local authorities need to take preventive measures against public displays of racism and violence, and have a coordinated early-warning mechanism to identify potential trouble spots. Countries with early-warning systems include Germany, Britain, the Netherlands and the Nordic countries (Oakley 1997).

Mainstream political participation of ethnic and national minorities and settled immigrants is very important. It is a powerful symbol of their belonging, and gives a true sense of mutual participation and a feeling of involvement in society. It cannot be achieved by having separate immigrant councils, which has been necessary in Germany because of the lack of political rights of immigrants.

Legal barriers to full participation must be removed, especially those which exclude immigrants or other minorities from mainstream political life. Security of residence and access to naturalization and employment in the public services are of real importance. Britain, the Netherlands and Norway have relaxed the nationality restrictions on public service employment, and this has enabled the latter two countries to set targets for the employment of ethnic minorities in public services. Belgium has recently broadened its nationality requirements, but in the remaining EU countries, much of the public service is closed to immigrants and subsequent generations unless they become naturalized citizens of the receiving country.

Other forms of participation of minorities in mainstream decision making are equally significant. Specific efforts should be made to ensure that there is fair representation in all public boards and commissions, in education, housing and tenants' associations, religious fora, as trade union officials, and in any other machinery.

Immigrant and ethnic minority women are often unofficial and unrecognized mediators between the generations, and between the immigrant or ethnic minority and majority communities. In France, there is an official scheme which recognizes the special role of women as mediators, 'Femmes Relais' (ADRI 1996).

In all EU countries, immigrants and ethnic minorities are active in trades unions, often in works councils, in joint committees and other workplace and industrial forums. A study in Belgium found that over half the sample of young people of immigrant origin were members of trades unions, with over 70 per cent of those of Turkish and Maghrebin origin active (Feld and Manco 1996) In the United Kingdom, ethnic minority people are more likely than average to be members of trades unions. This indicates that there is a commitment to improving conditions and a desire to take part in other areas of national life which should be encouraged and facilitated.

In many countries, ethnic minorities suffer disproportionately from unemployment. This is partly due to discrimination, but it is also structural and because minorities have had limited opportunities to gain skills and vocational training. All training programmes should be adapted to take this disadvantage into account. Governments have a special role to play in taking the lead, encouraging the private sector to take action, and in ensuring that public funding is adequate and earmarked for reducing these disadvantages. Sweden, Germany and Britain have all allocated additional funds for training disadvantaged ethnic minority people.

There is also a need for vocational and professional training to be adapted to the requirements of ethnically and culturally diverse societies, and for training to be flexible and able to adapt both the arrangements and contents to meet the particular needs of different groups. There are many examples of this type of training throughout Europe (Council of Europe 1995). Two of the more imaginative schemes are in France and Sweden. Rencontre in Dunkerque, France, is an independent centre which has been carrying out intercultural training for professionals of Maghrebian origin for work with enterprises who operate in these countries, who recognize the value of employing managers with bicultural skills, contacts and knowledge. In Sweden, International Engineers is a special labour office in Stockholm, devoted to finding jobs for ethnic minority engineers. The project also offers apprenticeship and customized training periods with industrial companies, networking opportunities and job-seeking training. Both of these examples demonstrate the need for intensive promotional efforts to involve employers, and the need for an agency to take the lead in planning coordinating action.

Incentives can be a powerful tool for local and central governments. The award of public grants and contracts can take into account the equal opportunity record of the bidding organizations. Partnerships with private corporations can be established to encourage investment and regeneration of decaying multi-ethnic areas. This has been a feature of the urban policy approach of France.

Training of public officials and managers relevant to the needs of a multicultural society is essential for all who work in public services and with minorities. Training of managers and public servants in behaviour and skills appropriate to working in ethnically and culturally diverse communities is a key requirement, especially for police forces who hold the line between different groups, and who must work with the tensions. Britain, the Netherlands and Germany have developed specific training for their police officers (Oakley 1994); there is now collaboration at EU level, and assistance has been given to police forces in central and eastern Europe.

Reducing ethnic inequality requires action by many different agencies and organizations. One clear lesson which emerges from many countries is the need for a national strategy to be sustained and coordinated. There are many different approaches to this. Some countries have found it best to set up a designated agency to coordinate, monitor progress and evaluate the effectiveness of interventions taken. Others have implemented the strategy through specific programmes in each ministry. However it is done, an objective evaluation of progress is needed to ensure that objectives are being met and that the momentum is maintained.

There is no blueprint; what is important is that someone is designated to take the lead in planning and for coordinating strategy and action, that all agencies involved are clear about their roles and action, and that progress is reviewed so that problems can be ironed out. For example, in Norway, this coordination is initiated by the Labour Ministry, in France by the Ministry of Social Affairs, and in the Netherlands in the Ministry of the Interior, which has a Minorities Integration Department.

Yet in many areas, the task of reducing economic or social exclusion is allocated to local projects organized by non-governmental organizations (NGOs), which often have difficulty in attracting partners from the big institutions. It is not possible to tackle such complex, often deep-seated, social and economic problems through isolated and fragmented action by small-scale pilot projects, typically run by NGOs. Visible and tangible support is needed from all the main institutions in society. Many excellent initiatives are undermined because of short-term, piecemeal funding, or because other agencies have not been involved, or had different or conflicting priorities. These initiatives are more effective if they are sustained and coordinated across the various agencies with relevant responsibilities and resources. This is partly a reflection of the low political priority given to reducing ethnic inequality.

Many European countries have been reducing the scale of public spending. Governments have fewer public resources for solving economic and social problems. New partnerships and methods of intervening are being tried, and there is awareness that all organizations in public life need to become involved in implementing solutions to complex social problems, particularly the business sector. Sweden and Britain have business-run campaigns to encourage this sector to adopt active policies, Sweden 2000, and Race for Opportunity.

However, the same few business corporations such as British Airways, BT, Volvo, and Levi Strauss, are involved in all European countries and the leadership is often lacking – it remains an uphill task to gain their wide support. A small number of transnational corporations are beginning to recognize that ethnic and cultural diversity can bring business benefits, but most have not.

Accurate data is needed at a variety of levels to measure progress and allow evaluation of policy interventions. Facts are also important to help generate public interest and concern, and to help dispel myths about immigrants. Britain and the Netherlands are two states which have accepted the need for ethnic registration and monitoring. Other countries rely on data which records birthplace or parental birthplace. There are key differences between these different approaches; the former being more dynamic but subjective, the latter being objective but more restrictive as the generations pass. These differences need to be reconciled at European level so that we have comparable information (Council of Europe 1997).

Application of policies to central and eastern Europe

Circumstances in Europe changed significantly after 1989, and from the mid-1990s, the Council of Europe membership was widened to include many of the new democracies of central and eastern Europe. These new democracies are redefining themselves, grappling with assertions of national identity and culture, and the need to reconcile these with the existing pluralist societies. Latent nationalism and assertions of ethnic identity are not always easy to manage, especially where there is insecurity created by the massive economic restructuring which these countries have undergone during the last decade.

Central and eastern European countries are experiencing immigration, albeit at a much lower level than was the case in western Europe. More significantly, many central and eastern European countries have significant national minorities within them, and these raise questions about community relations and equal opportunities. Although these questions arise in a different context, many of the principles which have been developed in western Europe in relation to populations of immigrant origin apply to policies for the treatment and integration of national minorities.

One important factor has been that several of the new member states are also aspirant members of the European Union. Their human rights record is one relevant criterion for acceptance. Moreover, exposure to the policies and practices of established pluralist democracies and participation in the debates and proceedings of a European intergovernmental institution have given them valuable experience of current European approaches to social policy and the rule of law.

There are welcome signs that some countries have accepted the need for positive measures to be taken. Hungary adopted a Decree in 1997 to implement policy measures to improve the living conditions of the Roma, including employment, research into discrimination with a view to supplementing existing legal provisions and promotion of police careers with young Roma school students. Bulgaria has a programme 'From Social Care to Employment', to improve the employment prospects of the Roma.

Concluding comments

It is important to get the problems into perspective, and focus on what can be achieved. It is clear from analysis of experience in the member states of the EU, and elsewhere in Europe, that many of the required solutions to racial discrimination and inequality are there. But the political leadership and determination are often missing, and this is needed to make a difference. Admittedly, governments cannot do everything, but they can influence what is done. Above all they can influence the climate of opinion. It is often a question of political and moral courage.

Much of what is being recommended does not require extra resources. It requires a refocusing of existing resources, so that funds are earmarked to meet the needs of the most disadvantaged. Again, this needs political courage. A review of the legal framework, in order that immigrants and ethnic and national minorities can exercise political rights and have security of residence, will make a big symbolic difference. This too needs political courage. The fact that the newly elected German government is, at the time of writing, considering an overhaul of that country's unfair citizenship laws is a welcome development in the EU's largest multi-ethnic member state.

References

ADRI (Agence pour le Developpement des Relations Interculturelles) (1996), *Roles et perspectives des femmes relais en France*, Paris: ADRI.

Ausländer in Deutschland (1995), a magazine published by Isoplan, Institute for Entwicklungsforschung, Wirtschafts und Socialplanung, Martin-Luther-Strasse 20, 66111 Saarbrucken.

Bundesministerium für Wirtschaft (1994), *Foreigners and the German Economy*, No. 139.

Bureau voor Economische Argumentatir (1994), *De economische betekenis van minderheden voor de arbeidsmarkt*, Hoofddorp.

Commission for European Communities (1995), *Migration Statistics*, Eurostat, Luxembourg: EC Official Publications.

Council of Europe (1991), *Community and Ethnic Relations in Europe*, Strasbourg: Council of Europe Press.

Council of Europe (1992), *Integration of Immigrants: Towards Equal Opportunities*, Strasbourg: Council of Europe Press.

Council of Europe (1995), *Legal Measures to Combat Racism and Intolerance in the Member States of the Council of Europe*, Strasbourg: Council of Europe Press. Belgium has the Centre pour l'Egalité des Chances et la Lutte contre le Racisms; Britain has the Commission for Racial Equality; the Netherlands has the National Bureau for Combating Discrimination (LBR); Sweden has an Ethnic Discrimination Ombudsman, and Denmark has the Board for Ethnic Equality. The legal basis of these agencies varies.

Council of Europe (1997), *Measurement and Indicators of Integration*, Strasbourg: Council of Europe Press (discussion and guidelines on policy indicators).

European Commission (1995), *The Demographic Situation in the European Union*, Luxembourg: EC Official Publications.

Feld, S. and Manco, A. (1996), *Famille, communauté et organismes publics: les reseaux de solidaritéens*, Liège.

Hyrsky, K. (1996), 'The Rocky Road of Immigrant and Ethnic Business in Finland', paper presented to the Second Irish Entrepreneurship Research Conference, November.

Migration News Sheet (1997), March, Brussels.

Oakley, R. (1994), *Police Training Concerning Migrants and Ethnic Relations*, Strasbourg: Council of Europe Press.

Oakley, R. (1997), *Tackling Racist and Xenophobic Violence in Europe: Case Studies*, Strasbourg: Council of Europe Press.

Stalker, P. (1995), *Les Travailleurs Immigrés*, Geneva: International Labour Organisation.

Tribalat, M. et al. (1991), *Cent Ans d'Immigration, Etrangers d'Hier, Français d'Aujourd'hui*, Paris: Institut Nationale d'Etudes Demographiques, Presses Universitaires de France.

6 The Cultural Short-cut: A Road to Exclusion? Notes on Identity Politics in the European Union

Peo Hansen

Since the 1980s we have witnessed a growing debate, within both academic circles and the media, around the issue of identity politics. Almost exclusively, identity politics has come to refer to the politicization and affirmation of separate ethnic, racial, cultural, religious and gender identities. It occurs mostly in the West among groups who oppose what they consider to be discriminatory state policies. Black separatism in the United States, the headscarf controversy in French schools, gay and lesbian street demonstrations, and the struggle for state-funded Islamic schools are just a few among countless examples where identity politics is said to be at work.

As few will have failed to notice, over the years, identity politics has acquired derogatory connotations. For example, it is suggested that it fragments society and undermines inclusive social policies, threatens universal principles of equal treatment, preaches segregation, and is essentialist, purist, tribal, and even racist and sexist. Thus, there is a need to question how the concept of identity politics is employed and, even more importantly, to question why it is that only certain groups and certain expressions have come to be associated with the politics of identity.

One of the problems with this conception of identity politics is that it excludes other sites where this politics is also being waged. If identity politics is indeed about the articulation of a particular identity and not just about some (minority) group engaging in it, then other such articulatory practices, taking place for instance at the level of the state, must be scrutinized as a type of identity politics as well. Julien and Mercer make a similar point regarding the common-sensical utilization of ethnicity, stating that: 'a one-sided fixation with ethnicity is something that "belongs" to the Other alone, thus white ethnicity is not under question and retains its "centred" position (1988:6).

By doing exactly this, but on yet another level, this chapter will focus on the politics of identity that is now being pursued by the European Union. Put simply, the major research question I seek to deal with here is how the EU goes about articulating an identity for itself. This task, however, does not set out from the common understanding of identity politics as something that is *a priori* harmful and excluding. Instead, such politics must be seen as potentially open-ended, depending on how it construes the identity it seeks to mobilize. The many different identity articulations in motion today must thus be contextualized; each being approached as having very different causes and effects. Most of all, they do not exist in isolation from each other but have to be seen as contingent and relational. Therefore, when minorities engage in identity politics, this might well be seen as a response to the identity politics emanating from the state, which in many cases has assigned identities for these groups as 'other', who cannot belong to the national community. Harvey makes this point succinctly:

> The demands of minority groups within larger social entities for the recognition of cultural heterogeneity tend to require a politics of identity, where culture is used as a means to an end. These are the terms in which dialogue with hegemonic groups is deemed possible, for it is only through an awareness of the ways in which one group's cultural assumptions systematically erase the presence of others that progress can be made and change achieved. (1996:30–1)

Bearing this in mind, I relate identity politics at the level of the EU to the situation for ethnic minorities with migrant backgrounds now living in the EU. The intention is to investigate whether or not we can detect any attempt from within EU institutions to articulate an alternative, less rigid and more inclusive Community identity, compared to those often exclusive national identities we see being pursued within the member states. These questions will mainly be situated in the context of three policy areas, central for identity construction in the EU: culture, education and citizenship. These areas, crucial for the consolidation of the nation state, were also given priority in the Maastricht Treaty as key areas for the creation of a cohesive European identity.

Below, I first outline my research approach to these matters. Secondly, I want to bring up some theoretical issues related to the politics of identity at the level of the European Union and, thirdly, display some concrete examples from EU policies on culture, education and citizenship, hinting at the types of representations of 'Europe' that the EU deems appropriate as sources of identification. Finally, I try to situate the identity politics under study in the context of the crisis of legitimacy facing the European Union today. Due to the limited scope of this chapter my discussion will mainly focus on the work carried out by the European Commission.

Broadening the focus of research on identity in the European Union

The work to establish greater popular cohesion across national borders among citizens within the European Union, and not only among the member states themselves as political entities, has been part of the Community project since the outset. Indeed, for many of the so-called 'Founding Fathers' and the subsequent Community engineers, federalists and visionaries, the long-term goal of European Community formation has been to dissolve the nation state as the primary unit of identification among people in the Community (Shore 1995; see also Bull 1993; Kourvetaris and Kourvetaris 1996).

However, it was not until 1973 that the Community put forth its first formal statement that explicitly addressed the issue of 'European identity' (see Tindemans 1976; Commission of the European Communities (CEC) 1988). In the 1973 Declaration on the European Identity, the member countries agreed 'that the time has come to draw up a document on the European Identity', which was followed by statements such as:

> The diversity of cultures within the framework of common European Civilization, the attachment to common values and principles, the increasing convergence of attitudes to life, the awareness of having specific interests in common and the determination to take part in the construction of a united Europe, all give the European Identity its originality and its own dynamism ... The European identity will evolve as a function of the dynamic of the construction of a united Europe. In their external relations, the Nine propose progressively to undertake the definition of their identity in relation to other countries or groups of countries. They believe that in so doing they will strengthen their own cohesion and contribute to the framing of a genuinely European foreign policy. (CEC 1973:119, 122)

Nevertheless, it was not until the launching of the 'People's Europe' concept in the mid-1980s that any real and explicit discussion of a 'European identity' took shape on the EEC agenda (see CEC 1985; CEC 1988). This concept was developed by the ad hoc Committee on a People's Europe, chaired by Pietro Adonnino and set up by the European Council in 1984 (see CEC 1985). The committee was asked to focus on future Community manoeuvres that would meet the 'expectations of the peoples of Europe by adopting measures to strengthen and promote its identity and its image both for its citizens and for the rest of the world' (cited in CEC 1988:6). From here on, the identity discussion became firmly embedded in European Union discourse, and initiatives to foster a strong identification with what is now the EU have been numerous. We can call this the EEC's, and subsequently the EC's, and now the EU's politics of identity.

Since the end of the 1980s much has been written on the issue of 'European identity' and the different processes of identity formation taking place inside the European Union. Within a great deal of the critically oriented research on identity in the EU, emphasis has been focused on the situation for migrants from the South and East, the exclusion of immigrants, the asylum policies implemented by both member states and intergovernmental groups (such as Schengen, Trevi, etc.), and on racism, Eurocentrism and 'Fortress Europe' (cf. Balibar and Wallerstein 1988; Mudood and Werbner 1997; Gordon 1989; Hadjimichalis and Sadler 1995; Miles and Thränhardt 1995; Rattansi and Westwood 1994; Rex and Drury 1994; Solomos and Wrench 1993; White 1999). Much of this work, however, only deals to a limited extent with EU institutions such as the Commission and Parliament, and the views emanating there on identity in the Union. Instead, the focus has predominantly been put on individual member states and intergovernmental groups. Certainly, since these are the most influential actors shaping the Union and its direction, there are important and obvious reasons for the dominance of this focus. But it is also important to take a closer look at the policies, recommendations and future goals that are articulated from inside the (supranational) EU machinery itself, such as the European Commission and the European Parliament. It should be mentioned here though that this perspective has been applied by, among others, Martiniello (1995); Morley and Robins (1995); Neumann (1998); Schlesinger (1991, 1993); Shore (1995, 1996); Shore and Black (1994).

A reason for adopting this perspective stems from the fact that the EU does not speak with one voice on issues pertaining to its migrants and non-white inhabitants. The European Parliament, for instance, has on several occasions expressed its disapproval of how the member states, the European Council and intergovernmental groups deal with the issues of racism, immigration and asylum. Speaking of the often adverse identities assigned to non-white minorities in the EU, the European Parliament has criticized intergovernmental groups, claiming that these

> ... treat migration and refugee matters very much as related to policing. And this has a very negative effect on public opinion. Associating migrants and refugees with police and national security could well feed racist ideas and could be used to legitimize certain forms of racist behaviour (extra identity control of those who are or look like 'foreigners'). (European Parliament 1990:133)

Another reason for taking this perspective into account is the limited expansion of authority and competence that the Commission and, to a lesser extent, the Parliament, has acquired in recent years. Also, with expanded supranationality anticipated in the future and, possibly, more transnational political organization through the European Parliament, it becomes important to obtain an in-depth knowledge of the type of Union identities that are being articulated by these EU bodies. Can one, for instance, detect any discourses that run counter to the often very exclusive, ethnocentric and, indeed, 'EU-rocentric' ones we see at the level of the member states and the intergovernmental EU bodies? Is it possible to foresee any potentially productive conflicts emerging here, or will Commission and European Parliament policies merely reinforce and reproduce a hegemonic discourse installed by member states and their intergovernmental cooperation?

Although some implicit and tentative answers to these last questions will surface when EU perspectives on culture, education and citizenship are presented and discussed, this chapter will not scrutinize these questions any further. They merit mention here since they form an important part of the research perspective that I seek to develop.

Approaching cultural difference in the European Union

Aware of the wide array of theoretical work on collective identity formation and mobilization in general, and the work on how these processes operate in Europe in particular, the unobtrusive purpose here is to think through just a few of the articulatory practices employed by the EU in its endeavour to construct a collective identity in the Union. Thus, the focus for the discussion here is the EU's conception of cultural 'difference', and how this conception is being engaged in the discourse on European identity.

Due to every identity's relational character, the application of difference in identity construction is central to any discussion of identity (Mouffe 1994; Connolly 1991; Eriksen 1993; Hall 1991). Indeed, difference can be said to constitute identity's partner term in that all identities are constructed through a process of differentiation between, for instance, 'self' and 'other', 'us' and 'them', 'Swedes' and 'immigrants', 'Europeans' and 'non-Europeans'. But if these binary opposites point to one aspect of the simultaneous politics of identity and difference – where the second term comes to signify the antagonists, those who are said to threaten the stability of 'our' identity, when in fact they provide the very building blocks (or the 'constitutive outside' (Mouffe 1994:107)) for that excluding yet parasitic identity – it is far from the only one. Stated differently, the application of difference is far from always being a straightforward process, reducible to two clear-cut and antagonistic identity categories. Rather it is always potentially amendable, depending on levels and contexts.

This last point is important to keep in mind, since the issue of difference can be treated rather simplistically, without nuances, in the debate about the European Union's approach to collective identity construction. Too often the European Union is portrayed as mobilizing around only one line of difference, one narrow and unified definition of European culture and identity; in other words, that the EU only operates with one uncomplicated and negative conception of difference to define its identity. However, drawing from EU documents that address the issue of European identity, one finds that difference, when referred to in the abstract, is often appropriated as something positive, as an asset said to belong inside the Union and which therefore should be preserved, included and negotiated, rather than reduced to one uniform level. As the former Swedish Commissioner Anita Gradin has put it: 'We are Europeans because we are so different, there we have the European identity' (cited in Lönnqvist 1995/96a, author's translation). In the same vein, the former Speaker of the European Parliament, Klaus Hänsch, once pointed out that 'There is no one European people or European culture, there are many' (Lönnqvist 1995/96b, author's translation).

With reference to this, at a surface level, one could argue that this points to a potential future transformation of traditional understandings of European identity. It enables a rethinking of the notion of 'European-ness' as something closely associated with (white) skin colour, the 'West' and other essentialist and supremacist identity markers, traceable to the colonial era. In other words, it recognizes the danger of organizing a collective identity around particularist and excluding notions of ethnicity, culture and religion. As it allows for the inclusion of differences, constructed as non-antagonistic, it becomes possible to envisage a situation different to that depicted by Gilroy when he states that 'the terms "black" and "European" remain categories which mutually exclude each other' (1990:74).

Aside from the merely rhetorical, however, actual EU policy construes the issue of difference in much more limited terms, seeing a 'European identity' comprising only what is said to be different national and regional cultural identities. Differences between recognized national and regional entities in the Union – a recognition which over the years has been increasingly emphasized in a variety of contexts – are seen as positive instances of difference and, as such, they are included in the Maastricht Treaty: 'The Community shall contribute to the flowering of the cultures of the Member States, while respecting their national and regional diversity and at the same time bringing the common cultural heritage to the fore' (Council of the European Communities, Commission of the European Communities 1992). Hence, this articulation can be said to disassociate itself from an identity formation through a process of levelling, and instead seeks to have difference and commonality constitute two sides of the same coin:

> On the one side, we see a disparate family of nations embracing many different cultures; on the other, a desire to develop a common identity, to make Europe 'European' – but without succumbing to the colourless uniformity of 'Europeanism' or to the temptation of blindly imitating the past. (CEC 1991:5)

Thus, difference is by no means always constructed as being of a dividing or mutually antagonistic nature. National and regional cultures, framed as bounded and essential entities but which still can be organized around the least common denominator of 'Europe' which provides the differentiated space with its unifying and 'natural' boundaries, are also differences destined to coexist in a pluralist harmony. A Union 'we' then, is indeed said to encapsulate differences, and no identity mobilization conducted by the EU is allowed to overlook what are conceived of as distinct and homogenous national and regional cultures.

But, as mentioned in passing above, this particular conception of cultural difference is limited and says nothing about those who are today considered too culturally different to be included in the official and hegemonic versions of national and regional cultures. Thus, it can be argued that an intensified differentiation *within* the nation state (and its recognized regions) which excludes ethnic minorities with migrant backgrounds from cultural belonging – both symbolically and materially, as mirrored in political, social and economic marginalization – is implicitly reproduced when 'EU-ropean' identity is being mapped out. By not addressing this issue, therefore, there might be a risk of excluding ethnic minorities with migrant backgrounds from yet another level of identity-negotiation (cf. Shore and Black 1994; see also Ireland 1996; White 1999).

To get a closer understanding of who will be included and who will be excluded from the process of European identity negotiations today, and in the future, we need to inquire further into how these questions unfold in specific policy areas. The discussion below should be seen as an introduction to this project.

The turn to culture: the shaping of culture, education and citizenship policies in the EU

By the mid-1970s we can detect an emerging awareness, even uneasiness, from within the Community organization about the fact that economic integration in itself had not, so to speak, 'blessed' Community institutions with enough legitimacy to make integration in other areas self-evident. The opening sentence of the Tindemans Report to the European Council in

1976, read: 'Why has the European concept lost a lot of its force and initial impetus?' In order to alter this precarious state of affairs the Report went on to argue for an expansion of Community competence and activity into areas 'closer' to the daily concerns of its 'citizens':

> No one wants to see a technocratic Europe. European Union must be experienced by the citizen in his [*sic*] daily life. It must make itself felt in education and culture, news and communications, it must be manifest in the youth of our countries, and in leisure time activities. (Tindemans 1976:12)

In some respects, the Tindemans Report, with its emphasis on a 'citizen's Europe', can be said to have laid the discursive foundations for the new strategies that were set in motion in the mid-1980s in order to win more popular support and thereby legitimacy for the Community project. As Newman notes: 'For most of its history, the EU has not talked of "citizens" but of "workers". However, ... during the 1980s, the emphasis shifted from the category of 'workers' to the category of "citizen"' (1996:152). These new strategies thus assigned much greater importance to the policy areas of culture, education and citizenship. Although these policy areas are sometimes defined as being outside the immediate economic realm, they are nevertheless considered fundamental to it since these policies, if successfully implemented, would create the legitimacy which further economic integration needs to rest upon.

Stated differently, this reorientation in terms of strategy reflected a widespread conviction among Community policy makers that, in order to rally more people behind the Community project and to strengthen a sense of European identity, the stress on 'common market' had partly to give way to a stress on 'common culture' (Morley and Robins 1995; Shore and Black 1992; see also Fontaine 1993). As the Commission put it, it is necessary 'for Community action to look beyond economic issues to the major concerns of day-to-day life', since that will 'help heighten the sense of belonging to a European culture and thereby strengthen the European identity' (CEC 1988:7, 11). Indeed, the Commission feels that 'new impetus for Community measures in the cultural sector is also an economic necessity' (CEC 1987:1). In this sense, development over the past ten years can be seen as conscious attempts by Community institutions to redefine the EU as primarily constituting a *cultural* community. As formulated by the European Parliament (1988): 'Europe is not only an association of economic interests but also a cultural unit, ... the integration of Europe must be built on the common foundations of European culture.'

With 'culture' being installed as the future foundation upon which European Union integration is to be built, the discourse on 'culture' has consequently influenced *not only* cultural policy *per se,* but has also come to structure the articulation of several other EU policies that address the issue of collective identity (cf. CEC 1996). Indeed, speaking of questions pertaining to identity formation and popular endorsement for the EU project, one could go as far as to say that the discourse on culture has acquired the status of a 'master' discourse.

Probing into how this discourse manifests itself in EU cultural policy, we can see that Union identity 'in the making' does not appeal to a cultural homogeneity that would break with recognized national and regional cultures. In this sense, reflecting the views of the Economic and Social Committee (1992), there have been no attempts to create an 'all-embracing "melting pot"' in the European Union. Instead, for the Commission 'unity in diversity' is said to constitute the starting point for cultural policy in the Union. In a document titled *The Community and Culture,* the Commission writes:

> European culture is marked by its diversity: diversity of climate, countryside, architecture, language, beliefs, taste and artistic style. Such diversity must be protected, not diluted. It represents one of the chief sources of the wealth of our continent. But underlying this variety there is an affinity, a family likeness, a common European identity. Down the ages, the tension between the continent's cultural diversity and unity has helped to fuse ancient and modern, traditional and progressive. It is undoubtedly a source of the greatness of the best elements of our civilization. (1983:1)

Further, in the Commission guidelines of 1987, under the heading, 'A fresh boost for culture in the European Community', the following statements are made:

> ... the Commission will be at particular pains to integrate the cultural dimension, which the Community citizen sees as being intimately linked to his [*sic*] feelings of identity and of belonging to the European Community ... that the creation of a larger market establishes a European area based on common cultural roots ... The unity of European culture as revealed by the history of regional and national cultural diversity is the keystone of the ambitious construction which aims at European Union. (1987:3)

As these quotations clearly indicate, 'culture', in European Union discourse, is mainly understood as that which signifies a bounded entity's shared beliefs, way of life, history, heritage, etc. It is an understanding of culture that emphasizes naturalness, rootedness and what it deems to be its inherent essence, unproblematically inserted under the headings of 'European', 'national' and 'regional' cultures.

The numerous references in EU documents to Greece as 'the cradle of European culture and civilization' (European Parliament 1988) is yet another example which points to this essentialist search for immaculate cultural roots. At work here, one may well argue, is an underlying statement which, borrowing from Bhabha, could be formulated as an 'appeal to a pure and settled past', from which a stable and overarching 'unicultural present' can be deduced (1989:39). The problem then seems to be one of selection, where only a privileged and highly exclusive segment of the multitude of cultural influences, experiences, narratives, histories and myths are deemed appropriate when 'EU-ropean' cultural identity is being carved out. For the Commission, 'European culture' and its assigned national and regional cultural building blocks are considered unproblematic, as something essentially 'good' in and of themselves. Martiniello refers to this view as the 'traditionalist and fundamentalist option' for the future development of the European Union, where '"European culture" is seen as a given, an admitted fact on the basis of which a European "community of destiny" should be developed' (1995:44).

As hinted at above, this discourse on culture does not restrict itself to the realm of cultural policy, but spills over into the European Union's work in the field of education and citizenship as well. Arguably, education policy as developed by the EU can be seen in some measure as a mere extension of the EU's cultural policy in that it largely builds on the latter's particular understanding of 'culture'. Hence, the EU seeks to 'strengthen in pupils and students a sense of European identity' through the promotion of an education policy that is 'based on the cultural heritage of the member states' (European Parliament and Council of the EU 1994:52). This approach is developed in 'the European dimension of education', which is the main education policy being drawn up by the EU. According to the *Green Paper on the European Dimension of Education*, teachers in the member states should 'learn to share and pass on the wealth of European cultures', and so 'develop a European perspective alongside national and regional allegiances' (CEC 1993:9–10). Furthermore, in the more recent *White Paper on Education and Training*, the Commission elaborates on the importance of improving students' knowledge about Europe's historical roots, cultural heritage and civilization:

> Knowledge of history ... is essential to everyone if they are to come to terms with their roots ... The penalty society pays for forgetting the past is to lose a common heritage of bearings and reference points. It is not surprising that, not knowing the history of European civilization, such expressions as, 'being out in the wilderness', 'having a cross to bear', 'Eureka !', 'the judgement of Solomon' or 'the tower of Babel' have lost their meaning ... European civilization has a

> long history and is very complex ... the legacy of a tradition which made Europe the first to bring about a technical and industrial revolution and thus change the world ... Being European is to have the advantage of a cultural background of unparalleled variety and depth. (CEC 1995b: 12, 50, 51)

Education thus takes on the role of passing on an official and highly selective version of European culture, its roots and what it means to be a 'European' which, in principle, resembles much of the traditional roles assigned to education when Western nation states made nationals of the majority of their inhabitants (cf. Anderson 1983). Furthermore, the discourse running through the passages cited above implicitly establishes an ethno-cultural understanding of what it means to be 'European', where only those who fully embody the 'history', the 'roots', the 'cultural tradition', the (Christian) 'civilization' and who take pride in the colonial era during which European states 'changed the world' are fully included in the 'European' identity. An education policy promoting an identity defined in such frozen and narrow cultural terms, therefore, excludes the great number of EU inhabitants who do not meet these implied ethno-cultural requirements, and risks giving further credence to the exclusionary processes already in place in the member states. Nowhere in the culture and education policies referred to here is there any real discussion of how this particular and ethno-cultural depiction of 'Europe' squares with the situation for ethnic minorities with migrant backgrounds. As Delanty notes: 'The official and codified version of European culture has nothing to say to the silent Europe of minorities' (1995:9).

Turning finally to the issue of citizenship and the European Union, a few distinctions between culture and education, on the one hand, and citizenship, on the other, need first to be spelled out. In terms of Community competence, 'Citizenship of the Union' was written into the Maastricht Treaty as a legal concept, whereas Community activity in the areas of culture and education explicitly excludes any interference with the member states' laws and regulations. Instead, according to the Treaty, Union institutions should seek to develop European cultural and educational perspectives alongside national and regional ones in the member states (see, among others, Council of the European Communities, Commission of the European Communities 1992; McMahon 1995).

Apart from equipping Union residents, living outside of the member state where they are citizens, with the right to vote and stand in elections for the European Parliament and for local office, EU citizenship does not provide any notable additions to the rights already guaranteed by citizenship of a member state (cf. Newman 1996: ch. 6; Closa 1994). To the extent that the new rights granted by EU citizenship alter the status of national citizenship, these alterations only affect positively the citizens of member states, and so create new hierarchies and cleavage structures. Stated differently, EU citizenship does not replace national citizenship, but rather underlines its importance, since people residing in the Union cannot acquire EU citizenship without first having acquired its counterpart in a member state. Thereby, as Newman expresses it, 'the determination of Union citizenship is solely a question for decision by MS [member states], following whatever internal systems they have for determining national citizenship' (1996:156). EU citizenship, regulated by the ever harsher citizenship laws in the member states, can therefore be said to reinforce the hierarchy within the nation state at the Union level between those with full formal citizenship and those with only residentship, the so-called 'denizens', to use Hammar's (1990) term (cf. O'Keeffe 1994; Martiniello 1995).

Moreover, the mechanisms of exclusion associated with EU citizenship are far from being only of a strictly legal character. The problematic also seems to stem from the fact that the articulation of EU citizenship has been located largely within the realm of cultural identification, rather than within the realm of constitutional or political identification (cf. CEC 1997). To cite the Commission yet again:

> Europe's cultural heritage has evolved over time ... and displays certain common characteristics that transcend national or regional differences. This interplay of diversity and constancy perfectly illustrates the regional, national and European roots of Europe's citizens. Community action in the field of cultural heritage can thus help to forge a European citizenship, based on a better understanding of both national culture and the culture of the other Union states. (CEC 1995a:1)

There is thus a strong case for arguing that EU citizenship, defined in terms of (ethno-)cultural belonging, is in keeping with the legal restrictions placed on EU citizenship since the majority of those inhabitants excluded from formal Union citizenship coincides with those inhabitants whose presence has failed to influence the cultural definition of the EU citizen. In that this cultural configuration takes no notice of the large number of *de jure* EU citizens who originate outside of Europe, it sharply outlines the deep problems that permeate the construction of 'Citizenship of the Union'.

Conclusion: cultural identity, exclusion and the problem of legitimacy

As the preceding discussion shows, the identity politics now being staged 'from above' in the European Union has opted for 'culture' as its organising principle. Thus, the Commission writes:

> The sense of being part of European culture is one of the prerequisites for that solidarity which is vital if the advent of the larger market, and the considerable changes it will bring about in living conditions within the Community, is to secure the popular support it needs'. (CEC 1987:1)

If this poses grave concerns for Union residents whose background falls outside the dubious conception of 'European culture', it also raises some serious doubts about the prospects of transnational democratization in the EU. Hence, EU identity politics says practically nothing about how transnational political, constitutional and social rights could be employed as sources of collective identification in the European Union.

Listening to Morley and Robins, the emphasis on cultural identity in the EU can be interpreted as an attempt to counterpoise the absence of any real political integration and democratic legitimacy (1995:181). The ethno-cultural articulation of EU citizenship is symptomatic of this in that it precludes any vision of a post-national and trans-ethnic Union citizenship based on socio-political rights, which in turn – as Habermas (1994) would have it – could foster a sense of constitutional patriotism and political identification that would subvert contemporary ethnic and cultural divisions. Contrary to the Habermasian ideal, however, what seems to be taking place in EU policy formulation is that citizenship, construed as a set of political and social rights, increasingly becomes separated from the issue of collective identity formation (Morley and Robins 1995:184). To quote Touraine: 'We now have an essentially economic vision of the state [or as in the case here: the supra-state] and an essentially cultural vision of society' (cited in Morley and Robins 1995:175).

In its principal meaning then, the European Union resembles Western European nation states, prior to the expansion of voting rights and large-scale popular mobilization from below, in that it seeks to disseminate a symbolic and mythical cultural identity rather than the practical tools with which a process of democratization could be initiated. Tarrow's reflection captures this: 'Europe is definitely in movement but there is little sign so far of a Europe of movements' (1994:1). In the midst of a drawn-out crisis of legitimacy, and with bleak prospects of some type of federal solution –

which seems inevitable if post-national democratization is to emerge (cf. Andersen and Eliassen 1996) – being agreed upon in the foreseeable future, the EU seems to have no other alternative than to grasp at the cultural straw. Hence, legitimacy is sought, so to speak, by taking the cultural short-cut. However, instead of creating legitimacy and popular support for the EU project, this cultural short-cut runs the risk of widening even further the several roads to ethnic, political and social exclusion already paved in the member states.

Note

Much of the research for this chapter was made possible by a grant from the Committee on Global Processes in a European Perspective, within the Swedish Council for Planning and Coordination of Research (FRN). The author is grateful for the valuable comments of Jan Engberg, Ragnar Haake and Carl-Ulrik Schierup

References

Andersen, S.S. and Eliassen, K.A. (1996), 'Democracy: Traditional Concerns in New Institutional Settings', in Andersen, S.S. and Eliassen, K.A. (eds), *The European Union: How Democratic Is It?*, London: Sage.

Anderson, B. (1983), *Imagined Communities*, London: Verso.

Balibar, E. and Wallerstein, I. (1988), *Race, Nation, Class: Ambiguous Identities*, London: Verso.

Bhabha, H. (1989), 'Down Among the Writers', *New Statesman & Society*, 28 July.

Bull, M.J. (1993), 'Widening Versus Deepening the European Community: The Political Dynamics of 1992 in Historical Perspective', in Wilson, T.M. and Smith, M.E. (eds), *Cultural Change and the New Europe: Perspectives on the European Community*, Boulder: Westview Press.

Closa, C. (1994), 'Citizenship of the Union and Nationality of Member States', in O'Keeffe, D. and Twomey, P.M. (eds), *Legal Issues of the Maastricht Treaty*, London: Wiley Chancery Law.

CEC (Commission of the European Communities) (1973), 'Declaration on the European Identity', *Bull. EC.*, 12 (Clause 2501).

CEC (Commission of the European Communities) (1983), 'The Community and Culture', *European File*, 5/83.

CEC (Commission of the European Communities) (1985), 'A People's Europe: Reports from the *ad hoc* Committee', *Bull. EC.*, Supplement 7/85.

CEC (Commission of the European Communities) (1987), *A Fresh Boost for Culture in the European Community*, COM(87) 603 final, Brussels, 14.12.1987.

CEC (Commission of the European Communities) (1988), 'A People's Europe: Commission Communication', *Bull. EC.*, Supplement 2/88.

CEC (Commission of the European Communities) (1991), *The European Community 1992 and Beyond*, Luxembourg: Office for Official Publications of the European Communities.

CEC (Commission of the European Communities) (1993), *Green Paper on the European Dimension of Education*, COM(93) 457 final, Brussels, September.

CEC (Commission of the European Communities) (1995a), *European Community action in Support of Culture*, COM(95) 110 final, Brussels, 29.03.95.

CEC (Commission of the European Communities) (1995b), *White Paper on Education and Training*, COM(95) 590 final, Brussels, 29.11.1995.

CEC (Commission of the European Communities) (1996), *First Report on the Consideration of Cultural Aspects in European Community Action*, COM(96) 160 final, Brussels, 17.04.

CEC (Commission of the European Communities) (1997), *Citizen's Access to Culture*, DGX, Culture, Culture Action (http://www.europa.eu.int)

Connolly, W.E. (1991), *Identity/Difference: Democratic Negotiations of Political Paradox*, Ithaca: Cornell University Press.

Council of the European Communities, Commission of the European Communities (1992), *Treaty on European Union* ('Title IX, Article 128'), Luxembourg: Office for Official Publications of the European Communities.

Delanty, G (1995), *Inventing Europe: Idea, Identity, Reality*, London: Macmillan.

Economic and Social Committee (1992), 'Opinion on the Citizens' Europe', *Official Journal of the European Communities*, No. C 313, 30.11.92.

European Parliament (1988), 'Resolution on the Founding of a Centre for European Culture and Civilization', *Official Journal of the European Communities*, No. C 262, 10.10.88.

Eriksen, T.H. (1993), *Ethnicity and Nationalism: Anthropological Perspectives*, London: Pluto Press.

European Parliament (1990), *Report Drawn up on Behalf of the Committee of Inquiry into Racism and Xenophobia*, Session Documents, 23.7, Series A, Document A3–195/90, Rapporteur: Mr Glyn Ford, Brussels–Luxembourg.

European Parliament and Council of the EU (1994), 'Common Position (EC) no. 33/94 ... with a view to adopting European Parliament and Council Decision 94/ ... /EC of ... establishing the Community action programme "Socrates"', *Official Journal of the European Communities*, No. C 244, 31.8.94.

Fontaine, P. (1993), *A Citizens' Europe*, European Commission, European Documentation series, Directorate-General for Information, Communication, Culture and Audiovisual, Luxembourg: Office for Official Publications of the European Communities.

Gilroy, P. (1990), 'The End of Anti-racism', *New Community*, 17(1).

Gordon, P. (1989), *Fortress Europe? The Meaning of 1992*, London: Runnymede Trust.

Habermas, J. (1994), 'Citizenship and National Identity', in Steenbergen, B. van (ed.), *The Condition of Citizenship*, London: Sage.

Hadjimichalis, C. and Sadler, D. (eds) (1995), *Europe at the Margins*, Chichester: John Wiley.

Hall, S. (1991), 'Europe's Other Self', *Marxism Today*, August.

Hammar, T. (1990), *Democracy and the Nation-State*, Aldershot: Avebury.

Harvey, P. (1996), 'Multiculturalism without Responsibility? The Contemporary Universal Exhibition', *Critical Quarterly*, 38(3), Autumn.

Ireland, P. (1996), 'Asking for the Moon: The Political Participation of Immigrants in the European Union', in Kourvetaris, G.A. and Moschonas, A. (eds), *The Impact of European Integration: Political, Sociological, and Economic Changes*, Westport: Praeger.

Julien, I. and Mercer, K. (1988), 'Introduction', *Screen*, 29(4).

Kourvetaris, A.G. and Kourvetaris, G.A. (1996), 'Attitudes Toward European Integration: Ethnic and Cultural Dimensions', in Kourvetaris, G.A. and Moschonas, A. (eds), *The Impact of European Integration: Political, Sociological, and Economic Changes*, Westport: Praeger.

Lönnqvist, S. (1995/96a), 'I Sverige har vi alltid trott på samarbete över gränserna', ['In Sweden we have always believed in cooperation across borders']; interview with Anita Gradin), *Europa*, 12/95–1/96.

Lönnqvist, S. (1995/96b), ' ... och på lördag skyller de på Bryssel', ['and on Saturday they are blaming Brussels']; interview with Klaus Hansch), *Europa*, 12/95–1/96.

Martiniello, M. (1995), 'European Citizenship, European Identity and Migrants: Towards the Post-national State?', in Miles, R. and Thränhardt, D. (eds), *Migration and European Integration: The Dynamics of Inclusion and Exclusion*, London: Pinter.

McMahon, J.A. (1995), *Education and Culture in European Community Law*, London: The Athlone Press.

Miles, R. and Thränhardt, D. (eds) (1995), *Migration and European Integration: The Dynamics of Inclusion and Exclusion*, London: Pinter.

Modood, T. and Werbner, P. (eds) 1997, *The Politics of Multiculturalism in the New Europe: Racism, Identity and Community*, London: Zed Books.

Morley, D. and Robins, K. (1995), *Spaces of Identity: Global Media, Electronic Landscapes and Cultural Boundaries*, London: Routledge.

Mouffe, C. (1994), 'For a Politics of Nomadic Identity', in Robertson, G. et al. (eds), *Travellers' Tales: Narratives of Home and Displacement*, London: Routledge.

Newmann, I.B. (1998), 'European Identity, EU Expansion, and the Integration/Exclusion Nexus', *Alternatives*, 23(3).

Newman, M. (1996), *Democracy, Sovereignty and the European Union*, London: Hurst & Company.

O'Keeffe, D. (1994), 'Union Citizenship', in O'Keeffe, D. and Twomey, P.M. (eds), *Legal Issues of the Maastricht Treaty*, London: Wiley Chancery Law.

Rattansi, A. and Westwood, S. (1994) (eds), *Racism, Modernity & Identity on the Western Front*, Cambridge: Polity Press.

Rex, J. and Drury, B. (eds) (1994), *Ethnic Mobilisation in a Multi-cultural Europe*, Aldershot: Avebury.

Schlesinger, P. (1991), *Media, State and Nation: Political Violence and Collective Identities*, London: Sage.

Schlesinger, P. (1993), 'Wishful Thinking: Cultural Politics, Media, and Collective Identities in Europe', *Journal of Communication*, (43)2.

Shore, C. (1995), 'Usurpers or pioneers?: European Commission Bureaucrats and the Question of "European Consciousness"', in Cohen, A.P. and Rapport, N. (eds), *Questions of Consciousness*, London: Routledge.

Shore, C. (1996), 'Transcending the Nation-State?: The European Commission and the (Re)-Discovery of Europe', *Journal of Historical Sociology*, 9(4).

Shore, C. and Black, A. (1992), 'The European Communities and the Construction of Europe', *Anthropology Today*, 8(3).

Shore, C. and Black, A. (1994), 'Citizens' Europe and the Construction of European Identity', in Goddard, V.A., Llobera, J.R. and Shore, C. (eds), *The Anthropology of Europe*, Oxford/Providence: Berg.

Solomos, J. and Wrench, J. (eds) (1993), *Racism and Migration in Western Europe*, London: Berg.

Tarrow, S. (1994), 'Social Movements in Europe: Movement Society or Europeanization of Conflict?, *EUI Working Papers*, No. 94/8, Florence: European University Institute.

Tindemans, L. (1976), 'European Union: Report by Mr. Leo Tindemans, Prime Minister of Belgium, to the European Council', *Bull. EC.*, Supplement 1/76.

White, P. (1999), 'Ethnicity, Racialization and Citizenship as Divisive Elements in Europe', *Divided Europe: Society and Territory*, London: Sage.

7 Public Policy in a Divided Society: Lessons from Northern Ireland

Mari Fitzduff

A failure of public policy

The outbreak of civil violence in 1969 in Northern Ireland, which lasted almost thirty years and cost over 3,500 lives, was significantly attributable to the failure of public policy in Northern Ireland since its inception as a state in 1921. Although the newly formed region of the UK contained within its borders a substantial number of Catholics who were unhappy with their status within Northern Ireland, few efforts were made by the newly elected Unionist government to sufficiently address their responsibilities involved in governing a divided society. Such a failure, with its concomitant patterns of inequity, biased voting systems, unrepresentative policing, a maintenance of ghettoization in education, housing and workplaces, and a significantly alienated minority created the context for the eventual development of a civil war which is only now approaching an ending.

The eventual political agreement reached in April 1998 through multi-party political talks, finally achieved a significant consensus on the principles, and in some cases the practice, necessary to govern a society divided on constitutional, political and cultural perspectives. Such a consensus was only possible because in the decades prior to the Agreement, public policy bodies in Northern Ireland had already significantly shifted their approaches to governance in a divided society. Without such previous refocusing, the Belfast Agreement would have lacked both credibility and hope.

This chapter highlights the attempts made since 1969 by policy makers and by public bodies in Northern Ireland to address their responsibilities in the governance of a divided society. It suggests that the journey for public policy makers has often been both slow and defensive, and has unfortunately often only been fuelled by the desperation engendered by the decades of violence. It also suggests, however, that many of the lessons learnt in Northern Ireland are worth recording. Such lessons may be particularly useful for those who need to examine the capacity of public policy to prevent significant tensions, or, as too often needs to happen, to restructure and refocus a society which requires a retuning to ensure the significant inclusion of its dissatisfied minorities.

Peoples apart

The existence of a divided society in Northern was the product of a system of plantation that was designed, from the seventeenth century, to ensure the continued separation of planters and natives in order to ensure orderly governance by the British through their settlers. Unlike the earlier plantations, where gradual integration between natives and settlers on the island became the norm, the later influxes developed an extremely divided society which has maintained most of its divisions to this day. Such divisions successfully combined to create what LeVine and Campbell (1972) have termed a 'pyramid-segmentary' structure, that is, a structure in which different categories of a social, political, cultural and theological nature rarely cut across one another, and segregation in the north of Ireland became the norm

When Protestants took power in Northern Ireland in 1921 they failed to address such segregation, and indeed established what was essentially a Protestant state, with little thought, and no strategic policies directed at ensuring the inclusion of a sizeable disaffected Catholic minority within the systems of the state. This meant that by the time of the civil rights movement in 1969, the divisions were structurally entrenched. The education system was almost totally segregated; the number of Catholic students attending state schools was less than 5 per cent. Most work situations were segregated, sports and other cultural activities were often divisive and sometimes violent occasions, the flying of the Irish flag was forbidden and the use of the Irish language was covert and deemed to be provocative. In addition, Catholics were effectively discriminated against in housing, jobs and political representation (Rose 1971). The police were seen as not only consolidating the divisions, but as largely representing and supporting the Unionist Protestant, hegemony: by 1969, Catholic members comprised only 10 per cent of the police force (Hamilton 1995).

When the Unionist government failed to adequately acknowledge and address the civil rights and equity concerns of Catholics, and when subsequent civil unrest proved both the biased and inadequate nature of the security approaches by the Unionist government, the Northern Ireland government was dismissed by Westminster, and direct political and security control for the region from London began. Such control was to be a key factor in ensuring the development of a variety of public policy initiatives which, over the next 27 years, were eventually to lead to a more equitable and culturally representative society in Northern Ireland – thus providing a more positive framework for the success of the Belfast Agreement.

A developing approach

Three principles now significantly inform ongoing public policy work related to the conflict in Northern Ireland. These are the principles of equity, diversity and interdependence (Eybin 1997) although the emphasis given to each of these foci has varied over the decades. Interdependence work, which focuses on issues of community relations, was the initial focus for public policy immediately following the civil rights campaigns, equity work dominated much of the 1970s and 1980s and diversity work and interdependence have become increasingly important in the 1990s.

Equity

Since the inception of the state in 1921, many Catholics believed that there had been systematic discrimination against them. Their perceptions were confirmed by the findings of the first official enquiry by the British government into such matters which was undertaken in 1969 when the Troubles erupted (Cameron Report 1969). This inquiry concluded that a sense of injustice had been a major contributory factor in engendering the violence. The British government declared in August 1969 that every citizen of Northern Ireland was entitled to the same equality of treatment and freedom from discrimination as obtains in the rest of the United Kingdom; a series of legislative reforms to address existing inequalities was introduced, first by the Northern Ireland parliament and after it had been dissolved in 1972, by the Westminster parliament. In 1969, the Parliamentary Commission Act (NI) established the office of the Northern Ireland Commissioner for Administration with powers to investigate complaints of maladministration by government departments, including discrimination on grounds of religious or political belief. In 1972, a commission was established to promote fairness in staff recruitment in the local councils, which had been so noted for their discriminatory nature. The government also established a working party to look at employment practices in the private sector. In 1973, the

Northern Ireland Constitution Act provided for a legislative assembly for Northern Ireland and made void any legislation by that body which discriminated on the grounds of religious or political belief. The Act also established the Standing Advisory Commission on Human Rights to monitor the effectiveness of laws against discrimination.

As discrimination in housing had been a major grievance, control of all public housing allocation was transferred from local council authorities to a regional authority, the Northern Ireland Housing Executive, which succeeded in having housing prioritized. Voting reforms were quickly introduced by the British government following its intervention in 1969. House ownership was no longer deemed a prerequisite for voting rights, and the multiple vote given to business owners was abolished, as both of these criteria had effectively discriminated against Catholics. Local council boundaries were redrawn more accurately to represent the reality of citizen distribution, and a proportional representation system of voting was introduced which increased nationalist chances of gaining power where their numbers were substantial enough, and increased the number of councils under nationalist control.

Employment inequities

Inequality in unemployment was a particular problem as major disparities in employment levels were confirmed by the Cameron and other reports. In 1971, it was estimated that 17.3 per cent of Catholic males were unemployed, compared to 6.6 per cent of Protestant males. In 1976, the Fair Employment Act was passed, making discrimination in employment on religious or political grounds unlawful and a Fair Employment Agency (FEA) was established to receive complaints of discrimination in employment and to investigate further the extent to which there was inequality.

From the mid-1980s, however, the 1976 Act came under increasing pressure for reform, as government statistics continued to indicate a significant unemployment gap between Protestants and Catholics. A new Act was introduced in 1989 under which the FEA was replaced by the Fair Employment Commission (FEC) which was given extra resources and powers by the government in pursuit of its task. These included a new body to handle cases of alleged discrimination, and the requirement that all employers with 25 or more employees had to register with the FEC and to monitor the religious composition of their workforce. In addition, indirect discrimination was made illegal and guidelines issued with the Act described legal affirmative action policies that employers could implement in their attempts to lessen the existing imbalances within their workforce.

By the early 1990s, after two decades of government attempts to address equity issues in Northern Ireland, the indicators still showed that the Catholic community in many areas remained seriously disadvantaged, for example, Catholic men were still twice as likely to be unemployed as their Protestant counterparts. In addition, 45 of the top 50 unemployment black-spot areas in Northern Ireland were almost exclusively Catholic. Research into the reasons for the continuing disparity also showed that although direct discrimination against Catholics was still playing a part in maintaining discrimination, the steps needed to redress the situation were now seen to be far more complex than merely introducing monitoring and legislative procedures.

Targeting social need

Faced with a major challenge of the continuance of marginalized ghetto areas (mainly Catholic, but also some Protestant areas) and the link between such areas and the use of paramilitary violence, the government decided that a major initiative was needed to address such alienation. This initiative, Targeting Social Need (TSN), was established under the auspices of the Central Community Relations Unit which had been set up in 1989 to promote community relations. The objective of this programme was to tackle areas of social and economic differences by targeting government policies and programmes more directly to those areas or sections of the community suffering the highest levels of disadvantage and deprivation.

Under this initiative, all government departments were in the first place required to analyse and monitor the impact on the community of their policies and actions and any differentials in such impact between the two sections of the community. Where a differential was found to exist, scope for remedial action was to be considered. In addition, a variety of new schemes were implemented. Existing schemes were augmented to ensure that they made a more effective contribution to the decreasing of disadvantage. These initiatives included work designed specifically to address disadvantage in Belfast such as the Making Belfast Work scheme (with funding of approximately £25m per year) which was designed to assist community participation and development, including economic development, in the most deprived areas of Belfast.

Extra attention was also given under the TSN programme to providing further opportunities for training, to increasing development work for indigenous industry creation, particularly in the most marginalized areas, and to ensuring that individual job creation agencies further biased their work towards those areas that were most seriously disadvantaged. Action for Community Employment (ACE), a scheme primarily aimed at the long-term unemployed was given substantially more resources, as long-term unemployment is proportionately higher among Catholics. More money was made available for housing renovations, and for community development, which the government agreed was often the first step necessary for communities to develop in confidence and expertise to a level enabling them to begin to address the hard necessities of economic and job development. In addition, five areas of particular rural disadvantage were also chosen for extra funding and development – all of which were predominantly Catholic areas.

Policy and fair treatment

As well as the above initiatives, designed to address issues of inequality by dealing with the wider context, in 1994, the government introduced a new initiative called Policy Appraisal and Fair Treatment (PAFT). The object of this initiative is to ensure that issues of equality condition policy making and action in all spheres of government activity, both in regulatory and administrative functions and through the delivery of services to the public. The guidance given through the initiative is designed to ensure that considerations of equality, equity and non-discrimination (not just in relation to religious/political affiliation, but also in relation to other areas of inequality) are in-built from the outset to the preparation of policy proposals, including legislation, other initiatives, and strategic plans for the implementation of policy and the delivery of services. These guidelines now apply to all Northern Ireland government departments and all government agencies.

Successes of equity work

Many of the initiatives designed to introduce more equity into the structures and systems of Northern Ireland have had some considerable success. Complaints are no longer heard about rigged voting, unfair housing allocations, or unequal educational funding. Twice as many Catholics are now employed at senior management level in the public and private sector than were employed ten years ago. Although they are still disproportionately less involved in the very senior positions in both the civil service and the private sector, over 50 per cent of the entrants to the civil service are now Catholic, notwithstanding the fact that Catholics now constitute 40 per cent of the population. In addition, the majority of entrants to both Northern Ireland's two universities are now Catholic.

The one substantial area of necessary redress remains unemployment, with its significant capacity to destabilize Northern Ireland. Statistics show that cities and towns with large Catholic ghettos and with high unemployment rates have the highest levels of violence (Poole 1990). The link between unemployment and violence is also noticeable on the Protestant side and studies in both Belfast and Derry/Londonderry show a similar connection between unemployment and support for loyalist paramilitaries. Although the IRA, the UVF and the UDA are on cease-fire at the time of writing, there are several splinter groups who continue to seek and use the dissatisfaction of young unemployed males to continue the conflict.

Diversity

Policing a diverse society

When civil unrest broke out in Northern Ireland in 1969, the fault lines within the police force were to render it in many cases counterproductive and inflammatory to the conflict. The force itself was seen as largely sympathetic to the unionists and it was in fact a mostly Protestant force, with a participation rate of only 10 per cent by Catholics in 1969, a rate which subsequently dropped to 6 per cent by 1994 (Hamilton 1995) . When the Troubles broke out, it quickly became evident that the police were unable to react to the emerging law-and-order needs in a way that was professional and unbiased. The Cameron Commission, set up by the British government in 1969 to examine the causes of the Troubles, implicated the police as a major problematic factor in the conflict and in particular police acts of misconduct, assault and battery, and use of provocative sectarian and political slogans (Cameron 1969). Both the Cameron Commission and the Scarman Tribunal, which were set up to investigate the grievances of Catholics, were particularly critical of the actions of the B Specials, a section of the police force with a particular history of bigotry towards Catholics.

Consequently, the reform of policing formed one of the main objectives of the British government. It was recommended that the B Specials be disbanded and that a new part-time force be established; the RUC were to be disarmed, a police authority was to be set up to provide a buffer between the police and the unionist government, and a complaints system was to be developed. Although the recommendations were generally welcomed by Catholics, they were in the main offset by the introduction of internment in 1971 which had resulted in the imprisonment without trial of over 1,500 people, almost all Catholics. The majority of those interned (most of whom were subsequently released without charge) had been imprisoned on the ill-informed advice of the police.

Since the late 1970s, however, there has been a gradual professionalization of the police, which helped to upgrade standards of impartiality in policing. Nevertheless, they are still viewed suspiciously by a sizeable element within the Catholic community partly because of historical attitudes and a perceived bias in their daily interactions with local communities and their methods of interrogation which many suspect went beyond the rule of law (CAJ 1992). Particularly since the early 1990s, the police themselves, under pressure from bodies such as the CRC, the CAJ and the Mediation Network, have begun to address more proactively the kind of training that could ensure that the interface between the security forces and Catholics (and increasingly with working-class Protestants) did not continue to be a problem in fuelling resentment and diminishing cooperation with the security forces. Both the Royal Ulster Constabulary (RUC) and the army have taken steps to increase the quality of their recruits, and selection programmes are now in place to try and identify bias on the part of would-be trainees.

In 1993, the RUC, in cooperation with the Mediation Network and other conflict resolution bodies, began to develop its own programmes to deal with issues of sectarianism among the force, and to promote and encourage a greater respect and understanding among its staff for the differing cultural and political traditions in Northern Ireland. Such training is now an integral part of the initial training of all recruits entering the force, and has also been introduced as part of the in-service training of established police personnel.

Since the 1994 cease-fires, there has been a substantial amount of community interest in addressing the issue of policing. Dozens of debates, facilitated by the Police Authority, community groups and justice groups, have taken place across Northern Ireland and the arguments around future developments in policing became one of the most passionate debates in the pre-Agreement period. In May 1996, the government published a White Paper which contained proposals for the reform of policing structures, that is, the legislative framework within which the police will operate. And in 1997 a Fundamental Review of policing was undertaken which was conducted jointly by the government, the RUC and the Police Authority on the future policing needs of the community. And, as part of the Belfast Agreement, an Independent Commission on Policing for Northern Ireland has been set up to 'inquire into policing in Northern Ireland, and, on the basis of its findings, bring forward proposals for future policing structures and arrangements, including means of encouraging widespread community support for those arrangements'.

Such activities, with their emphasis on consultation, and learning from international experience, should eventually help to secure a more professional and impartial approach to policing in a society that in many ways still remains both culturally and politically divided.

Cultural diversity

For the entire period of the existence of the state, expressions of cultural and political identity have been contentious. Flag-flying, the use of the Irish language, language and unionist and nationalist parades, have all been seen as a threat to the political realities and aspirations of the other side. In a contested territory, such expressions have a significant potential to accrue into civil disorder.

Since 1921, many such expressions on the part of nationalists in Northern Ireland were deemed illegal and legislation passed to deal with these issues often provoked tension rather than eased it. Several legislative Acts (1951 and 1954) outlawed the flying of the Irish flag, and allowed the police to take action against any use of symbols that was likely to cause a breach of the peace. In the case of the nationalists, it therefore often became a conscious act of rebellion to fly the Irish tricolour, while the unionists for their part often insisted that the full rigour of the law should be brought to bear upon such displays, thus ensuring continuing conflict between the communities and the police.

Laws were also passed restricting the use of the Irish language by forbidding the use of Irish-language street signs (1949) or the use of any language other than English in court (1739), and all transactions with the government had to be conducted in English. By 1992, however, over 550 Irish-language street signs had been erected in nationalist areas in clear defiance of the law. Many nationalists also began to use the Irish language and its lack of official support as a cultural weapon with which to challenge the authorities; signs appeared in Catholic West Belfast which read 'British soldiers speak English – what language do you speak?' in an effort to encourage people to speak Irish as a political gesture.

In broadcasting, there were many issues that were a source of considerable contention to the nationalist minority. There was an exclusion on the reporting of cultural issues, including sport, that was of interest to the minority nationalist population, and the Irish language was banned from radio and television for almost the first fifty years of the Northern Ireland state. Such exclusion of language and other cultural expressions of nationalist identity from public life – when such expressions were both permitted and funded in Scotland and Wales – was a symptom of the fear of the Unionist government. They felt that permitting such expression would encourage political instability, and thereby threaten the existence of the state itself. Such exclusion, however, inevitably fuelled the resentment and hostility of Catholics and increased their sense of alienation from the government. Such alienation was a considerable factor in both assisting the start of paramilitary violence, and in its continuation.

Following the Civil Rights campaign, the new-found culturally assertive capacities of the nationalist community began to achieve some successes in the early 1970s when the British Broadcasting Corporation (BBC) was persuaded to introduce occasional radio programmes in the Irish language. Although there was considerable resistance from many unionists, the BBC persisted with the experiment, and were eventually persuaded to introduce a regular Irish-language programme in 1981, followed by some schools broadcasting in 1985. In 1991, the BBC broadcast its first television production in Irish. Although the total hours broadcast in Irish are still minimal, particularly when compared to those available in Gaelic in Scotland, or in Welsh in Wales, the barriers to the use of Irish in broadcasting have now substantially disappeared.

Other public policies addressing diversity have also begun to ensure statutory validation for cultural diversity in language and symbols, and state resources for such validation. Much of this has been due to the work of the Cultural Traditions Group (CTG) who are a group of academics, practitioners and policy makers. Drawn from both the nationalist and unionist communities, it operated under the auspices of the Community Relations Council (CRC 1994). Many within this group recognized that the negative government response to the Irish language had been both short-sighted and unnecessary. They established and achieved government funding for the Ultacht Trust, a group set up on a non-sectarian basis to develop and fund the Irish language, and which included on its management committee members from the unionist tradition. The government was also persuaded to fund those schools that taught through the medium of Irish on the same basis as other schools, and to assist with the funding of a daily newspaper in Irish.

In addition to its work on the language, the CTG also helped to develop further the work of the broadcasting companies by encouraging, and in some cases funding, initiatives which exemplified cultural diversity programming. Although there is little evidence that such programmes on their own were significant in changing attitudes (Nolan 1993) they did help to ensure local programming which exemplified an ethos of diversity.

In 1992, the Secretary of State for Northern Ireland announced that where there was a local demand, street names in Irish could be erected alongside the English name. Correspondence in Irish is also now dealt with by the government, and although there is as yet no official policy on publishing official documents in Irish, this does happen when requested, for example, the Belfast Agreement was published in Irish.

The use of the Irish language, and expressions of nationalist and Irish identity, have now receded as a significant source of political tension. The community is now used to hearing regular Irish-language programmes on radio and television, the tricolour usually flies freely, without official interference, and street names in Irish are now accepted as delivery addresses by the postal services.

In 1991, the CTG organized the first ever Cultural Traditions Fair in Belfast, through which they brought together many groups with very different cultural and historical perspectives to provide an open exhibition for each other and for the public. It was a unique undertaking in Northern Ireland, as it brought together groups that had been in the main suspicious and hostile to one another for most of the life of the state. Some years later, the CTG organized a Symbols exhibition which included hundreds of artefacts – flags, banners, sashes, epaulettes and religious symbols – from all traditions which were commonly perceived to give offence or cause hostility (McCartney 1994). The Symbols exhibition, held first in the Belfast City Hall (usually perceived to be a symbol of unionist rule), became a very visual testimony that political and cultural diversity was a reality that had to be addressed, and not avoided. Both the Fairs and the Symbols projects helped to break down many barriers of prejudice and ensured a much more positive context for the eventual agreements on cultural pluralism that were made in the Belfast Agreement.

Interdependence

A first approach

Following the re-emergence of sectarian violence in 1969 in Northern Ireland and particularly in the aftermath of the riots in Belfast and Derry/Londonderry in August 1969, the British Labour Home Secretary, James Callaghan announced the establishment of a Ministry for Community Relations and a Community Relations Commission (the Community Relations Act, 1969). Thus began the history of public policy attempts to foster improved community relations between the two major communities in Northern Ireland.

The Ministry of Community Relations was charged with the promotion of policies which would improve community relations. It was also made responsible for administering funds to statutory bodies and voluntary organizations for what were considered to be worthwhile projects, and with the funding of the Community Relations Commission which was established a month after the establishment of the Ministry. The Commission was charged with the promotion of activities relevant to the field of community relations, and the terms of reference for the Commission were almost identical to those of the Race Relations Board of Great Britain (Race Relations Act 1968). It was to be concerned with promoting harmonious community relations through various programmes, advising the Minister on community relations issues and carrying out research that was deemed relevant to its objectives.

In approaching its task of promoting community relations, the Commission decided to adopt as its main strategy the initiation of local community development programmes across Northern Ireland. Its analysis of this as the preferred approach was based on the belief that communities which lacked self-confidence were more likely to relate aggressively to one another. Furthermore, it believed that the problem, particularly for people in more socially marginalized communities, of relating to the structures of power, contributed to feelings of helplessness and resentment which in turn contributed to community tensions. The Commission's belief was that the process of community development, could help address these problems, and thus assist in resolving existing and developing conflicts (Hayes 1972). The Commission subsequently channelled most of its resources into this oblique approach – an approach with which the Ministry of Community Relations had little sympathy.

In the event, both the Ministry and the Commission had a short life. A proposal to the Ministry for a substantial expansion of the community development programme of the Commission was dismissed, not surprisingly in view of the Ministry's scepticism and suspicions about the use of community development. The chairman of the Commission subsequently resigned, and this was followed a few months later by the resignation of the director, in April 1972.

The Commission itself survived until the Sunningdale Agreement in April 1974, when it was abolished by the newly formed Assembly for Northern Ireland in one of the first actions taken by the incoming Minister for Community Relations. The main reason generally suggested for such a decision was that the Ministry (and in particular the civil servants servicing it) was not alone in becoming increasingly suspicious of the possible radical nature of some of the Commission programmes whose outcomes they felt to be uncertain or possibly counter-productive (Hayes 1972). The newly elected politicians of the power-sharing executive also believed that they as elected representatives should shoulder the major responsibility for hearing people's concerns, and translating such concern into action, without the use of what they saw as an independent body.

Assessments vary as to the success or otherwise of these first government attempts at promoting community relations. There appears, however, to be agreement that the process of community development remains an important method of facilitating participation between government and communities; this belief has continued to underpin many programmes subsequently initiated and funded in the last two decades which have concentrated on securing community involvement in programmes designed to address issues of local social and economic need.

Renewal of interest in community relations work

The mid-1980s saw some signs that the government might again be considering addressing the more effective development of community relations work. In 1985, the Standing Advisory Commission on Human Rights commissioned a report on the current state of the work and its potential for future development (Frazer and Fitzduff 1986). This reported on the under-resourced, underdeveloped and unstrategic nature of much of the work. It also outlined the beginnings of a theoretical framework for its development, and suggested some practical structures that should be considered if the government intended to take the work seriously. Among these suggestions were the creation of a specialist community relations unit within the Secretary of State's office and the creation of an independent community relations body.

The suggested functions for the specialist community relations unit included advising the Secretary of State and other ministers on all aspects of promoting better community relations; working to eliminate discrimination; ensuring that all government policies, for example, in housing, health, industry, economic development and education, were geared to improving community relations, and ensuring that adequate funding was made available for the further development of the work. The central functions suggested for the independent agency were that it should ensure a focal point for all organizations active in the field of community relations, develop training in community relations work, increase public awareness of the need for the work at all levels within Northern Ireland, and give advice to government, in particular through the proposed government unit.

The report suggested that there was a need for positive support from government in promoting such work at all levels, and not just at the voluntary sector level and it suggested that the major factor in ensuring the development of such work was the government departments themselves. It hence suggested that any government unit should be located centrally, rather than in a separate ministry, because of a conviction that locating it within a particular ministry could leave it marginalized, rather than at the centre of the policy-making processes of all departments. In the event, both major suggestions of the report were implemented. In 1987, the Central Community Relations Unit (CCRU) was set up, responsible to the Central Secretariat, which was located at the heart of government, and funded through the Department of Finance and Personnel. Although it received an overall remit for the development of community relations work, the Department of Education remained responsible for the development of community relations work with young people and children.

The newly formed CCRU immediately started a consultative process to assess what its strategic approach should be in developing community relations work. It consulted with a wide range of statutory bodies, particularly with those who had been involved in community relations work and eventually, in January 1990, the CRC was inaugurated. The members of the Council were drawn from the statutory, private, voluntary and community sectors with one-third of them being appointed by the minister.

Community relations 1990–98

In drawing up its initial strategic plan, the CRC decided not to concentrate on developing more 'reconciliation' groups, or to depend upon the work of such existing groups. While recognizing the valuable work undertaken by many of them, the CRC was not convinced that work through such agencies could reach the wide spectrum of people necessary to ensure the effectiveness of its programmes. It therefore expanded its remit to include bodies who had not significantly recognized their remit in promoting community relations, for example, business, church and sports groups, health and education boards, and many groups from the voluntary and community sector. It also worked closely with the trade unions who had, since the late 1980s, been developing anti-intimidation and anti-sectarian programmes for the workplace. The amount of money which was invested in such work increased to approximately £7 million per annum by 1997. As the theoretical framework for such a focus expanded (Fitzduff 1989), the work began to engage a much wider spectrum of people, including those who had previously been cynical of the 'peace and doves' stereotype attached to the work. It therefore became more possible to build a coalition of people and organizations addressing both the 'softer' issues such as understanding and cooperation, as well as the 'harder' issues of inequality, rights, policing and political and constitutional differences. Such initiatives were extremely important in facilitating the community discussions on the issues that accompanied the multiparty talks and that preceded the Belfast Agreement.

The work of the Department of Education, which had a particular remit for the promotion of community relations work with children and young people was also highly significant. By the early 1990s, programmes within schools designed to increase understanding among children and young people, for example, Cultural Heritage, Mutual Understanding and Contact programmes, were an obligatory part of every schoolchild's curriculum. By 1990, a common history curriculum was being taught in all schools in Northern Ireland, whereas before 1990 Catholic and Protestant schools taught different versions of history. By 1994, a common religious curriculum was in place. Significant resources were also allocated to the development of integrated education, and by 1998 over thirty of these had been developed . Although they still only cater for about 3 per cent of the school population, their development has ensured that an increasing number of state schools are 'transforming', that is, being allocated resources to become more plural in their student representation and their cultural ethos.

In addition, a district council community relations programme begun in the 1990s means that every one of the 26 district councils now has at least one full-time community relations worker addressing needs in its area. As each of these programmes has had to ensure an overall commitment from what are often very divided councils, their very existence has marked a substantial sign of progress in the field. The evidence is that where such relationships have been active for at least two years, relationships between communities have significantly improved (Knox and Hughes 1994).

In recent years, it has been recognized that many legislative and policy approaches to both equality and diversity work have not actually increased understanding and cooperation between community, and that in some cases they can, if not handled carefully, increase segregation and ghettoization. Therefore, the development of a Policy Appraisal for Sharing and Separation (PASS) programme is now also being considered (Hadden et al. 1998). Such a programme would require of all government departments and governmental agencies that they scrutinize their various public programmes and initiatives to ensure that, where appropriate, they increase the number of choices available for shared living and work possibilities for both communities. In this way, it is hoped to decrease the patterns of segregation which still continue to dominate Northern Ireland society, and which increase the difficulties of developing successful community relations strategies.

Lessons learned

Unfortunately, the experience in Northern Ireland (as elsewhere) has been that it often takes community violence, or the threat of violence, to ensure the attention of government to issues of inequality and alienation. This has had particularly harrowing consequences in Northern Ireland, where the historical fears and suspicions between the two communities, as well as the unionist hegemony in government, has meant that public policy approaches to addressing such issues have been unusually difficult. Given the nature of such fears, it eventually took the dismissal of the unionist government in 1972, and the advent of direct rule from Westminster, to ensure that progress was made. In addition, the Anglo-Irish Agreement which was signed in 1995 and which gave the Irish Government an official role in addressing issues of concern to Catholics, ensured that such progress would be maintained. Most reforms continued to be fought by the unionist community. However, significant improvements have now been secured by Catholics on many issues of inequality, albeit slowly in some areas such as employment, and albeit primarily by many within the middle classes (O'Connor 1994). This has substantially decreased the alienation and hostility felt by the majority of Catholics towards the state, which, it is hoped, will in turn considerably reduce the likelihood of any major support by Catholics for a return to the support of paramilitary violence.

Many reforms within the civil service and other public bodies were also made more possible by the changing nature of the public sector itself (Chief Executives Forum 1997). The UK Financial Management initiative of the early 1980s was followed by the Rayner programme of efficiency scrutinies, the Next Steps programme of reform of government and the Citizen's Charter, all of which were applicable to Northern Ireland. Therefore, the public sector in Northern Ireland was in any case facing significant challenges of professionalization, downsizing and public accountability – all of which processes enabled reforms regarding equality and diversity to be obliquely, if not directly, addressed.

By the 1990s, the government had also learnt the usefulness of a multitrack approach to the problems in Northern Ireland. Whereas in the 1970s and 1980s it had tended to concentrate on either an equality or a security response to the problems of Northern Ireland, by the 1990s, a more integrated approach had been developed to address the many-faceted nature of the conflict. Such an approach included ensuring that security policies did not further alienate communities and increase the support for paramilitarism, undertaking economic development in such a way that it was not seen as a loss for any one community, developing more contextualized approaches to equality work, more significantly resourcing community relations work, undertaking more creative and courageous approaches to political dialogue and significant increasing support for community development (Fitzduff 1989).

The latter approach, that is, of more substantially resourcing community development, was to prove very significant for the eventual agreement that was reached in April 1998. The resource input into community development activities by the government – which was seen as at least one possible avenue for constructive activities as violence raged on the streets – began to pay significant political dividends. Such work, in the absence of local democracy, had provided for community participation in governmental consultation processes about social, economic and political issues. By the 1990s, however, it had also helped to generate a new breed of 'community' politicians who developed loyalist, republican and feminist thinking in a way which significantly enriched the political mix of parties who were eventually able to sign the Belfast Agreement. Parties such as the PUP, the UDP, the NIWC and Sinn Fein all have considerable experience at community and social politics. Such experience in the past has often provided them with fruitful contacts gained from their collective experience in addressing local social issues together, and should augur well for the social and economic tasks that face them as representatives in the new Assembly.

If the breakdown of Northern Ireland into civil war was substantially due to the failure of state public policy to address issues of inequality and inclusion, it is probably now true to say that the more substantial development of such policy, albeit mainly under direct rule, has helped to provide for a legislative and programmatic approach to such issues in a way that should substantially help to underpin the Belfast Agreement. The pity for many, of course – particularly those who have suffered so substantially in the course of the conflict – is that such developments were so long and so fragmented in their coming. But perhaps that is the salient lesson of every conflict for every government: that there is a need for those responsible for public policy to be much more aware of the murmurings of those who are feeling left out on the sidelines of society, and to be much braver in addressing issues of equality, pluralism and inclusion. And it appears particularly important that such responses should happen long before the murmurings turn into hostility and alienation that may eventually take many years to control, and be very costly for both people and government alike.

References

CAJ (Committee on the Administration of Justice) (1992), *Adding Insult to Injury*, Belfast: CAJ.

Cameron Report (1969), *Disturbances in Northern Ireland: Report of a Commission Appointed by the Governor of Northern Ireland*. Belfast: Her Majesty's Stationery Office.

Chief Executives Forum, Joseph Rowntree Foundation (1997), *People and Government, Questions for Northern Ireland*, Belfast: Chief Executive's Forum.

CRC (Community Relations Council) (1994), *Giving Voices: The Work of the Cultural Traditions Group*, Belfast: CRC.

Eybin, Karen (1997), *Training for Community Relations Work*, Report to Central Community Relations Unit, Northern Ireland Office.

Fitzduff, Mari (1989), *A Typology of Community Relations Work and Contextual Necessities*, Belfast: Policy and Planning Unit, Northern Ireland Office.

Fitzduff, Mari (1992), 'Northern Ireland – A Case Study in Parallel Necessities' in Rothman, J. (ed.), *Practising Conflict Resolution in Divided Societies*, Jerusalem: Leonard Davies Institute.

Frazer, Hugh and Fitzduff, Mari (1986), *Improving Community Relations*, Belfast: Standing Advisory Commission on Human Rights.

Hadden, T., Rainey, B. and McGreevy, G. (1998), *Equal but not Separate. Communal Policy Appraisal*, Belfast: Fortnight Supplement, Fortnight, based on a report commissioned by the Community Relations Council.

Hamilton, Andrew (1995), *Policing a Divided Society*, Coleraine: Centre for the Study of Conflict, University of Ulster.

Hayes, M (1972), *The Role of the Community Relations Commission in Northern Ireland*, London: Runnymede Trust.

Knox, C. and Hughes, J. (1994), *Community Relations and Local Government*, Coleraine: Centre for the Study of Conflict, University of Ulster.

LeVine, Robert and Campbell, Donald (1972), *Ethnocentrism: Theories of Conflict, Ethnic Attitudes and Group Behaviour*, New York: Wiley.

McCartney, Clem (1994), *Clashing Symbols?*, Belfast: Institute of Irish Studies, Queen's University.

Nolan, Paul (1993), *Screening the Message*, Belfast: Central Community Relations Unit.

Poole, Michael (1990), 'The Geographical Location of Violence in Northern Ireland', in *Political Violence*, Belfast: Appletree Press.

Rose, Richard (1971), *Governing Without Consensus: An Irish Perspective*, London: Faber.

8 Multipoverty Europe: Reflections on Migration, Citizenship and Social Exclusion in the European Union and the United States

Carl-Ulrik Schierup

A proliferating multiplicity of *misère du monde* confutes tales of universal citizenship and solidarity in faltering European welfare states:[1] a permanently unemployed section of the population facing increased distress due to diminishing public unemployment security schemes and shrinking income-tested social assistance, the growing category of the homeless, the feminization of poverty and the problems of poor single-parent households,[2] increasing concentration of unemployment and poverty among the young, the enclavization of the disadvantaged in socially and culturally sealed-off neighbourhoods, the growth of low-wage informal urban enclave economies and occupational ghettos marginal to national labour market regulation and social security systems, the molecular warfare among criminalized[3] urban 'tribes' in socially polarized and segmented cities.[4] These issues have all become a shared contemporary concern of the European Union, from Kiruna to Malaga. They belong to the 'paradoxical', 'horrifying' and 'alarming' facts (Gaudier 1993) of a so-called 'new poverty' and processes of social exclusion, growing rather than receding, within one of the world's most powerful economic blocks (Room et al. 1989; Teekens and Van Praag 1990).[5]

Most of these contemporary practices of social exclusion bear an irrefutable tinge of racialization or ethnicization.[6] This means that they constitute increasingly widespread practices and forms of exclusion which particularly hit migrants and new ethnic minorities (that is, visible as well as less visible minorities with a relatively recent immigrant background). These practices, publicly rationalized and legitimized in ethnic, racial and cultural terms,[7] give rise to various forms of what we may call *ethnicized* or *racialized poverty*.

With their distinctive racial and ethnic bias zones of poverty, many western European cities bear increasing resemblance to the United States' urban ghettos, marked by multiple forms of social and cultural isolation, institutional impoverishment and exclusion from social rights of citizenship. As in the US 'Sun Belt', racially, ethnically and culturally rationalized social exclusion is being exacerbated through the presence of a substantial population of non-documented immigrants (Africans, Asians, eastern Europeans), often living under sub-human conditions, and deprived of elementary civil, political and social rights. These so-called 'margizens' of the European Community are particularly numerous in France and in southern Europe (Portugal, Spain, Italy, Greece).[8] In Germany, Austria and Switzerland, a polarization of society and the polity along ethnic lines is being reproduced through the perpetuation of legal-institutional practices modelled on the matrix of the discriminatory guest-worker policies of the 1960s. In the Nordic countries, an official rhetoric of 'integration' has to an increasing extent come to function as a synonym for exclusionary institutional practices, which cause social marginalization, urban segregation and political isolation.[9] Within most of western Europe, new restrictive refugee regimes based on the principles of so-called 'temporary protection' may, as their supposedly unintended effect, come to add to a growing category of socially marginalized and ethnically or racially delimited population groups.

Ethnicized and racialized social exclusion constitutes, to a more or less poignant degree, a common problem for all member states of the European Union. This problematic takes different forms, depending on the current character and the history of national polities, welfare regimes, as well as particular national policies of immigration and incorporation of immigrants and new ethnic minorities (cf. Faist 1995; Soysal 1994).[10] The national variation of ethnicized or racialized social exclusion and contingent forms of poverty in the Union as a whole[11] are related to the more general problem of the 'post-Fordist' restructuring (e.g. Liepetz 1987; Crompton and Brown 1994; Kennett 1994) and the ways in which it is articulated in different member states. It is in the same way important to distinguish between variations concerning prevalent European and North American (particularly US) trajectories concerning the articulation of our times' ethnicized poverty. On this premise I set out, in the following, to identify some of the prevalent academic conceptualizations of ethnicized and racialized exclusion and poverty in the European Union and in the United States. In conclusion, the question of a transatlantic conversion, which has become a major theme for European debates on ethnicized poverty, is raised. A possible, but still not given, scenario of a general Americanization of the welfare regimes of an emerging multipoverty, multi-ethnic Europe, this chapter argues, constitutes one of the most powerful challenges to the European Union facing the Third Millenium.

The negation of citizenship: from 'poverty' to 'social exclusion'

The shared reason for the development of a new poverty in western Europe since the mid-1970s has been identified as the *contraction of the welfare state,* a process increasingly expressed in the exclusion of a number of population segments from established rights encoded in national charters on social citizenship (for example, Dahrendorf 1985; Schmitter-Heisler 1991). So conceived, the so-called 'new poverty' equals *exclusion from social citizenship.* The concept of citizenship is that presented by T.H. Marshall in his now classical work, *Citizenship and Social Class.* Marshall defines 'social citizenship' as that 'whole range [of rights of citizenship] from the right to a modicum of economic welfare and security to the right to share to the full in the social heritage and to live the life of a civilized being according to the standards prevailing in the society' (1992: 8). These rights are, as conceived by Marshall, the most recent among the rights of citizenship on the basis of which, historically, the status of the citizen has progressively become instituted in western European societies. Social rights of citizenship have been closely contingent on the establishment and consolidation of the modern European welfare state and its institutions in the twentieth century, particularly those concerned with the social services and education.

The idea of 'exclusion' from social rights of citizenship (that is, 'social exclusion'), in the Marshallian sense, became a guiding thread for defining and analysing 'poverty' within the framework of the Poverty Programme of the European Commission. As operationalized in the *Background Report* to the European Poverty Programme the poor are, in this sense, defined as 'persons whose resources (material, cultural and social) are so limited as to exclude them from the minimum acceptable way of life in the Member State in which they live' (CEC 1991: 1). This definition is the basis on which the Commission has produced evidence that there is a considerable overall, widespread and growing poverty in Europe which is, at the same time, variable in extent and forms.[12] It is, in fact, an approach to poverty that strongly echoes the so-called 'relative perspective' on poverty as publicized through the influential writings of Peter Townsend (for example, 1979 and 1987); a perspective that now enjoys widespread acceptance among social scientists and policy makers. In the subsequent work of the Commission, 'social exclusion' has been forcefully adopted as a theoretically-based concept for identification, analysis and policy formation related to groups exposed to conditions of enduring and multiple deprivation.

The Marshallian concept of social citizenship was explicitly adopted as the basis for the work of the Observatory on National Policies to Combat

Social Exclusion, which was founded by the Commission of the European Communities in 1990. Seeking a precise and theoretical content of the notion of exclusion, the Observatory defines social exclusion 'first and foremost in relation to the social rights of citizens'. Social exclusion can, accordingly, 'be analysed in terms of the denial – or non-realisation – of social rights' (Room et al. 1992: 13–15). The Observatory includes other types of rights of citizenship – that is, Marshall's civil and political dimensions[13] – in its analyses, only in so far as they, in concrete cases, appear important for the analyses of the exclusion from or realization of social rights (pp. 16ff). It investigates what social rights (to employment, housing, health care, child care, etc.) individuals have in the individual member states, and it makes use of studies of multiple, persisting and cumulative disadvantage (in terms of education, training, employment, housing, financial resources), and 'whether those who suffer such disadvantages have substantially lower chances than the rest of the population of gaining access to the major social institutions' (ibid.). The general orientation here is, argues del Castillo, on social exclusion as 'it relates directly to the contemporary challenge to one of the cornerstones of justice or ... the system of "social contract" associated with democracies since the Second World War, namely, the equality of opportunity which should be guaranteed by law' (1994: 616).

Migrants and ethnic minorities: a neglected issue

Accordingly, considerable official and academic attention has, during the 1980s and 1990s, been devoted to matters of poverty and social exclusion in the European Union. However, the work of the Commission as well as that of individual social scientists has, as a whole, suffered from what critics have identified as one of the serious soft spots so often present among protagonists of the Marshallian paradigm, that is, their apparent blindness to matters of ethnicity and the social position of immigrants (for example, Turner 1990). A number of important national surveys, studies and academic discussions on social exclusion and poverty from the 1980s and 1990s contain, with notable exceptions,[14] quite inadequate material, or lack data altogether, concerning the situation of immigrants and ethnic minorities;[15] too often as well, the studies lack a discussion as to this apparent scarcity. This problem has also been pronounced concerning comparative compilations of information on social exclusion and poverty under the jurisdiction of the EU (for example, Teekens and Van Praag 1989; Room et. al. 1989, 1992).

A marked lack of attention from mainstream research to practices and trends concerning ethnicized social exclusion and contingent manifestations of poverty is at present, as a matter of fact, being partly redressed. There is certainly, and particularly from the 1990s, a growing interest from international bodies (like the European Commission, the OECD, ILO and UNESCO) in setting up systematic studies and documentation on various aspects of social exclusion like, for example, labour market discrimination and residential segregation. Apart from the attention from national governments as well as the Commission, concerning social exclusion, private organizations, specialized in migration and ethnic relations, have made efforts to produce compilations of data on single countries as well as for European comparative purposes.[16] To this comes a multitude of theoretically informed empirical studies – often at local or city level – carried out by individual researchers among the growing number of academic specialists on migration and ethnic studies in different European countries. They serve as important sources on the basis of which a view of the multiplicity of ethnicized social exclusion in the Union can be sketched out.

The so-called 'underclass' and the declining welfare state

Among the early local-level studies on social exclusion of new ethnic minorities are those conducted by John Rex and associates in British cities (for example, Rex and Moore 1967; Rex and Tomlinson 1979). These studies demonstrate how, contingent on competition between racially defined minorities and the majority and uneven ethnically structured power relationships in society, immigrant minorities are alienated from the welfare state struggled for by the British working class, and thus from the benefits of social citizenship.

In *Colonial Immigrants in a British City*, Rex and Tomlinson (1979) use the notion of the 'underclass' in order to describe this state of marginalization of the 'immigrant community'. This should not be confused with the way in which the term 'underclass' is used by the New Right, which embodies rather the opposite meaning (cf. Close 1995). In the British New Right discourse, the distinctive feature of 'the underclass' is rather that of an *excessive use of the welfare services*, which is seen to develop into a pathologic 'culture of dependency'.[17] This is a question that I shall return to in the following section, as I consider possible moral-political pitfalls embodied in the 'underclass' terminology, as well as critique as to the more general theoretical and analytical value of the approach for setting up comparative research on the ethnicization of social exclusion in Europe. For, despite its obvious ideological-political usurpation by the New Right in Britain, 'the underclass' has continued to be an important theme of discussion and analytical concept for British leftist academics and has also entered wider European circulation (for example, Rex 1988; Cross 1992a *passim*; Kloosterman 1994).

A sketch of the meaning of 'underclass' in the wider European context has been proposed by Ralph Dahrendorf (1985).[18] While the focus of the local studies from the 1960s and 1970s by Rex and associates was on social exclusion due to racism, inter-ethnic relations of power and market competition in an *established* welfare state, the focus has now moved on to major structural and social disjunctions in welfare states in crisis and decomposition. Setting out, like Rex and associates, from T.H. Marshall's concept of citizenship, and focusing particularly on social rights of citizenship, Dahrendorf defines the underclass as an increasingly sizeable and composite section of the population that is excluded from full rights of citizenship. He links an emerging underclass in western Europe in general with the wider range of problems connected with citizenship and social exclusion in welfare states marked by crisis, contraction and declining social rights. Exclusion brands a number of marginalized and poor categories of the population, among them immigrants and racially excluded new minorities. The contraction of the welfare state has created a 'crucial boundary ... between the majority class and those who are being defined out of the edifice of citizenship" (Dahrendorf 1985: 98).

An important merit of the underclass debate, as here represented by Rex and Dahrendorf, is the contribution it has made to make visible the social exclusion of immigrants and ethnic minorities in Europe – a fact possibly related to the term's origins in the United States, where social exclusion has always been inextricably linked with issues of migration, 'race' and 'ethnicity'. It carries, moreover, in line with the focus on exclusion as represented by the approach of the Commission, the issue of ethnicized poverty out of the realm of an ill-defined and diffuse notion of 'the new poverty' (Room et. al. 1989) and into the terrain of the specific historically instituted legal and social frameworks of citizenship of European states. By doing so, the questions of exclusion and poverty can be framed in terms of the moral-political premises (of citizenship) on which modern welfare states have been erected as well as in terms of challenges to the social policies set to protect the 'social compact' upon which the cohesion and social stability of the post-Second World War western European nation states have rested (for example, Wieviorka 1993; Naïr 1992).

By setting the problem within a wider context concerned with social rights and the moral and political predicaments of the welfare state (cf. Schmitter-Heisler 1991), the British 'underclass' perspective, as represented by Rex and associates, focused, moreover, the issue of ethnicized exclusion in a more radical way than more habitual approaches to issues of immigration and citizenship in the European context. They go beyond a conventional focus on exclusion/inclusion in the sense of formal and overall membership, that is, membership as simply meaning the access to nationhood in a formal legalistic sense: 'To have legal rights is not necessarily to be accepted completely in society' (Rex and Moore 1967: 15). Said in other words, the focus on racialized exclusion from the 'social contract' of the welfare state opens up the whole question of the relationship between what has been called 'formal' and 'substantial' citizenship.[19] If set in a complex and flexible analytical framework marked by a focus on the articulation of structured inequality *and* agency,[20] this dichotomy (that is, of formal and substantial citizenship) is inextricably related to another; that is, the dichotomy and intricate political problematic embodied in the relation between the so-called 'passive' and 'active' dimensions of citizenship (Turner 1990). These are diacritical issues for the development of theory and political practice for a democratic intercultural European *welfare society* (for example, Rein and Rainwater 1987; Ålund and Schierup 1991) of new post-Keynesian times.

New Right versus liberal approaches to 'the underclass' and poverty

When this is said, the substantial criticism that has been directed at a wider subsequent academic and public–political circulation of the notion of 'the underclass' should not be neglected. It is essential to consider this, particularly facing suggestions for adopting the term as a more general currency in research on ethnicized exclusion in western Europe (such as the discussion in Cross 1992b).

One forceful argument, with which we shall be concerned first, has to do with the moral–political pitfalls latently present in well-intended leftist/liberal discourses on 'the underclass'. 'The underclass' is a term that was all too easy to appropriate for the purposes of a Thatcherite New Right and its stigmatizing 'blame the victim' discourse on the welfare-dependent poor, argues Ruth Lister (1992; see also, for example, Close 1995; Bottomore 1992. Lister continues:

> Those who invoke the development of an 'underclass' to make the case for the restoration of full citizenship rights to the poor are playing with fire. They are using a stigmatising label to make the case for non-stigmatising politics. At the same time, the Right is arguing that part of the answer to dealing with the devel-

> opment of an 'underclass' lies in the revival of social stigma: 'Social stigma is an essential ingredient of social order and must, slowly and cumulatively be restored'. Overall, the policy lessons drawn from Murray's [New Right] 'underclass' thesis combine a counsel of despair – since central Government is 'powerless' to intervene – with calls for tougher social control and law and order policies.

The effect, Lister warns,[21] 'could be to denigrate the struggles of the poor and the efforts of those who work with them, whilst giving comfort to those who wish to whip up "moral panics" and cut back on social spending'.

Making use, in her criticism, of reference to the underclass thesis of the American New Right campaign against welfare spokesman, Charles Murray (1989), Lister points to the fact that the Thatcherite appropriation of the 'underclass' discourse in Britain (as so many other elements of Thatcherite ideology), is built on import from the American New Right's well-worn intellectual armoury in the war on the welfare-dependent 'undeserving poor' of the inner-city ghettos in the United States (as argued by Katz 1989). But similar narratives speaking of the non-working, 'undeserving' culturally alien 'stranger' within, who drains the welfare assistance of state and local communities, is standard in current nationalist–populist lore all over Europe.[22] Setting the 'underclass' discourse into general circulation within Europe might produce similar results as in Britain, in the form of providing armoury to the New Populist Right's crusades against morally destitute and 'parasitic' immigrants and new ethnic minorities, allegedly undermining public budgets and, thereby, endangering the lives of a decent and hard-working 'autochtonous' population. This possible danger is one good reason among others to take a closer look at the development of the US poverty debate, for which 'the underclass' has long been a pivotal conceptual hub – for liberals as well as for the New Right.

Tenets of the American debate

It was, in fact, Gunnar Myrdal (1964) who, with a term translated from his Swedish vernacular, first introduced the term *underklass* – 'underclass' – into the international vocabulary of social science. Studying New York's ghettos in the early 1960s, he maintained that the 'underclass' was the term that best described the condition of a population, socially and culturally apart, consisting of 'unemployed and gradually unemployable families at the bottom of society'. He tended, at least still in 1964,[23] to see the largely black ghetto underclass as a sort of social residuum left behind by liberal American reformism while, 'for the majority of people above that level, the increasingly democratic structure of the educational system creates more and more liberty'.[24]

During the 1980s and 1990s, given economic restructuring and extended social crisis in large American cities, a resurging post-Myrdalian American underclass debate bifurcated into two main directions focusing, respectively, on the so-called 'culture of poverty' and the impact of macro-structural change.[25]

Remoulding theses on 'cycles of deprivation' from the 1960s and 1970s (for example, Leacock 1971) and hinging on to conceptions of a problematic 'culture of poverty',[26] *New Right* intellectuals (e.g. Murray 1984; Mead 1988) and politicians have focused on the development of an allegedly uncooperative and 'irresolute mentality' and an unsound psychological dependency on welfare among the unemployed inner-city ghetto 'underclass'.[27] A problematic sense of pride and attitudes of fatalism and defeatism are perceived as expressed in unwillingness to take those many low-quality jobs that are indeed available. The welfare poor are hereby, largely due to their own agency or lack of such, seen to be caught in a vicious cycle, unable to accumulate sufficient work records for qualifying for more attractive jobs in the labour market. Poor people's inefficacy is in turn, according to the neoconservative approach of Lawrence M. Mead, understood 'to be the result primarily of weak socialization … erratic parenting (and failure) to internalize goals such as work and self-reliance with enough force to feel them as obligations' (1988: 134). The 'culture of poverty' encourages 'voluntary nonwork', 'breakdown of the work ethic', and asocial and menacing criminal behaviour among adolescents. The cure is seen in 'Workfare' – that is, in making welfare benefits for able-bodied, working-age people dependent on employment-related activities, such as vocational training, job-seeking activities and entrepreneurship, and a systematic change in attitudes concerning engagement in low-wage, low-status jobs. New Right approaches to *how* Workfare should be implemented vary considerably, however. They range between forcible neoliberal 'swim or sink in the labour market' therapies (for example, Murray 1984) implicating a minimal involvement of the central state, but trust in *local* communities and neighbourhoods, to proposals for authoritative neoconservative government policies, opposing permissiveness and *laissez-faire* (for example, Mead 1989).[28]

An alternative *liberal* approach to the 'underclass' – in fact a direct inheritor to the Myrdalian liberal discourse on poverty – distances itself not only from the simplicity and moralistic discourse that generally distinguishes the New Right's 'culture of poverty' thesis (for example, Wilson and Wacquant 1989; Anderson 1989; Sullivan 1993; McLanahan and Garfinkel 1993), but even from mono-causal leftist explanations of underclass formation in terms of 'racism' (see, particularly, Wilson 1978). A number of studies by liberal researchers locate the primary causes of social exclusion and the realities of ghetto culture in processes of macro-structural change and not in internalized, self-reproducing patterns of socialization (for example, Wilson 1987; Waldinger 1992; Kasarda 1989, 1993). They point to two major economic processes, *uneven economic growth* and *deindustrialization*, both largely beyond the control of the underclass constituents. Also the perception of the role of the state and social policy is qualitatively different. The alternatives to welfare and a growing underclass are seen in universal social programmes and adequate public institutions (schools, child care, health care) sustaining the reproductive and socialization functions of poor families and in macro-economic policies of *employment* (for example, McLanahan and Garfinkel 1993) that will raise the income level and security among the inhabitants of the inner cities (for example, Testa et. al. 1993).

The most systematic research and analysis of the growth and conditions of the inner-city 'underclass' in the liberal tradition have been done by William J. Wilson (1987). An important tenet of his argument is the so-called 'spatial mismatch hypothesis', pointing to the mismatch between the location of employment and residence in the inner city. He argues that the historical dimension of discrimination and a relatively late process of migration from rural areas in the South to industrial metropolitan centres made large sections of the black working class particularly vulnerable to the processes of deindustrialization taking place since the 1970s. It was the time when the major manufacturing industries and most jobs in the new service economy started massively to be located out of the old working-class neighbourhoods of central cities. Despite the passing of subsequent anti-discrimination legislation and the creation of affirmative action programmes, this has created a permanently high rate of joblessness among black people. This has triggered a concentration of poor people, an increasing number of poor single-parent families, and a permanent dependence on welfare benefits. These adverse processes have been exacerbated by the exodus to the suburbs of white *and* many black middle-class and established working-class families. These, Wilson maintains, had earlier – through investment of economic resources in the building-up of a diversified network of institutions (stores, schools, banks, community organizations, churches), and through 'reinforcing societal values' – made it meaningful even to lower-class people to anticipate some upward mobility. The combined effects of deindustrialization, uneven economic growth, out-migration of the resourceful, and the evacuation of the inner cities from its economic, political, social and cultural institutions have, consequently, created extended and spatially concentrated urban enclaves of deprived, the opportunities of whom are bounded by their social and cultural isolation in relation to the mainstream of the nation.[29] In so far as there exists a 'culture of poverty', the values of the ghetto result in its adaptation to structural change and can be expected to change when objective circumstances change.

In his comprehensive and polemic review of the US poverty debate, *The Undeserving Poor: From the War on Poverty to the War on Welfare* (1989), Michael B. Katz finds considerable sympathy for the liberal approach. He points, particularly, to the endeavours of William J. Wilson to rephrase a moralistic American academic, popular and political debate on poverty – focusing on an 'underclass' of menacing non-working teenage black youth, and the immorality of young poor single mothers on welfare – while pointing to the macro-economic dimensions of joblessness, the complete inadequacy of the Conservative Workfare strategy, and the inextricable necessity of formulating new broad reform strategies linked to economic and social policy. However, given the rhetoric that surrounds it, Katz (1989: 234) concludes that sticking to the underclass label is bad liberal strategy.

Aside from the moral judgement it implies, the term 'underclass' focuses public debate on a *particular subset of the poor*. It deflects attention from comprehensive social policies and encourages targeted approaches that historically have isolated their beneficiaries and reinforced the stigma attached to poverty and relief. 'Underclass' also revives discredited notions of the culture of poverty by emphasizing the behaviour of poor people rather than the sources of poverty.

The way 'underclass' has been formulated by the New Right has since long come to occupy a hegemonic space in mainstream American political discourse, Katz maintains. The tenet of his argument rests on his key thesis that 'underclass' has helped to diffuse an image of poor people as split into two sharply divided groups: the 'deserving poor' – homeless, harmless, helpless, grateful and deserving of 'charity' – and the 'undeserving' – that is, the amoral, demanding, culturally alienated, ungrateful and menacing inner-city (black) 'underclass', to be disciplined through Workfare. Insisting on 'underclass' helps to perpetuate the powerlessness of the poor in general by strengthening the barriers for so long dividing them (p.235). Finally, the New Right's appropriation and massive exploitation of the 'culture of poverty' thesis should lead to an extreme caution when using the term 'culture' as an epithet for describing the behaviour of poor people in general. 'For culture, like underclass, is used with such imprecision and in such varied ways that it has become more a barrier than an aid to understanding' (p.234).

Post-Fordism: multiform poverty and the question of a transatlantic convergence

Nevertheless, the 'underclass' continues to serve as an important conceptual vehicle for critical liberal–leftist discourse on both sides on the Atlantic. At the same time, while carrying Myrdal's term into widening circulation, contemporary interventions have increasingly come to represent 'underclass' as a growing, persistent and increasingly complex social category symptomatic of new times, rather than a relict of past repression (for example, Dahrendorf 1985; Schmitter Heisler 1991; Lash 1994,). This, however, has provoked another important critique of the 'underclass' approach, questioning its appropriateness as a general analytical and comparative category in the context of the emergence of an increasingly complex ethnic division of labour contingent on the post-Fordist transformation of economy and society.

One strand of this critique concerns the overall value of 'underclass', as developed by Wilson and associates for analysing social exclusion in complex post-Fordist urban settings. A range of contemporary studies, in North America as well as Europe, expose the multiplicity of ethnicized / racialized social exclusion and poverty in alternative terms, arguing that there is a need for a more dynamic and discriminative analytical framework. One example is the study by Roger Waldinger (1992) of 'Native Blacks, New Immigrants' and what he calls the 'post-industrial transformation' of New York. Waldinger maintains that there is an interdependence between the formation of a deprived, welfare-dependent black ghetto population and the upsurge of new groups of migrant working poor, like the numerous clandestines, for example, who occupy completely different positions in the larger society's political and moral economy. He questions the mismatch thesis in favour of a careful analysis of the interaction between population dynamics and labour demand and urges for more attention to the complex processes by which America's increasingly variegated minority populations adapt to the 'post-industrial' economies in which they live. The clue is to be found in a more comprehensive study of the post-industrial transformation that fundamentally remoulds the labour market and the class structure, and imposes new limits and demands on public policy.

In *The Informational City*, Manuel Castells (1989) maintains that the formation of the black welfare ghetto was rather the result of a culture of resistance, than a 'culture of poverty'; that is, the black working class became 'unemployable', not because of welfare, and not even simply because of the evacuation of jobs from the areas where the traditional industrial working class used to live, but because of its genuine labour union tradition and working-class militancy which served it well during the heyday of Fordism. In this sense, a heavy import of new low-wage, non-protected migrant labour from, principally, Latin America became a strategic element in a changing class struggle, associated with the establishment of a new mode of economic development: the informational society, in the division of labour of which the rise of an ethnic niche economy has become an integrated element.

A number of contemporary studies in western Europe indicate a similar perspective (for example, Lash 1994; Faist 1995). They describe a situation marked by a complex division of labour where ethnic and racial categorization takes on new economic and moral–political functions. This structures a situation marked by a highly complex and multifarious positioning of a whole range of working/non-working ethnic/racial minority groups among the socially disadvantaged. They certainly all have in common that they are incorporated in society as excluded (formally and/or substantially) from 'normal' historically won social rights of citizenship in European nation states. But they are excluded in different ways and with different consequences, that is, as welfare-dependent ethnic minority (national) 'citizens', as undocumented (non-national) labour migrants in the informal sub-minimal wage service economy, as super-exploited short-term migrant 'contract workers', etc. (Jones 1993; Cross 1995; Roseman et al. 1996; Ålund 1997.) Seen in this perspective, the truly disadvantaged and ethnicized 'new poor' become so much more than an 'underclass' *residuum* left behind by an affluent society (Myrdal), or the *faux frais* of industrial relocation (Wilson). They all constitute, but in importantly different ways – as working poor, labour reserves, or 'deserving'/'undeserving' non-working Others – indispensable cogwheels for the political and moral economic order of the third (micro-electronic/informational) industrial revolution.

These and other obvious transoceanic similarities concerning the development of social inequality and ethnic divisions of labour in the US and Europe, have given good reason to discuss the issue of convergent development. In his article, 'European Cities, the Informational Society, and the Global Economy', Castells (1994) indicates, for example, that a transatlantic convergence concerning the development of contemporary US and western European cities is taking place. This is related to the universal forces of the new (micro-electronic) technological revolution, globalization and economic restructuring. It involves, among other things, the arrival of millions of new immigrants and their overwhelming concentration in ethnic niches belonging to a proliferating 'informational' network economy within an increasingly socially polarized urban–societal space. This is consistent with the logic of global convergence, embodied in a number of contemporary studies on globalization and migration, for example, the influential work of Saskia Sassen (1988, 1994, 1996) on so-called 'global cities'.

Others – for example, Gary Freeman in 'Migration and the Political Economy of the Welfare State' (1986) – have pursued the theme of convergence in the sense of predicting an inevitable 'Americanization' of European social policies as they encounter a globalized economy marked by intense competition, interdependence and extreme inequality. Also, continued mass immigration is an inevitable feature of globalization. In shrinking welfare states under global pressure, migration becomes a source of highly divisive conflict. It will provoke a growing fragmentation along lines of ethnicity and 'race' of the broad consensus necessarily circumscribing any developed system of national social redistribution. A deepening division of society expressed in terms of an ethnic division of labour will serve to rationalize new forms of social exclusion. The dilemma is, Freeman maintains, impossible to solve within the framework of the 'closed systems' of national distributive welfare states which – whether we like or not – in the longer run, will be forced to open up themselves fully to the forces of the free market and global migration. Given that we accept the basic presuppositions of this scenario, we may, in line with Stephan Leibfried (1992: 255), expect a general 'Americanization' of European social, and, particularly, poverty policies.

This is, however, where yet a critical contextualization of the liberal 'underclass' thesis comes in. Using a comparative and inductive approach, several empirical studies (for example, Kloosterman 1994; Wacquant 1995) reach the conclusion that 'underclass', as applied in the American context (given the US's traditionally 'small' and presently deteriorating welfare state) is in fact not directly applicable to the conditions prevailing among disadvantaged urban populations in European countries. This is so, these studies confirm, at as least so far as it concerns more developed welfare states on the continent, like Holland, France, Germany and the Scandinavian countries. Even given the present crisis, they still embody elaborate welfare systems qualitatively different from those of the US. As a consequence, and in spite of their relative deterioration, disadvantaged neighbourhoods in European cities, inhabited by large proportions of new ethnic minorities and immigrants do – in terms of social security as well as their integration into the national institutional system in general – present a qualitatively different universe than do isolated black underclass ghettos in the United States.

Towards an 'Americanization' of European social policy?

Facing theses of convergence it is, accordingly, important to observe the continued existence of a number of qualitatively different welfare regimes across Europe and North America. And we must not necessarily believe that we have reached 'the End of History'. We can project several equally realistic future scenarios for the European Union and the western European welfare states (cf. Balbo 1993). The contingencies of their respective likeliness are dependent on the outcome of current political struggles, within nation states as well as on the level of the Union. This perspective also implicates that the American way to the informational society is only one among several, as argued by Stephen S. Cohen (1993) in a geo-economic analysis of strategic long-term alternatives for the European Union, the United States and Japan. And it is definitely neither the most humane nor the most socially or economically proficient.

An American development strategy, based on large-scale immigration of cheap, super-exploited and very often non-documented labour (in popular speech called 'the great American job-machine'), employed in a swelling and poorly regulated informal sector, combined with consecutive, *ad hoc* but destructive, attempts to dismantle the welfare state, has not only led to the formation of large disadvantaged population groups and new bitter social conflicts. It is a strategy that has brought about an economy badly equipped to match the intensified competition among the leading economic blocs of the twenty-first century. The proficient alternative for the EU is, analysed in this perspective, definitely *not* to copy the United States; that is, to indiscriminately open up itself to the blasts of globalization and a free market, and to dismantle remaining high protective welfare-state arrangements. For the 'welfare state' is much more than a closed system based on an ethos of distributive justice. It constitutes a comprehensive system for managing social reproduction and political–economic development that *could* be made to conform to new challenges. Therefore, Cohen warns: 'Before Europe, in some futile quest for lower costs, sets out to dismantle its social protection system, it would be well advised to study the ironies of America's "cost savings" in such critical areas as child care, health, and social stability ... seen in the context of a realistic image of a modern production system' (1993: 147).

Concluding the argument, two main analytical points can be drawn. One relates to the necessity of forging an efficient and discriminating comparative framework that is capable of capturing the historical and current uniqueness of different types of national welfare regimes and regimes of incorporation (of migrants and ethnic minorities) in Europe (for example, Esping-Andersen 1990 and Soysal 1994) and not least the highly different ways in which they respond to the forces of globalization. Such a framework should endeavour to evade the obvious discursive and analytical pitfalls embodied in the 'underclass' notion, while continuing to refine critical comparative potentialities relating to the mutually linked categories of 'social exclusion' and 'social citizenship' and to their contingence on changing national 'welfare regimes'. The other is related to the need for analysing the 'Social Dimension' of European integration in a perspective capable of accounting for different alternative options concerning the ways in which the *Union* as a *whole* may respond to the present encompassing transformation of economy and society and, contingent on this, to the demands, problems and opportunities related to international migration and the formation of increasingly poly-ethnic societies within its borders. All the emergent forms of ethnicized new poverty and processes of racialized exclusion inhibit salient features of a profound structural nature, which by far exceed the domain of a residual 'social problem' and the capacities for reform of national welfare regimes in crisis. They add salient demands and challenges to the complex but increasingly urgent task of adding a forceful 'social dimension' to the domains of an ongoing supranational economic and political integration in an intercultural Europe.

Notes

1 *'Misère du monde'* alludes to the title of a volume edited by Pierre Bourdieu (1993) exposing the vast multiplicity of contemporary forms of poverty in France.

2 See, however, the comparative analyses by Hobson (1994) and Hobson and Takahashi (1996) who argue that, in contrast to a number of other European countries, lone mothers in Sweden have not been a socially stigmatized social category. This is seen as being mainly due to their firm inclusion into rights of social citizenship and general welfare schemes. It is a situation that could be taken to be rather general concerning the Scandinavian welfare states, which in this respect expose a striking contrast seen in relation to the situation in, for example, Britain. But this situation might change (ibid.) considerably due to current reform and cuts in the welfare system.

3 The notion of 'criminalized' employed in the sense as, for example, used by Keith (1993).

4 The expression of 'molecular warfare' was coined by Hans Magnus Enzensberger (1994) in his book *Civil Wars: From L. A. to Bosnia.*

5 For a critical discussion of the notion of 'new poverty', see Room et al. (op. cit.).

6 The concept of 'racialization' has been particularly elaborated by Robert Miles (e.g. 1993). A collection of valuable theoretically informed and empirically documented studies of racialization within different social spheres was published in the book *Racism, the City and the State,* edited by Cross and Keith (1993). The term 'ethnicization' has been used as a concept for ideological and institutional practices which – contingent on political, economic, and cultural claims and relations of power – lead to the systematic, institutionally embedded exclusion of ethnic minorities (Ålund and Schierup 1991; Schierup 1993; Faist 1995). Racialization might be a more readily employable term in the British context (given a particular historical and etymological anchoring and a still prevalent and broad discourse on 'race' in the UK), and not readily transferred into common usage on the continent (given the generally very particular and narrow connotations of the notions of 'race' and 'racism', historically and in current public and scientific discourse, outside the UK context).

7 For a detailed analysis of the complex interrelationship and dynamics of exclusion and stigmatization typically involved in processes of ethnicization/racialization rationalized in terms of 'culture', see Schierup's (1993) study of the Danish case.

8 The notion of 'margizens', sometimes used as a term for the undocumented immigrants of western Europe (e.g., Martiniello 1994) enjoying almost no civil, socioeconomic and political rights, alludes to and complements the more established concept of 'denizens' (Hammar 1990): that is, citizens of an extra-communitarian state legally settled in Europe and (varying in quality and extent between countries) possessing substantial rights. For numbers and a sympathetic discussion of the role and status of undocumented immigrants in Europe, see, for example, Collinson (1993).

9 For example, the detailed exposé of the Danish case by Schierup (1993). Collinson (1993) provides a comparative discussion of changing migration policies in different western European countries.

10 The term 'new ethnic minorities' (introduced and defined by Castles et. al. 1984) refers to minority groups (with a recent migrant background) formed in western European immigration countries during the period after the Second World War.

11 Most national surveys on living conditions and social exclusion lack adequate material on immigrants and ethnic minorities. This problem is still more pronounced concerning large comparative compilations of information on poverty and social exclusion, like those of the poverty programme of European Community (see, for example, the compilation of Teekens and Praag (1990) on policy issues, research options and data sources on poverty in the European Union, where discussions of criteria for analysing the distribution of poverty among ethnic groups are conspicuously absent except – and this is rather symptomatic – for the contribution from the US) and the European Observatory on Social Exclusion.

12 For seminal discussions on the European Commission's perspective on poverty and social exclusion see, for example, Close (1995: 30ff), Strobel (1996), and del Castillo (1994).

13 Marshall conceived social rights as complementary to *civil* rights, that is, 'the rights necessary for individual freedom-liberty, of the person, freedom of speech, though and faith, the right to own property and to conclude valid contracts, and the right to justice' – and to *political* , that is, 'the right to participate in the exercise of political power' (Marshall 1992). He argued, based on his conception of British history, that civil rights were historical achievements of the seventeenth century and political rights of the eighteenth.

14 The most notable exception is that of Britain, which is the by far best-researched western European country in this respect.

15 For example, the important anthology on deprivation and poverty, edited by Ferge and Miller (1987)

16 For example, the European Centre for Work and Society in Maastricht.

17 Close (1995: pp.45 ff.) referring to the British debate, among others, in an interview with the former Prime Minister, Margaret Thatcher.

18 See also the critical review and appraisal of Dahrendorf's conception of the underclass by Schmitter-Heisler (1991).

19 For example, Brubaker (1989), Brubaker and Rogers (1992), Castles (1994); see also the discussion by Bottomore (1992: 66 ff.); cf. Barbalet (1988).

20 For example, as attempted in Rex and Moore (1967) and Rex and Tomlinson (1979); see also, later theoretical considerations in Rex (1988).
21 Quoting a liberal intervention in the British underclass debate from *The Sunday Times* by Thompson (1989).
22 For example, the critical analyses by Hjarnø (1993), Schierup (1993), Freeman (1986), Wieviorka (1993).
23 Looking critically back on *The American Dilemma* during the early 1970s, Myrdal's optimism concerning the potentials of American liberal reformism had become thoroughly jeopardized (see, further, Schierup 1995).
24 See also the commentary on Myrdal by John Rex (1988).
25 For general overviews on the underclass debates in the USA and Europe see, for example, Katz (1989, particularly Chapters Four and Five), Roche (1992) and Schmitter-Heisler (1991). See also, for example, Greenstone (1991), who – purporting a third 'multicultural' approach – argues that the 'culture of poverty', and the structural approach are equally flawed, each in their way, in that they underestimate the particular rationality and potentials of the culture of the underclass. The collected volume, *The Urban Underclass*, edited by Christopher Jencks and Paul E. Peterson (1991), provides a varied sample of theoretical–analytical perspectives and a number of useful case studies.
26 'Culture of poverty' is a term originally coined by Oscar Lewis (1968), based on his studies of the lives of poor people in Middle America. Lewis was criticized by Ulf Hannerz (1969) for failing to distinguish clearly between causes and symptoms of a life in poverty (see also Wilson 1993: 4–5). For a critical discussion of the 'culture of poverty' thesis, see also Katz (1989, particularly Chapter One).
27 See also the informative review of New Right and liberal perspectives on the underclass by Roche (1992, particularly Part II, *passim*).
28 In his review of disputes on social citizenship Maurice Roche (1992, particularly Chapters 4–6) provides a review and a seminal critique of New Right conceptions of 'culture and poverty' and of conceptions of 'Workfare'.
29 This widespread trend towards the accumulation of massive spatially isolated economic, political and cultural deprivation in major metropolitan areas of the United States has been summarized in the notion of the 'impacted ghetto' (Hughes 1991).

References

Ålund, Aleksandra (1997), *Multikultiungdom: Kön, etnicitet, identitet*, Lund: Studentlitteratur.

Ålund, Aleksandra and Schierup, Carl-Ulrik (1991), *Paradoxes of Multiculturalism: Essays on Swedish Society*, Aldershot: Avebury.

Anderson, E. (1989), 'Sex Codes and Family Life among Poor Inner-city Youths', *Annals of the American Academy of Political and Social Science,* January, pp.59–78.

Balbo, Laura (1993) 'Our European Futures: Alternative Scenarios', unpublished research note, University of Ferara.

Barbalet, J.M. (1988), *Citizenship: Rights, Struggle and Class Inequality*, Stony Stratford: Open University Press.

Bottomore, Tom (1992), 'Citizenship and Social Class, Forty Years on', in Marshall,

T.H. and Bottomore, Tom, *Citizenship and Social Class*, London and Concord, MA: Pluto Press, pp.55–93.
Bourdieu, Pierre (ed.) (1993), *La misére du monde*, Paris: Seuil.
Brubaker, W. Rogers (ed.) (1989), *Immigration and the Politics of Citizenship in Europe and North America*, Lanham, New York, London: University Press of America.
Brubaker, W. Rogers (1992), *Citizenship and Nationhood in France and Germany*, Cambridge, MA: Harvard University Press.
Castells, Manuel (1989), *The Informational City: Information Technology, Economic Restructuring, and the Urban–Regional Process*, Oxford: Blackwell.
Castells, Manuel (1994), 'European Cities, the Informational Society, and the Global Economy', *New Left Review*, 204, pp.18–32.
Castillo, Yepes del (1994), 'A Comparative Approach to Social Exclusion: Lessons from France and Belgium', *International Labour Review*, 133 (5–6), pp.613–33.
Castles, Stephen (1994), 'Democracy and Multicultural Citizenship: Australian Debates and their Relevance for Western Europe', in Bauböck, Rainer (ed.), *From Aliens to Citizens: Redefining the Status of Immigrants in Europe*, Aldershot: Avebury, pp.3–28.
Castles, Stephen et al. (1984), *Here for Good: Western Europe's New Ethnic Minorities*, London and Sydney: Pluto Press.
CEC (Commission of the European Communities) (1991), *Background Report: The European Poverty Programme*, Luxembourg: Office for Official Publications of the European Communities.
Close, Paul (1995), *Citizenship, Europe and Change*, Houndmills and London: Macmillan.
Cohen, Stephen S. (1993), 'Geo-Economics: Lessons from America's Mistakes', in Carnoy, Martin et al. (eds), *The New Global Economy in the Information Age*, Houndmills, Basingstoke: Macmillan.
Collinson, S. (1993), *Europe and International Migration*, London and New York: Pinter Publishers.
Crompton, Rosemary and Brown, Phillip (1994), 'Exclusion, Post-Fordism and the 'New Europe', in Brown, Phillip and Crompton, Rosemary (eds), *A New Europe? Restructuring and Social Exclusion*, London: UCL Press, pp.14–32.
Cross, Malcolm (1992a), *Ethnic Minorities and Industrial Change in Europe and North America*, Cambridge: Cambridge University Press.
Cross, Malcolm (1992b), 'Introduction: Migration, the City and the Urban Dispossessed', in Cross, Malcolm (ed.) (1992a).
Cross, Malcolm (1995), '"Race", Class Formation and Political Interests: A Comparison of Amsterdam and London', in Hargreaves, Jeremy Leaman (ed.), *Racism, Ethnicity and Politics in Contemporary Europe*, Aldershot: Edward Elgar.
Cross, Malcolm and Keith, Michael (eds) (1993), *Racism, the City and the State*, London and New York: Routledge.
Dahrendorf, Ralph (1985), *Law and Order*, Boulder, CO: Westview Press.
Enzensberger, Hans Magnus (1994), *Civil Wars: From L.A. to Bosnia*, New Press.
Esping-Andersen, Gøsta (1990), *The Three Worlds of Welfare Capitalism*, Cambridge: Polity Press.
Faist, Thomas (1995), 'Ethnization and Racialization of Welfare-state Politics in Germany and the USA', *Ethnic and Racial Studies*, 18(2), pp.219–50.
Ferge, Z. and S. M. Miller (eds) (1987), *Dynamics of Deprivation*, Aldershot: Gower.
Freeman, Gary P. (1986), 'Migration and the Political Economy of the Welfare State', *Annals of the American Academy of Political and Social Science*, 485, May, pp.51–63.

Gaudier, Maryse (1993), *Poverty, Inequality, Exclusion: New Approaches to Theory and Practice*, Serie Bibliographique No. 17, Génève: Institut International d'Etudes Sociales.

Greenstone, Robert (1991) 'Culture, Rationality, and the Underclass', in Jencks, Christopher and Peterson, Paul E. (eds), *The Urban Underclass*, Washington: The Brookings Institute.

Hammar, Tomas (1990), *Democracy and the Nation State*, Aldershot: Avebury.

Hannerz, Ulf (1969) *Soulside: Inquiries into Ghetto Culture and Community*, New York: Columbia University Press.

Higham, J. (1993), 'Multiculturalism and Universalism: A History and Critique'. *American Quarterly*, 45(2), pp.195–219.

Hjarnø, Jan (1993), 'Causes of the Increase in Xenophobia in Denmark', *Migration*, 18(2), pp.41–62.

Hobson, Barbara (1994), 'Solo Mothers, Policy Regimes, and the Logics of Gender', in Sainsbury, Diane (ed.), *Gendering Welfare States*, London: Sage, pp.170–87.

Hobson, Barbara and Takahashi, Mieko (1996), 'Genusperspektiv på det sociala medborgarskapet: En studie av ensamstående mödrar', in Palme, Joakim and Wennemo, Irene (1996), *Generell välfärd: Hot och möjligheter?*, Stockholm: Nordstedts.

Hughes, Mark Alan (1991), 'Formation of the Impacted Ghetto: Evidence from Large Metropolitan Areas', *Urban Geography*, 11(3), pp.265–84.

Jencks, Christopher and Paul E. Peterson (eds) (1991), *The Urban Underclass*, Washington: The Brookings Institution.

Jones, Trevor (1993), *Britain's Ethnic Minorities*, London: Policy Studies Institute.

Kasarda, John D. (1989), 'Urban Industrial Transition and the Underclass', *The Annals of the American Academy of Political and Social Science*, 501, January, pp.26–47.

Kasarda, John D. (1993), 'Urban Industrial Transition and the Underclass', in Wilson, William J. (ed.) *The Ghetto Underclass: Social Science Perspectives*, Newbury Park, London and New Delhi: Sage.

Katz, Michael B. (1989), *The Undeserving Poor: From the War on Poverty to the War on Welfare*, New York: Pantheon Books.

Keith, Michael (1993), 'From Punishment to Discipline? Racism, Racialization, and the Policing of Social Control', in Cross, Malcolm and Michael Keith (eds.) *Racism, the City and the* State, London and New York: Routledge, pp.193–209.

Kennett, Patricia (1994), 'Exclusion, post-Fordism and the "New Europe"', in Brown, Phillip and Crompton, Rosemary (eds), *A New Europe: Restructuring and Social* Exclusion, London: UCL Press, pp.14–33.

Kloosterman, Robert C. (1994), 'Amsterdamned: The Rise of Unemployment in Amsterdam in the 1980s', *Urban Studies*, 31(8), pp.1325–1344.

Lash, Scott (1994) 'The Making of an Underclass: Neo-liberalism versus Corporatism', in Brown, Phillip and Crompton, Rosemary (eds), *A New Europe? Restructuring and Social Exclusion*, London: UCL Press.

Leacock, E. (ed.) (1971), *The Culture of Poverty: A Critique*, New York: Simon and Schuster.

Leibfried, Stephan (1992), 'Towards a European Welfare State? On Integrating Poverty Regimes into the European Community', in Ferge, Zsuzsa and Eiving Kolberg, (eds), *Social Policy in a Changing Europe*, Frankfurt am Main and Boulder, Colorado: Campus Verlag and Westview Press.

Lewis, Oscar (1968), 'Culture of Poverty', in Moynihan, Daniel Patrick (ed.), *On Understanding Poverty: Perspectives from the Social Sciences*, New York: Basic Books.

Liepitz, Alain (1987), *Mirages and Miracles: The Crisis of Global Fordism*, Thetford: The Thetford Press.
Lister, Ruth (1992), *The Exclusive Society: Citizenship and the Poor*, London: Child Poverty Action Group.
McLanahan, Sara and Irwin Garfinkel (1993), 'Single Mothers, the Underclass, and Social Policy', in Wilson, William J. (ed.), *The Ghetto Underclass: Social Science Perspectives*, Newbury Park, London and New Delhi: Sage.
Marshall, T. H. (1992 [1950]), 'Citizenship and Social Class', in Marshall, T.H. and Bottomore, Tom, *Citizenship and Social Class*, London and Concord, MA: Pluto Press, pp.3–54 (reprinted from Marshall, T.H. (1950), *Citizenship and Social Class*, Cambridge: Cambridge University Press).
Martiniello, M. (1994), 'Citizenship of the European Union: A Critical View', in Bauböck, R. (ed.), *From Aliens to Citizens: Redefining the Status of Immigrants in Europe*, Aldershot: Avebury, pp.29–48.
Mead, L. (1988), 'Jobs for the Welfare Poor', *Policy Review*, Winter, pp.60–9.
Mead, L. (1989), 'The Logic of Workfare', *The Annals of the American Academy of Political and Social Science*, 501, pp.156–69.
Miles, Robert (1993), *Racism after Race Relations*, London: Routledge.
Murray, Charles (1984), *Losing Ground*, New York: Basic Books.
Murray, Charles (1989), 'Underclass', *Sunday Times Magazine*, 26 November.
Myrdal, Gunnar (1964), *Challenge to Affluence*, Gollancz: London.
Naïr, Sami (1992), *Le regard des vainqueurs: les enjeux français de l'immigration*, Paris: Grasset.
Rein, Martin and Lee Rainwater (1987), 'From Welfare State to Welfare Society', in Esping-Andersen, Gösta (ed.), *Stagnation and Renewal in Social Policy*, Armonk, New York: M.E. Sharpe.
Rex, John (1988), *The Ghetto and the Underclass: Essays on Race and Social Policy*, Aldershot: Avebury.
Rex, J. and Moore, R. (1967), *Race, Community and Conflict: A Study of Sparkbrook*, London and New York: Oxford University Press.
Rex, J. and Tomlinson, S. (1979), *Colonial Immigrants in a British City*, London: Routledge.
Room, Graham, Lawson, Roger and Laczko, Frank (1989) '"New Poverty" in the European Community', *Policy and Politics*, 17(2), pp.165–76.
Room, Graham et al. (1992), *Observatory on National Policies to Combat Social Exclusion, Second Annual Report*, Brussels: Directorate General for Employment, Social Affairs and Industrial Relations, Commission of the European Communities.
Roche, Maurice (1992), *Rethinking Citizenship: Welfare, Ideology and Change in Modern Society*, Cambridge: Polity Press.
Roseman, Curtis C., Laux, Hans Dieter and Thieme, Günter (eds) (1996), *EthniCity. Geographic Perspectives on Ethnic Change in Modern Cities*, London: Rowman and Littlefield.
Sassen, Saskia (1988), *The Mobility of Labor and Capital: A Study in International Investment and Labor Flow*, Cambridge: Cambridge University Press.
Sassen, Saskia (1994), 'The Urban Complex in a World Economy', *International Social Science Journal*, 139, pp.43–62
Sassen, Saskia (1996), 'Rebuilding the Global City: Economy, Ethnicity and Space', in King, Anthony D. (ed.), *Re-Presenting the City: Ethnicity, Capital and Culture in the Twenty-First Century Metropolis*, Houndmills and London: Macmillan.

Schierup, Carl-Ulrik (1993), *På kulturens slagmark: mindretal og størretal taler om Danmark*, Esbjerg: Southern Jutland University Press.

Schierup, Carl-Ulrik (1995), 'A European Dilemma: Myrdal, the American Creed and EU Europe', *International Sociology*, 10(4), pp.347–69.

Schmitter-Heisler (1991), 'A Comparative Perspective on the Underclass: Questions of Urban Poverty, Race, and Citizenship', *Theory and Society*, 20, pp.455–83.

Soysal, Yasemin Nuhoglu (1994), *Limits of Citizenship: Migrants and Post-national Membership in Europe*, Chicago: The University of Chicago Press.

Strobel, Pierre (1996), 'From Poverty to Exclusion: A Wage-earning Society or a Society of Human Rights?', *International Social Science Journal*, 148, pp.174–89.

Sullivan, Mercer L. (1993), 'Absent fathers in the inner city', in Wilson, William J. (ed.) *The Ghetto Underclass: Social Science Perspectives*, Newbury Park, London and New Delhi: Sage.

Teekens, Rudolf and Bernard M. S. Van Praag (eds) (1990), *Analysing Poverty in the European Community: Policy Issues, Research Options and Data Sources*, Eurostat News, Special edition 1–1990, Luxembourg: Office for Official Publications of the European Communities.

Testa, Mark, Astone, Nan Marie and Krogh, Marilyn (1993), 'Employment and Marriage among Inner-city Fathers', in Wilson, William J. (ed.), *The Ghetto Underclass: Social Science Perspectives*, Newbury Park, London and New Delhi: Sage.

Thompson, Kenneth (1989), *Sunday Times*, 3 December.

Townsend, Peter (1979), *Poverty in the United Kingdom*, Harmondsworth: Penguin.

Townsend, Peter (1987), 'Conceptualising poverty', in Ferge, Z. and Miller, S.M. (eds), *Dynamics of Deprivation*, Aldershot: Gower.

Turner, B.S. (1990), 'Outline of a Theory of Citizenship', *Sociology*, 24(2), pp.189–217.

Wacquant, Löic, J.D. (1995), 'The Comparative Structure and Experience of Urban Exclusion: "Race", Class, and Space in Chicago and Paris', in McFate, Katherine, Lawson, Roger and Wilson, William Julius (eds), *Poverty, Inequality and the Future of Social Policy: Western States in the New World Order*, New York: Russell Sage Foundation.

Waldinger, Roger (1992) 'Native Blacks, New Immigrants and the Post-industrial Transformation of New York', in Cross, Malcolm (ed.), *Ethnic Minorities and Industrial Change in Europe and North America*, Cambridge: Cambridge University Press.

Wallerstein, Immanuel (1990), 'Culture as the Ideological Battleground of the Modern World-system', *Theory, Culture and Society*, 7(2–3), pp.31–56.

Wieviorka, Michel (1993), 'Tendencies to Racism in Europe: Does France Represent a Unique Case, or is it Representative of a Trend?', in Wrench, J., and Solomos, J. (eds), *Racism and Migration in Western Europe*, Oxford: Berg Publishers, pp.55–66.

Wilson, William J. (1978), *The Declining Significance of Race: Blacks and Changing American Institutions*, Chicago and London: The University of Chicago Press.

Wilson, William J. (1987), *The Truly Disadvantaged: The Inner City, the Underclass, and Public Policy*, Chicago and London: The University of Chicago Press.

Wilson, William J. (ed.) (1993), *The Ghetto Underclass: Social Science Perspectives*, Newbury Park, London and New Delhi: Sage.

Wilson, William J. (1994), *Citizenship and the Inner-city Ghetto Poor*, London, Thousand Oaks and New Delhi: Sage.

Wilson, William J. and Wacquant, Löic J.D. (1989), 'The Cost of Racial and Class Exclusion in the Inner City', *The Annals of the American Academy of Political and Social Science*, 501, January, pp.8–25.

9 Migration and Social Policies in Northern and Southern Europe: A Comparative Perspective

Giovanna Campani

Migratory and integration policies

Migratory policies represent, as Schnapper writes, an 'ensemble of measures and social practices adopted along two complementary axes: ruling and controlling the entry, the stay and the employment of non-nationals; treating the populations already settled' (1992: 29). Still, the connection between the two axes is quite problematic, the first one having to do with restriction, control and repression, the second with social policies.

Different migratory policies and integration models existed in Europe in the period between the end of the Second World War and the introduction of immigration control (the so-called 'stop-policies') in the mid-1970s (Campani 1987). After the closing of the European borders, the importance of illegal (or undocumented) migration grew. Southern Europe became also an immigration area. The new context cannot be understood without examining changes which have taken place in European societies: such changes have questioned the concept of integration, which had been considered until recently the solution and the destiny for immigrant groups.

Lapeyronnie points out that the model of integration of immigrant or ethnic minorities in Europe is strictly bound to a representation, an image of the society, in national and modern terms: 'The integration of immigrants doesn't work differently from the integration of natives, individuals and groups. It means their identification to a national, modern culture and their functional incorporation in the social system' (Lapeyronnie 1990: 168).

It is precisely this model of integration which is going through a crisis, because of the changes which have taken place in European societies, concerning both the organization of work and the labour market (the industrial system) and the traditional integration structures, such as the school, the family, the Church, the state (the social system and the nation state). These changes have modified the model which structured the unity and the division of the social system: the unity was based on the nation state; the division was based on the class conflict. The class conflict structured social, political and intellectual life on the basis of the industrial relations.

As Wievorka writes: 'The social question cannot be, nowadays, separated by the cultural fragmentation' (1996: 14). This doesn't mean that the social question must be interpreted through 'cultural differences', but that different cultural orientations can be at the centre of social conflicts.

In this context where cultural fragmentation and social exclusion are strongly connected, integration processes follow new dynamics which are complex and various. National migratory policies seem to play a minor role in integration processes, in comparison with other variables, depending on the local contexts (and the existing resources at local level), but also on immigrants' organization forms, like networks and associations. This is particularly evident in southern Europe where immigration has assumed, since the beginning, specific characteristics.

Migratory and integration policies in Europe: different models in the post-war years

As Noiriel (1988) writes, in Europe the role of migration and of migrants has been underplayed, unlike in the United States and in Canada, where migration has been a constitutive dimension of the society. 'The nation-states of Europe have defined themselves as "temporary labour recruiting countries" and reserved for immigrant resident an outsider status of 'birds of passage' (Piore 1979), while at the same time setting assimilation as 'the ultimate goal' (Morokvasic 1994: 461) Schnapper writes: 'Until 1960, France, country of unitarian tradition and ideology, wanted to ignore that it was a country of immigration. The other European countries, included the United Kingdom, in spite of the Irish immigration, conceived themselves as emigration countries more than immigration countries' (1992: 13).

In a general frame of not recognizing migration as permanent, European countries have shown important differences in migratory and integration policies and in the social representation of migration. Such differences depend on the economic, political and social history of each country, and also on their specific idea of what constitutes a nation. Migratory policies are 'one dimension of the national elaboration' (Schnapper 1992: 17). In other words, the integration of immigrants is a *particular* dimension of the national integration.

Emile Durkheim noted that the nation was a mystical, obscure idea (quoted by Liauzu 1996), which is in fact based on contradictory principles: in the etymological meaning of 'nation' (coming from the Latin for 'birth'), there is the idea of birth, community, blood, nature; however, since the eighteenth century, the nation has been considered, through the French Revolution, as a conscient, political, will. On one side, the representation which is often made of the nation reflects this mystical, obscure idea: myths of the origin, national heroes, often legendary; on the other, the nation is founded on a political pact, and it is never established just once, but goes through a continuous process of elaboration, re-elaboration, inclusion and exclusion. The opposition between the biological community and the political will is expressed by the 'ideal/typical' opposition between France and Germany.

The French republican idea of nation has a strong universalistic tension. Michelet wrote: 'This nation, considered as the asylum of the world, is much more than a nation; it's a living brotherhood.'[1] In fact, even in French political thought, there are two different ideas of the nation, represented by different political forces, opposing each other: the expression of the will of the citizens and the republican tradition, and the nation-community, inspired by the German model of *Volk*. The two ideas of nation have been represented, during the Second World War, by Vichy, from one side, and by the Resistance on the other. After the Second World War, the republican idea has become the predominant one, while the other idea is nowadays exploited by the National Front of Jean Marie Le Pen.

The case of Germany is even more complex than the French one: 'The idea of the nation as creation of the History and of the Jura is very different from the idea of ethnic community, of blood and of culture which the nationalist German thought has developed in a rigorous way since Herder' (Liauzu 1992: 72–3) Germany is still, in some way, an 'ethnic nation-state', which has eliminated the universalistic elements of the national idea, to keep just its particularistic dimension (Schnapper 1992). As Schnapper writes:

> The Federal Republic of Germany has been created around democratic values, the State of right and Human rights. Still, in the Constitution, it is affirmed the unity of the German people, in spite of its [previous] division between RFA and RDA. Consequently, the juridical measures keeping the principle of the Volk have not been eliminated. Especially, the right to the nationality is still strongly based on the principle of the 'jus sanguinis' [blood right]. (1992: 65)

This has of course a great influence on migratory policies. The German Constitution made it very difficult for foreigners to obtain German citizenship. Though a few million immigrants have lived in Germany for many years, the right of citizenship hasn't changed, in spite of some new rules for children of immigrant workers, who were born in Germany and who have completed four years of school there.

In migratory policies, the ideal/typical opposition between the French and German models is represented by assimilation and by the *Gastarbeiter* system. The '*Gastarbeiter* policy' was followed in Germany and Switzerland: 'guestworkers', come to the 'host' country for a period of time, in order to accomplish a limited task. In these countries, the purpose of migratory policies has been, for many years, mainly to control and to reduce length of stay. In comparison with Germany and Switzerland, France and Britain had fairly liberal immigration policies. Immigrants could settle and, eventually, become citizens. France represented for many years the example of an assimilationist policy of immigrants, being practically the only European country which has known, since the last century, a massive immigration movement which has strongly influenced demographic and economic growth, as well as the social mobility of the French population (Liauzu 1996). It is estimated that 10 million French people are of foreign origin.

France has progressively elaborated a policy of 'naturalization' (citizenship), based on the *jus solis* (right of the soil), according to which the second generation of immigrant origin, born in France, becomes automatically French citizens. This has been changed, only recently, by the right-wing coalition government directed by Balladur and has been substituted with the voluntary choice by immigrant children at age 18. The present Socialist government has reintroduced the old system, showing how this idea of citizenship is substantive to the republican idea of nation.

The law on citizenship is one instrument which should make easier the process of assimilation. Another instrument of assimilation has been the education system, charged with the transmission of national values. The great laws which established the French school system date back to the Third Republic, in 1881, 1882 and 1886. The French school has herited the values and ideals of the Enlightenment and French Revolution. The state monopoly of education as opposed to Church – was realized during the Revolution in 1793–94. The Third Republic (1870–1940) made the school system the guarantor of national unity, through the principles of a free compulsory secular schooling aimed at reducing cultural differences. The French school system in fact expresses integration 'à la française', universalistic and equalitarian. In presenting republican values as universal, the secular education system has played an important role in the assimilation of generations of immigrant children. It is precisely in the education system that the signs of the crisis of this assimilation have appeared with the famous 'affaire' of the 'foulard' (headscarves). (This debate was raised in the French schools by the wish expressed by some Muslim girls to wear a headscarf in the classes. According to the school director, the secular rules of the school didn't allow this practice.)

The new context of international migration and the crisis of the national societies

Both the *Gastarbeiter* system and the assimilation model belong to the past. Already at the end of the 1970s, it had become apparent that the arrival of immigrants could not respond only to economic rationality, as foreseen by the *Gastarbeiter* model: 'We wanted arms and men arrived', said the Swiss writer Max Frisch. At the same time, the economic crisis which took place in Europe in the mid-1970s and the introduction of immigration control reduced the previous mobility of workers (mainly from southern Europe and South Mediterrean countries). As a result, Germany accepted the need to develop an integration policy for settled immigrants.

In the 1970s, from the introduction of the immigration control, two main phenomena characterized migratory processes:

- Immigration into Europe no longer responded to a demand for labour, but become more and more dependent on 'push' factors.
- 'Pull' factors have been represented by the general attractiveness of the Western world, and of Europe in particular, and by 'niches' existing in some economic sectors, mainly informal ones, as will be illustrated in the analysis of the Italian case.

The existence of these 'niches' in southern Europe has certainly encouraged immigrants, rejected by the northern European countries, to seek employment there. Considering that this type of employment has often been illegal, it has not allowed the immigrants to regularize their status. The presence of illegal immigrants has been progressively growing in southern European countries, which traditionally have not legislated on immigration.

As a consequence of these characteristics of migratory flows, a strong dichotomy between policies has emerged concerning the entry of the newcomers and the integration policies, and creating a rupture between already settled immigrants and the newcomers. The very restrictive policies imposed on immigrants are even justified by the development of integration policies for those already settled. This dichotomy is certainly one of the issues which must be considered in the analysis of the integration perspectives: the image of immigration as a threat is negative even for the settled groups, especially in a context where xenophobia and racism are growing. Particularly in southern Europe, the combination of restrictive and integration policies cannot function: immigration there is a recent phenomenon and the immigrant communities are as yet unstructured. The laws giving legal status to illegal immigrants (who were the majority in some periods, at the beginning of the trend), need be considered, as well as legal instruments to make integration possible.

Other general social and structural changes in Europe also bring into question the process of integration of immigrants, in particular, the same idea of integration – as 'functional incorporation in the social system' – which needs a progressive identification with the modern culture.

The crisis of the French assimilation model is a good illustration of present changes. The French assimilation model has in fact been put into question both by the multicultural approach, that is, the idea of the necessary respect which has to be given to immigrant cultures, *and* by the changes which have taken place in the economic system, both at national and international level as well as in French society. From the 1970s onwards, it has not been a question any more of assimilation, but of the 'republican integration model'. In this model, it is possible to keep specific elements of culture, language or religion, but these elements should not structure particular political identities, recognized as such inside the public space. In fact, even this model is going through a deep crisis.

As Wievorka writes: ' The reference to the republican model, if it doesn't become full of nostalgia or incantatory, risks becoming mainly repressive – referring to a pure and rigid conception of secularism, and the implementation, above all, of a police management of the urban crisis, for example' (1996: 40, translation Campani)

The assimilation model, and, later, the republican integration model, came about in France because of, firstly, the existence, until the 1970s, of 'an integrated system', as Wievorka writes, formed by 'the system of industrial social relations, secondly the institutional system reinforced by the republican values – liberty, fraternity, equality – and thirdly, a culture, and, most of all, a national identity attributed in a contradictory way, both to political openness and to nationalistic closure' (1996: 33, translation Campani).

The assimilation processes could take place in France, because of the combination of a specificity, the 'universalistic' idea of nation, combined with the social relations of the industrial society, the class system, the workers' strong identity and the connection between work or employment and social rights. This was particularly so in a period of full employment known as the *trentes glorieuses* (thirty glorious years). The crisis of the republican integration model corresponds with a process of 'cultural fragmentation', expressed by the development of cultural identities, searching for a specific political expression, and to the decline of the national, industrial society. This means that the crisis of institutions ensuring the transition of norms and values such as the family, the school, religion, etc., occurred simultaneously with change in the organization of work which created a greater flexibility and the informalization of the economy. This in turn corresponds with the decline of the working class and the working-class movement, and with the growth of inequalities, of social exclusion and poverty. In other words, a national crisis occurred in the model of integration which affected natives as well as immigrants.

The connection between cultural fragmentation and social exclusion has emerged precisely in relationship to immigrant groups, some of whom were traditionally 'peripheral workers', occupying the most difficult and dangerous jobs in factories, or working in peripheral and informal sectors. This connection is emerging dramatically for the new migratory flows, which cannot, as we have seen, find any other economic role than in peripheral or informal sectors, in both northern and southern Europe.

The perspectives of multiculturalism

The crisis of the republican integration model must also be understood in the frame of the development of globalized social relations. In circumstances of growing globalization, Giddens writes, the nation state is too small for the great problems of life and too big for the small problems of life (1990). Giddens also notes that globalization also means pressure to obtain more local autonomy and a regional cultural identity.

The development of globalized social relations reduces some aspects of feelings connected to the nation as a whole, but can reinforce more localized 'nationalist' feelings. The globalization processes and the crisis of the national model of integration correspond with the development of ethnic and regional identities and movements. Such identities and movements present themselves more often as exclusive rather than inclusive in front of the others. Immigrants' communities can also be organized around exclusive identities (Gallissot 1993). Still, immigrants in the European countries tend to organize themselves around issues of discrimination, segregation, exploitation and the search for equal opportunities.

On the other hand, the 'diasporas' (Gallissot 1993) seem to be more adapted to face the present reality not only with their transnational and extra-territorial identification, but also with the circulation of goods and persons, maximizing the opportunities of work and success.

The answer to the crisis of integration cannot easily be found in the idea of multiculturalism, which represents in fact 'one of those new worldwide floating concepts, which, travelling from continent to continent are communicated easily and quickly to sometimes unexpected recipients and with sometimes surprising results' (Radtke 1992, quoted in Schierup 1996). Multiculturalism certainly means a change in the representation of the society, which could have an impact on the school system (the idea of intercultural education for all), structured around the representation of the nation state. But the ideological construction of multiculturalism is very problematic, insisting more on cultural differences than on a genuine project of common life (Schierup 1996).

Schierup analyses Sweden, the only European country where the idea of multiculturalism 'developed in what may be characterized as a genuinely state-sanctioned official political ideology' (1996: 4). The debate between universalism and recognition of difference goes beyond the dichotomy between two 'political choices'. It also raises the issue of 'limitations and opportunities of the social structure, power relationships and material preconditions'. Schierup refers to Rex (1985) and wonders which political and economic institutions will support a genuine project of common life:

> It is the kind of universalism, which Rex understands as embedded in the political and economic constitution of the welfare state, that represents the foundations on which a democratic and just multiculturalism could be built. It is, Rex says, a society which, in its 'main structures' is committed to 'equality of opportunity'. A multicultural society – being thus already a welfare state society – represents a society which in its main structures 'must find a place for both diversity and equality of opportunity'. (Schierup 1996: 22)

According to Schierup, this vision comes close to the Swedish conception of multiculturalism: 'in 1975 spelled out in the main long-term perspectives of Swedish immigrant policy: "Equality, partnership and freedom of choice"' (1996: 22). But he remarks also that this framework was conceived when the 'classical' Swedish welfare state was already 'on the verge of eclipse'. Even in Sweden, the discourse of multiculturalism appeared more centred on 'freedom of choice':

> The idea of 'being different' has, given the predominance of primordial and naturalized conceptions of ethnicity and culture, underpinned increasingly problematic processes of differential institutional treatment adjusted to an emerging unequal ethnic division of labour. This, in fact, could be taken to represent a rather general development (Wievorka, 1992), articulated, during the past twenty years, in different ways and to varying degrees in different economically advanced European societies of immigration. (Schierup 1996: 23)

Schierup considers then that the decline of the labour movement and its political ideology has left the place to an 'enclavization' of society, where the central place is occupied by new middle strata, oriented towards professional mobility, competition, personal and cultural identity and individualistic social and political attitudes. In this context, the communal horizon of the welfare state project which John Rex speaks about is replaced by a postmodern preoccupation with particular cultural identities. In other words, social injustices are translated into cultural differences.

The issue is not just multiculturalism, but the collapse of any reasonable universalist conception of citizenship, social welfare and democracy. Immigration just reveals the new tendencies, issues and problems of European society. The crisis of the welfare state, which makes multiculturalism problematic, is connected not only with the decline of the working-class movement and ideology, but with the changing nature of work in society: in other words, with the end of what the French sociologist Robert Castel calls the 'salary society'.

The end of the salary society

The crisis of the industrial system has an important impact on the organization of work and the condition of workers. The French sociologist Robert Castel speaks of the end of the salary society (*société salariale*): the salary society was the economic, social and political system where the majority of the members found, in the fact of being employed, of receiving a wage, a salary, a principle of social identity (Castel 1995: 372).

But the salary society is also 'un mode de gestion politique qui a associé la propriété privée et la propriété sociale, le développement économique et l'acquisition des droits sociaux, le marché et l'Etat' (a model of political management which has associated private and social property, economic development and social rights, market and State) (Castel 1995: 372).

Two more basic aspects have characterized the salary society in its history – economic growth and growth of the welfare state: 'So that the end of this combination could be considered an effect of the economic crisis, but, mainly, the questioning of this sophisticated montage – construction – of economic factors and social regulations which has allowed the existence of the modern salary system' (Castel 1995: 372). Today the shift to a service economy, the principle of flexibility in work and in wages, unemployment and job instability have pushed many workers into peripheral sectors and destabilized those who thought they were secure.

The end of the salary society has had different consequences: the phenomenon of social exclusion has taken a new dimension through the growth of unemployment and the precariousness and the destabilization of work. The role of work in social identities has also been limited, and this has opened a new space for identities which seemed about to disappear, such as family cohesion, inscription into a community, etc.

Even if Castel's analysis mainly refers to France, the processes he describes concern more or less all European countries. The question of social exclusion or of disaffiliation has become central in the political debate as well as in the social sciences, for native-born citizens as well as for the immigrants, practically all over the European Union.

Still, the salary society, as well as the welfare system, assumed specific forms in the southern European countries, being combined with a large informal sector of non-guaranteed workers, a sector which occupies a central role in national production. As we have already remarked, the arrival of immigrants in southern Europe can be understood as a response to the existence of this large sector. For this reason, the situation of immigrants in southern Europe is very specific, but is also a sort of prefiguration of what is beginning to happen in northern Europe with new flows of population.

In fact, in industrial societies, according to Mingione (1983), technological progress and the processes of tertiarization (shift to services) of the economy, produce dualistic forms. These tend to split on different poles, often in antinomic opposition: high/low productive development, in connection with the use (or not) of technology; inclusion/exclusion from the guaranteed areas; continuity/discontinuity of services; regularity/irregularity of contractual positions in relationship to different employment forms, and security/precariousness of work and living conditions.

As a consequence of these processes, labour markets need a quota of low-qualified, highly flexible workers, having little professional content, and willing to endure long working hours and irregular wages. In southern Europe, such a labour force can be both native and immigrant. However, immigrants would cover jobs which the local labour force does not accept (Pugliese 1990), because, even inside the informal economy, these jobs are under the level of income and general work conditions considered socially acceptable by native-born residents. Still, as far as other jobs in the informal economy are concerned, natives and immigrants experience objective competition.

The difference between natives and immigrants lies mainly in the fact that the former have a much more structured network of social local relations than that possessed by immigrants. This is a form of compensation for the precarious work conditions. The condition of non-protection (lack of institutional guarantees, norms, etc.) makes immigrants more subject to the risk of insecurity and marginality. The existence of a network of social local relations can be considered a basic aspect in countering vulnerability, and, in the case of immigrants, necessary to ensure integration processes. These networks are constituted both by the family, the community and by the social services or the solidarity associations existing in a specific area. The Italian case is a good example of the conditions of immigration in a labour market where the informal economy is very important.

The Italian case

Immigration into Italy for the purpose of work is a quite new phenomenon in the general landscape of migrations in Europe. In Italy, the passage from being a country of emigration to one of immigration took place in 1975, a year when, for the first time since the unity of the country in 1870, the migratory balance showed more arrivals than departures. In around twenty years, the foreign presence has multiplied by five. In December 1996, according to the Ministry of the Interior, the residence-stay permits issued numbered around one million. The importance of the foreign presence has emerged after the promulgation of the three regularization laws (Law 943 in 1986, Law 39 in 1990 and the Decree Dini in 1995), together with humanitarian permits (for ex-Yugoslavs and Somalis), family reunification and study permits.

Laws 943 and 39 have not only given a legal status to some immigrant workers, who were on the national territory: they have 'legitimized' their presence in Italy. This introduces the 'universal' principle of equality of rights, including economic and civil rights, independent of the nationality of origin. Still, the universal principle of equality of rights at the economic and civil level exists in stark contrast to the real position of the immigrants in the labour market and in Italian society.

Since the start of immigration into Italy, in the 1970s, the role and function that the immigrant presence has had in internal labour-market dynamics (macro-level) and on the regional and local labour market (micro-level), have been important topics of debate, both inside the trade unions and within the academic field. According to Pugliese (1990), the presence of immigrants inside national and local labour markets cannot be understood and interpreted without considering the segmentation which characterizes these labour markets.

In Italy, the central labour market works in the factories, within both the public and and private sectors, supported by solid systems of guarantee and of trade union and social security protection. Outside the central labour market, there are peripheral markets, which can be thought of as concentric circles in relationship to the proximity to or from the 'central market'. The extreme peripheral labour market is characterized by the most precarious and discontinuous forms of subordinated autonomous work.

The peripheral labour markets are characterized by dynamics concerning small enterprises, where forms of non-institutional employment are common and where general guarantees are less important, being constantly negotiable in a direct manner among the interested parties. In the most peripheral labour market are the most precarious jobs, often half illegal, such as street selling, daily labour in agriculture, unskilled labour in construction and in the porterage services. In this labour market, immigrants are the majority.

This segmentation into a central labour market and peripheral labour markets explains the apparent contradiction existing between the active presence of immigrants and high unemployment in Italy. The native-born unemployed are not interested in working in the most peripheral labour markets.

Still, as an effect of productive recessions of limited or generalized character, a few native-born workers, who refuse for a time to enter into the peripheral labour markets, tend to come back to the marginal market, even in conditions similar to that of immigrants, provoking situations of competition. The situations of competition can often lead to so-called 'ethnic conflicts', as was the case in the summer of 1993 in the Pouilles, where immigrants arrived in search of work as harvesters and were violently chased away. In fact, competition is often viewed by the Italians as an ideological matter, without any real understanding of the concrete conflictual dynamics for the occupation of specific jobs.

But, if for native-born residents the passage from employment to unemployment finds a minimum of guarantees in the family and society (indirect wage), for immigrants, this passage means a process of going from a relatively positive existence to mere subsistence.

The effect of citizenship, and the benefits which citizenship implies for the natives, play a main role in the discrimination against immigrants working in the same labour market sectors. Consequently, among natives and immigrants there exists, in many ways, a difference in 'vulnerability' to conditions of employment and unemployment.

We have already noted that the existence of local networks of protection and solidarity (family, community, local services) can play an important role in decreasing vulnerability. Without considering their existence as the only protection against the risks of social exclusion, they have assumed a new role in the crisis of the welfare system and of guaranteed work. The Italian case shows also how the great differences between local conditions, as far as the possibilities of employment and the offer of social services are concerned, influence the processes of integration far more than the national migratory policy. We can speak of 'niches of integration' or, on the contrary, 'niches of marginality' for specific local areas. In the 'niches of integration', immigrant communities and networks can play an important role, for example, in the development of ethnically-based business, as in the case of the Chinese in Milan and Tuscany (Campani 1996).

Conclusions

Changes in European national industrial societies have challenged migratory policies and integration policies elaborated in the 1950s, 1960s and 1970s.

What appears clearly is that neither the state, even if it maintains a regulating role, nor the labour market can be considered any longer as pillars of the integration processes. The eclipse of the welfare state represents also a major change, opening the way to phenomena of social exclusion.

In this context, where the same idea of integration is questioned, processes of incorporation in the receiving societies seem to be much more complex and differentiated than in the past. They seem to vary from one ethnic group to another, from one local context to the other. Though these are common tendencies all over Europe, the state migratory and integration policies of southern Europe, which are very recent, have great difficulties in responding to the new migratory flows. As we have seen, these difficulties lie in the political and economic contexts: closing of borders (and consequently illegal migration), the crisis of the nation state and of the structures of integration, the development of an informal economy and of segmented labour markets, and processes of social exclusion. In this context, is it still possible to talk of incorporation and integration of immigrants at a national level? In southern Europe, the local reality seems to be more effective in the integration processes than national policies. For example, the incorporation of immigrants in Brescia, in northern Italy, an area of small industries and of good social services, has little to do with the marginality of immigrants surviving in Villa Literno, near Naples, waiting for precarious jobs in agriculture.

In recent years, the importance of local integration has been underlined in research on immigration. Considering local aspects means insisting on the importance of networks, the system of interactions between individuals and groups, families and communities, social services and associations, local and national authorities. This is also a possible analytic perspective which would regard integration processes as more participative.

Still, local policies and custom cannot alone respond to the issues raised by immigration: because state policies cannot offer the frame for integration any more, the challenge presented is to the whole of Europe. A common European policy shouldn't be reduced to 'ruling and controlling entry', in a repressive manner: it should also give to immigrants, as individuals and communities, their place in the construction of Europe.

Note

1 'Cette nation, considérée ainsi comme l'asile du monde, est bien plus qu'une nation; c'est la fraternité vivante' (Michelet, *Le peuple* (1846: 327), quoted by Liauzu (1992).

References

Campani, G. (1987), 'Le politiche di stop', in Sergi, N. (ed.) (1987), *L'immigrazione straniera in Italia*, Rome: Edizioni Lavoro.

Campani, G. (1996), 'I Cinesi in Toscana: economia etnica, distretto industriale, globalizzazione', in Cespi, *I diritti della civiltà*, Rome.

Castel, R. (1995), *Les métamorphoses de la question sociale*, Paris: Fayard.

Censis (1979), *I lavoratori stranieri in Italia*, Rome: Istituto Poligrafico e Zecca dello Stato.

Chiapparugi, M. (1983), L'immigrazione straniera in Italia: quadro di riferimento teorico', *Studi Emigrazione*, 71, September, p.415.

Gallissot, R. (1993), *Pluralisme culturel en Europe*, Paris: L'Harmattan.

Giddens, A. (1990), *Consequences of Modernity*, Cambridge: Polity Press.

Lapeyronnie, D. (1990), *Intégration et Sociétés Nationales, i Adri, L'intégration Locale des Minorités Immigrees en Europe*, Paris: CNTPT.

Liauzu, C. (1992), *Race et Civilisation*, Paris: Syros.

Liauzu, C. (1996), 'Migrazioni nella ricerca e nell'insegnamento storico in Francia', in Campani, G. (ed.), *La rosa e lo specchio*, Naples: Ipermedium.

Mingione, E. (1983), 'Gli immigrati in Italia', *Inchiesta*, 62, October–December, p.21 and 'Gli immigrati in Italia: mercato del lavoro, marginalità e povertà', paper, Messina.

Morokvasic, M. (1994), '"In and Out" of the Labour Market: Immigrant and Minority Women in Europe', *New Community*, 19(3), pp.459–83.

Noiriel, G. (1988), *Le creuset français*, Paris: Seuil.

Piore, M. (1979), *Birds of Passage: Migrant Labour and Industrial Societies*, Cambridge: Cambridge University Press.

Pugliese, E. (1985), 'Quale lavoro per gli stranieri in Italia', *Politica economica*, September, p.70.

Pugliese, E. (1993), *La sociologia della disoccupazione*, Bologne: Il Mulino.

Pugliese, E. (1990), 'Gli immigrati nel mercato del lavoro', *Polis*, IV, l April, p.71.

Pugliese, E. and Macioti, M.I. (1990), *Gli immigrati stranieri in Italia*, Bari: Laterza.

Rex, J. (1985), 'The Concept of a Multi-Cultural Society', *Occasional Papers in Ethnic Relations*, no. 3, Warwick: Centre for Research in Ethnic Relations.
Schierup, C. (1996) 'Multiculturalism, Neo-Racism, and the Changing Welfare State: Nordic Trajectories', Euroconference No. 14 Racism and Anti-racism in Europe – New Dimensions, Sonderborg, 27–30 June.
Schnapper, D. (1992), *L'Europe des immigrés*, Paris: François Burin.
Wievorka, M. (1992), 'Tendencies to Racism in Europe: Is the French Experience Exemplary or Unique?', paper presented at the Conference organized by the University of Warwick and Birbeck College, University of London, Kenilworth, 20–22 September.
Wievorka, M. (1996) (ed.), *Une société fragmentée?*, Paris: Editions La Découverte.

10 Intercultural Education in the European Union from a 'Southern' Viewpoint

Anna Frangoudaki and Thalia Dragonas

Introduction

Among the most powerful beliefs of our time is that European civilization has a special cultural quality and an unique historical advantage which gives it a permanent superiority over all other communities in history, down to the present (Blaut 1993). Intercultural education, addressing mainly the European conception of culture, still dominant in all EU countries, aims to deny this belief of cultural superiority.

European Union policy considers the educational system to play an important role in fighting the negative stereotypes, assumed by each national group, about the 'other'. Thus, intercultural education is considered the main means of achieving the goal summarized by the motto 'Unity in diversity'. It is seen as capable of accomplishing harmonious coexistence and the collaboration of member states, through respect and acceptance of national differences in culture and language. A great number of EU programmes finance common projects on education, and encourage teachers' and students' mobility among countries. The target is to get to know the 'other', learn their language, and become familiar with their culture in order to acknowledge similarities and understand differences, learn from the other cultures, and finally appreciate the wealth resulting from cultural contact and mutual influences.

Intercultural education, defined as the transmission of values and assumptions, through which differences are recognized and respected, rights are acknowledged, collaboration is learned and practised, and new perspectives are taught (Troyna 1989), is closely related to the belief which recognizes the standards and values of the northern and western industrialized zones of Europe as prototypical while regarding other cultures as inferior.

The impact of intercultural education

The influence of intercultural ideas is notable in all EU countries and, as far as their incorporation in education is concerned, developments have been radical. In some countries, mainly those with a colonial past, intercultural education has stemmed from the actual necessity of providing education to extensive numbers of minority groups. In such countries, the development of intercultural education reflects the adoption of policies which span a wide spectrum of ideologies: the 1960s followed a model of assimilation of minority population in schools which gradually gave way to a model of integration through respect of differences. Subsequently, integration moved to the more recent idea of cultural pluralism which aims at establishing truly intercultural schools in a multicultural society. In the UK, for example, the situation for many years has been marked by attempts to assimilate immigrant children, mainly through efforts to teach them the language of the host country. Gradually, the ideology implicit in intercultural education evolved to include the preservation of mother-tongue identity, literacy and values (Troyna 1992). The most important critique of that policy refers to the emphasis placed on the knowledge of other cultures rather than on anti-racism (Troyna and Williams 1986; Troyna 1993; Sarup 1991; Siraj-Blatchford 1994). The 1980s witnessed in Britain a movement towards the racialization of the discourse on education. Racialization denotes explicit reference to perceived racial differences with an intent to minimize racial inequalities and discrimination. However, many writers and practitioners claim that no real progress has been achieved in the clarification of either the nature of racism in education, or the specific processes which are responsible for discriminatory practice (Troyna 1992). Moreover, anti-racist ideology in education is considered to have basically fallen short in showing how racism functions as a fundamental organizing and discriminating structural variable, in the context of other forms of discrimination, such as class and gender (Troyna 1992; Gilroy 1987; Rattansi 1992; Cohen 1992).

In France, once the goal of assimilation was abandoned, intercultural education focused on integrating children from other cultures by taking into consideration their cultural differences. Thus, information on other cultures and people, their history, literature, customs, habits and food was introduced into the school curriculum. This model is today criticized for ethnographic practices which identify cultural differences as exotic. The fundamental goal of intercultural education was thus lost, since children with 'exotic' cultures were seen as a deviation from the cultural norm, an idea strongly implying the authoritarian notion of 'normality'. Again the teaching of the mother tongue has proved to be fundamental. Another important policy adopted has been the teaching of various ethnic minority languages at school as optional courses, offered to the entire school population and not only to those for whom these are mother-tongue languages (Henry-Lorcerie 1986).

Yet other European countries, Greece among them, still today, for mainly historical and social reasons, consider themselves monocultural entities. In such countries, evolution has also been radical. They have had recently to face intercultural education as part of the transformations produced by the EU. Thus, the notion of monoculturalism is starting to lose its mythical quality. Cultural diversity is viewed by many as a characteristic of modern societies, and the practice of stereotyping and prejudice is becoming part of a debate questioning its relation to the social and political dangers concealed in an intolerant society (Dragonas et al. 1996).

Education and the notion of national culture

In the field of intercultural education, developments have been radical, and the influence of intercultural ideas has spread to all EU countries. Still, the actual implementation of intercultural education has an important barrier to surpass: the ethnocentric conception of culture inherent in all educational systems. Despite the extensive differences among EU countries, one may claim that, with no exception, all educational systems are ethnocentric. They socialize children, that is, they induce a symbolic code to represent society, and instigate a sense of belonging to this society. The socialization process leads to identification with the national group, and with the construction of national identity (Percheron 1974; Billig 1995). Furthermore, education within EU countries is based on the principle of transmitting, to younger generations, one language and one culture, considered to be the national language and culture. The mere notion of 'a' national culture implies cultural homogeneity within the nation state although such a tenet is unfit to resist any kind of historical or social documentation. Nation states contain various cultural entities, distinct from the dominant group, as well as populations with multiple cultural loyalties and double identities. In some cases these even have additional languages, such as, for example, Breton and French, or Catalan and Spanish. Moreover, European nation states include populations differentiated not only by culture, but also by other differences, including economic inequalities. Economic differences not only divide nation states, but also cut across national frontiers, distinguishing agricultural from industrial zones, developed from underdeveloped areas and the north from the south: 'Most nation states are stratified polyethnic states, using a variety of mechanisms to maintain their social and economic stratification, usually presented with an accompanying rhetoric emphasising societal cohesion' (Gundara and Jones 1992b: 392).

Contrary to these realities, the educational system in all European countries sets, as its main target, the transmission of the national language and culture. The notion of a national culture is either fictitious or it excludes important parts of the population in each country. Moreover, it not only implies the idea of nations having a homogeneous culture, but also a clear national idiosyncrasy. This conception, in its extreme logic, disguises the idea of cultural purity. It also implies the taxonomic idea of national 'authenticity'. The claim of authenticity is even less fit than homogeneity to represent national realities. Masked in the notion of national culture, it is an old taxonomic myth invented in the past for the same reasons it survives today. It helps justify the social division of economic privileges and social power. The definition of nation, whenever studied empirically, has proved to be extremely vague, and the characteristics conferred to the nation's members have been observed to change over time, precisely in order to justify concentrations of power and wealth among the allegedly authentic members of the national entity (Citron 1989). Ultimately, the latent idea of national authenticity is a disguised acceptance of inherited social superiority. The old aristocratic privilege, denied in the Declaration of Human Rights: 'All men are born free and equal', becomes a national privilege, since equality is limited to the citizens of the nation state. This ideological process has permitted a slight slide towards an authoritarian use of the democratic principle, ensuring that the 'authentic' citizens of the nation state are equal.

Further evidence of an authoritarian process is the actual use of the concept of citizenship among EU countries. Theoretically, citizenship should be the only indicator of belonging to a country, applied equally to all groups of citizens or else it would be impossible to be both a citizen and a member of a minority group. Nevertheless, one can think, for example, of a case whereby a British and English-speaking pupil, born in England of Caribbean parents who obtained British citizenship before the child's birth, who belongs to a minority group which suffers discrimination. Similarly, in France, a pupil born of Algerian parents with French citizenship, or in Germany, a pupil born of Turkish parents with German citizenship, both belong to minority groups. Furthermore, in all European countries one can find the case, even more relevant to discriminatory minority status, which refers to the great difficulty involved in answering the question 'Who is a

Jew?' In fact, the very notion of 'the' national culture is the basis on which cultural differences are determined, integration interpreted, and the conception of minority formulated. Discriminatory ideas, attributing minority status to human groups, derive from the myth of the existence of a national cultural authenticity, stemming from the national ideologies of the previous century.

Although very important changes have taken place in all European countries, national educational systems still reproduce, through the traditional notion of nations, the conception of social groups as fundamental entities, each perceived as a group of people, related by a common language and common origins/ancestors, and having a history and a culture of its own. Research data, on the conception of nation held by 15-year-olds, show that a very traditional conception is dominant. Adolescents from several countries (including most within the EU),[1] see nations as 'natural entities, unified by common origin, language, history and culture' and, in large percentages, accord primary importance to their own nation (Angvic and Von Borries 1997).

Despite the fact that analysis has extensively shown that culture is socially differentiated, the educational system in each country reproduces a traditional conception of national culture. The working classes and the middle and upper strata do not share a common culture (Coleman and Rainwater 1978; Bourdieu 1979). The same applies in the case of the national language versus linguistic variations among social classes. For example, according to linguists, the language spoken by the working classes in London is a linguistic system distinct from formal standard English (Harris 1980). Also, as the work of Basil Bernstein (1971, 1977) has shown, difference in language among social categories is so pronounced that school reproduces social inequality, mainly by treating pupils of various social backgrounds as speakers of the same language.

The notion of national culture disguises social evaluation and prejudice. As far as culture transmitted by schools is concerned, there is accumulated evidence that it consists of the dominant culture in each society. The possibility of handling the interpretative keys of this dominant culture has been analysed as a social marker of 'distinction', as coined by Pierre Bourdieu (1979), in the sense of social superiority. Social superiority distinguishes the élite from the majority of the population in all European countries. Dominant culture is moreover seen as high culture, represented by a catalogue of renowed names, including, for example, Praxiteles, Michelangelo, Aeschylus, Shakespeare, Molière, Goethe, Cervantes, Descartes, Confucius, Hegel, Galileo, Einstein, etc. Beside this high culture, determined by social class, and by widely international sources of reference, there is another culture, evaluated as low. It is determined by kinship organization, customs and habits, cooking, tools, rules and taboos, sexual practices, etc., and is considered as 'ethnic' culture (Guillaumin 1994). Low culture's ethnological description applies to the so-called southern zones of Europe, and to the popular social classes of the European states, as well as all the 'other' non-European civilizations. The dominant culture acknowledges some EU people, as well as all non-European people, as objects of study, rather than subjects of history, and describes them as having folklore, rather than culture, and making handicraft, rather than art.

Education and discriminations

In all European countries, the selection of knowledge transmitted by schools has a tendency to accord primary importance to the dominant group, and to evaluate its real or alleged characteristics and practices as most worthy (Preiswerk & Perrot 1975). This evaluation, together with the myth of a homogeneous national culture, indirectly promotes the idea of the right of each national entity to defend its own culture. Once the mere notion of this right becomes crystallized, racism may take the form of a legitimate position, despite the fact it is widely lacking consensus in all countries, particularly after the Second World War.

Thus, the social phenomena of xenophobia and rejection of 'foreign' cultures seem to be spreading in the European Union. This is the case with the New Right in the UK which claims the just demand of British citizens to protect their own culture, and introduces this claim by reference to the 'invasion' of 'foreign' cultures in the country (Barker 1981). The xenophobic phenomena take, in some countries, the disturbing form of social movements, as is the case in France, with the unexpected effect of the positions promoted by the *Front National*.

The dominant culture is presented, by EU educational systems, as the national culture, and this metonymy is the basis of the reproduction of social discrimination. As the sociology of education has long documented, the elitist view of culture, mentioned above, turns school into an inefficient institution, particularly regarding the education of children from working-class backgrounds. On the one hand, the language and culture of the working classes are not taken into consideration by the school system, thus producing, in EU countries, masses of low-achieving pupils from working-class families.[2] On the other hand, school culture implies the inferiority of working-class culture and language, to the point that not only the syntax but also the accent of popular urban varieties of any national language are considered by school as indicators of social inferiority (Halliday 1978).

Pupils are evaluated and selected on the basis of their acquaintance with the dominant culture, a process through which social origin determines their school achievement. According to these findings, discrimination is based on prejudiced social knowledge, through which they are also reproduced. As far as education is concerned, in all EU countries, low achievement in school is seen to involve either cognitive or genetic deficit, or cultural deprivation. Theories based on genetic causes of high or low human intelligence have today very little support within the academic community.[3] They do, nevertheless, in many countries, indirectly affect school practices since the mental capacities of pupils are often taken for granted as being either high or low by 'nature'. On the other hand, cultural deprivation theories are more important for the topic we are dealing with in this chapter, as these examine the effects of cultural poverty on various groups of children. We suggest that this notion of poverty is again a product of taxonomic evaluation. There are no social groups sharing a culture, while others are just deprived of culture, as implied in the theory of cultural deprivation. There are different cultures, only they are categorized in such a way that some cultures are ranked so low that they are perceived as having an absence of culture.

Europe has a past of industrial development which has had serious consequences for the environment, and has produced profound social inequality. Great economic diffferences, observed in EU societies, have shaped ideologies of antagonism, disdain of human groups and violence. At the same time, Europe has had a past of colonialism, expansionism and violent struggles for the formation of a multitude of independent nation states. This past has shaped such ideologies to legitimize territorial claims, expansionism and wars, as well as dominance of 'other' peoples. These ideologies are at the same time the foundation of what feminist analysts have called the 'patriarchal society'. As feminist critique has shown, acknowledgement of one discrimination does not eliminate others. Nevertheless, it has also shown that discriminatory ideas are intricately interrelated. Thus, for minority populations in the EU, discrimination is twofold, both social and ethnic (Gundara and Jones 1992a). Furthermore, according to the novel analytical view of industrial societies offered by feminist social scientists, as long as the right of some people to dominate other people is accepted at all and, as long as the right of men to dominate the other half of humanity is seen as natural, a tolerant European society will never come into being.

Despite the very important steps which have been taken during the last decades against sexism, the gender parameter has not actually been fully incorporated within the social sciences, except by women analysts (Michard-Marchal and Ribery 1982). During the 1960s and 1970s, when the sociology of education expressed the notion of a clear social determination of school success and failure and its application in all industrialized countries,[4] the gender dimension was absent from all analytical work, with the exception of that by the renowned French sociologists, Bourdieu and Passeron (1970). Nevertheless, in this work there is a relevant paradox concerning gender, not acknowledged until the feminist critique revealed it. The analysis of the two French sociologists suggests that reproduction of social inequality through the school is the result of the existence of a system of relations of dominance between social classes. Surprisingly, no such system of relations of dominance between genders is suggested to support the reproduction of gender inequality in education (Mosconi 1994).

Much has changed during the last decades in European society as to the access of women to education at all levels (Baudelot and Establet 1992). Yet, there is still a pronounced inequality in educational opportunities for both ethnic minority and working-class children, as well as for girls (Driessen & Jungbluth 1994). Women enjoy the outcomes of a successful education in such lower percentages relative to men, that the notion of 'false success' has been used.[5] There is evidence on the differential outcomes in terms of educational access, attainment, and choice of field of study (Stromquist 1990). These differences affect the economic independence of women in the north-western European countries (Dekkers 1994).[6] Despite important changes in women's roles, there is a gendered division of knowledge in the educational system of all EU countries. Access to knowledge, as well as the relation to it, is still definitely gender biased. The 'hard' sciences are still predominantly male territory, while at the school level, the view that mathematical achievement is not beyond the abilities of the female gender is only beginning to be accepted (Phillips 1993). It is suggested that there is a gender-specific aspect of the hidden curriculum through which school perpetuates traditional gender socialization (Delamont 1990), and that important gender differences are detectable in the contents of school knowledge (Isambert-Jamati 1990). Finally, feminist analysis on gender educational inequalities detects severe limits in the state's ability to improve women's conditions (Stromquist 1990). Gender discrimination has a particular importance for intercultural education, since gender equity applies to both boys and girls and crosses all racial, ethnic and class boundaries. Moreover, gender discrimination is closely related to the traditional conception of nations, since all national ideologies are fundamentally sexist (Fourier & Vermes 1994).

Intercultural education and the multivariant aspect of Eurocentrism

As already mentioned above, intercultural education has been criticized for not attacking racism directly. Racism, as a social phenomenon, and the complex process through which it determines ethnic, racial or cultural units, is a vast subject outside the scope of the present text. Nevertheless, racism has an important impact in schools (Kelly and Cohn 1988; McCarthy and Crichlow 1993). In that sense there is a need to identify the function of education in shaping social identities, through taxonomies and evaluations of human groups.

Research on the way other civilizations are described in the school textbooks of all Western countries is relevant to the need for change of the evaluative ideas about the superiority of what is called 'Western civilization'. According to research findings, pupils in European schools are taught, *inter alia*, that Africa is composed of tribes, not of nations, that the Americas before their 'discovery' were inhabited by people to whom Europeans brought 'language' and 'religion', and that the model of the industrial Western society is the unique model of progress in the world (Preiswerk and Perrot 1975). The superiority of the Western industrialized zone, implicit in the 'understanding' of the world from a Western point of view, leads to a legitimation of another taxonomic idea, indirectly evaluating cultural influences as positive or negative, according to the source of influence. Western influences in all other parts of the world are referred to by the terms of development, evolution, or progress. At the same time, the presence of populations from 'other' cultures in EU countries is often described as a harmful influence, endangering the cohesion or the specificities of national cultures. Thus, the evaluation of cultures is the basis on which are formed the assumed dangers for one's culture deriving from contact and intermixture.

Dangers presumed to threaten national cultures because of 'foreign' influences seem to have a serious persuasive impact on various social groups, in the EU countries. Among the products of this persuasiveness is the fact that large numbers of people declare feeling under threat of losing part of their national cultural features because of cultural contact with 'other' peoples. This discourse on threat to national cultures would not spread effectively unless it was based on the assumption of inferiority/superiority of cultures and peoples. As analytical approaches of this sense of threat show, it often emerges among strong and dominant groups or countries. All discrimination, as well as any

> ... modern forms of ethnicism and racism do not seem to have developed out of fear, but rather because of the will to dominate and exploit others, to maintain one's privileges, and so on. Indeed, most minority groups that are the target of racism are relatively small and hardly constitute a threat. (Van Dijk 1993: 172–3)

The ethnocentric character of European educational systems produces a contradiction that calls for clarification. Cultural diversity, as well as cultural intermixture, is not only an historical fact, it is also a social reality in every country. National cultures in the EU, as well as in many other countries, are the product of multiple counter-influences from all sides. European countries of today, especially their big cities, are multinational, multi-ethnic, multilingual and multireligious. If schools, in contradiction with these realities, continue to present culture as national and indirectly as pure, it is as if they teach children to disregard what they themselves witness. The answer to the existence of this contradiction may well be that racism is socially situated, that is, it is part of so-called Western culture and deeply embedded in it.

The ethnocentric aspect of schools is accountable for all kinds of discrimination detected in the educational system. For the same reason, education is particularly important in fighting sexism, as well as racism and social discrimination. Schools could maximize or minimize discrimination between social groups, if they directly confront institutional sexism, racism and social division. All kinds of social discriminations are directly or indirectly connected to school, and thus they can be reproduced by it, or they can be attenuated and transformed.

In terms of educational policy, European curricular systems have systematically overlooked the contribution to human knowledge and progress of substantial groups of people, such as non-majority indigenous groups within particular states of the European Union, first- and second-generation immigrants representing a great range of cultures and all those countries on the periphery of the European Union whose status as European is increasingly marginalized (Coulby 1995).

Thus, the main barrier for intercultural education to being understood as wealth, resulting from cultural contact and mutual influence, is the nineteenth-century taxonomy, which is, still today, directly or indirectly, categorizing and segmenting human groups. These taxonomies have been invented in order to justify domination and exploitation of 'other' people by European states. The national educational systems in the EU have for a long time shaped imperialist images of deference and legitimation of dominance (Mangan 1993). They are still openly used or implied in order to legitimize social division of wealth and power, as well as domination.

A united Europe is a very important goal and a great challenge for the future. In each country the idea of a united Europe helps those forces which desire a more pluralistic perspective (Gundara and Jones 1992b). Yet, this concept is still opposed by traditional nationalist ideology, prevalent in EU countries, presenting each nation state without differing internal interests. According to this ideology, all members of the national entity appear to have perfectly common interests, which only contrast with interests of other nation states. It is beyond the scope of this chapter to refer to the extensive international bibliography contesting this image of nation states, having no internal boundaries or comprising social groups with no conflictual interests. Nevertheless, we suggest that traditional nationalisms are not only an obstacle to the unity and collaboration of the EU, but they are at the same time a potential barrier to the possibility of collaboration among EU and the so-called eastern European countries, as well as to the harmonious integration of populations of non-European origin.

A point of view from the south of Europe

The reasons accounting for the intensification of nationalist and cultural racisms, in both western and eastern Europe, are issues open to further research. National identity is, in almost all European countries, increasingly loaded with xenophobia and racism (Solomos 1986; Wievorka 1994). In an attempt to explain contemporary European racisms, there are positions which suggest that we are witnessing, instead of an increase of racism, an intensification of nationalist cultural racisms, being the product of the crisis of the nation state, in view of the globalization of Europe. As a result of this emerging globalization, national tradition and identity are perceived to be under threat, and this requires a reaffirmation of 'our own people', as well as the exclusion of those 'others', whose presence destroys the alleged cohesion and homogeneity of the national culture (Miles 1993).

We believe that the crisis of the nation state seems to be a reality going beyond the formation of a broader European entity. This crisis, which is responsible for the intensification of xenophobia, is at the same time a product of the evaluation among nation states which ranks them in order of importance. A united Europe is a definite challenge through which a new world begins to counter the old, and traditional nationalisms may undermine the demand for the constructinon of a new European identity. They, nevertheless, may as well produce an European identity, shaped to fit traditional ethnocentrism by only broadening national frontiers to those of the EU.

The belief, mentioned above, according to which European 'Western' civilization gives this community of people a permanent superiority over all 'others' in the world, has recently been defined as 'Eurocentrism'.[7] This belief, firmly grounded in the Western world, renders inferior not only all non-European cultures, but also other less dominant cultures in each country, whether regional or social, as well as those countries considered to belong to the periphery or the south of Europe. The southern countries, according to the same stereotype, are considered to be less developed, as far as both their economies and cultures are concerned. In the process, old nationalisms may gradually be replaced by a new Euro-chauvinism.

An example of the negative effects resulting from a tendency towards Eurocentrism is informed by recent research data on xenophobia in the Greek educational system. According to this data (Frangoudaki and Dragonas 1997), after important changes during the last ten to fifteen years, and a significant effort to adapt school knowledge to EU ideas and values, Greek school textbooks contain a highly ethnocentric conception of history and culture which is placed in an extremely Eurocentric context. On the other hand, high percentages among a representative sample of Greek school teachers have a very Eurocentric view of culture, and a particularly xenophobic attitude towards the new populations of immigrants. The 'superiority' of European culture seems to be the main message, produced directly or indirectly by information provided or by omissions, statements or silences, throughout every school textbook. At the same time, this superiority leads to firm beliefs among Greek teachers, as detected in evaluations as well as in contradictions, and to very ambivalent attitudes towards the EU. Greek teachers are very largely in favour of the EU, but one-third among them fear that European integration could threaten the survival of the Greek language and culture, and they are mostly very critical of the values of the so-called technocratic society, 'introduced' by the EU.

Alleged European superiority is related to the definition of the national culture, contained both in school textbooks and the teachers' discourse. Greek culture is described in school books as having two main traits: an uninterrupted historical continuity since antiquity, and a powerful ability to resist influences from other cultures, resulting in the conservation of the main cultural characteristics of Ancient Greece. The majority among teachers deny the existence, in today's Greece, of all cultural influences other than European. At the same time, they systematicallly underline the impact of Ancient Greek culture in the development of European civilization.

The analysis of the above data suggests that the denial of cultural influences, detected both in school textbooks and the teachers' discourse is legitimated by the alleged superiority/inferiority of cultures. If Greek[8] culture is a product of history and social evolution, that is, if it is the consequence of cultural counter-influences and intermixture, then the 'superiority', rendering Greeks equal to the 'superior' Europeans, is lost in an 'infamous' blend of Turkish, Middle Eastern, Sephardim, Slav and Arab influences. On the other hand, the great emphasis in school textbooks on an uninterrupted cultural continuity since antiquity, as well as the claim put forth by Greek teachers that Ancient Greek culture is the only source of the national culture (either directly or through the European civilization shaped by Greek antiquity), seems to be the result of justifications needed to support national self-esteem. The fictitious 'Greekness' of the direct linear and uninterrupted link with the glories of Greek antiquity, untouched by 'inferior' cultural influences, bears the great contradiction of the mere existence of these influences. The analysis of this contradiction suggests that the emphasis on uninterrupted continuity, as well as the irrational denial of other influences, are a disguised expression of felt inferiority. It means that the national social and cultural present is seriously undervalued.

In almost all countries of the European Union, every positive mention of Greece is a reference to Greek antiquity. In the political discourse of official representatives of other European countries, as well as in the media, the sole positive reference ever made to Greece (or anything which is Greek), monotonously refers to Ancient Greece. Naturally, there is a long tradition of neoclassicism in most European countries. However, the fact that almost every positive mention of Greece pays tribute solely to Ancient Greece, produces a latent message of implied comparison. This repeated reference to the importance and universal value of Greek antiquity functions as a pejorative euphemism through the continuously implied contrast between the prestigious past and the insignificant present. It is as if political leaders and journalists of other European countries consider the ancient past not only superior but also more 'civilized' than the Greek present.

Greek national identity is seen by its bearers as needing to be defended. In other words, a significant part of the educational authorities in Greece seem to deny present culture and history by using it as a screen on which the highly prestigious values of antiquity are projected. Through the return to an idealized past, they seek to share the high evaluation accorded to Ancient Greece. We believe that one of the principal factors informing the 'context of situation' of this experienced inferiority in national identity is, *inter alia,* the conjuncture of the country's participation in the European Union with the dominant belief in the superiority of European civilization. There are, of course, multiple reasons for the crisis of the Greek national identity, most of them outside the scope of this chapter. However, we suggest that because of the country's membership of the Union, among other reasons, certain Greek intellectual groups and educators refuse to recognize themselves in the 'underdeveloped' and 'levantine' image reflected in the European mirror. They attempt to escape the inferiority they see in this identity by refusing to identify themselves with those 'Modern' Greeks around them who are culturally so distant from their noble Ancient Greek ancestors.

Antiquity is seen as the emblem distinguishing Greek people from their 'southern' and 'oriental' inferiority, by rendering them equal members of the aristocratic European 'family'. Finally, this crisis of evaluation of the national culture is related to some further contradictory data. Greek teachers appear to have an openly xenophobic attitude towards new populations of immigrants. In unexpectedly high percentages, they declare their opposition to the presence of immigrant populations, attributing to them increases in criminality and unemployment, as well as the deterioration of neighbourhoods. They also claim that they would not be against the presence of 'foreign' populations, if these populations had some economic status and 'a' culture, as do the citizens from other EU countries. Also, according to the same research data, teachers believe, almost unanimously, that Greek people are not racist. Probably the most telling detail in this respect is the explanation some teachers provide for their rejection of immigrants from non-European and non-western European countries. They claim that an increase of populations, from either outside Europe or eastern Europe, who are described as poor, uneducated and lacking culture, intensifies underdevelopment and other levantine characteristics of the society, thus blocking Greece's way towards European progress.

According to the above, we suggest that the increase of xenophobia and the intensification of racism are part of a vicious circle of discriminatory ideas embedded in the belief in the superiority of western European culture. We also suggest that Greek society, according to the analysis of current social phenomena, could easily replace the notions of traditional nationalism and monoculturalism by a broader and 'higher' European identity which excludes and renders inferior people from non-EU countries.

On the main objectives of intercultural education

Feelings of inferiority are, for all human groups, reason enough for xenophobia and discriminatory thinking and practice. The inferiority of one's own image is projected on to the 'other', thus relieving the pressure of having to deal with it. The actual threat, experienced from the presence of 'others', derives from differences in economic strength and power of decision making among various nation states. Yet national communities, as a rule, do not wish to acknowledge this threat, preferring to displace it on to the presence of particular social groups.

Profound social inequality, unemployment, deprivation, isolation and an environment of misery, next to the luxury and technological sparkle of the consumption society, in many European cities, produce what Pierre Bourdieu has called 'la misère du monde' (1993). This imposed misery is seen as the main reason for hostility and anger observed against 'foreigners' by members of the working as well as the lower middle class. These people, because of unequal economic development, the absence of state protection, and unemployment, are in a social and economic situation which deprives them of the merest sense of dignity. According to Bourdieu, they revolt against the injustice perpetrated against them by reference to a recent past, when their French identity provided them with a profound sense of dignity, as hard working people. They feel humiliated by this class degradation and they turn their despair against the only visible enemy, held accountable for their 'misery', the socially excluded foreigners living next door, in their own – formerly purely French – neighbourhoods.

Social injustice and racism not only victimize and harm the self-esteem of minority populations in the EU nation states, but also produce separatist cultural movements, mirroring the quest for cultural homegeneity put forth by the dominant national groups.[9] If intercultural education means the acquisition, by all children, of a sense of self-worth, then the acknowledgement of racism, social discrimination and sexism, by the agents of change, is vital. This acknowledgement cannot function unless prejudiced social knowledge, through which discrimination is reproduced, is challenged in schools.

All discrimination is related to the social division of wealth, power and privileges, that is, to the domination of some human groups by others. If domination is seen as social control, then it is understood as having not only a social but also a cognitive dimension. Explanations for occurrences, events and societal problems cut across both the cognitive and the social and are based on widely held, shared beliefs in the form of social and collective representations which construct cognitive schemas and produce attitudes. Thus, intercultural education can be effective if it reinforces fundamental change in schools, since the educational system is, in the societies of the so-called Western world, among the most important institutions involved in the production and reproduction of social representations. Interiorization of meanings, conceptions, interpretations, principles and evaluations, determine the relation of individuals to culture which, in turn, engenders their attitudes and practices. Eurocentrism, expressing a belief in European superiority, has been defined, not only as prejudice but also as 'science', in the sense that it includes a set of beliefs that are statements about empirical reality, accepted as true by educated and usually unprejudiced Europeans, considering them to be supported by facts. They are beliefs based on history, geography and social sciences, reproduced by élite groups in European countries (Blaut 1993).

Intercultural education, as mentioned in the beginning of this chapter, has developed considerably, from an assimilation model to a search for schooling appropriate for minority pupils, aimed at preserving their identity without isolating them from the rest of the population. The importance of mother-tongue teaching, as part of the process to conserve pupils' identity, has in some countries, as for example in the UK, quite a large consensus although it may, in some cases, be contested as impossible to put into practice (Porcher 1981). The problem of language teaching, both of the mother tongue for the preservation of the pupils' identity, as well as of the language of the country for purposes of integration, is seen as a fundamental issue for intercultural education in many EU countries (Driessen 1994).

One aspect to be considered, next to sensitivity over current educational issues and the acquistion of knowledge for new practices, is that the main reason for school underachievement of minority pupils is not the fact that they are natural speakers of another language. The main reason is social inequality, connected, in most cases, with minority-group status, as well as racism. Children of diplomats, or international civil servants, or academics, educated in countries where other languages are spoken, do not seem to have any problems at school, either with bilingualism or with levels of achievement. There is evidence pointing to the close relation of school performance to social factors. Research on the reasons differentiating school achievement between high- and low-achieving immigrant children in French secondary schools shows that the main differentiating factors are social (Zeroulou 1988). If data are grouped according to ethnic and linguistic factors, school achievement of native French children is far superior to that of immigrant children. However if, with the same data, social parameters are isolated, there is no longer an apparent ethnic differentiation, and school achievement reflects social parameters (Vallet and Caille 1995).

According to the above, we suggest that, in the development of intercultural education, the provision of new knowledge through differentiated pedagogical approaches, is very important.[10] Traditionally, the curriculum and the whole school experience keep children, particularly the younger ones, away from problems connected with politics and sexuality. From a psychological point of view, silence over these matters may have the effect of rendering children unable to understand the secrecy involved. After all, children are part of everyday politics and sexuality and can well understand the events taking place around them.

If intercultural education was to introduce new knowledge in schools, adapted for each age level, on the history of the issues related to interculturalism, such as the history of colonialism and sexism, it might provide children with interpretations which have a powerful impact, helping them to put in context the problems of the present. The history of colonialism and sexism could provide children with answers on why such events took place in the past, how and why the ideas on these issues evolved up to today, and how values, beliefs and practices change over time and space. Such new knowledge in schools would permit teachers and students to proceed by acknowledging inequalities and discriminations in their historical discourse, and thus follow the very important steps towards effective forms of intercultural, anti-racist, and anti-sexist education that have developed in the past 20 years. In many EU countries, commitment to combating racial and gender discrimination in education has produced knowledge, as well as possible strategies for anti-racist and anti-sexist teaching approaches and teaching materials. Racism, sexism and social discrimination awareness, understood as the acknowledgement that the discriminatory taxonomy of human groups is inherent in all aspects of European society, that it evolved considerably in the past, and is still evolving today, could have another last, important impact. The widespread understanding that this taxonomy is damaging to all children, in the sense that it is harmful not only to the victims of such discriminations but to everybody, can be achieved through the 'recontextualization' (Bernstein 1990) of the notions of nation, national culture and ideas of homogeneity and purity, implied in these traditional terms, as well as notions of race and sex seen as natural taxonomies.

Intercultural education can be a means of change, if pupils in the EU understand that social inequality, mass unemployment and poor living conditions in consumer societies lead to social unrest and violence, which could victimize both the privileged and unprivileged; that racism and antisemitism, being irrational and worn-out taxonomies of human groups, leads to suffering among the alleged inferior human groups while, at the same time, dangerously opening the way to violence and destruction, of the 'apocalypse now' kind, for the alleged superior group; and, that sexism contributes to the impossibility, for all humans, of finding sexual fulfilment or happiness. Finally, intercultural education can be a means of change if pupils understand that the notion of cultural purity, intrinsic in all discriminatory ideas, is based on an indirect claim for the elimination of differences. The mere formulation of this idea may take the monstrous form of eliminating the different groups and this is not only something that has happened in the past (as is the case of Nazism), it is also happening in the present, as the extreme example of the war in Yugoslavia has shown.

Notes

1 These data are derived from a large study, investigating historical awareness by means of a questionnaire, of more than 30,000 15-year-olds in Belgium, Bulgaria, the Czech Republic, Denmark, Estonia, Finland, France, Germany, Greece, Hungary, Iceland, Israel, Italy, Lithuania, Norway, Palestine, Poland, Portugal, Russia, Slovenia, Spain, Sweden, Turkey, Ukraine and the UK. See Angvic and Von Borries (1997).

2 See, for example, Coleman (1966); Boudon (1973); Bowles and Gintis (1975); Bourdieu and Passeron (1964, 1970).

3 The famous IQ debate has a very rich bibliography. See for example, Block and Dworkin (1976); Lewontin et al. (1984).

4 See note 2.

5 In providing information about educational success with no equivalent professional outcome, the monthly supplement of *Le Monde* on education entitled its issue on gender: 'Girls: A False School Success'(*Le Monde de l'Éducation*, 1990).

6 In the rest of the world, as far as gender inequality in education is concerned, illiteracy is mainly a women's characteristic. For example, according to estimates by UNICEF, in 1990 there are more than 900 million illiterate adults in the world (half of the earth's population), and two-thirds of these are women.

7 On the term of Eurocentrism and its content, see Clay and Cole (1992); as well as Amin (1989), and the controversial reviews and articles on this book.

8 In this chapter, we do not follow the tradition, according to which the word 'Greek', in all European languages, means Ancient Greek, and today's language (and people) have the name of Modern Greek(s). We use the adjective Greek to indicate everything relevant to the present society, while Ancient Greece is always referred to as 'Ancient'. We suggest that the traditional meaning of the word 'Greek' is a symbolic product of the primary importance accorded to Ancient Greece, in juxtaposition with the Greece of today. An example of the impact on ideological values of such insignificant semantic differences would be an analogy: if, for example, the Italians and their language were named Modern Latin(s).

9 An example of this phenomenon could be the animated and controversial debate of the right of minority pupils in French secondary schools to wear the Muslim head scarf in class (Wievorka et al. 1996).

10 An example of such an approach constitutes the material produced by the Department of Early Childhood Education at the University of Athens (Androussou 1996).

References

Abdallah-Pretceille, M. and Thomas, A. (eds) (1995), *Relations et apprentissages interculturels*, Paris: A. Colin.

Amin, S. (1989), *Eurocentrism*, New York: Monthly Review Press.

Androussou, A. (1996), 'Moi et l'autre: Un voyage. Materiel educatif interculturel pour lecole primaire', in Dragonas, T., Frangoudaki, A. and Inglessi, C. (eds), *Beyond one's own Backyard: Intercultural Teacher Education in Europe*, Athens: Nissos.

Angvic, M. and Von Borries, B. (eds) (1997), *Youth and History: A Comparative European Survey on Historical Consciousness and Political Attitudes among Adolescents*, Hamburg: Korber-Stiftung.

Barker, M. (1981), *The New Racism*, London: Junction Books.

Baudelot, C. and Establet, R. (1992), *Allez les filles!*, Paris: Seuil.

Bernstein, B. (1971), *Class, Codes and Control: Theoretical Studies towards a Sociology of Language*, vol. 1, London: Routledge.

Bernstein, B. (1977), *Class, Codes and Control: Towards a Theory of Educational Transmissions*, vol. 3, London: Routledge.

Bernstein, B. (1990), 'Social Class and Pedagogic Practice', *Class, Codes and Control: The Structuring of Pedagogic Discourse*, vol. 4, London: Routledge.

Billig, M. (1995), *Banal Nationalism*, London: Sage Publications.

Blaut, J.M. (1993), *The Colonizer's Model of the World: Geographical Diffusionism and Eurocentric History*, New York: Guilford Press.

Block, N.J. and Dworkin, G. (eds) (1976), *The IQ Controversy*, New York: Pantheon Books.

Boudon, R. (1973), *L'inegalité des chances*, Paris: A. Colin.

Bourdieu, P. (1979), *La distinction: critique sociale du jugement*, Paris: Les Editions de Minuit.

Bourdieu, P. (ed.) (1993), *La misère du monde*, Paris: Seuil.

Bourdieu, P. and Passeron, J.-C. (1970), *La Reproduction*, Paris: Les Editions de Minuit.

Bowles, S. and Gintis, H. (1975), *Schooling in Capitalist America*, New York: Basic Books.

Citron, S. (1989), *Le mythe national: l'histoire de France en question*, Paris: EDI.

Clay, J. and Cole, M. (1992), 'Euroracism, Citizenship and Democracy: The Role of Teacher Education', *International Studies in Sociology of Education*, 2(1), pp.75–88.

Cohen, P. (1992), '"It's Racism that Dunnit": Hidden Narratives in Theories of Racism', in Donald, J. and Rattansi, A. (eds), *'Race', Culture and Difference*, London: Sage.

Coleman, J. (1966), *Equality of Educational Opportunity*, Washington: US Government Printing Office.

Coleman, R.P. and Rainwater, L. (1978), *Social Standing in America: New Dimensions of Class*, New York: Basic Books.

Coulby, D. (1995), 'Ethnocentricity, Postmodernity and European Curricular Systems', *European Journal of Teacher Education*, 18(2/3), pp.143–53.

Dekkers, H. (1994), 'Equal Opportunities in Education and the Economic Independence of Women in North-West Europe. A Comparative Study of the Situation in Norway, Sweden, the UK, Germany, and the Netherlands', in Driessen, G. and Jungbluth, P. (eds), *Educational Opportunities: Tackling Ethnic, Class and Gender Inequality through Research*, New York: Waxmann.

Delamont, S. (1990), *Sex Roles and the School*, London: Methuen.

Donald, J. and Rattansi, A. (eds) (1992), *'Race', Culture and Difference*, London: Sage.

Dragonas, T., Frangoudaki, A. and Inglessi, C. (1996), 'Unpacking Intercultural Teacher Education: From Monoculturalism to Respect of Human Rights', in Th. Dragonas, A. Frangoudaki and Ch. Inglessi (eds), *Beyond one's own Backyard: Intercultural Education in Europe*, Athens: Nissos.

Driessen, G. (1994), 'Moroccan Children Acquiring Arabic in the Netherlands. Mother Tongue Instruction as a Means of Combating Educational Disadvantage', in Driessen, G. and Jungbluth, P. (eds), *Educational Opportunities. Tackling Ethnic, Class and Gender Inequality through Research*, New York: Waxmann.

Driessen, G. and Jungbluth, P. (eds) (1994), *Educational Opportunities. Tackling Ethnic, Class and Gender Inequality through Research*, New York: Waxmann.
Fourier, M. and Vermes, G. (eds) (1994), *Ethnicisation des rapports sociaux: Racismes natio-nalismes, ethnicismes et culturalismes*, Paris: L'Harmattan.
Frangoudaki, A. and Dragonas, T. (1997), *'Ti ein' i patrida mas;' Ethnokentrismos stin ekpaidefsi* ['What is our country?' Ethnocentrism in education], Athens: Alexandria.
Gilroy, P. (1987), *Problems in Anti-racist Strategy*, London: The Runnymed Trust.
Guillaumin, C. (1994), 'Quelques considerations sur le terme "culture"', in Fourier, M. and Vermes, G. (eds), *Ethnicisation des rapports sociaux: Racismes natio-nalismes, ethnicisme et culturalismes*, Paris: L'Harmattan.
Gundara, J. (1990), 'Societal Diversity and the Issue of "the Other"', *Oxford Review of Education*, 16(1), pp.97–109.
Gundara, J. and Jones, C. (1992a), *Long-term Unemployed and the Elderly in Migrant Communities in Europe*, Council for Cultural Cooperation: Manhattan Publishing Company.
Gundara, J. and Jones, C. (1992b), 'Nation States, Diversity and Interculturalism: Issues for British Education', in Ray, D. and Poonwassie, D.H. (eds), *Education and cultural differences: new perspectives*, New York: Garland Publishing Co.
Halliday, M.A.K. (1978), *Language as Social Semiotic: The Social Interpretation of Language and Meaning*, London: Arnold.
Harris, R. (1980), *The Language Makers*, London: Duckworth.
Henry-Lorcerie, F. (1986), 'Education interculturelle, changement institutionnel. L'experience française', *Sociologie du Sud-Est*, 49–50, pp.103–126.
Isambert-Jamati, V. (1990), *Les savoirs scolaires: Enjeux sociaux des contenus d'enseignement et de leurs réformes*, Paris: Editions Universitaires.
Kelly, E. and Cohn, T. (1988), *Racism in Schools: New Research Evidence*, London: Trentham Books Ltd.
Lewontin, R., Rose, S. and Kamin, L.J. (1984), *Not in our Genes: Biology, Ideology and Human Nature*, New York: Pantheon Books.
McCarthy, C. and Crichlow, W. (eds) (1993), *Race, Identity and Representation in Education*, New York: Routledge.
Mangan, J.A. (ed.) (1993), *The Imperial Curriculum: Racial Images and Education in the British Colonial Experience*, New York and London: Routledge.
Michard-Marchal, C. and Ribery, C. (1982), *Sexisme et sciences humaines*, Lille: Presses Universitaires de Lille.
Miles, R. (1993), *Racism after 'Race' Relations*, London: Routledge.
Mosconi, N. (1994), *Femmes et savoir: La societé, l'école et la division sexuelle des savoirs*, Paris: L'Harmattan.
Percheron, A. (1974), *L'univers politique des enfants*, Paris: A. Colin.
Phillips, A. (1993), *The Trouble with Boys*, London: Pandora.
Porcher, L. (1981), *The Education of Children of Migrant Workers in Europe: Interculturalism and Teacher Training*, Strasbourg: Council of Europe.
Preiswerk, R. and Perrot, D. (1975), *Ethnocentrisme et Histoire: l'Afrique, l'Amerique Indienne et l'Asie dans les manuels occidentaux*, Paris: Anthropos.
Rattansi, A. (1992), 'Changing the Subject? Racism, Culture and Education', in Donald, J. and Rattansi, A. (eds), *'Race', culture and difference*, London: Sage.
Ray, D. and Poonwassie, D.H. (eds), *Education and Cultural Differences: New Perspectives*, New York: Garland Publishing Co.
Sarup, M. (1991), *Education and the Ideologies of Racism*, London: Trentham Books.

Siraj-Blatchford, I. (1994), *The Early Years: Laying the Foundations for Racial Equality*, London: Trentham Books.

Solomos, J. (1986), 'Trends in the Political Analysis of Racism', *Political Studies*, 34(2), pp.33–324.

Stromquist, N. (1990), 'Gender Inequality in Education: Accounting for Women's Subordination', *British Journal of Sociology of Education*, 2, pp.137–53.

Troyna, B. (1989), '"A New Planet"? Tackling Racial Inequality in All-white Schools and Colleges', in Verma, G.K. (ed.), *Education for All: A Landmark in Pluralism*, London: The Falmer Press.

Troyna, B. (1992), 'Can you see the join? An historical analysis of multicultural and antiracist education policies', in Gill, D., B. Mayor and M. Blair (eds), *Racism and Education*, London: Sage.

Troyna, B. (1993), *Racism and Education: Research Perspectives*, London: Open University Press.

Troyna, B. and Williams, J. (1986), *Racism, Education, and the State: the Racialization of Education Policy*, London: Croom Helm.

Vallet, L.-A. and Caille, J.-P. (1995), 'Les carrières scolaires au college des élèves étrangers ou issus de l'immigration', *Education et Formations*, 40, pp.5–14.

Van Dijk, T.A. (1987), *Communicating Racism. Ethnic Prejudice in Thought and Talk*, London: Sage.

Van Dijk, T. (1993), *Elite Discourse and Racism*, London: Sage

Wieviorka, M. (1994), 'Racism in Europe: Unity and Diversity', in Rattansi, A. and Westwood, S. (eds), *Racism, Modernity and Identity on the Western Front*, Cambridge: Polity Press.

Wieviorka, M. et al. (1996), *Une société fragmentée? Le multiculturalisme en débat*, Paris: La Decouverte.

Zeroulou, Z. (1988), 'La reussité scolaire des enfants d'immigrés: L'apport d'une approche en termes de mobilisation', *Revue Française de Sociologie*, XXIX, pp.447–70.

11 Out of Mind, Out of Sight: Education and Older Migrants

Jagdish Gundara and Crispin Jones

The process of ageing, and being older people, conjures up ideas, images and stereotypes which have a profound impact on the way in which, at an individual and collective level, this process is perceived and dealt with. Indeed, the very terms used to describe older people carry considerable cultural baggage with them, and colour the potential and limitations of this period of human life. In this chapter, the term 'older people' is used to stress the continual links between people, irrespective of age.

Clearly, the concept of old age is socially constructed. This is not to deny the physical and intellectual consequences of becoming older. But despite this, it is clear that meanings and evaluations of ageing are differentially constructed in different cultures and also in the same culture over time (Featherstone and Wernick 1995). Our current Western postmodern obsession with the body beautiful means that a healthy and beautiful body is now a powerful cultural imperative, a denial of ageing. There is a significant gender bias at work as well, taking different shape in different cultures. Within dominant cultures within Europe, male ageing is seen as mainly a physical weakness. To compensate, many such older men are seen as wise. Women are less fortunate, primarily being seen as having lost their sexual allure. Indeed, for many centuries, older single women were seen as threatening, often being associated with witchcraft and mistreated accordingly. That is not all: older men can have relationships with younger women, but the converse is still seen in a mainly negative light. Similar patterns exist in relation to class and status, maintaining existing cultural patterns of domination and subordination.

Issues surrounding older people are thus obviously complex, the more so as they are not simply grounded in our personal experiences. For example, the experience of growing old in a society where only youth is privileged, is different from a society where old age is revered and privileged. In a society where old age ceases to have cultural value, major dislocation is created. Thus, many who have come to Europe from societies where ageing carries with it a status and a role in the family and the community have found to their shock that being an older person in their new environment now carries little or no status. They have also seen, within one generation, the nature of their families change dramatically, their own status loss being located within a more general sense of confusion and loss about the role of the family in late modern society. One consequence has been that for many older people from migrant communities, their sense of family, and their place and status within it, no longer has a reassuring sense of solidarity, comfort and reality for them. Such people are not alone. Older people in traditional rural areas of Europe have similarly seen an erosion of their status, as the nature of rural societies and economies have transformed, not least because of the continuing migration of the young to the urban areas within their own and other states.

At the same time, these changes have brought about an increasingly negative perception of older people. Moreover, a negative view of older people may not only contribute to older people being seen as 'the other' on to whom fears and hopes are projected, but may also contribute to a view of the older people from certain migrant communities as being 'the others' who are beyond the pale. As demographic change leads to an increase in the numbers of older people, this view of the 'otherness' of certain older people within Europe requires a qualitative shift in our thinking, to ensure that all such people are seen as an integral and integrated part of society. The physical, social, cultural and economic issues and problems of older people cannot simply be viewed on an individualistic basis but have to be seen in holistic terms as being issues for society as a whole and therefore as presenting, like many similar issues, social possibilities as well as social problems. The profound implications of this are that older people, perhaps particularly those from the migrant communities, ought not to be left to rely on themselves, on kith and kin or voluntary agencies, but should be seen as central concerns of European national governments and intergovernmental organizations. The resonance of ageism, particularly in economically and racially stratified European societies, raises acute problems for those who may already also be socially and sexually discriminated against.

As was suggested above, many of the older people who have settled in Europe in the post-Second World War period have had to make significant changes during their settlement in Europe. As they have become more settled, their younger generations have adapted, albeit to varying degrees, to the social, cultural and economic patterns of life in European conurbations. These changes have exacerbated the stress which is often found between generations. These and other issues indicate that the problems at the underlying levels for the older people of the newly settled communities, as well as for older people generally, may require understanding which is not only related to eliminating discrimination and changing social policy. The complex social processes involved in the construction of ageing within the context of societal diversities in Europe consequently still require further research and action.

Unlike in Europe, there has been tremendous enthusiasm concerning issues of educational gerontology in the United States, although there has been little impact of this on federal government policy. In the European context, there has been very little influential scholarly work done on the range of educational issues as they pertain to the older people (Peterson 1980; Glendenning 1985). However, despite such caveats, one of the most important developments has been the definition of educational gerontology undertaken by Peterson, albeit related to British developments. However, it may be useful to widen its usage to European societies generally, to ascertain whether its implications for educational gerontology can be further refined in this broader context. His definition of educational gerontology can be summarized as the creation of effective models and subsequent provision for older adults, the research into such issues and the support, at all levels, of professionals and others who do educational work with older adults (Peterson 1980).

Such a framework also resonates with the earlier recommendations made by Brian Groombridge (1960) for more daytime provision, the promotion of education for retirement and the need for professionals like social services workers to emphasize creative and satisfying needs in relation to older people. His continuing concerns about the role of broadcasting were also highlighted and yet, since he wrote in 1960, there does not seem to have been very much progress made. Moreover, such an integrated social policy provision for older people, which related to a person's whole life, would have an added bonus in that it is likely that such activity would help to ensure that the older people themselves would enjoy better mental and physical health. Such policies have the potential to lower the high social cost of old age as well as enhancing the quality of older people's lives. This reduction of social cost is of importance, not only because of the current widespread reduction of resources in relation to social policy issues but also because of the increased pressure on such support systems as the number of older people increase across Europe. More consideration, therefore, ought to be given to the interrelationship of education, leisure and health for older people. Such action is desirable as the work in all three areas interweaves; thus work in a concerted manner is likely to be more effective than working in a compartmentalized way. Such measures can help to ensure a larger autonomous older people population which is not a burden on the state, because they are physically, mentally and socially independent.

However, the realization of any concerted effort and action for universal provision is not in the offing. This is particularly the case if the issues are seen in the broader context outlined in the rest of this volume. Visits to housebound older people from marginalized migrant community groups in London by one of this chapter's authors demonstrated poignantly the loneliness and purposelessness felt by a lot of them. Many looked blank and some even said that they had nothing but death to look forward to. These views help support the view that a critical issue in respect of effective educational provision is dealing with the diminution of roles and functions of these older people and the sense of alienation that such feelings may engender.

In addition, since a number of these respondents had long ago come from rural farming backgrounds, they either had distant and perhaps inappropriate models of old age from that past life, or had sparse and equally inappropriate models of being old in a migrant community in a seemingly relentless and still alien urban environment. There may be useful lessons to be learnt from the older people in rural European farming communities, where similar structures for dealing with old age may still exist, as remembered by the older people in the migrant communities, particularly those communities with origins in rural areas of less developed countries (LDCs): this is clearly an issue worthy of further study.

The marginalized older people respondents in London conveyed a strong image of life which held no joy, companionship and for many with no facilities or inclination for collective worship, not even spiritual solace. Many saw their days as devoid of any meaningful activity or contact. They felt remorse for being lonely and alone, as well as fatalistic about the future. It is difficult to convey these complexes and the morass of guilt and shame many felt at being alone, perhaps abandoned by families. The loss of contact with families and grandchildren to give their lives an anchor and meaning was particularly noticeable.

In other visits, among the older people of the South Asian community in London, the question of shame and guilt was particularly an issue because they felt that they could not, as one said, 'show their face to anyone' from their communities. The respondents could be seen in two categories. The first was made up of those who had spent their working lives here and were somewhat more attuned to living and functioning in Britain and were thus somewhat better able to cope. The second group was made up of older people who had come as dependants of their children. In their case, the issue of the city and the country becoming even stranger as they grew old was very evident. Hence, those who were seen as 'the other' by the dominant community, in fact, began to feel that they did not belong and had become estranged from the wider society within which they lived.

The loss of status, role and respect which both groups felt they deserved, but which they felt they were denied, added to a lack of well-being. Apart from mental stress as well as illness, they were seldom able to communicate to medical and paramedical personnel what, in fact, were their problems. In the case of those who did not speak English and where an interpretation and translation service was patchy or non-existent, this language gap added to their problems. Moreover, there was evidence, from some of those who could clearly communicate about their symptoms and aliments, that they were treated callously and, in fact, they felt they were ignored as patients who required attention.

When the respondents were further questioned about educational provision, their responses demonstrated that these were conditioned by their other preoccupations about life. The issues raised earlier of a holistic and universal view of the needs of the older people came to the fore at this point. It requires the inclusive provision described earlier, where their educational needs are part of a larger parcel of social policy needs, in turn making the educational provision more meaningful and rooted. So, how might education best respond? An education worker can only be a 'barker for custom' as Eric Midwinter (1982) states, if (s)he is not only culturally attuned but also if (s)he is able to establish credentials in the context of wider concerns and needs of the older people within that broader concept of provision. The functions which Midwinter defines in this larger context, which is inclusive of the three roles of a professional educational worker, are as a 'barker, broker and booster'.

The tasks of being a 'barker' or recruiter, of being a 'broker' or educational enabler, and of being a 'booster' or morale and confidence builder are clearly difficult ones, best realized in an institutional setting that has a more holistic and universalistic framework than is normal. If such a context of a holistic and universal social provision is taken as given, then these are issues for tutors and educators of older people. It is, of course, a precondition that tutors have to be culturally attuned and have the appropriate attitudes. However, the attitudes of tutors in themselves are not sufficient, because such attitudes and their cultural empathy only assist in the process of education. There is more importantly an extremely broad question of the knowledge and skills of tutors who are to engage with work with older people in a culturally diverse Europe. This raises fundamentally important questions concerning the training of tutors with appropriate skills and knowledge, as well as the maintenance of these attributes through their own continuing education. This also presumes a sympathetic attitude on the part of the provider institutions, at the level of policy and delivery. The underlying issue, however, is that of using the positive attitudes of tutors to empower them to work within these difficult contexts.

Of the respondents interviewed from the marginalized communities, there was a large number who themselves accepted the myths of their own reduced capacity to learn, particularly because of their age. It is at this level that the stark realities of the brutal prospects for this older community become clear. If future generations of older people within the migrant communities are not to meet with a drastically dismal end to their lives in Europe, not only is a total reappraisal of the social delivery to them required but there is also a need for a major injection of resources. There is also a greater need to ensure that the older people are brought into a more meaningful relationship with their own families and communities. These relationships would help not only the older people themselves, but also their tutors to cope with a legacy of a lifetime of intractable problems. The legacy includes not only a denigration of their immigrant cultural origins but the added notion of feeling strange and estranged in their country of settlement, accompanied by notions of inferiority, weakness, narrowness and inadequacy because of being 'old', 'older people', 'aged' or 'old aged'. These seem like an extremely powerful set of weapons operating against the teaching and learning process of older people, particularly those from minorities. These are not necessarily intractable problems: there is an important educational task of ensuring how not only such images can be deconstructed but how images which are more realistic become operationalized. The demythologizing of the images of older people would make easier the task of appropriate and relevant service delivery.

While the field of social gerontology in relation to education might be underdeveloped, the area of ethno-gerontology is even less examined. It is therefore critical at this stage before ethno-gerontology is more defined, that current issues of definition are examined. Are the needs to be defined on the basis of the ethnicity, national origins, religion or social class of these groups? A holistic approach, which is not only based on the 'needs side' of this phenomenon but also on the ways in which communities wish to plan appropriate provision is important. Hence, if ethno-gerontology as a field is to make any genuine contribution, it ought to take on fundamental concerns about the misuse of definitional frameworks which have resulted in inappropriate provision being made. For instance, are factors of racism and the denial of access the basis on which we need to analyse the issues? If this is the case, the ethnicity of the group in question may not be the relevant operative consideration. Hence, as the Forum on the Rights of the Older People to Education (1983) stated: 'Worse educated as children and young persons than any of their successors in our population, they should now have access, as of right, to all the intellectual, cultural and aesthetic facilities and practical skills which in their own judgement they need and desire' (1983: 15).

The need to make the families, either in the homes of the older people or in the residential institutions, aware of the needs and concerns of the old people concerned is also essential. The question, as far as the migrant populations are concerned, is whether the residential homes themselves are suitable for them. The advantages of service provision in a holistic manner in homes as well as in residential institutions would be to foster self-reliance and independence among the older people by improving their mental and physical health. Hence, seen as a preventative measure, it would ensure that the subsequent demand on public and private resources for curative and cumulative needs would be obviated.

Older people from these migrant communities, as well as other working-class older people who have not had adequate access to education, would, under this system, be given assistance in coping with practical and social as well as psychological problems in a changing world. This would, therefore, enhance and encourage the older people to make an actual contribution to society, as well as strengthen the potential of their contribution. Among a group of the older people spoken with, a number were extremely active in several local institutions, including health services, community organizations and school governing bodies. Their confidence in having acquired knowledge and skills in this society, as well as their knowledge of other languages and experiences in other parts of the world, was seen as a positive strength and an asset. An even more useful insight was how they had seen their working lives as really a sacrifice to support their families. However, now that their families had grown up and left home, these older people, unlike those who were isolated, were extremely interested in developing their self-awareness and knowledge, thus fulfilling dreams and aspirations which they had not been able to do earlier. They also brought complex and interesting cultural insights into this process.

Since both getting older and learning are lifelong processes, it is extremely important that some of the aspirations of older people are seen by their educators as requiring continual support through development of suitable courses and educational activities. Many old people, for instance, received very little pre-retirement education although employers, trade unions and pre-retirement associations, as well as more normal educational institutes, could all provide this. However, many older people from the migrant communities are intimidated by educational institutions and feel that they would be excluded because of their age, or that, because of their specific cultural needs and demands, the provision would not be adequate. Hence, institutions need to institute positive measures to encourage access by older people to attend educational institutions, including concessionary fees. Such provision should also be offered in premises suitable for the older people, particularly as some of the provision in school buildings with long corridors or stairs is neither welcoming nor suitable. Transport can also be a major asset or a hurdle and needs careful consideration. A coordinated provision for older people which is sometimes able to cater for special groups, like women or men in separate groups, should also be seen as part of legitimate demand. Finally, the providers should also ensure that their programmes are valid for a culturally diverse ageing population.

One way round some of these issues is greater use of distance learning. The role of distance learning, certainly for those who in this instance have become housebound, requires further exploration, attention and development. A forum of older people, gathered together to express their own needs and to be involved in developing their own educational projects seems crucial not just for distance-learning programmes but for all learning of older people.

Within the provision for older people the needs of women from the migrant communities require particular attention. This is because of unequal access during their earlier education, leaving a legacy for later life. The needs of widows from these communities, whose levels of educational attainment may have been extremely low in the past, require greater resources, skilled tutors and in many cases better-educated women tutors who are more sensitive to their needs. Needs for tailored courses for women, particularly where social custom and religion forbid contact with men, may require special consideration. Counselling is needed to ensure that confidence, often lost during working lives or during work as housewives, is re-established. In most cases, there may be a need to re-establish confidence, particularly for non-traditional provision. The denial of equal opportunities to this group is a complex issue because of the range and levels of barriers to access throughout life, which come home to roost in old age. In the case of women, the need for education to cope with life with little social support has become more essential as the social structures of their own families have changed. There is a particular need to inform such women of what is available, to inspire them and stimulate their mental facilities to ensure they do not slip into senile dependency and to ensure that this inspiration is met with an involvement which is supported.

However, there may be problems, which Diane Norton describes as the age 'ghetto' (Council for Educational Advance 1984), when the specific needs of a peer group are met separately. Provision which has plurality is important, so that peer group or single-sex provision is supplemented by multi-age and multi-group provision to allow for women to choose the provision they require. The stereotype of single-sex provision for all Muslim women may not necessarily be an advance. Similarly, the need for a pedagogy which pays greater attention to pace, quality and clarity of instruction of the older learner may have greater relevance to those who have not done well in their earlier schooling.

There is also a continuing need to monitor provision to ensure that it meets the needs of older students. This is necessary not only to ensure that access to provision is a reality but to evaluate the structural and resource implications of a class, since older people too have a right to education. Since the take-up of such educational provision by older people is extremely low, estimated by to be between 1 or 2 per cent of a cohort group in the UK context (Midwinter 1984: 203), the barriers to take-up require more detailed analysis as well as action.

A further major barrier to education for older people from minorities in a culturally diverse Europe is the need to re-examine the knowledge basis of what is considered important and to ensure that the curriculum is inclusive of knowledge from a broad cultural pool. If it is not, it will only replicate the inequalities. Knowledge from all cultures has potential relevance to all communities and not specifically to migrants. The Eurocentric basis of knowledge misinforms all and alienates many.

The need to retrain the older people after the age of 55 requires attention as does the issue of education for those who are over 70. Both these groups require access to educational programmes and materials which are redesigned to meet the needs of these learners and take into account their strengths and weaknesses according to their age and experience. While the over-55s may require retraining with credentials or qualifications, those who are over 70 may be more interested in 'participative learning'.

A range of conditions may affect the learning processes of all these older people, however. These may include a partner's death, vulnerability to crime, coping with authorities and seemingly unloving families and a range of health problems. The older people from various migrant communities, therefore need to be educated through self-help which would assist them in building their coping skills and self-esteem. Moody defines the 'hard path' and the 'soft path' as two options available in such situations. While the 'hard path' may reinforce 'learned helplessness', the 'soft path' by stressing 'self-help' may allow these older people to bolster their confidence (Moody 1986). The contemporary stress on maintaining a rigid separation between learning, work and leisure requires a certain amount of reconsideration.

An example of such work at an intercultural level is provided by the Older Women's Project based in London. In this project, older women from different cultural groups are brought together. One question was: why only women? Their response to the issue is that at the age of 60 there were twice as many women as men, rising to four times as many over the age of 80.

Since none of the statutory social policy agencies make any provision for their needs, the need for this group became obvious and the Project was established in 1985, with an advisory body of older women from various backgrounds. This women's group works together collectively, with no leaders, although tutors do act as resource persons. Not only were health issues, physical exercise, self-defence, yoga and assertiveness training engaged in but they even brought in belly dancers to perform for them. They are not a middle-class group which deals with issues from safe material situations, but a group of working-class women who had experienced various disadvantages. The group has an equal opportunity policy and despite the fact that they are a multi-national group, they have few religious or racial problems. In fact, when racist language was used, the group was able to confront its members without the group breaking up.

A further issue for both male and female older people is the social mobility of the younger generation from the inner city. This is an issue for families where the older people were left after the younger generation had moved away. In some cases, older Asian women themselves felt that they had had enough of the constraints and limitations placed on them by the extended family and wanted a certain amount of space to become creative and acquire a sense of fulfilment. The functions of well-trained tutors to be facilitators for women is of critical importance to increase their potential. Hence, for women in such groups, a predetermined provision is not necessarily required, as the provision needs to be negotiated in consultation with them.

A second example of such work is a centre based in London which provides another type of provision. The Milap Centre, based in the Southall area of London, is not a single-sex provision for older people but contains men and women, and is multifaith and multi-national. The fact that this centre in a fairly traditional Asian neighbourhood provides service to a multifaith and multi-national community allows us to question the way in which further developments including research and action ought to be determined. The work of the Milap Centre, with its membership of 1000 men and 337 women, does mean that there are fewer women members than there ought to be. It in fact requires single-sex provision for men and women, as well as mixed provision. The fact that a significant number of women are going to this Day Centre is a testimony to this need. This Centre also provides evidence of Asian women who would like to learn new things and open their minds to a different set of experiences. Their interests testify to the notions of releasing the resources which they have acquired and the need to enhance their potential. The Women's Project and the Milap Centre testify to the strength of the case for entitlement to a lifelong and permanent education for women, which is often currently denied them.

These projects also help in breaking the stereotype that older people are consumers and not producers.

A further consideration ought to be for large numbers of older people from migrant communities who can take part in a very different type of operation, namely more formal higher education. If all the educational provision is to exist within a framework and has universal and international implications, then the British University for the Third Age (U3A) is an important project, since it can open up many avenues for this potentially large constituency.

As a new development in education for older people, such university provision started in France in the 1960s. The Third Age replaces 'old age' and is defined as an age of activity and participation in social life and leisure. It centres on the autonomy of older people and is presented as a period of self-realization, free from work and family responsibilities, a concept in total opposition to the traditional view of old age. There are active U3A groups in a number of areas throughout Britain offering opportunities to participate in weekly lectures, small group seminars, recreational activities, practical craft work, research projects and social functions. Each group is set up on a local basis and each group is different. There is no uniform method or way to constitute such a group. Some have highly intellectual activities, others emphasize practical skills or entertainment. They are all based on the principle of skills exchange, with the aim of making older people aware of their aesthetic and intellectual potential, in order to improve the quality of life for older adults and to create an agency where there is no distinction between those who teach and those who learn and where as much as possible of the activity is voluntary, freely given by U3A members to U3A members. The attraction of U3A is that it is run by older people for older people and no money changes hands. U3A groups give their members an autonomy to determine their own needs and make provision for those needs themselves. They give the U3A members a sense of worth which society by definition has taken away from them (Dee and Bowen 1986).

A similar programme to U3A in the USA is the elder hostel programme which is an international network of colleges and universities providing liberal arts education to retirement-age people. A study was conducted in 1982 of elder hostel programmes to discover 'the personal, social and general intellectual growth' perceived by the older people (Brady 1983). The very general conclusions revealed that elders were unanimous in their enthusiasm for the courses. Brady suggests that 'the knowledge that older students are experiencing various types of personal, social and intellectual growth should serve to encourage professional educators concerning the efficacy of their expressive type adult education programmes' (1993: 132).

Roger Cann (1989) supports this perspective when he argues for the need for a range of learning experiences to supplement the formal provision of classes. He sees a need for a more informal approach to learning which includes the scope for 'incidental learning':

> An important aspect of learning is the creation of confidence in confirming of changing an individual's opinion. If opportunities are given for people to test their knowledge and abilities against others in a supportive environment, then incidental learning can create personal satisfaction and contribute significantly to changes in attitudes and perceptions (Cann 1989: 74).

This potential contribution of older people in an intercultural context requires an empowerment of the hitherto disenfranchised groups, if the strengths of Peter Laslett's eloquent arguments for U3A are to be realized (Laslett 1989). This is important because currently the provision probably does not have an intercultural dimension, integrally reflected in its offerings of negotiated learning.

However, discussions about appropriate provision have to take place within an understanding of the greatest impediment to learning the minority communities face, namely poverty. In the UK the migrant communities are overrepresented among groups which are living below the poverty line. In a survey undertaken by Age Concern in the UK, less than 45 per cent of older Asians interviewed received any pension (Hearnden 1984). This is an indication of various things: many are ignorant that they can claim state welfare benefit or pension benefit, while others choose to ignore making a claim out of pride and embarrassment. Also, it is likely that many of the older people do not have the appropriate English-language skills to realize their entitlement to support. Many older Asians, Cypriots, Chinese, Vietnamese, Poles and others in the UK have these difficulties. An approach on the part of social policy agencies, which does not take into account the needs of economically poor linguistic and religious groups, places them in a situation of double jeopardy due to discrimination against the ageing population in general. There are, however, even graver problems confronting older, isolated women and/or illiterate women because they are triply jeopardized, due to the gender discrimination that is endemic in society.

The above issues obviously ought to be dealt with in conjunction with other areas of need within the social policy area. All older people, including those from the migrant communities, are themselves a resource and one which needs to be reassessed as Europe's population ages. Their 'cost effectiveness' in a whole range of social policy areas, including education, is represented by the enormous amount of voluntary work being done by older people, particularly 65–75-year-olds. The caring by this group even within families of other members of the family, including older people, is an added bonus which is not imposed on the social and educational system. Yet, as racism and sexism limit the potential of large numbers of people, so does ageism which makes for a powerful and lethal combination. Such questions as ageism, sexism and racism will obviously be returned to again and again as the migrants who arrived in Europe and who are retiring after a lifetime of work increase in numbers, while the prejudices remain the same.

This chapter bases its case for educational provision for older people from minorities not only on compassionate grounds, but also in the genuine interests of society. The more preventative and comprehensive social policy provision there is, the more economic it is for society, because it helps to postpone their expensive institutionalization. Their physical, mental, familial and social well-being ensures that they do not have to rely on the state to look after them. The strong family structures of many migrant communities are, in fact, an invisible saving for the state because of the caring which goes on outside society's institutional framework. An educational provision which strengthens this is obviously useful for such structures of self-help. Such educational provision which, within the larger social policy provision, is able to utilize the knowledge and experience of the older members of the migrant communities in order to help them teach as well as learn needs to be supplemented by providing guidance and counselling, since a number of the older people harbour insecurities about their ability to do either.

However, if the educational needs of the older people migrants can be closely examined and, as a result, practical policies can be implemented, great benefit will follow and not only to the individual older people concerned. If European society can provide effective educational opportunities for such people, in all their richness, the effect on the communities within which they live will be marked. The older people themselves will have more of a contribution to make, to society at large and to their community in particular. This in turn will encourage those members of the migrant community who are currently (and correctly in many cases) disenchanted with the way the wider society deals with their community to start to perceive that society values their presence and the contribution that they have made to the postwar prosperity of much of western Europe. To this end, the EU and the Council of Europe should work towards a Charter of Rights for Older People in a European intercultural context.

References

Battersby, D. (1987), 'From Andragogy to Gerogogy', *Adult Education*, pp.4–11.

Bengston, V.L. (1978), 'Ageing in Minority Populations: An Examination of the Double Jeopardy Hypothesis', *Journal of Gerontology*, 33(3).

Bornat, J. et al. (1985), *A Manifesto for Old Age*, London: Pluto Press.

Brady, E.M. (1983), 'Personal Growth and the Older People Hostel Experience', *Lifelong Learning*, 7(3).

Cann, R.C. (1989), 'Incidental Learning', *Adult Education*, 57.

Centre for Policy in Ageing (1990), *Older People and Education After 1990*, Conference Report, London: ILEA.

CEA (Council for Educational Advance) (1984), *Report on Day Conference on Educational Needs of Women, the Older people, the Unemployed*, London: CEA.

Dee, M. and Bowen, J. (1986), *Library Services to Older People*, London: British Library.

Elmore, R. (1988), 'Sociological and Social Policy Dimensions of Educational Gerontology', *Journal of Educational Gerontology*, 1(1), April.

Featherstone, M. and Wernick, A. (eds) (1995), *Images of Ageing: Cultural Representations of Later Life*, London: Routledge.

Fenton, S. (1987), *Ageing Minorities: Black People as they Grow Old in Britain*, London: CRE.

Forum on the Rights of the Older People to Education (1983), 'A Statement', unpublished ms.

Glendenning, F. (1983), 'Educational Gerontology: A Review of American and British Developments', *International Journal of Lifelong Education*, 2(1).

Glendenning, F. (ed.) (1985), *Educational Gerontology: International Perspectives*, London: Croom Helm.

Groombridge, B. (1960), *Education and Retirement: An Enquiry into the Relevance of Education into the Employment and Learning in Later Life*, London: National Institute of Adult Education.

Groombridge, B. (1987), 'Older Students: The Perception of Educational Provision in Great Britain', *Journal of Educational Gerontology*.

Hearnden, D. (1984), 'Britain's Other Elders', *New Age*, No. 25.

Hibbert, P. and Ralph, O. (1986), *Report on the Education of Ethnic Minority Older People in the London Borough of Haringey*, London Borough of Haringey.

Laslett, P. (1989), *A Fresh Map of Life*, London: Weidenfeld and Nicholson.

Lebon, A. (1982), *Maintenance of Cultural Links with the Country of Origin – Possible Effects of these Links on Integration and Insertion in the Host Country*, Council of Europe, CDMG, rev. 16.

Midwinter, E. (1982), *Age is Opportunity: Education of Older People*, London: Centre for Policy on Ageing.

Midwinter, E. (1984), 'The Social Determinants of Educational Policy in the United Kingdom', *Educational Gerontology*.

Moody, H. (1986), 'Education in a Ageing Society', *Daedalus*, 115(1).

Norman, A. (1985), *Triple Jeopardy: Growing Old in a Second Homeland*, London: Centre for Policy on Ageing.

Peterson, D (1980), 'Who are the Educational Gerontologists?', *Educational Gerontology*, 5(1), Jan./March.

UDACE (1988) *Learning Later: The Policy Paper*, Leicester.

Woodbury Down Memories Group (1989), *Woodbury Down Memories: the History of an LCC Housing Estate*, London: Woodbury Down Memories Group.

12 Youth and Interculturalism in Europe

Roger Hewitt

Introduction

There have been two major movements generating youth intercultural trends across Europe in recent years. The first of these has been that inclusive movement in which new contexts have been provided for youth cultural activities in the realms of musical production and consumption, sports, art and video projects, etc., articulated in relation to specific ethnic community bases. Simultaneously, other cultural innovations have taken place that merge elements from differing cultural points of departure into new 'hybrid' or syncretic forms that somehow articulate 'youth' in a way that breaks with past absolutisms of all kinds and creates new freedoms of combination and movement at the cultural and the social level. These inclusive aspects have been positive in registering the fact that the notion of what it is to be 'European' is not the simple story it was once commonly presented as being.

The second movement is far less positive. This has been the trend towards white community closure, racism and xenophobia evident in the rise of political parties of the racist right and in the increase in the number of incidents of racial harassment and assault in a number of European countries. This issue is not, of course, in itself just a youth-related matter. However, the prominence of young males in the 15–25 age range in the profile of perpetration of racist incidents is a pan-European phenomenon. Furthermore, as musical and fashion stylistics have also come to provide a vehicle and expressive form amongst young people for a significant if small component in this racist activity, the ideological content of youth cultural forms cannot today, any more than in the past, be taken to be 'essentially' anti-conservative, anti-racist or positively intercultural. Youth culture is itself a politically malleable instrument. For this reason, struggles at the cultural level are particularly pertinent for the role of youth in the development of interculturalism in Europe.

This chapter will sketch in some of the ways in which these starkly diverging movements have been evident across Europe, and indicate the ways these may be affected by social policy.

Cultural change and innovation

Language

One of the most impressive features of the growth of visible youth cultural products by young members of minority ethnic communities is the facility with which they transcend linguistic boundaries. Even in some of the most socially and linguistically complex of situations, either some *lingua franca* emerges as the medium of cultural exchange, or young people develop hybrid communicative forms themselves, drawing in lexical and grammatical fragments from several disparate sources. Linguistic innovation has, of course, often been associated with youthful experimentation – the absence of the common observance of cultural and linguistic barriers, or merely the kind of word-play evident in back-slang, pig-latin or the constant re-invention of street slang. Where several languages are played with in this way and made to serve both communicative and expressive ends, a kind of spontaneous interculturalism is generated that serves a number of complex social, cultural and sometimes political purposes.

In the UK, this process was first documented with regard to the 'London Jamaican' or 'Black English' of second- and third-generation young people of African-Caribbean parentage (Sutcliffe 1982; Sebba 1993). The role that this relocated, emergent street language had in the articulation of a new, vibrant urban black youth culture in the UK during the 1970s and 1980s, soon itself became taken up into a much wider, international pattern in which black speech forms became adopted and adapted by other ethnic groups, both minority and majority (Hewitt 1986; Rampton 1995). Here, the hybridization of linguistic forms generated a flexible local multicultural vernacular that was capable of local inflection by whatever other local sources were socially pertinent – Turkish, Punjabi, Cockney, etc. – creating local blends that can be taken as emblematic of mixture and crossover at the level of the social itself. Certainly they indicated a higher degree of social contact between young people of differing ethnic backgrounds than had ever been evident in the past – at least as far as northern Europe was concerned.

What was once mainly true for urban youth mainly in the UK very rapidly became also commonplace for youth in many of the newly emergent urban centres within Europe where economic and political migrants made their homes. Berlin, Paris, Amsterdam along with the migrant settlement towns outside of the large conurbations of Sweden and Denmark, all began to produce the new kinds of social relationship between indigenous majority ethnic youth and the new and old minority ethnic groups and with them established new frontiers of linguistic innovation. The Swedish suburban area of Rinkeby is almost itself symbolic of this process. Although the processes flagged-up by the phrase 'Rinkeby-Swedish' are no different from those also evident in other ethnically mixed suburbs, such as Alby in Stockholm, or Rosengard in Malmo, 'Rinkeby-Swedish' (*Rinkebysvenska*), became the focus of an ideological exercise in national identity, conducted mainly in the press, with headlines such as 'Rinkeby-Swedish Takes Over', raising a debate about the influence of immigrant groups on the national culture (Kotsinas 1992). Such reactions are indicative of the fact that cultural crossovers of all kinds can be the site of considerable contestation and backlash because they are seen as potentially transformative.

Music

Perhaps even more pervasive have been the transformations in youth musical culture throughout Europe in recent years. In particular, the ubiquity and political utility of rapping and rap-derivatives, as well as the digitalization of the music industry has changed the face of musical consumption and production. While mainly black American commercial performers tend to dominate mass-market CD and cassette sales, European home-grown musical production and local audiences have created their own forms and productive relationships within the musical culture. The background to this is to be found in the early widespread penetration of hip-hop culture from its original genesis in the US during the 1970s.

The advent of North American – especially New York – hip-hop culture had a distinctive impact on African-Caribbean youth in the UK, in Holland and in pockets elsewhere in Europe. There were four main aspects to it. Two of these, graffiti art and break-dancing were at the time the most visible aspects as far as those outside of the culture were concerned. Graffiti art in particular began to adorn, as it still does, many public spaces, including walls beside public transport systems, abandoned buildings, fences and other roadside sites. The art styles were for the most part directly borrowed from the styles that had been developed by the young black New York hip-hop subway artists. These had become widely known through the graffiti book *Subway Art* by Martha Cooper and Henry Chalfant, and were also reproduced in the colour supplements to some of the Sunday newspapers. As with the American graffiti art, each artist would have his or her 'tag' (artist's name) that was always somewhere appended to the often large and always boldly colourful designs. Although graffiti art was particularly taken up by black adolescents, it was inevitably not confined to them, and the subsequent spread of hip-hop graffiti throughout Europe and, indeed, much of the rest of the world, has crossed many ethnic borders.

The capacity of graffiti art to transform the environment in positive ways and serve young people from diverse ethnic backgrounds is particularly evident from a series of youth art projects that were initiated throughout the mid-1990s in Berlin. The simple act of providing young people with large public wall-spaces, which they were permitted to use for their art work, provoked an explosion of creativity amongst groups of young urban artists working on the hip-hop tradition. Spaces were in a constant state of elaboration and transformation as groups and individuals jostled to outdo each other in inventiveness. These vibrant surfaces combined an exacting aesthetic with ethnic exuberance and social and political comment in a way that could almost be taken as a metaphor for contemporary urban transformation and grassroots interculturalism. The photographic record of these activities has yet to be published, but one account of this exciting work can be found in an article by Ulrich Puritz entitled 'Sexy "Kanake"' (1998).

The second most visible aspect of hip-hop culture was break-dancing, sometimes called 'B-boying'. Although it was most often performed in clubs, during the early 1980s, it was often to be encountered in street contexts and even made regular appearances in some of Europe's busier tourist spots. Generally performed by small (but sometimes large) groups of black boys (very rarely girls), it incorporated gymnastical feats with slick dance routines performed to the distinctive sharp beat of post-soul and disco electronic drum-machine percussion. It had been made popular beyond its original US bases particularly through the films *Flashdance* and *Breakdance (The Movie)*, and always displayed a strong continuity with earlier American soul music.

The other main aspects of hip-hop culture to be taken up by African-Caribbean youth, particularly in the UK, were rapping itself – of all the hip-hop elements the most enduring – and the hip-hop vocal group performances in which bass and percussion sounds were simulated by the human voice beneath a rapped vocal top line. Again this was predominantly a male expressive form within the culture and, although not widely popular, hip-hop vocal groups were very much a part of the UK black youth cultural scene during the mid-1980s. Rap, of course, started out as a live verbal art performed in Bronx discos in the US in the mid-1970s. By the end of the decade, the first rap records began to appear, quickly followed by radio shows and a proliferation of creative DJs who created the musical sounds over which the rappers, known as MCs, talked their raps. At that time it was the music that was considered as primary, the rapping as secondary. By the mid-1980s, the balance had begun to tip towards the rappers but by then it was already becoming mainly a studio-recorded, rather than a live performance, art. Secondly, in the first wave of hip-hop music it was the DJ, such as Grandmaster Flash and Afrika Mambaata, who through their live mixing of sounds through dual-deck record-players, developed the various effects, including stylus scratching, possibly the best known of the hip-hop DJ trademarks. But after 1981 when the first 'mix' *record*, 'Grandmaster Flash and the Wheels of Steel', was released, gradually the record *producer* replaced the DJs as the prevailing creative force: rap as live performance became far less important than the production and consumption of rap records (Sexton 1995). Countervailing this tendency in the UK, however, was the already vigorous Jamaican 'toasting' tradition, which was highly participatory, permitting many young performers the chance to 'have a go' at the microphone at parties and blues dances. Here something of the hip-hop influence was felt in live performance, although the UK followers of pure rap increasingly contented themselves with underground and mainstream recordings. Of all of the hip-hop elements, however, it has been rap which has endured and developed, leaving graffiti art somewhat locked into its early styles (although it is still widely practised by black and white youth alike); break-dancing has disappeared altogether. British-born black youngsters have, to some extent, developed a UK counterpart to the American rappers and, where they do so successfully, have their dedicated followers amongst black British youth. This same pattern is also evident elsewhere in Europe.

The elaboration of technological components of the music scene has also brought with it a further shift. Nowadays much musical production occurs through a mixture of computed-generated and otherwise synthesized sounds, into which may be added digitally produced 'samples' – pre-recorded musical extracts of voices or instruments which are electronically mixed together by a producer. Such recordings are themselves subject to reinterpretation either by further 're-mixes' by other producers, or by DJs using multiple turntables during live performances in dance clubs (or both). Who counts as a 'recording artist' thus includes singers and musicians as it always has, but also record producers (who by no means need the facilities required by large record companies but can operate on a fairly small (corner of the bedroom) scale), DJs (whose special skill is in inspired and spontaneous mixing) and MCs who rap, toast and more generically 'chat' their own 'lyrics' in the clubs. Thus there is a perpetual feedback, remodification and cross-referencing inherent in this human/electronic musical interface.

The technological means to create music in these ways is becoming increasingly available to even the very young – some youngsters as young as ten and eleven years old have sound mixers and double-decks, even if not of the top standard; as a result, the kind of position once occupied by, say, the guitar amongst young would-be music creators, has been overtaken by the turntable and the mixer. The culture which grows out of this is almost inevitably very much a rhythm-based and primarily dance-oriented culture with its social life predominantly taking place in clubs, parties and over the soundwaves, particularly of the illegal pirate radio stations that flower, sometimes only briefly, on the urban airways. This musical youth culture, with its local inflections and variations, extends throughout Europe, particularly through 'rave' and post-rave dances, from southern Spain to the Arctic Circle. It is probably the most powerful metaphor for the social facts of mixture and interpenetration of national and ethnic identities currently active across Europe, drawing in diverse musical forms, as well as metropolitan and Third-World linguistic resources.

Rap is now the pre-eminent expressive mode of young people's contemporary vocal forms, being adopted particularly but not exclusively by ethnic minority youth and often blending at least three languages including minority ethnic, majority local/national and – in recognition of its American origin and reference – English. Thus Turkish, German and English may all feature together within a single rap delivered with pungent political messages and a distinctively European urban content. In Germany the creative dynamism and political pointedness has also been elaborated and taken up into other expressive forms, such as the African-German Rap-Theater, a company which performs socially critical plays for young people, using rap and rap sensibility as its main communicative vehicle. Rap has been similarly harnessed to both aesthetic and political ends in Sweden. One locally well-known collective of young people comprising Chilean, Somalian, Turkish, Kurdish and other minority young people in an almost exclusively immigrant town on the outskirts of Gothenberg, raps in Swedish, English, Spanish, Turkish and Amharic, with different verses delivered by in different languages within the same rap. Their lyrics are intelligent and subtle and their themes are the exclusion of minorities, local street-political struggles with the far right and the international struggle of the Third World diaspora for equality and rights. Unsurprisingly, the black South African rap group Black Noise, following a tour of Sweden on which they ran rap workshops and came to meet the group, have now actually signed them up to tour with them (Sernhede, forthcoming). Such an event underscores the international dimension and political significance of such European youth trends.

Against the drift of this mass movement amongst young people, is the far less influential but nevertheless disturbing presence of attempted interventions by far right racist groups setting out to underscore their neo-Nazi message through musical allegiances. Since the emergence of the skinhead bands in the UK in the early 1980s – most notably 'Oi Music' – a small but proactive subculture has developed. Explicitly racist groups, such as Skrewdriver and No Remorse – both UK bands – are regarded as foundational for similar groups scattered across the globe. Indeed, the very slenderness of their following has spurred many racist organizations to use all the means of modern communications technology – in particular the Internet and the widespread use of websites – to spread its messages of hate and draw together distant allies. At the same time, a small but significant underground circulation of illegal CDs produced and distributed by far right organizations and individuals is becoming evident. Although there appears to be more activity in this area in the United States with groups such as Rahowa and distributors such as Resistance Records, there is some impact of 'White Power Music' including, paradoxically, White Power Hip-Hop also evident in Europe. However, because the importation and public playing of this music is illegal in most European countries, performances and dances are restricted to non-advertised, secretly organized occasions in remote or obscure venues in the UK, Germany, Scandinavia and elsewhere. Such activities are a warning against assuming that youth cultural forms are in themselves intrinsically progressive. On the contrary, they are politically and socially highly manipulable; hence the need for permanent vigilance and clear anti-racist strategies.

Sport

Another area of considerable cultural importance with regard to interculturalism and youth is sport, both with regard to participation and as a spectator activity. There have been in recent years a number of attempts to counter the presence of racist and socially exclusive practices in sport in several European countries. The UK once had a very severe problem with racism on the football terraces in particular, and football matches were especially targeted by racist political organizations selling their newspapers and distributing racist literature. Legislation to curb hooliganism and racism at football matches began to be introduced in the early 1980s but to little effect. In recent years, however, football clubs and various football organizations such as the Professional Footballers' Association, have sought to find new ways of curbing racism at all levels, from the racial abuse of black football players, to the selling of racist literature and the underrepresentation of ethnic minorities amongst spectators due to fear.

A number of football clubs have taken a lead in positively setting out to build links between their supporters' clubs and local minority ethnic communities. In Sheffield, a project called 'Football Unites – Racism Divides' is one of four European Commission-funded projects, with funding from the EC Cities Anti-Racism Project. It is a multi-agency project which has brought together the Sheffield Youth Service, Sheffield United Football Club, South Yorkshire Police and various local community and youth organizations. Other anti-racist projects, such as 'Show Racism the Red Card,' an anti-racist education project using video and based in the north-east of England, has been developed jointly by Youth Against Racism in Europe, the Independent Newcastle United Supporters' Association and the Racial Equality Councils of Tyne and Wear and Cleveland. It has harnessed high-profile professional footballers as positive role models for young people. Other similar important initiatives have been taken by clubs such as Leicester City which ran a 'Let's Kick Racism Out of Football' campaign, extending club-run coaching and outreach schemes to all sections of the community. Free tickets have also been given out to local Asian young people to encourage them to attend matches.

In south London, three major national clubs – Charlton Athletic, Millwall and Crystal Palace – two of which once had a major problem with organized racism, now have built up an effective anti-racist partnership which underscores the value of multi-ethnic communities and the need to confront racism at all levels in professional football. At the same time, these clubs have cooperated in supporting a move to persuade local authorities to endorse an anti-racist policy applying to the use of all of the public playing fields under their control, thus attempting to tackle some of the less obvious forms of social exclusion in local amateur football, particularly as it impacts on young people. Again in the UK, another London club, Leyton Orient, in the East End, chose to commission a play to be written about racism in football, specifically to be performed for young people. The ARC Theatre Ensemble developed the play with their play writer, Clifford Oliver, who chose the theme of the exclusion of Asian players from amateur and professional football. It took as its starting point the stereotypical ways in which Asian young men and women are commonly represented and how, despite the existence of vigorous Asian football leagues in the UK, Asian players are almost universally ignored both at amateur and professional level. The play was widely acclaimed and toured first the UK and then a number of other European countries, playing mainly to young people in schools and youth clubs (AGARI 1996).

Similar projects to some of these UK examples have been also mounted elsewhere in Europe. In Bologna, Italy, the Ultra Football Projetta works directly with young racists. In Dortmund, the Dortmund Fun project has two to three workers who work on the streets in anti-racist outreach work with young people; and in Vienna, Austria, there is a Fair Play project which, in the summer of 1998 has run the first World Anti-racist Football Championship.

In all of these cases, policy initiatives made by both local authorities, sports associations and individual clubs have had a significant effect on encouraging a wider participation in the sport by young people from minority ethnic communities and broadened the social base at all levels; although football is the flagship sport at present, already other sports are also beginning to examine their practices and their effects on young people.

Racism and youth

Despite the broad trend towards forms of spontaneous interculturalism and anti-racism amongst young people, however, minority ethnic youth across Europe still suffer the effects of social exclusion and racism. Furthermore, it is a sad fact that white males in the 15–25 age range feature as the most prominent group in the profile of perpetrators of racist harassment and assault across the continent. The racism experienced by European minority ethnic youth, however, is not only or even mainly that perpetrated by white adolescents. That is true both within and beyond the European Union. Harrowing reports, for example, by Roma children in the Czech Republic, demonstrate that the full effects of racism combine both casual abuse and bullying at the level of immediate social contacts, with indifference and hostility at the level of officials and authority figures, such as teachers and police. Callousness about routine racist name-calling and bullying appears to be rife in the Czech Republic with regard to the Roma, and applies equally to the elderly as to the young (Conway 1996).

It would be a mistake to attribute the apparent tide of racism in some countries to the activism of the far right. In some countries, there certainly is a rise in the visible membership of racist political organizations and related groups. In others, however, probably the majority, neo-Nazi activism is of little numerical significance to the profile of racial assaults and harassment. These are more mundane but because they often involve nearby neighbours they can be very insidious and undermining. One report on racial harassment in an east London borough captured this aspect of racial harassment with its title, *Beneath the Surface* (Waltham Forest Council 1991), which emphasized that even though many incidents may be small and – to those not on the receiving end of them – insignificant, the pattern of intimidation set up by acts of vandalism, racist graffiti and name-calling are linked through fear to the more dramatic acts of violence and assault. Combined, they create the conditions for the daily misery and anxiety that many thousands of black and minority ethnic families endure every day all across Europe.

Young people, including small children, have been heavily implicated in racial harassment in many European countries. In Germany, reported cases of racial violence rose steadily in the early 1990s and young people were implicated in a high proportion of them (Bjorgo and Witte 1993; Hazekamp and Popple 1997). In Holland, France, Belgium, Spain and Italy, the 1990s have also seen a rise in racial incidents (Fekete and Webber 1994). The same is also true for the UK, although there is the persistent analytical problem of distinguishing rises in reported incidents with a rise in incidence itself. Robert Miles has argued for considerable caution when looking at such figures and deciding that we are seeing a new phenomenon – a new 'Euro-racism' as it came to be called in the early 1990s, derived from a 'Fortress Europe' mentality (Webber 1991; Miles 1994). In fact, the consequences of the European Union have been far more varied than the early predictions led many to believe.

The motors of racism in Europe can be divided between those which – as with the Roma and the Czech Republic – combine state racism either by commission or omission with street racism and quotidian harassment and abuse, and 'backlash racism' in which equalities and rights gained by minority ethnic communities are reacted against by sections of the majority communities (Witte 1996). Young people can and have been implicated in both of these forms, although inevitably they are generally less attuned to the rights issues than adults. In the UK, however, there has been, in some parts of London and elsewhere, a backlash by young whites to some of the anti-racist and multicultural educational delivery. Studies of young people in south London, where there have been a significant number of racist attacks in which young white males have been involved, (ICIS 1992; Hewitt 1996), found that, although anti-racist and multicultural policies and practices have been effective with a majority of young people, there was a large minority of young people in some areas who not only remained unaffected, but who had developed clear hostility to anti-racist messages and multiculturalism. These reactions were in some cases derived from a clumsily implemented anti-racism which worked on a model of racism as 'prejudice plus power equals racism' and which seemed to have little understanding of the role of social class in the generation of forms of consciousness – including racist consciousness.

It is clear from this research that any attempt to work with racist youth or young people on the verge of being drawn into racism and racist activism, will need to be particularly sensitive to not just 'getting the message right' but making sure that there is a very comprehensive understanding of how such messages are received. This means paying attention to the understandings and world-views of such young people and working from that starting point, rather than assuming the high political or moral ground and believing that all that has to happen is for the truth to be proclaimed. In the UK, there have been several projects working with white racist youth that have abandoned the older style of 'preachy' anti-racism, and which now take a less confrontational, more subtle and audience-sensitive approach. Although these approaches are new, there are already signs that with certain types of young people they do offer much more hope of success. One of these, the Bede Project in Bermondsey, south London, has recently published an account of its work which contains training and discussion exercises which make it an invaluable resource for youth and community workers, teachers and those involved in detached anti-racist work with young people (National Youth Agency 1997). Another project based on the same premises was initiated in the London Borough of Greenwich under the European Commission's Cities Anti-Racism Project. Here there has been the same focus on approaching the understandings of young white people, particularly through group work. In conjunction with this project a video, *Routes of Racism,* was made by the International Centre for Intercultural Studies, Institute of Education, University of London. This video is specifically designed for showing to young white people who are either explicitly racist or who may be drawn to racism. Greenwich Council, in south London, have published a manual to go with the video and have trained youth workers in its use. Both the video and the manual are currently being piloted by Greenwich Youth Services. Both of the above departures from traditional anti-racist practice in the UK are derived from a specific problem arising from a too-doctrinaire anti-racism, as it was developed in the 1970s and 1980s. They point the way both for a broader approach in the UK and as a useful warning on the development of anti-racism and interculturalism elsewhere in Europe.

References

AGARI (1996), *Alive and Still Kicking: A Report by the Advisory Group Against Racism and Intimidation,* London: Commission for Racial Equality.

Bjorgo, T., and Witte, R. (eds) (1993), *Racist Violence in Europe,* London: Macmillan.

Conway,L. (1996), *Report on the Status of Romani Education in the Czech Republic,* Prague: HOST.

Cooper, M. and Chalfant, H. (1994), *Subway Art,* London: Thames and Hudson.

Fekete, L. and Webber, F. (1994), *Inside Racist Europe,* London: Institute of Race Relations.

Hazekamp, J. and Popple, K. (1997), *Racism in Europe: A Challenge for Youth Policy and Youth Work,* London: UCL Press.

Hewitt, R. (1986), *White Talk Black Talk: Inter-racial Friendship and Communication amongst Adolescents*, Cambridge: Cambridge University Press.

Hewitt, R. (1996), *Routes of Racism: the Social Bases of Racist Action Amongst Adolescents*, London: Trentham Books.

International Centre for Intercultural Studies (1992), *Sagaland: Youth Culture, Racism and Education. A Report on Research Carried Out in Thamesmead*, London Borough of Greenwich, reprinted 1993, 1996.

Kotsinas, U.-B. (1992), 'Immigrant Adolescents' Swedish in Multi-Cultural Areas', in Palmgren, C., Lovgren K. and Bolin, G. (eds), *Ethnicity in Youth Culture*, Stockholm: University of Stockholm.

Miles, R. (1994), 'A Rise of Racism in Europe? : Some Sceptical Reflections on its Nature and Extent', *New Community*, 204, pp. 547–62.

National Youth Agency (1997), *Blood, Sweat and Tears*, London: National Youth Agency.

Puritz, U. (1998), 'Sexy "Kanake"', in Gogolin, I., Kruger-Potratz, M. and Meyer, M. (eds), *Pluralität und Bildung*, Opladen: Leske und Budrich, pp. 25–41.

Rampton, B. (1995), *Crossing: Language and Ethnicity Among Adolescents*, London: Longman.

Sebba, M. (1993), *London Jamaican: Language Systems in Interaction*, London: Longman.

Sexton, A. (ed.) (1995), *Rap on Rap*, New York: Delta Books.

Sernhede, O. (forthcoming), *Youth, Music and Politics*, Gottenberg: University of Gottenberg, Department of Social Work.

Sutcliffe, D. (1982), *Black British English*, Oxford: Blackwell.

Waltham Forest Council (1991), *Beneath the Surface: An Inquiry into Racial Harassment in the London Borough of Waltham Forest*, London: The Race Unit, London Borough of Waltham Forest.

Webber, F. (1991), 'From Ethnocentrism to Euro-racism', *Race and Class*, 32(3), pp. 11–19.

Witte, R. (1996), *Racist Violence and the State*, Harlow: Longman.

13 Racist Violence and the European Community

Paul Iganski

Racist violence, or violence motivated by racism, anti-Semitism or xenophobia, has presented a serious social problem across Europe in recent years and provided a formidable challenge for social policy. Whilst some countries are beginning to recognize the problem, there has been uneven policy activity across the European Community. Scholarly analysis of the problem of racist violence is also in its infancy. The limited sociological literature on the phenomenon published in the UK to date has largely focused on conceptualizing the causes of violence. The emerging literature has neglected anti-Semitic manifestations and violence against historically persecuted groups such as Gypsy/Roma communities. Significantly, there has also been little scholarly evaluation of policy intervention.

In the early 1990s, it was commonly claimed, on the basis of official statistics, that European countries were experiencing a 'rising tide' of racist violence (cf. Read and Simpson 1991). However, some circumspection about claims of a worsening epidemic of violence might be justified. As Miles has suggested, a rise in incidents recorded by police statistics might represent a greater willingness on the part of victims to report incidents, and it may even represent a greater willingness by the police to record them (1994: 554). By the same token, we might also be circumspect about claims of a homogeneous 'rise of racism' across Europe, for as Miles also argues 'there is very considerable uneven development, and explanation must retain a reference to national specificity' (1994: 552). These observations are not intended to negate the significance of the phenomenon of racist violence and violence motivated by anti-Semitism and xenophobia, but rather to indicate that although there are a number of common factors that precipitate violence (Bjrgo and Witte 1993; Husbands 1993), understanding of the causes must be rooted in the specific spatial locations and the socioeconomic and political circumstances in which incidents occur.

The extent of racist violence, irrespective of whether it is on the increase, indicates that it is a significant social problem. The phenomenon necessitates the targeting of policy initiatives at the specific spatial, socioeconomic and political contexts in which violence occurs involving police, social services, education and housing authorities. But there are also some common policy measures, and particularly legislative measures, that transcend spatial boundaries. This chapter scrutinizes a number of such measures proposed by the institutions of the European Community. The scale of the problem of racist violence and the European Community policy response are first briefly discussed.

A 'rising tide' of racist violence?

The Commission of the European Communities observed in 1993 that 'nearly all countries report increased numbers of racist incidents and attacks on foreigners and individuals belonging to ethnic, racial or linguistic minorities' (CEC 1993: 7). In France, for instance, according to official statistics the number of incidents recorded each year has increased throughout the 1990s. Seven racially motivated murders were recorded in 1995 (Institute for Jewish Policy Research 1996: 117). In Germany there was a tenfold increase in the number of racist attacks between 1990 and 1991 (CEC 1993: 9). In 1996, 8,730 'far-right' offences were recorded by the Bundesamt für Verfassungschutz (Federal Office for the Protection of the Constitution) which included 2,232 offences against foreigners, although violent incidents against foreigners fell by nearly 20 per cent between 1995 and 1996 (Institute for Jewish Policy Research 1997: 162). In England and Wales the number of incidents recorded annually has risen throughout the 1980s and 1990s. In 1995–96, for instance, 12,222 incidents were reported to the police compared to 7,734 in 1992, and 4,383 in 1988 (UK Home Office 1997: 8). In the Netherlands the number of racist attacks and other incidents also appears to have risen across the early 1990s. In 1994 the number of incidents recorded by the Criminelle Inlichtingen Dienst (Criminal Investigation Service) nearly doubled. But there was no further increase in 1995 and a fall in the number of recorded incidents in 1996 (Institute for Jewish Policy Research 1997: 207).

In the context of the history of the movement of people into and across Europe the minority ethnic groups subjected to racist violence – Turkish communities and asylum seekers in Germany, North Africans in France, African-Caribbean and Asian communities in Britain, to name a few – are relatively recent settlers compared to other long-established communities. But even historically victimized groups such as Gypsy/Roma communities have recently been targeted in racist attacks. However, contemporary scholarly analyses of racist violence in Europe, published in the UK, largely concentrate on violence against black and Asian communities. Attention to violence against other communities, and particularly historically victimized groups, such as Gypsies and Jewish communities, has been limited. The neglect is significant in the light of arguments by some commentators that Gypsies, for instance, are the most 'vilified' minority in Europe (Brearley 1996: 3).

The collapse of communist regimes in eastern Europe in the 1990s and the associated decline in the authoritarian climate has provided fertile ground for historic enmity against Gypsies to surface with a new virulism in countries which include those on the 'fast track' to European Community membership. In the Czech Republic, for example, a number of murders have resulted from anti-Gypsy violence orchestrated by neo-Nazi groups, and far-right political parties have publicly demonstrated their hostility to Gypsies. In 1994, racist attacks tripled in number compared to the previous year, with the great majority targeted at Roma. In 1997 violence and discrimination against Roma in the Czech and Slovak Republics resulted in Roma seeking asylum in Canada, France and the United Kingdom. Violence and discrimination against Roma in other countries of central and eastern Europe have also produced similar movements of asylum seekers (Minority Rights Group International 1998). Extreme violence against Gypsies has also occurred in recent years in the member states of the European Community. In the early 1990s, thousands of Romany refugees in Germany, fleeing persecution in Romania, Poland, and the former Yugoslavia, were subject to forced repatriation, and many incidents of violence occurred (Brearley 1996: 22). In Italy in 1995 a five-year-old Roma boy in Pisa was maimed by a bomb hidden inside a children's book. The 'White Brotherhood' later claimed responsibility. In March 1995, two Romany children begging on the Pisa–Florence motorway were maimed by a bomb hidden inside a doll. In Austria, in February 1995, four Roma were killed in an explosion when trying to remove mock gravestones urging Gypsies to return to India placed near the entrance to their encampment. Responsibility for the murders was claimed by the 'Bavarian Liberation Army' (Brearley 1996: 15).

In many countries racism in the shape of hostility against visible minority ethnic groups has been far more extensive than anti-Semitism. Despite the lack of reliable evidence it is also apparent that in many countries the extent of anti-Semitic incidents appears to have peaked in the mid-1990s. Therefore, Jews in contemporary Europe are not a victimized group – at least compared to their past history of victimization and compared to the contemporary experience of other more visible minority ethnic communities. Nevertheless, many extreme incidents of anti-Semitism continue to occur in addition to everyday manifestations of hostility, and the extent of anti-Semitism remains a concern for many Jews. Hertzberg, for instance, argued in the early 1990s that 'Anti-Semitism may or may not be growing more virulent today, but every recent study, both in the United States and Europe, shows that at least seven out of ten Jews believe it has increased to the point where they should be particularly concerned about it.' (1993: 51).

In France, the beginning of the 1990s was marked by an extreme manifestation of anti-Semitism. On 10 May 1990, Jewish tombstones in Carpentras were desecrated and the body of a man buried two weeks earlier was disinterred and mutilated. The incident attracted widespread condemnation amongst the French population – many taking part in street demonstrations – and it was unequivocally condemned by the French government and broadcast media. But it was immediately followed by an escalation of anti-Semitic and racist incidents. However, compared to the consistent rise in reported racist incidents, there appears to have been no consistent trend in anti-Semitic incidents according to available statistics. Whilst there was decline in the number of reported anti-Semitic incidents overall, in 1994 a spate of incidents occurred in February and March of that year seemingly associated with the massacre of Muslims by a Jewish settler in Hebron. There was a further decline in incidents in 1995. In September of that year, though, in the first car bombing in mainland France since 1982, fourteen people, including six children, were injured when a bomb exploded outside a Jewish school in the Lyon suburb of Villeurbanne. Suspicion centred on the *Groupement islamique armé* – committed to the establishment of an Islamic state in Algeria and opposed to the French Government for its support of the ruling regime (Institute for Jewish Policy Research 1996: 122). In 1996, there was little change in the number of recorded anti-Semitic incidents compared to the previous year and events in Israel again appear to have provided a spark for a number of the incidents (Institute for Jewish Policy Research 1997: 148).

In the Netherlands, anti-Semitism has essentially been a residual problem (Institute for Jewish Policy Research 1993: 43) compared to the number of racist incidents, and there has been no consistent trend across the 1990s in terms of a rise or fall in the number of incidents. However, in 1994 three synagogues were attacked – possibly for the first time since the Nazi occupation of the Second World War. Two of the attacks occurred in February following the Hebron massacre. Swastikas were daubed on a monument to Dutch victims of the Sachsenhausen concentration camp at Vught in September on the day it was unveiled (Institute for Jewish Policy Research

1995: 171). The number of anti-Semitic incidents appears to have peaked in 1994 as only relatively minor incidents were reported in 1995 and only a few incidents reported in 1996 (Institute for Jewish Policy Research 1997). In Britain the Board of Deputies of British Jews reported a year-by-year rise in recorded anti-Semitic incidents up until 1994 and a decline since. In 1996 227 incidents were recorded with physical assaults constituting 6 per cent of the total (Institute for Jewish Policy Research 1997: 297).

It is not possible to make reliable comparisons between European countries about the extent of racist violence as recording processes and definitions of incidents vary. However, it is probably the case that in each country the number of reported incidents severely understates the real extent of violence. For example, the UK Home Office estimated on the basis of the British Crime Survey that nearly 382,000 racially motivated offences were committed in 1995 (over 30 times more than the number of incidents recorded by the police); of these 238,000 were committed against white people and 143,000 against people from black and Asian minority ethnic groups. For the minority ethnic groups the number of racially motivated offences represented 15 per cent of the estimated total number of offences committed against them, compared to 1 per cent for whites (Percy 1998: 16). The disparity between such survey findings and police statistics on racist incidents has been subject to little systematic research. Whilst some police forces have been increasingly sensitive in their handling of racist attacks, reported dissatisfaction with the police response in general to racist incidents (cf. Gordon 1993) provides some clues to the reasons for under-reporting by victims and for the under-recording of attacks by the police.

The European Community policy response

The extent of racist violence across the European Community member states has exposed the failure of many countries – and the European institutions – to ensure basic rights for substantial numbers of their citizens. As Social Affairs Commissioner Padraig Flynn argued in 1995: 'I do not believe that we can credibly claim to support the concept of a Citizen's Europe which, for example, sets welfare standards for farm animals but remains utterly silent on the subject of racism' (CEC 1995).

'Utterly silent' is perhaps an unfair accusation as the European Parliament, for instance, has expended considerable resources gathering evidence about racist violence from expert witnesses and others, and then making policy proposals first in the Evrigenis Report in the mid-1980s (European Parliament 1985), followed by the Ford Report in 1991 (European Parliament 1991), and most recently by the Kahn Report (European Parliament 1995). Policy implementation, had, however, been limited to the extent that the European Parliament Committee on Civil Liberties and Internal Affairs concluded in 1993 that 'despite repeated demands and recommendations it has made since 1986, Community measures against racism and anti-Semitism are still unsatisfactory' (European Parliament 1993). One of the strongest measures was the adoption in June 1986 of a Joint Declaration Against Racism and Xenophobia – by the European Parliament, the Council, representatives of member states meeting within the Council, and the Commission – which 'vigorously' condemns 'all forms of intolerance, hostility and use of force against persons or groups of persons on grounds of racial, religious, cultural, social or national differences'. But the impact of the Declaration was limited. It had no binding force as it was a declaration of principle only, rather than a recipe for policy intervention.

In October 1993 a 'Declaration and Plan of Action on Combating Racism, Xenophobia, Anti-Semitism and Intolerance' was adopted by the heads of states and governments of the 32 member states of the Council of Europe. The European Council meeting in Copenhagen in June 1993 also reiterated its resolve to challenge racism and xenophobia, and in December the European Parliament adopted a 'Resolution on Racism and Xenophobia' which called upon 'Member States to move on from making statements and declarations on racism and xenophobia and to adopt as soon as possible practical measures at national and Community level to combat the phenomenon, particularly by implementing special legislation'. In 1994, approval was given at the European Council meeting in Corfu in June to a Franco-German initiative to establish an overall policy strategy across the European Community. A Consultative Commission chaired by Jean Kahn was set up in September 1994 to formulate the strategy. It was instructed to 'make recommendations, geared as far as possible to national and local circumstances, on co-operation between governments and the various social bodies in favour of encouraging tolerance, understanding and harmony with foreigners'. The Consultative Commission's final report was produced for the Cannes European Council summit in June 1995 (European Parliament 1995) although the UK's representative Baroness Flather abstained from the report, finding some of the proposals 'particularly difficult to accept'.

The recommendations made by the Kahn Commission provide a starting point for potential legislative intervention against racist violence. But arguably many of the recommendations were formulated with a degree of generality that demonstrates little sensitivity to the conflicts over 'rights' which impede legislative provisions. Legal instruments against racism and anti-Semitism confront a dilemma of striking a balance between the potentially conflicting rights enshrined in international treaties of the right to freedom of expression and the right to the freedom of not being subjected to hatred on the basis of 'racial', ethnic, or religious identity, especially if the hatred leads to discrimination or violence. The conflicts involved are discussed below.

Legal instruments against violence motivated by racism, anti-Semitism and xenophobia

Outlawing 'racially motivated' violence

Many manifestations of racism and anti-Semitism, such as physical assaults, verbal threats, and damage to property, for instance, are generally prohibited by the criminal law in European countries irrespective of the motivation involved. There have been calls, however, to take account of motivation in the prosecution of incidents, and although the Kahn Commission stopped short of advocating the establishment of a specific offence of racially motivated violence, it did recommend penalty enhancement in cases of racially motivated crime (European Parliament 1995: 49). The UK Government has recently gone further by outlawing 'racially aggravated offences' (UK House of Lords 1997).

Calls for the establishment of a specific offence of racially motivated violence are usually justified on the grounds that the impact of the incidents concerned extends much further than the immediate acts committed, and constitute qualitatively more serious offences than the same acts of violence committed without such motivation. Proponents of legislation commonly argue that it would play an important role in setting standards of public behaviour, and provide an unambiguous expression of government and public abhorrence of the incidents concerned.

Some major objections have been raised in the UK, however, to legislation specifically outlawing racially motivated violence (UK House of Commons 1994a), and it is instructive to consider some of them with a view to evaluating the conflicts involved. Chiefly, the need to account for racist motivation raises fundamental questions of social justice in terms of potentially infringing the rights of the accused. It had been suggested in the UK, where courts have been required by the Criminal Justice Act 1991 (Part I, Sections 3(3) and 7(1)) to take racist motivation into account in sentencing, that a lesser burden of proof might be applied for deciding about motivation compared to evidence for the crime of violence for which the defendant is being tried. For instance, in voicing his opposition to legislation, Michael Howard, the UK Home Secretary in 1994, argued that the task of gathering evidence about racist motivation would provide 'an unnecessary complication' for the police and the prosecution to be able to prove it beyond reasonable doubt:

> After all, if there is a racial element in the offence, that is something which would have to be proved to the standard of the criminal burden of proof – beyond reasonable doubt. Whereas if the court is satisfied – without necessarily being satisfied to the same extent – that racial motivation was a factor, it could take it into account in sentencing. (UK House of Commons 1994b: 65–66)

Such a basis for penalty enhancement raises questions about the just treatment of offenders, as arguably a higher sentence should not be imposed unless a court is satisfied of culpability beyond reasonable doubt. Perhaps more fundamentally, though, evidence which might be used to justify penalty enhancement or to secure a conviction under an offence of racially motivated violence – perhaps membership of an extremist political organization, or things that the offender said before or after an incident, or even beliefs that they hold – may not in themselves be unlawful. The prosecution of racially motivated offences would therefore constitute restrictions on freedom of thought, expression and association, which had not been *a priori* proscribed. The justification of using such evidence must seriously be in doubt unless the offence is regarded as a distinct act in itself and not simply as an act of violence with the addition of the particular motivation. It would seem incautious to establish provisions for either penalty enhancement or to outlaw racially aggravated crimes without a more informed basis to policy development. There is a need to evaluate existing provisions for penalty enhancement – in countries where they exist – to determine the nature of evidence that might be used to indicate racist motivation, as well as any conflicts that such evidence might present in terms of the just treatment of offenders, the means by which evidence might legitimately be obtained, and the weight with which the evidence might be considered by the courts. All of these issues are yet to be explored by policy research.

Incitement

The Kahn Commission proposed that 'a clear prohibition on incitement to racial hatred should be explicitly and unequivocally included in the criminal law' (European Parliament 1995: 49). Behind such a call for the curbing of freedom of expression is perhaps the common-sense assumption that 'hate speech', or 'hate expression', leads to, or provokes, violence and discrimination.

Most countries in Europe, including former communist countries, have enacted laws against incitement to racial hatred, indicating broad approval for constraints on freedom of expression in cases where there is a probable association between hate expression and violence and disorder. There is, though, considerable variation across Europe in the degree to which laws against incitement are applied. In some countries – Denmark, France, Germany, and the Netherlands – the laws appear to have been actively applied, although the number of prosecutions accounts for a very small proportion of the number of recorded racist incidents (Kohl 1993).

In contrast, little use has been made of provisions against incitement to racial hatred in Great Britain and Northern Ireland (Colliver 1992). A fundamental limitation of the provisions in the Public Order Act 1986 outlawing incitement against racial hatred lies in the stringent – but yet ambiguous – language used to define exactly what is unlawful. The Act refers to the stirring up of racial 'hatred'. But 'hatred' is a very severe sentiment which may exclude many other reactions which might lead to unlawful behaviour. The Board of Deputies of British Jews has proposed in consequence that 'hatred' should be extended to include 'hostility or contempt' (UK House of Commons 1994b: 100). The Act also refers to the 'stirring up' of racial hatred, which implies an active instigation on the part of the offender, excluding milder impulsion such as encouragement or advocacy. Incitement is also defined to occur through the use of words or material which are 'threatening, abusive and insulting', and the strength of feeling conveyed by these words arguably excludes many relatively more moderate and subtle expressions, which could be just as likely to stir up racial hatred.

It is possible that many expressions, even very moderate expressions of dislike or prejudiced ideas, may either directly provoke or contribute to unlawful acts by striking a chord with particular individuals – who already adhere to such sentiments but needed a provocation to act on them – or, in combination with other expressions, have a cumulative effect for some individuals or, in a broader way, by contributing to societal norms which may eventually lead to unlawful behaviour. But to outlaw all these forms of expression would require draconian legislation, which would probably be practically unworkable, even if it were desirable. It would also shift the onus on to the predisposition of those who are provoked, rather than the intentions of those who provoke.

The ambiguities inherent in defining incitement may be removed by limiting provisions to the prohibition of expressions that are intended – or should have reasonably been anticipated – to lead directly to violence or other unlawful behaviour. The onus then would be on prosecuting authorities to prove the intent behind the words used, or in the absence of intent, an impact that should have been reasonably anticipated. The actual causal link between the words and subsequent unlawful action would also have to be proved or, in the absence of some action, the potential for action to be provoked would have to be demonstrated by reference to past experience. If the condition of impact is removed from the sentiments expressed, the law would serve to regulate the expression of ideas, beliefs, attitudes and opinions which in themselves would not be unlawful, unless they were already prohibited. If such a regulation was imposed, there would be a serious conflict with the rights to freedom of expression enshrined in international treaties and declarations and, in the extreme, it would arguably provide the potential for the repression of political rights and the rights of government critics.

If prohibitions against incitement to racial hatred are to be actively applied, ambiguities in legislative definitions about forms of expression defined as unlawful need to be resolved to provide clear parameters for police and prosecuting authorities. Arguably, to inform policy development, an evaluation needs to be made of the justifications used to circumscribe freedom of expression in countries where the condition of impact is absent from prohibition of expressions of 'hatred'. Similarly, an evaluation needs to be made to determine how rights to freedom of expression have been preserved, again, in countries where the condition of impact is absent.

Holocaust denial

The Kahn Commission called for the establishment of Holocaust denial legislation in all member states of the European Union, arguing that 'there should be specific offences of Holocaust-denial and the trivialisation of other crimes against humanity' (European Parliament 1995: 49). Holocaust denial might perhaps be regarded as a specific case of 'hate speech'. It has been outlawed in a number of European countries, most of them member states of the European Union (Austria, Belgium, France, Germany and Spain). Switzerland is the only non-EU country in Europe to have established such legislation. There is, however, little uniformity of provision in the countries where legislation has been established, with variation in the type of offence prohibited. There are differences in the provisions for bringing prosecutions and provisions for hearings, variation in the penalties that might be imposed, and variation in the relationship between Holocaust denial legislation and other legal provisions, such as laws against racial discrimination and incitement to racial hatred.

The case for outlawing Holocaust denial centrally rests upon a moral repugnance towards denial or distortion of the facts of the Holocaust. But repulsion alone arguably cannot justify prohibition, as there are countless other distortions of historical events, many also under the guise of academic scholarship, which are not subject to similar calls for prohibition. It would have to be demonstrated, therefore, that Holocaust denial is uniquely offensive. Such a requirement might be difficult to sustain when confronted by claims to prohibit other distortions of historical events. Or might a demarcation line be drawn to invalidate claims concerning events that occurred before a particular point in time? How might that time-point be decided? Whilst the Holocaust was unique in the modern industrialized world, there have been other cataclysmic acts of genocide, for instance, in Cambodia and more recently in Rwanda.

A refusal of competing demands for legislation would present a morally questionable proposition that the historical tragedy of one group is less serious than another. The definition of Holocaust denial would also be problematic as there are many more subtle ways of attempting to distort the historical record than boldly stating that the Holocaust was a lie. Very complex legislative provisions would be required to outlaw all of the possibilities, and in effect, the legislation would be defining historical truth. There is a need, therefore, for a wide-ranging debate about the merits of establishing legislation that would incorporate the prohibition of Holocaust denial in a broader framework of legislation against the trivialization of other crimes against humanity – as the Kahn Commission suggested. This would address some of the moral dilemmas discussed above, although the practical difficulties would remain.

Outlawing far-right groups

The conflict between the right to freedom of expression and the right to freedom from hatred on the basis of 'racial', ethnic, or religious identity has fuelled a controversy about whether far-right political organizations, whose members espouse and promote 'racial' hatred, should be banned (prohibitions against some far-right groups have been established in the Netherlands, Germany and Austria). The debate has been fuelled by the apparent growing support for such groups over the last decade; both for groups who participate in electoral processes and for those who eschew democratic politics, the links established by some groups across Europe and the Atlantic, and the involvement of some members of far-right groups in racist attacks.

Whilst the significance of far-right groups differs from country to country across Europe, they share a number of common perspectives, in particular, that there is an indigenous way of life and culture in their countries that is under threat by 'outsiders'; that there is an indigenous population in their countries who have a prior claim to jobs, housing and other social and welfare resources, ahead of 'outsiders', and that the presence of 'outsiders' constitutes a threat to the economic and social welfare of the indigenous population.

The Kahn Commission stopped short of calling for an outright ban, but it proposed that 'it should be possible within the law to curb the activities of groups with a record of racist activities, where those activities threaten the security or safety of ethnic minority groups' (European Parliament 1995: 49). Opponents of a ban argue that the prohibition of named groups would be practically ineffective as they would simply reappear under another name and, if they were forced underground, monitoring of their activities would be more difficult. Even more, a ban might create martyrs out of leaders of such organizations, and artificially inflate their significance in the public eye. There is perhaps, though, a more fundamental objection which reiterates much of the argument in this chapter. A ban on membership of many of the groups in question would constitute a prohibition of political expression on the basis of subscription to ideologies that in themselves are not unlawful. If members of far-right groups are involved in unlawful behaviour, such as violent attacks on minority communities, then their activities would be subject to the ordinary provision of the criminal law as discussed above, and provisions for incitement against racial hatred.

Conclusions

The proposed use of legal instruments against racism and anti-Semitism encounters a fundamental conflict between the right to freedom from hatred on the basis of 'racial', ethnic or religious identity, and the right to freedom of expression. The European Parliament's legislative proposals to date have provided little direction for resolving the conflict involved. As there is a dearth of comparative policy research on the potential, and the effectiveness, of legal instruments against racist violence and violence motivated by anti-Semitism and xenophobia, there is a need for policy learning from the measures that have been established. Legal instruments are not, of course, the only potential policy measures that could be used, but they potentially have a significant declaratory value. Legislation can play an important role in setting public moral standards. It can also provide a means of redress for victims of racist incidents. But legislation can only be effective if it is actively enforced; otherwise those who violate the law will soon realize that they can act with impunity.

References

Björgo, T. and Witte, R. (1993), *Racist Violence in Europe*, Basingstoke: Macmillan.

Brearley, M. (1996), *The Persecution of Gypsies in Contemporary Europe*, London: Institute for Jewish Policy Research.

Colliver, S. (ed.) (1992), *Striking a Balance: Hate Speech, Freedom of Expression and Non-discrimination*, London: Article 19.

CEC (Commission of the European Communities) (1993), *Legal Instruments to Combat Racism and Xenophobia*, Luxembourg: Office for Official Publications of the European Communities.

CEC (Commission of the European Communities) (1995), Press release IP/95/614 19 June, 'Commissioner Flynn calls for European legislation to combat racial discrimination'.

European Parliament (1985), *Committee of Inquiry into the Rise of Fascism and Racism in Europe*, Report on the findings of the inquiry (Evrigenis Report), Luxembourg: Office for Official Publications of the European Communities.

European Parliament (1991), *Committee of Inquiry on Racism and Xenophobia*, Report on the findings of the inquiry (Ford Report), Luxembourg: Office for Official Publications of the European Communities.

European Parliament (1993), *Report of the Committee on Civil Liberties and Internal Affairs on the Resurgence of Racism and Xenophobia in Europe and the Danger of Right-wing Extremist Violence* (DOC EN\RR\225\225100), Luxembourg: Office for Official Publications of the European Communities.

European Parliament, Committee on Civil Liberties and Internal Affairs, (1995), *Consultative Commission on Racism and Xenophobia* (DOC EN\CM\274\274586), Luxembourg: Office for Official Publications of the European Communites.

Gordon, P. (1993), 'The Police and Racist Violence in Britain', in Björgo, T. and Witte, R. (eds), *Racist Violence in Europe*, Basingstoke: Macmillan.

Hertzberg, A. (1993), 'Is Anti-Semitism Dying Out?', *New York Review of Books*, June 24, pp. 51–2.

Husbands, C. (1993), 'Racism and Racist Violence: Some Theories and Policy Perspectives', in Björgo, T. and Witte R. (eds), *Racist Violence in Europe*, Basingstoke: Macmillan.

Institute for Jewish Policy Research (1993), *Antisemitism World Report 1993*, London: Institute for Jewish Policy Research.

Institute for Jewish Policy Research (1995), *Antisemitism World Report 1995*, London: Institute for Jewish Policy Research.

Institute for Jewish Policy Research (1996), *Antisemitism World Report 1996*, London: Institute for Jewish Policy Research.

Institute for Jewish Policy Research (1997), *Antisemitism World Report 1997*, London: Institute for Jewish Policy Research.

Kohl, H. (1993), 'Freedom of Speech and Hate Expression: The German Experience', *New Community*, 20(1), pp. 147–54.

Miles, R. (1994), 'A Rise of Racism and Fascism in Contemporary Europe? Some Sceptical Reflections on its Nature and Extent', *New Community*, 20(4), pp. 547–62.

Minority Rights Group International (1998), *Roma/Gypsies: A European Minority, Update (March 1998)*, London: Minority Rights Group International.

Percy, A. (1998), 'Ethnicity and Victimisation: Findings from the 1996 British Crime Survey', *Home Office Statistical Bulletin*, Issue 6/98, London: Home Office.

Read, N. and Simpson, A. (1991), *Against a Rising Tide: Racism, Europe and 1992*, Nottingham: Spokesman/Nottingham Racial Equality Council and European Labour Forum.

UK Home Office (1997), *Racial Violence and Harassment. A Consultation Document*, London: Home Office.

UK House of Commons (1994a), *Racial Attacks and Harassment*, Home Affairs Committee, Third Report, Vol. I, London: HMSO.

UK House of Commons (1994b), *Racial Attacks and Harassment*, Home Affairs Committee, Third Report, Vol. II, London: HMSO.

UK House of Lords (1997), *Crime and Disorder Bill*, London: HMSO.

14 The International Migratory Movement of Women

Giovanna Campani

Sisterhood is powerful, but sisterhood can also be misleading unless contextualized. (Anthias and Yuval-Davis 1983)

Introduction

Women have always played an important part in the history of international migratory movements, shaping the composition of populations in countries and continents. It is estimated that 46 million people migrated to the United States between 1820 and 1970. From the nineteenth century to the Second World War, the ratio of women to men migrants was about one to three. After 1945, they were more numerous than men.

In nineteenth-century Europe, within rural–urban migrations women were more migratory than men. They became wet nurses, nannies, maids and workers in the cities. The images that literature has left of these migrant women are not as heroic as those of the colonial epoch or of the American frontier.

Until the middle of the nineteenth century, inter-European migrations can be considered as an international variant of regional migration. But, after the development of large industries, organized immigration was established, particularly in France, directing labour towards the industrial centres which needed it most. Though recruitment policies were mainly concerned with men, some economic sectors, such as the garment and glass industries and, of course, domestic service, demanded a female labour force. However, European historical research, relatively sparse on migratory movements in general, has said very little about these women's migrations.

After the Second World War, during the 1950s and 1960s, migration to northern Europe was largely planned as temporary, mobile labour, recruited mainly from southern Europe to work in industry and construction. In this model, women were not considered as subjects in the migratory process. Migratory policies considered immigrants as male without women and children. According to these policies, women followed men and deserved the dependent status of 'migrant's partner (companion)', corresponding to the juridical status given by family reunification laws. These expressed a patriarchal conception of gender and family relations. Consequently, women are forced by immigration laws into the role of wife, with their working lives constrained by minimum residential requirements before being allowed to work. On the other hand, women who come with a worker status are often hindered in their family life, by being forced to leave their families in the country of origin.

The model of temporary labour migration functioned only for a short period as processes of stabilization of immigrant groups could not be prevented. After the introduction of immigration control, around the mid-1970s, family reunification became an important way of entering Europe for non-communitarian citizens. A consequence of the stabilization process was the increase in the number of women arriving, the majority through family reunification. In the European Community, between 1960 and 1980, the percentage of women in the immigrant population increased from 30 to 45 per cent. There are now about six million migrant women, constituting almost half of the 12,800,000 migrants in Europe (Eurostat 1992). In spite of growing unemployment in the EU, the percentage of active immigrant women has increased since 1980 in almost all European countries (OECD 1992).

The context of international migration has changed. Nowadays, the world-wide dimension of diversified flows involve more and more countries and, in spite of closed borders, clandestine migrants and refugees who have precarious economic positions, often in the services industry. Women have become a more and more consistent part of these new flows. The internationalization of the labour market has shown a new tendency to draw on the cheap labour of women both in the Third World and in advanced societies. The new context is characterized by the re-emerging demand for migrant women in traditional women's jobs, as domestic workers and in the sex industry. Old and new are mixed in the present phase. After the crisis in the welfare state and policies of structural adjustment, we are witnessing the simultaneous revival of high-risk capitalism, processes of world-wide cultural homogenization and sweeping changes in women's status and role in the developing societies from where migrant women now come. Migration is an integral part of the process of the structural transformation of developing societies, and is pertinent for understanding social change in general and gender roles in particular.

There has been a shift in the perception of migrant women from passive followers of their husbands to independent actors, due to the increasing number of migrant women, their growing presence in the labour market and, under the influence of feminism which made gender a primary focus of attention within the theory and practice of the human sciences (Anthias and Yuval-Davis, 1992), placing it at the centre of political struggle. This shift first took place in the United States, later in the UK, and then was slowly followed by the rest of northern Europe and, finally, by southern Europe. In the US and UK, one reason why reflections on the relationship between gender, ethnicity, race and class were developed earlier and went further than in France and in Germany, is precisely the existence of a 'black feminism', involving immigrant and minority women.

Black feminism developed a critique both of white feminism, accusing it of ethnocentrism, and a Marxist approach to gender and class which either ignored race or reduced it to a dependent variable. Within the last decade, class, race and gender have become the new 'trinity formula' within the area of 'race relations'. The critique of white feminism, proposing a model of women which connects race, gender and class, has allowed the relationship between migration and social change to be considered in terms of gender roles in a complex and subtle way, going beyond the model of Western culture as the only possible model for immigrant women's emancipation.

The position of migrant women must be analysed within the context of gender relations, paying attention to the way in which gender and class processes differentially affect women from different ethnic and racialized social groups. This chapter tries to develop some of the issues involved in women's migrations and their position in receiving labour markets. The new context of international migration and its impact on women's migration is also analysed, with particular attention paid to France and Italy. Finally, integration policies and problems, particularly at local level, taking these two countries as examples, are discussed.

Migration, gender, race and ethnicity

The concepts used in the sociology of migrations often have a contested status, being embedded in ideological constructions connected to different criteria and policies of inclusion/exclusion of migrant groups. Examples are the term *gastarbeiter* (instead of *fremdarbeiter*) used in Germany, black and ethnic minority as used in Britain, *extra-comunitari* in Italy and *minoritées immigrées* in France.

Miles and Rathzel distinguish between migrant and immigrant:

> The former usually refers to a person who is spatially mobile, either within a nation-state or between nation-states, while the latter identifies a person who enters and becomes a permanent resident in a nation-state, other than his or her birth. A difficulty arises in that many 'migrants' subsequently become 'immigrants' while many 'immigrants' do not in fact settle as originally intended. Moreover, these transitions are less to do with personal choices and more a function of state intervention. Hence, we shall use the two notions interchangeably to refer to any person who is spatially mobile across a national boundary. (1991: 2)

Both macro- and micro-approaches are constantly present in the sociology of migrations. The micro-approach is particularly important in understanding the social action of migrant women in the context of macro-trends, as well as their subjective perspective to migration, for example, as rupture from the traditional social boundaries.

To understand processes involving migrant women, for example, their position in the labour market of the receiving society, it is important to connect gender with race and class. Feminist research has shown that so-called sexual roles change from one culture to another and were therefore not produced by the 'natural and universal' difference of sex. Gender is a socially constructed category, questioning the 'essentialist and universalist idea that biology is destiny' (Stolcke 1992: 89).

The category of gender means a critique of the process of naturalization of social differences and social discrimination: 'Gender and race, unlike class, relate to a particular representation of a "biological", "physiognomic" or "natural" difference. The importance of the material reality of economic relations and other political and ideological relations will produce however different organizing principles at different times' (Anthias and Yuval-Davis 1992: 112).

According to Stolcke (1992), in modern Western society, there is an homology and an ideological–political boundary between the notions of sex and race, gender and ethnicity: both construct and justify social discrimination and gender discrimination, imputing them to supposed 'natural' facts: 'The main character of the class society in this aspect is the general tendency to naturalize social inequality' (Stolcke 1992: 100).

Wallerstein tries to explain racism and sexism starting from the productive processes, which are at the origin of class society. He considers racism and sexism necessary to the present division of labour in the capitalist world economy (Balibar and Wallerstein 1990). Racism means ethnicization of the labour force: a part of the labour force is condemned to particular types of unpleasant jobs and to low wages – meritocratic criteria alone would not justify this relegation in these jobs and wages. Women are not only discriminated against in jobs and wages but also undertake an important amount of unrecognized work to allow reproduction in households where wages are so low that they would not ensure the survival of the family without the free work of women, the young and old people. Homework has been historically determined by industrialism and, in both its capitalist and so-called 'socialist' forms, has given proletarian women the task of reproducing, looking after and maintaining the labour force.

It is important to consider how class divisions are concretely articulated through gender and race. Women of the upper class take part in the oppression of women of the lower class; areas and sectors of insertion in the labour market vary from one ethnic group to another and inside each group, women's position can differ. Thus, Anthias and Yuval-Davis (1992) affirm that class difference is not only grounded in the productive processes, but is also historically constructed in relation to the history of race and gender.

The specific forms of inequality and discrimination connecting with and articulating class, race and gender must be analysed in each historical and societal context. Consequently, it is problematic to refer to an essentialist idea of femininity or women's experience as opposed to masculinity or male experience, ignoring class and race differences.

As far as immigrant women are concerned, it is not enough to describe the discrimination they suffer as a 'triple burden' (class, race and gender) because 'it treats forms of subordination and oppression through race, sex and class as cumulative rather than articulating or intersecting together to produce specific effects' (Anthias and Yuval-Davis 1992: 100).

To understand the specific situation of migrant women in the receiving countries, we consider two sets of gender relations, the one of the receiving society and the one of the immigrant group. Gender relations are not static: on the contrary, migration is often connected to social change affecting gender relations and women's role and status, particularly in developing countries. We have then to consider the impact of this double set of gender relations in the distribution of immigrant women in the labour market and in the integration processes:

> Gender stratification in the host country affects not only nationals, but also immigrant women. Gender stratification refers to a system of ranking in which males are favoured incumbents in positions of authority and responsability. With reference to labour markets of industrial economies, it also means stereotyping of occupations as 'women's work' or 'men's work' and, in general, a

> monetary devaluation of women's work. The result is that migrant women are found in some jobs and not in others as a result of their gender, nationality (or race) and class. (Boyd 1991: 5)

Given the existence of gendered and racialized labour markets, and of sexism and racism in the receiving societies, emigration does not necessarily mean progress for women from the rural sending societies, nor does it open the way to emancipation from the oppression of traditional societies. Migration for women means a mix of gains and losses – this is particularly true in that migration laws often constrain women in the role of either wife or worker, making the other more difficult. To paraphrase Alba De Cespedes, 'nobody turns back', or retraces her steps: the issues for a better life are not in the traditional 'community', but in overcoming the present situation using a combination of cultural values, belonging to different worlds. In any case, white feminists cannot answer for black and immigrant women, who must find their own ways, starting from their complex position as social actors.

International migration and the demand for women's labour

Contemporary international migration movements differ from earlier migrations to northern Europe from the 1950s to the 1970s when immigration controls were tightened. Migrations now have a world-wide dimension, reaching regions which had not been or had been scarcely touched until now, both as sending and receiving countries. Asia has become a continent of migration, including countries like Japan where immigration was unknown. Eastern Europe is again becoming a region of emigration, after a long period of closed borders.

In Europe, we are now witnessing the natural growth of already established immigrant groups and the diversification of new flows, including flows to former emigration countries, such as Italy, Spain and Greece. Different authors have tried to determine what variables are new and what remains unchanged, compared to the past, both at the macro- and the micro-level. Melotti (1990), for instance, considers present migrations not as a traditional labour migration, but as a general population movement from South to North, following the socioeconomic breakdown of the Third World and, more recently, eastern Europe. This approach considers immigration in terms of North–South relations,with the South increasingly marked by poverty, worsening economic conditions, civil wars and social conflicts.

According to this analysis, push factors are much more important than pull factors. Furthermore, European labour markets no longer need immigrants. Thus, in the Western world, migration coexists with unemployment. Policies of closed borders and the drastic filtering of new arrivals are the sad response to these unwanted flows. The consequence is the growing importance of clandestine migration, with the only possibilities of legally entering Europe now being either family reunification or refugee status, which is increasingly difficult to achieve.

An alternative approach focuses on socioeconomic changes taking place in the receiving societies. These include changes in national and international labour markets due to industrial restructuring, increasing flexibility in productive processes, the development of the informal economy, tertiarization and segmentation of labour markets.

Venturini (1989) writes that migration flows are no longer attracted by an overall quantitative imbalance in the labour markets of receiving countries but rather by sectorial imbalances which may even arise in situations of unemployment. It results from the 'segmentation' process in labour markets and applies mainly to jobs at either the lowest or highest rungs of the occupational ladder. Thus, in spite of high unemployment among local populations, there are areas in European labour markets where there is still a demand for an immigrant labour force, particularly for female labour. Present international migration flows show a significant rise in female participation. This is a major trend with, of course, national variations. Women now represent nearly half of the world's migrant population. While this rise is partly due to family reunification, the number of active women migrating alone for employment purposes is also increasing. Flows of active women in the international labour market correspond both to a slackening in the international demand for male labour, and to a growing demand for traditional female jobs (Lim 1989). At the same time, socioeconomic changes in the industrial countries, including loss of social security and of 'guaranteed' jobs, create new space for the employment of immigrant women in labour-intensive sectors, mainly in the textile and garment industries. This involves immigrant women of both the new flows and established ones. The employment of immigrant women in European and international labour markets reveals one of the main aspects of the new migratory process: the economic transfer of immigrants from the industrial sector to the service sector, including services to private persons and to the informal economy.

The increase in the number of women immigrants is just one of the changes in the composition of migrant groups and flows. The number of immigrants with high school qualifications, and those from urban areas, is also increasing. There are more women, more students and more middle-class migrants.

In Third World countries, social and cultural changes are destroying social, and cultural barriers to emigration. For example,the restructuring of the traditional family, 'anticipatory socialisation' through the mass media; and, in general, the diffusion of Western models through consumption, life-styles and urbanization. ('Anticipatory socialisation', developed by Alberoni and Baglioni (1965), refers to the fact that immigrants from south to north Italy already knew, through the mass media, the socioeconomic reality existing in the north and thus, were prepared for it.) The micro-approach reveals the importance of emancipatory motivations, influenced by dreams of the West, among the reasons for departure, particularly for women.

Domestic work

Internationally, there is a growing demand for traditional female jobs such as maids, nurses and entertainers. Immigrant women have traditionally been recruited for domestic work. In the present situation, the internationalization of flows is not influenced by proximity and/or traditional boundaries between sending and receiving countries. For example, there are maids from the Philippines in Kuwait and from Peru, in Italy. Greece, Italy and Spain recruit foreign maids, as do both the rich industrialized Asian countries, such as Hong Kong and Singapore, and the 'oil monarchies' of Saudi Arabia, Kuwait, United Arab Emirates, Bahrain and Oman. Latin America though has the world's highest percentage of household employees. After a period of decline, services to private persons, including female domestic staff, gardeners and chauffeurs, has revived jobs which had almost disappeared within industrial Europe during the postwar years.

Women of some national origins are 'more migratory' than others and more 'specialized' than others in services to private persons. These include women from the Philippines, Sri Lanka, Eritrea, Cape Verde, Mauritius and Salvador. This is due both to economic and cultural factors and to the migratory policies of the countries of origin. For example, the women who presently constitute half of Filipino 'overseas contract workers' are spread all over the world as maids, nurses and entertainers. Data for the period 1980–86 shows an increase in Filipino women migrants from 36 per cent in 1980 to 46 per cent in 1986. In Asia, particularly Hong Kong, Singapore and Japan, 90 per cent of Filipino workers are women, mainly maids, nurses and entertainers. Filipino maids are also in the Gulf and Saudi Arabia and in Europe. The migration of Filipino women is influenced by the processes of change in women's status in the Philippines, for instance, women's schooling (many cleaning women have college degrees), and women's position in the labour market (male wages are still higher). In addition, high unemployment means that there are few possibilities of finding a job at all, and many Filipinos have internalized a Western consumption model. The government of the Philippines also encourages emigration to obtain foreign currency: 'Worldwide, 3.2 million Filipinos labour abroad and send home about $ 3 billion – no mean sum' (*The Nation*, 5 October 92).

Sri Lanka also encourages women's migration, particularly to the Middle East, through official government bureaux for the placement of domestic workers abroad. There is great pressure on women to leave, even though their experience in the Middle East is often unfavourable. Thailand has also become a country of emigration, exporting maids and entertainers, mainly to Hong Kong, Singapore and Japan, but also to western Europe and the Middle East. The authorities in Bangkok are starting to worry about a shortage of housemaids for rich Thai families, as maids are better paid in Hong Kong than in Bangkok. Western 'anticipatory socialization' and the destructuration of traditional family structures through mass Western tourism and the sex industry has also encouraged migration.

Mauritius has a long tradition of exporting maids to Europe. Since the 1970s, Cape Verde has supplied maids to rich families in Italy. The Catholic Church, and especially the Capuchine Fathers have played an important role in channelling this immigration. Cape Verde women also work as maids in Spain and Portugal while Portuguese women are still domestic helpers in France and Britain but are seldom live-in maids. Since the 1960s, Eritrea has furnished domestic helpers for rich Italian families. Following their civil war, Somali women arrived in Italy to work, mainly as maids.

Latin American women migrate both within South America, for example, from Colombia to Venezuela, or from Bolivia to Argentina, and to western Europe. In Italy, since the 1970s, maids have been recruited from Salvador and, more recently, from Peru.

Women do not generally migrate alone from the Islamic countries, but there are exceptions, for example, Egyptian women going to the Middle East as nurses, teachers and maids. Indonesian women go to Singapore as maids, as do Muslim Sri Lankan women.

According to *The Manila Bulletin* (1 January 1990 and 20 February 1990), there are 3,000 Filipino maids in London and around 100,000 in Italy; 81,000 in Hong Kong (*The Nation*, 5 October 1992); and between 30,000 and 35,000 in Singapore (*The Straits Times*, 18 April 1990). There are about 6,000 Thai maids in Hong Kong (*Bangkok Post*, 4 February 1990) and as many in Singapore (*The Straits Times*, 18 April 1990). There are around 250,000 Sri Lankan maids in East Asia and the Middle East (*Sunday Morning Post Magazine*, 3 December 1990). Before the Gulf War, there were 86,000 Sri-Lankan women (80 per cent maids) in Kuwait (*Arab Times*, 20 December 1989). In 1985, there were more than 63,000 maids in Kuwait, comprising around 60 per cent of immigrant women labour.

The Anti-Slavery Society (1990) estimates that there are between 30,000 and 60,000 foreign female domestic workers in Britain, mainly from the Philippines, Colombia, Nepal, India and Sri Lanka. In Italy, the INPS (National Institute for Social Security) data speaks of 220,000, legally resident, foreign maids (more than 52.2 per cent) in 1989. They come from the Philippines, Eritrea, Cape Verde, Sri Lanka, Mauritius and Salvador. In Spain, Ministry of the Interior data on legal non-national residents show that from 1980 to 1988, the number of Asians increased from 13,240 to 24,747. More than 90 per cent of Asians work in the domestic sector (Weinert 1991). In Portugal, immigration is mainly composed of PALOP (*Paises de Expressao Oficial Portuguese*), from Angola, Cape Verde, Guinée Bissau, Mozambique and Sao Tomé. In 1988, the Services for Foreigners of the Ministry of the Interiors, gave the number of 38,900 regular residents from the PALOP, 69 per cent being from Cape Verde. An estimate, combining different sources, speaks of around 60,000 irregular immigrants (Do Ceu Esteves 1992). As we have noted already, among Cape Verde immigrants there are many women, mainly working as domestic helpers. In Greece, immigrant maids are mostly Asian, largely from the Philippines. While working conditions for maids vary from one country to another, 'the general picture emerging from the literature, research work and newspaper reports, is that foreign female domestic workers are highly exploited both in the developed and in the developing countries' (Weinert 1991: 2).

As resident women now refuse to undertake live-in domestic work, foreign women have been substituted and have revived this job in industrial countries where it had been in decline in the postwar years. Nowadays, there is a broadening of the social groups demanding maids: 'The increasing phenomenon of migrant women working as domestic servants can equally be attributed to the growing wealth of the rich countries, enabling families to pay for households; a demand that cannot be met by the resident workforce, owing to the work's low social status, low pay and precarious working conditions' (Weinert 1991). In fact, the phenomenon is complex and can be attributed to different factors, including the development of professional activity and mobility among resident women without the corresponding provision of adequate social services. There is a clear connection between the lack of social services, particularly for children and old people, and the increase in demand for immigrant maids in Italy and Greece. This is reflected in governmental policies which, in spite of closed borders, issue entry visas to immigrants arriving on domestic work contracts, as Italy did until 1990. In Singapore, the government openly, 'recognizes that hiring foreign maids helps to encourage our women, especially those with marketable skills and qualifications, to continue working and raise families' (*The Straits Times*, 20 December 1989). In fact, Singapore tries to discourage the growing demand for maids by imposing a monthly tax on domestic workers. But it has exempted married women who work, as well as professional women who are widows and divorced, recognizing the social function maids perform in relation to the national women's professional life (*The Straits Times*, 20 December 1989). With reference to Italy, Pugliese adds another element:

> On the one hand, the recourse to maids is a necessity, determined by the lack of social services in our country: families with just one parent or with both parents working are forced to look for this type of service. On the other hand, the preference for an archaic relationship with the maid, available all day long, expresses a certain type of mentality, reaffirming old habits which, with the civil development of our country during the sixties, seemed largely overcome. (1991: 57)

Pugliese's observations would seem to be widely applicable, particularly in southern Europe. The master–servant relationship decribed by Pugliese is also the product of a too-rapid 'modernization', without the progressive interiorization of the values expressed by what we could call the 'social democratic' model of industrial society. It is not by chance that in Sweden and Denmark, live-in domestic work has practically disappeared. The Italian middle class and *petit bourgeoisie* whose high living standards are recently acquired, still consider maids as a status symbol. Paradoxically, this mentality combines the old and new: it corresponds in fact to the new ideologies glorifying the free market, privatization and individualism. Present policies encouraging privatization, the demolition of public services and cuts in state expenditure, have led to a decline in social services for children and old people which allowed women to work and, thus, have indirectly favoured the development of privately provided services. The recourse to immigrant maids by the women of the 'rich' world contributes to the oppression of women from poor countries, which risks polarizing the relationship between white women, who are increasingly entering the professions, and ethnic minority women, who are at the bottom.

The sex industry

The sex industry is flourishing all over the world and is recruiting more and more immigrant women from Asia, Africa, eastern Europe and Latin America. In Asia, Japan is the main recruiter of immigrant women for the 'entertainment industry' from Southeast Asia (the Philippines and Thailand). According to Japanese sources, annually around 50,000 women are officially recruited. There is also extensive recruitment of illegal female workers who are promised high-paying, respectable jobs but end up in the underworld of prostitution rackets.

According to POEA (Philippines Overseas Employment Agency) sources, between 1975 and 1987, there were 167,155 work contracts issued for Filipinos to Japan of whom 95 per cent were women 'entertainers'. In the same period, total contracts for 'entertainers' reached 172,465, 95 per cent of them for Japan. The remaining 5 per cent were distributed between Singapore, Hong Kong, the Middle East, Italy and Greece (PASEI *Gazette*, vol. l, No.l, 5/90).

The abuse of Asian women migrating to Japan is very often denounced by the Asian press:

> Upon arrival, they are 'sold' to the managers of bars and clubs for over US$ 20,000. It was argued that in order to recoup this fee most managers forced women into prostitution. Moreover, the women did not receive the wages they were officially promised. The club managers routinely confiscated the women's passports and return tickets and threaten to reveal their illegal status if they complain. Legal recourse is exceedingly difficult because the women are purposely ill-informed concerning the identity of their recruiters and even their bosses. This problem is compounded by their lack of knowledge of the Japanese language. Even in the rare circumstances that legal action is taken, women are usually deported prior to their case being heard. It was argued that the root of the problem is fourfold: (l) the basic violation of the human rights of illegal workers even by those in authority – rather than being seen as persons whose rights have been violated, they are seen as criminals; (2) discrimination against foreigners in a basically xenophobic society; (3) discrimination against Asians who hold lower status in Japan than other foreigners; and (4) discrimination against females in general which is a reflection of the low status of women in Japanese society. (Appleyard et al. 1992)

The 'entertainer' traffic to Japan is just one aspect of the global sex industry. In Europe, the number of immigrant women in prostitution is growing because of the development of trafficking from Eastern Europe, Africa and Latin America.

Immigrant women and the European labour market

A distinction needs to be made between immigrant women already settled and who generally came through family reunification, their daughters, the so-called second generation, and the women arriving with the new flows. There are also distinctions to be made according to national groups and within the EU, between migrant women coming from member countries, mainly from Portugal, Spain, Greece, Italy and from countries outside of the EU, largely from the Third World and eastern Europe, whose citizens are 'third class workers in the European hierarchy', as pointed out by Phizaklea (1992).

European labour markets are of course racialized and gendered, and labour market discrimination concerns all women. Women's activity rate is lower than that for men; women show a much higher tendency to work part-time, are concentrated in some sectors, mainly services, and are disproportionately found at the bottom of the pay scale. The unemployment rate is higher for women than for men in all European countries with the exception only of Britain (EUROSTAT 1992). Since the mid-1970s, at the European Community level, an effort has been made to improve women's situation in professional life. Different directives of the Council of the Ministers of the European Community (1975, 1976, 1978, 1986) have promoted the principle of equal salaries, equal opportunities to accede to employment, vocational education, professional promotion and work conditions, including the self-employed. The success of these actions is uncertain, but, in any case, these efforts to improve women's situation have excluded immigrant and minority women.

All over Europe, in the 1980s, the number of foreign workers has increased and, in spite of high women's unemployment, immigrant women have increasingly entered the labour market. This is because of the arrival of flows of active women and because immigrant women already settled and 'second-generation' girls are both increasingly choosing to work. 'Even when family reunification has prompted migration, the desire of wives to enter the labour force quickly turns family migration into a form of labour migration' (Boyd 1991: 3).

In all European countries, the lowest percentage of foreigners is in administration, a sector generally open only to nationals. They are more likely to be found in construction, manufacturing and in generally unskilled jobs than the native-born although unemployment rates are not necessarily always higher for foreigners. As far as women are concerned, their position in the labour market is generally worse than that for men.

Phizaklea(1992) points to the risk of polarization between highly qualified people and those with limited or no skills: this polarization appears even more evident among women. On the one hand, there is a movement of European women into managerial and professional jobs and, on the other, immigrant women are clustered at the bottom of the economic scale. Europe is reproducing a tendency which appeared clearly in the United States in the 1980s among white and black women.

The informal economy is developing all over Europe, not only in countries where it is traditionally important, like Italy. It segments the labour market, generating patterns of flexibility following the crisis of the Fordist–Taylorist model. It could be argued that these changes – segmentation of production, diversification of economic activities which reflect a proliferation of small and medium-sized self-employed activities, the development of subcontracting chains at the time when big manufacturing complexes are concentrating and automating their operations, and, simultaneously cutting back on their requirements for directly employed workers – have had the effect of stimulating self-employment which has increased in the 1980s, after a period of decline between 1969 and 1979 (Palidda, 1991). In the 1980s, self-employment has increased more or less evenly in all European countries.

The increase concerns immigrants who traditionally oriented themselves towards self-employment. Nowadays there is an interaction between economic change and immigrants' social action and dynamism – a mixture of negative and positive factors in the development of self-employment among immigrants in general and immigrant women in particular. Certainly, the self-employed activities of both immigrants and native-born citizens often alternate between the official and unofficial economy. Indeed the problem of legal regulation of economic and social relationships arises in more or less all European countries, precisely because the economic changes which have taken place have generated patterns of flexibility which are difficult to monitor (Palidda 1991).

Considering the economic context which is characterized by patterns of flexibility generating the informal economy, illicit work and exploitation, and the tendency towards the immersion of economic activities into social relations systems (family/networks/'work at home', etc.),it is little wonder that women are the first victims of the lack of social guarantees and of overwork in self-employment. On the other hand, we also have to consider the development of self-employment among immigrant women. On this point, opinions differ.

Palidda considers that the immigrant today is

> ... no longer the illiterate or semi-literate labourer of former times. He [*sic*] has a new sensitivity to technological innovation, and he seems to be increasingly ready to adapt to new professions. The self-employed worker of immigrant origin who minimises his risk and reinvests his profits in property rather than in his trade is tending to disappear. (Palidda 1991: 7).

Morokvasic's research on self-employed women presents a glowing picture:

> I had in front of me brave and determined women, women not being afraid of risks. For some of them, 'everything can be done'. They possess the character necessary to every person – woman or man, immigrant or not – wanting to start

> business. Still, they are not, and they do not think that they are 'exceptional'. Often just surviving, they appreciate independence in their activities and they wouldn't change it against a more comfortable material situation through waged work. (1988: 103)

More pessimistically, Anthias (1991: 30) remarks that, in Britain, 'self-employment is largely structured by lack of opportunities in paid employment either as a result of racism or the result of limited educational or other skills in relation to the requirements of the labour market.' Anthias refers to case studies showing that Asians and Cypriots turn to self-employment as a viable alternative to limited job opportunities. According to Anthias, networks and familial relations are central factors in understanding self-employment. Traditional kinship structures, for example in Asian and Mediterranean societies, and their familial ideology, allow for successful self-employment. But this can also mean exploitation of women and children who help in the family business.

Morokvasic suggests that in the cultures of origin, there is not only a familial ideology but also cultural elements and competences specific to women:

> They have recourse to their original knowledge and for their commercial or productive activity they give value to some elements of their culture which would remain unknown ... Oriental dance, latin, chinese or indian cooking, 'afro' coiffure ..., 'black' beauty products, Portuguese food, etc. ... all this is part of the everyday life in the big European cities. (1988: 104)

Integration policies at the European level

The present European migratory model seems to be characterized by policies of closed borders and integration measures for immigrants already living in the country. Integration policies, however, face difficulties caused by rising xenophobia and racism in all European countries.

Questions concerning immigration from outside the EU, the rights of refugees and freedom of movement inside the EU, are dealt with by non-elected organizations such as the Schengen Group of Ministers, the Trevi Group and the Ad hoc Working Group on Immigration.

Three aspects of integration policies are examined: naturalization laws, school insertion for children and social insertion. Naturalization laws within Europe differ between those countries preferring the *jus sanguinis* (nationality through 'filiation' as in Germany or Luxemburg) and those practising the *jus solis* as in France, Holland or Britain. School insertion has given rise to a debate around different recommendations by the European Community and the European Council, including the possibility of immigrant children keeping their language and culture of origin. Interest in immigrant women has in effect started with the problem of schooling. The difficulties immigrant children face in the different European school systems has pointed to the importance of the role of the mother.

While in Britain and Holland it is a question of integration policies for ethnic minorities, France is more concerned with the integration of individuals than of groups. The fields of intervention include: immigrant children's schooling, the retraining of the long-term unemployed, promotion of some categories of the population including women, the young and those with qualifications, housing, and health services, as well as campaigns against discrimination.

Women are considered a special category. There is still no general European policy addressing immigrant women other than recommendations concerning laws on family reunification. Measures on equal opportunities for women do not specifically address the issue of immigrant women.

The case of France

Since the nineteenth century, France has been a country of immigration, due to both labour shortages and demographic needs. These needs became particularly urgent because of France's heavy losses during the First World War. As a result, French governments have had fairly liberal policies in terms of family reunification which encouraged women's immigration. France always held to the *jus solis* policy, dating back to the French Revolution, allowing for the naturalization of immigrants' children. Italians and Belgians migrated to France in the last century, Italians and Spanish between the two World Wars, again Italians and Spanish after the Second World War, followed by the Portuguese. Since the middle of the 1960s, the most important groups of immigrants came from the Maghreb (Algeria, Morocco, Tunisia).

From the 1950s onwards, the majority of immigrant women arrived through family reunifications: Italian and Spanish first, Portuguese and Maghrebians during the 1970s. Presently, family reunification is the main way to get into France. In 1990 women formed 45 per cent of the total immigrant population. The fact of entering through family reunification schemes does not mean that immigrant women did not enter the French labour market: their labour rate was quite high in the years after World War II, reaching 32 per cent in 1946 but declined in the following years before rising again in the 1980s.

In France, immigrant women are more likely to be found in manufacturing than French women, twice as likely to be unemployed and less likely to be found in the more 'desirable' sectors of women's work. Nevertheless, the gap between French and foreign women's job levels has at an aggregate level shrunk over the last decade (Phizacklea 1992).

To analyse their insertion into the labour market, we have to consider nationality and the distinction between foreign and naturalized women for each national group. We have also to consider the importance of unofficial and undeclared work, including domestic work, child care and family businesses, which is much higher among immigrant than French women. Analysing an old immigrant group, the Italians, Palidda (1992) considers that it is important to distinguish between immigrant women who remain foreign nationals and those who become naturalized and whose labour rate is higher than that of French women. The labour rate of immigrant women has varied in time and according to nationality.

In France, there exists an image of Muslim women as passive and completely dependent on their husbands and children and who are not allowed to work outside of the family because of familial constraints. The culturalist explanation is, however, insufficient to explain the low labour rate of Maghrebian women: we also have to consider the articulation between gender, race and class which is at work here. Gender relations inside and outside the community must be considered but also class position and local labour markets. We have also to consider the tension involved in change which characterizes, if not all immigrant Maghrebian women, at least some of them: their daughters go to school developing a strategy of emancipation typical of all girls and succeed much better than their brothers.

The case of Italy

Italy was a country of emigration until the end of the 1960s, the flows being mainly directed from southern Italy to Germany and Switzerland. During the 1970s, limited flows of immigrants started to arrive: political refugees from Latin America, Vietnam and Eritrea; 'border immigrants', for example, Tunisians in Sicily working on fishing boats and in agriculture, Yugoslavs in Frioul and Trieste working mainly in construction; maids from Cape Verde, Eritrea, Mauritius, Salvador and, later, the Philippines and Sri Lanka. Maids were given a special resident permit which did not allow them to change jobs. Women were among the first to arrive in Italy and always constituted an important part of immigration because of the high demand for maids.

In comparison with other European countries, Italy has a particularly large informal economy and greater segmentation of the labour market. Italy's labour market acts to encourage illegal immigration. In Italy, immigrants mainly enter the informal economy, either taking jobs Italians have abandoned or creating new jobs for themselves, as in the case of street-vendors. The occupational areas which attract foreign immigrants are hawking, domestic work, small cleaning enterprises, catering and so forth, in the tertiary sector, and fisheries and some agricultural activities, in the primary sector. Recently, the industrial sector has started to absorb immigrants, but the process is limited to some regions and sectors, for example foundries.

Women are mainly employed in the domestic sector, as live-in domestic helpers. This specific type of insertion has not allowed immigrant women to have an independent family life. Almost all of them have either left their children at home with their families or have left them in institutions. In some national groups, as the Filipinos or Cape Verdians, the ratio of men to women is very unbalanced as women constitute between 70–90 per cent of the population. Invisible to Italian society – with the exception of their free days, usually Thursday and Sunday afternoon – immigrant women have developed a limited social life involving informal networks (female members of families, sisters, cousins, aunts, 'friendship groups') or formal associations, supported by the Church or by the trade unions. Mobility for immigrant women is rare and, given the present critical situation of the Italian economy, prospects for the future do not appear hopeful.

There has been a passage from live-in domestic work to domestic help but even this small professional promotion has been limited by the difficulties and expense encountered in finding accommodation. A further possibility is employment as nurses in hospitals. Some, especially Filipinos, already work in private clinics. But, as conditions of entry to Italian schools of nursing are very strict and, because of the employment crisis, this possibility will probably vanish.

In contrast to economically active women who arrived alone in Italy over the last twenty years, family reunification is very recent, dating back to Law 943 of 1988 and Law 39 of 1990. It is very limited because of the precarious situation of male immigrants who are unable to guarantee a stable job and accommodation. This migration mainly concerns women from the Maghreb.

A special case is the one of Chinese immigrants, coming directly from the People's Republic of China. They are either self-employed (restaurants and leather handcraft) or employed inside the community by Chinese employers. They have succeeded in reproducing in Italy the model of economic–family organization of their world diaspora. In the Chinese group, about 40 per cent are women who are very active in the family economy.

In Italy, there are no specific policies concerning immigrant women. The 'invisibility' of immigrant women is very often denounced by Italian feminist groups and by the few immigrant women involved in associative life, some of whom have a quite important media image, for example, Maria Lourdes Jesus, a former maid from Cape Verde, who presents a television programme, *Not Only Black,* for immigrants. In general, the participation of women in immigrants' national associative life is very rare.

In contrast, at local levels immigrant women have succeeded in creating networks and associations, sometimes helped by the Church and the trade unions. Integration policies in Italy are often left to voluntary associations. The most lively associations are those for Latin American women, followed by the Filipino women.

Policies directed towards immigrant women are organized either by the *Assessorati* for social policies, which have sometimes opened the so-called 'Centers for Foreigners' or by the *Consulte Emigrazione-Immigrazioni.* In some cities – for example, Turin, Milan and Bologna – there are 'Centers for Foreigners' which often coordinate all the policies directed at immigrant women; in other places, the *Consulta* organizes *ad hoc* projects for immigrants. Local authority intervention on behalf of immigrant women varies from one town to another but most provide assistance with finding accommodation and meeting places, counselling on health problems (contraception, abortion, pregnancy) and the training of mediators able to communicate with immigrant women. The initial problem identified is that of providing hostel accommodation for immigrant women. In Turin and Milan, hostels for women have been opened with around thirty beds each. Local authorities have tried to involve immigrant women and their associations in the management and organization of the hostels.

Another main problem concerning immigrant women is the limited use made of social and health centres. This is due to high percentages of illegal women, the ignorance of Italian legislation, cultural differences and so forth. In Bologna, a centre for immigrant women and their children, dealing with health questions has been opened and in Turin, there is a project aimed at opening a service of health counselling for African prostitutes. The centres have tried to help immigrant women form their own associations but have not always succeeded in this. Organization among immigrant women is still rare and uncoordinated.

Conclusion

It is very difficult to form conclusions in a situation as changeable as that which characterizes immigrant women. It is a positive factor that immigrant women are now less invisible than they were in the past. Research has recognized them at a time when they started to emerge as actors responsible for their own destiny. The development of associative life, for example, has been important in the development of participation of immigrant women. Black feminism is also another important aspect, creating an interesting connection between anti-racist struggles and anti-sexist struggles, no longer in a dogmatic way, but in a complex and dialectic manner which considers the point of view of black and minority women.

Still, social policies specifically for women are lacking, at EU, national and local levels. As Phizaklea (1992) observes, even if the aggregate data on occupational distribution of majority and minority women, in some European countries, show that the gap between them is not as wide as it was ten years ago, we have to interpret this very carefully as too many variables are excluded, such as unemployment, illegality and exploitation. There is a risk of economic polarization between workers who are native-born and immigrants, particularly those at the bottom – immigrant women from the Third World. Women migrants find themselves confined in traditional female jobs, particularly domestic work and the sex industry, where super-exploitation is normal. Will the efforts of immigrant women to become more autonomous overcome these constraints?

References

Alberoni, F. and Baglioni, C. (1965), *L'integrazione dell'immigrato nella società industriale* [The integration of the immigrant in industrial society], Bologna: Il Mulino.

Anthias, F. (1989), 'Gendered Ethnicities and Labour Market Processes in Britain', paper presented at the Conference 'Transitions' Science Center for Social Research/Labour Market and Employment Unit, May 13/14, Berlin.

Anthias, F. and Yuval Davis, N. (1983), 'Contextualizing Feminism: Ethnic Gender and Class Divisions', *Feminist Review*, 15.

Anthias, F. and Yuval-Davis, N. (1992), *Racialized Boundaries: 'Race', Nation, Gender, Colour, Class and the Anti-Racist Struggle*, London: Routledge.

Anti-Slavery Society (1990), *Domestic Workers*, Report to the Working Group on Contemporary Forms of Slavery, London.

Appleyard, R.T., Nagayama, T. and Stahl, C.W. (1993), *Report on Conference on International Manpower Flows and Foreign Investment in the Asian Region, in ILM*, Bangkok: ILO.

Balibar, E. and Wallerstein, I. (1990), *Race, nation, classe, les identités ambigueés*, Paris: Editions la Découverte.

Boyd, M. (1991), 'Migrant Women and Integration Policies', paper presented to the International Conference on Migration, OECD, Rome.

Do Ceu Esteves, M. (1991), *Portugal, Pais de Imigraçao* [Portugal, country of Immigration], Lisboa: Istituto de Estudio para o Desenvolvimento, Caderno 22.

Lim, L.L. (1989), 'The Status of Women in International Migration', paper for the Meeting on International Migration Policies and the Status of Female Migrants, United Nations.

Melotti, U. (1990), 'L'immigrazione straniera in Italia: da caso anomalo a caso esemplare', [Foreign Immigration to Italy: from anomaly to model], in Cocchi, C. (ed.), *Stranieri in Italia*, Bologna, Istituto Cattaneo.

Miles, R. and Rathzel, N. (1991), 'Migration and the Process of Nation-building', paper presented at the Conference 'Transitions', Science Center for Social Research/Labour Market and Employment Unit, Berlin, May 13/14.

Morokvasic, M. (1988), 'Entreprendre au féminin en Europe: cas des immigrés et des minoritées en France, Grande Bretagne, en Italie, au Portugal et en Republique Federale d' Allemagne: Motivations, Situations et Recommandations pour Actions', Commission des Communautés Européennes, Direction Générale de l'Emploi, des Affaires Générales et de l'Education.

Palidda, S. (1991), 'Le travail independant des immigrés dans huit pays Européens de L'OCDE', Rapport pour la Division des Politique de Main d'Oeuvre de L'OCDE, à paraître dans SOPEMI.

Palidda, S. (1992), 'Eurocentrisme et Realités Effectives des Migrations', *Migrations Sociétés*, 24(4).

Phizacklea, A. (1992), 'A Single or Segregated Market?: Gendered and Racialized Divisions', BSA Conference, University of Kent, Canterbury.

Pugliese, E. and Macioti, M.I.(1991), *Gli Immigrati in Italia*, Laterza: Roma-Bari.

Stolcke, V. (1992), 'Es el sexo para el género como la raza para la etnicidad?', *Mientras Tanto*, Barcelona 48.

Venturini, A. (1989), 'Emigrazione e Immigrazione (Emigration and Immigration) in Ministero del Lavoro, Occupazione e politiche del lavoro', Rapporto, Roma.

Weinert, P. (1991), 'Foreign Female Domestic Workers: Help Wanted', Geneva: International Labour Office.

15 Housing Policy and Segregation in Europe: Defining Race as the Problem

Sidney Jacobs

Introduction

Europe emerged from war in 1945 with its cities and much of its housing and industrial infrastructure in ruins. Prewar problems of grossly inadequate working-class housing were greatly exacerbated by extensive bomb damage. Thus, immigrants to western Europe, especially during the early period of reconstruction, entered housing markets in which decent, affordable accommodation was at a premium. Perceived to be in direct competition for housing with the native working class, immigrants encountered racism on a massive scale, seemingly within all sectors of the housing market, the public as much as the private. With little or no provision made for their accommodation and largely excluded from social housing until, at the earliest, the 1970s, newly arrived immigrants mostly found refuge in inner-city, slum property. When finally allowed access to social housing, ethnic minority tenants tended to be concentrated on the worst estates, which often merely replicated the poor conditions of the private sector. Although there have been improvements since including, in many places, large-scale urban rehabilitation schemes and considerable movement into both owner occupation and better-quality social housing, the general picture of ethnic minority populations residentially concentrated in areas of relatively poor housing is still largely in evidence half a century later.

Although virtually all of humanity now appears to be represented in Europe, working-class ethnic minority groups are, despite their heterogeneity, invariably poorly housed. Excluding decently housed middle-class enclaves of foreign professionals and business people, a similar pattern, of poor-quality housing emerges wherever ethnic minorities have settled during the postwar years, irrespective of either the country or the minority involved. This pattern broadly holds despite very significant differences between European states, in historical and cultural traditions, citizenship rights, immigration controls, anti-discriminatory legislation and the diversity of their welfare systems, labour and housing markets. For instance, as Kemeny writes, 'despite its much vaunted welfare state, immigrant housing in Sweden shows remarkably similar patterns to those of other countries whose housing markets are much less closely regulated and organized than the Swedish housing market' (1987: 154). In Germany, where the vast majority of postwar immigrants and their offspring are denied citizenship, their housing conditions seem roughly comparable to that of ethnic minorities in Britain where most are British citizens. In France, the 500,000 *Harkis* – Algerians and their descendants, who were granted citizenship for having served in the French army during the Algerian war of independence – appear to experience similar levels of discrimination as do others of Algerian origin (Blanc 1991: 145).

The literature has identified a multiplicity of factors influencing the formation of ethnic minority communities, including ethnicity, racism, class, length of residence in Europe, citizenship, links to the country of origin and so forth, with much of the debate focusing on issues of spatial concentration. In particular, researchers seem preoccupied by questions about the voluntary nature or otherwise of these concentrations. In other words, do ethnic minorities freely choose where to live or is this largely forced upon them? Here, it is assumed that, all other things being equal, people do not normally choose to live in unpopular locations in poor-quality housing. It is argued that the central issue is not so much ethnic minority concentrations as the quality of their accommodation. In summary, the position adopted in this chapter is that, although a complex combination of factors are usually involved, including elements of both choice and coercion, the essential key to our understanding of ethnic minority housing in Europe is racism. In the discussion that follows, European traditions of segregation are first examined. The analysis then turns to contemporary examples, focusing on common reactions to the formation of ethnic minority concentrations, in particular, the adoption at one time or another, in most European countries, of quotas and dispersal policies. Ethnicity as a primary explanation for the creation of these residential concentrations is then considered and rejected. Finally, some aspects of the politics of 'ghettoization' are explored. Through limitations of space, the discussion is largely based on material drawn from Britain, France, Germany and the Netherlands rather than Europe as a whole.

European traditions of segregation

In July 1723, Handel moved into his London house in Brook Street where he lived until his death in 1759. Yet, as a foreign national, he was 'debarred from either owning a freehold property or undertaking a long lease (Burrows 1996: 118). Thus, even Handel fell victim to discriminatory practices common throughout Europe in which housing and property rights were traditionally linked to nationality, religion and race. Ethnic minorities frequently suffered forced segregation, persecution and banishment. Medieval Europe, for instance, confined Jews to ghettos, in the hope that 'segregation and repression would break the back of stubborn Jewish resistance to conversion' (Wistrich 1992: 37). In Rome, the Jewish ghetto 'was the most desperately cramped, and its inhabitants were the poorest in Italy, forbidden to own property, forced to wear yellow badges and red hats and excluded from most professions ' (Rodin 1997: 412). During the nineteenth and early twentieth centuries, in a wide-ranging number of European cities, ethnic minorities were commonly segregated from the majority population, usually within poor and overcrowded tenements. Examples of minorities, listed by Carter (1992: 383), who lived in 'those urban neighbourhoods with the worst housing conditions', include the Flemish in Brussels, the Irish in Liverpool and the Greeks in Istanbul, who were forced to settle outside the city walls as they were forbidden to purchase 'any Ottoman dwellings' (1992: 380).

Within contemporary Europe, the link between housing and nationality is perhaps best preserved in Jersey's complicated and 'probably unique' housing policy. Jersey has twelve different categories of residents, each having differing rights of access to housing. Thus, while wealthy immigrants are allowed, under certain conditions, to buy freehold properties at the top end of the market, the housing of temporary residents, permitted to neither rent nor buy, must be provided by their employers. Migrant workers, mostly of Portuguese, British and Irish origin, employed on a seasonal basis in tourism and horticulture and without any apparent housing rights at all, 'tend to either live in accommodation attached to the farms and hotels where they are employed, or they rent rooms or other lodgings on a weekly basis without lease' (Kemeny and Llewellyn-Wilson 1998: 264).

Clearly, to the extent to which workers are deprived of civil, residential and housing rights, their position within the labour market is weakened, allowing both employers and the state to exercise almost total control over their lives and the terms and conditions of their work. Hostel accommodation in particular, as Castles and Kosack (1973: 13) suggest, allows control '24 hours a day'. To illustrate, they quote a representative of the German mining industry who 'proudly stated: the hostels belong to the mines, so the foreign workers are in our charge from start to finish'. Although hostels have since been largely phased out, some have survived. For instance, Hargreaves points out, in France in 1990, 'almost 100,000 foreigners – virtually all men, and 85 per cent Africans – still lived in hostel accommodation' (1995: 70).

During the period of postwar reconstruction when immigrants first began to arrive, Europe had only very recently emerged from the barbarism of Nazism, and its stench must, in many places, still have lingered in the air. But, even discounting the corrupting influences of the Nazi years, there are numerous other examples, both historical and contemporary, of segregation in Europe. In Northern Ireland, there is an almost complete residential polarization between the Protestant and Catholic communities. Elsewhere, in the former Yugoslavia, and in parts of the former Soviet Union, 'ethnic cleansing' violently destroyed existing secular, multicultural societies. Colonialism was, of course, also widely influential. Indeed, the colonial world in which Europeans insisted upon almost total segregation and social distance from native populations, emerged in 1945 still largely in place. Racial segregation, in other words, was very familiar indeed to Europeans, especially to the ruling classes and others with direct experience of the colonies. In these terms, postwar immigrants to Europe entered an essentially hostile white world already well versed in racist ideas and practices. Throughout the colonial period, white settlers chose mostly to live apart from local populations and European-style towns and cities were specifically built for that purpose. 'The settler town', as famously depicted by Fanon, 'is a strongly-built town, all made of stone and steel. It is a brightly lit town; the streets are covered in asphalt ... the settler's town is a well-fed town, ... a town of white people, of foreigners' (1967: 30). In contrast, 'the native town is a hungry town, starved of bread, of meat, of shoes, of coal, of light ... It is a town of niggers and dirty arabs.' Under colonialism, indigenous peoples were generally debarred from owning land and property within the so-called 'white' areas. Their presence, if tolerated at all, was usually only in their capacity as servants and menial labourers. In China, for example, the well-known park notice, 'Dogs and Chinese not admitted', recalls the arrogance of colonial rule. Land ownership was always a central issue and rigid, spatial segregation was the inevitable result. Colonial segregation only began to be dismantled with Indian independence in 1947 and Chinese liberation in 1949, but otherwise remained largely intact until the 1960s. It was only then that white supremacy in the American Deep South was first seriously challenged. In Africa, from Algiers to Cape Town, white minorities, although increasingly resisted, retained political power during most of this period, with the last bastion, the apartheid regime in South Africa, surviving until the 1990s.

The survival of racial segregation, throughout the colonial world, into the late twentieth century, would not have gone unnoticed in Europe. It was precisely during this period that significant numbers of immigrants arrived. Europeans, in the main, wishing them to stay as briefly as possible and to take up only menial, inferior and poorly paid jobs, showed little regard for either their welfare or housing needs. Given the severity of housing shortages, it is hardly surprising that competition for accommodation emerged early on as an issue of racial friction. Indeed, in Britain in the 1940s, anticipating this very problem, anti-discriminatory legislation, especially within the privately housing rented sector, was proposed by a government minister but was not acted upon for almost two decades (Gupta 1983: 120–2). Whatever other reasons impelled postwar immigrants to settle close together in the poorest districts of Europe's towns and cities, the colonial legacy of racism and xenophobia, expressed in contemporary forms, must loom large as an explanation. What was new in Europe was not anti-black racism but its large-scale domestic application. Certainly the few who had settled in pre-war Europe tended to suffer intense discrimination. Thus, in Britain, as Richmond found, the small, long-established, black communities, mostly of seafaring origin, were all 'located in the poorest quarters of towns', were all 'at least partially isolated from the rest of the community' and were all 'regarded by their respective city authorities as a "problem"' (1955: 254). Among these, about 60 families, belonging to the 'Moslem' community in Tyneside in north-east England, were rehoused by the council on an estate 'in which white families are not found' (Collins 1952: 21). Segregation within council estates was clearly then, but is no longer, regarded as permissible. The early postwar immigrants were largely housed within the private sector as it was, Castles and Kosack observe, 'rare for immigrants to get council houses' (1973: 13). They generally received the worst type of housing, paying extortionate rents for inadequate facilities. In Britain, this was largely in 'slums and run-down lodging houses, in France *bidonvilles* (shanty-towns) and overcrowded hotels, in Germany and Switzerland camps of wooden huts belonging to the employers and attics in the cities'. Hargreaves suggests that 'the *bidonvilles* exemplified the way in which unbridled market forces tended to create dense, ghetto-like concentrations of economically weak ethnic groups' (1995: 69). By the mid-1960s, 75,000 people, 80 per cent of them foreigners, were officially classed as living in *bidonvilles,* 'though the true figure was probably three times as high'.

After 1945, it appears that Europe's initial impulse, in response to the immigrant presence, far from being humanitarian, veered towards a desire for separation and segregation. In many European countries, it was assumed that migrant workers would not settle permanently. Thus, their poor housing was seen as a temporary problem requiring, at best, temporary solutions. However, it slowly dawned upon Europe's political leaders, including even the Germans who continue to insist that theirs is not a country of immigration, that these were permanent settlements. This realization was accompanied by increasing alarm at the prospect of American-type black ghettos forming in the urban heartlands of Europe. It was hardly an auspicious beginning. In housing terms, the damage done during those early years is still to be fully undone. Housing programmes aimed at improving conditions have often been inadequately financed, poorly conceived and, not infrequently, even informed by racist assumptions, as were, for example, dispersal policies. In those instances where living conditions have since been successfully improved, it has generally not been before a whole generation, or more, of ethnic minority children have grown to adulthood in the slums of Europe.

Dispersal policies

Power, in her study of unpopular housing estates in five European countries found that residents commonly felt 'trapped in, or coerced into, estates which were marginalised, stigmatised and rejected by mainstream society' (1997: 3). Examining the most extreme cases, what she calls symbolic housing estates, four of the five contained substantial ethnic minority populations. These ranged from 30 per cent in Les Minguettes, near Lyons, and 40 per cent in Taastrupgaard, near Copenhagen to almost 50 per cent in Broadwater Farm in north London and 70 per cent in Kolnberg, near Cologne. Almost all the residents on the fifth estate, Ballymun in Dublin, were Irish Catholic. Although ethnically homogeneous, Ballymun suffered levels of social malaise similar to the other estates. These findings eloquently dispel the misconception that ethnic minorities are responsible for urban decay. However, this does not mean that Ballymun was indistinguishable from the other estates. While the bulk of the residents on all of these estates most likely exist on the margins of society, casualties of the market economy, the ethnic minorities among them, unlike the Irish on the Dublin estate, would also have suffered intense racism; this fact, it is argued, is central to understanding their situation. Care must be taken not to simply subsume 'race' within broad categories of either class or poverty. In his highly perceptive analysis of the American ghetto, Wacquant attacks 'the dilution of the notion of ghetto', arguing that simply to designate all urban areas of 'widespread and intense poverty' as ghettos, 'obfuscates the racial basis and character of this poverty and divests the term of both historical meaning and sociological content' (1997: 341).

So-called 'sink' estates are, of course, almost as old as social housing itself, long pre-dating postwar immigration to Europe. For instance, in Britain, in 1946, Lewis Silkin, the Minister of Town and Country Planning in Labour's postwar Government, singled out for criticism the building of the Becontree Estate in London, consisting of '25,000 houses all of one type' but lacking the basic amenities 'essential to create a balanced community'. He described this as 'one of the greatest blunders ... made in the inter-war years' (1946: 65). However, after 1945, many newly constructed housing estates replicated the very blunders Silkin identified. At their worst, these estates, whether high or low rise, are vast, essentially featureless wastelands, badly designed, cheaply and shoddily built, in blocks and uniform rows, isolated and easily identifiable from a distance as housing for outcasts and the poor. Within these areas, services are typically indifferent, non-existent even; schools are run down, overcrowded and meagrely resourced; job opportunities are limited, shops expensive and transport unreliable with few, if any, public amenities within easy reach. It is here, on some of the worst estates, that Europe's new ethnic minorities tend to be housed. For example, in England, the 44 local authority districts with the highest concentration of deprivation have 'nearly four times the proportion of ethnic minority residents' than the rest of the country (Social Exclusion Unit 1998: 15).

A strength of Power's study is that it plots the process of decline within the worst estates, clearly showing that it was not caused by the presence of ethnic minorities. On the contrary, as she stresses, 'the growing minority communities were a consequence, not a cause of unpopularity' (1997: 279). Her findings confirm a familiar pattern of decline within social housing, initially occurring for a variety of reasons, including poor design and construction; undesirable location; bureaucratic, insensitive and incompetent management; and the growing popularity and accessibility of owner occupation. The departure of the more affluent and upwardly mobile residents, leading to high turnover and vacancy rates, invariably creates both deterioration and a sense of siege among those remaining. Once an area acquires the reputation and stigma of a 'dump' estate, only the poorest and most vulnerable, with no other housing choice, are willing to accept offers of accommodation there. Kolnberg, for example, was originally intended for high-income professionals but the investors' expectations were never realized and as a result 'standards plummeted and only disadvantaged tenants who suffered discrimination in the wider housing market were willing to live there' (Power 1997: 171). In another of Power's symbolic estates, Broadwater Farm, 75 per cent of allocations in 1975 were to homeless families (Gifford 1986: 21).

Growing poverty within social housing tends to be accompanied by declining public expenditure, cuts in essential services and the neglect of repairs and maintenance, ushering in the early onset of physical blight. At about this stage, ethnic minority tenants commonly begin to be allocated in large numbers to what are already extremely unpopular estates. This, in turn, precipitates additional flight, as described by Power, a 'scramble to leave by white households' and, from prospective tenants, increased 'resistance to moving in' (1997: 281). Thus, for example, between 1985 and 1987, no German tenants at all moved into the Kolnberg estate: 'Alongside the new Turkish occupants, the asylum-seekers, people dependent on social assistance, one-parent families, unemployed and single people, *300 Gypsies* came to Kolnberg where flats were available' (Power 1997: 174–5, emphasis added). Given the intensity of existing hostility commonly expressed towards Gypsies in Germany, the very willingness to house them at all is testimony to the depths of the estate's unpopularity among Germans. Indeed, by 1987 it was known 'as the worst estate in the country'.

Although clearly not responsible for the physical deterioration, ethnic minority residents are invariably blamed for it and for much else besides, in particular, for rising levels of unemployment, crime, drug abuse, prostitution, violence and vandalism. In Kolnberg, crime rose to nearly four times the rate for the city of Cologne. Although 'managers maintained that "drop-out" Germans were the cause of most problems, not immigrants', it was, of course, the Turkish community who were generally 'blamed for the social collapse and spiralling conditions' (Power 1997: 175). In their study of urban renewal in Rotterdam, de Jong and Verkuyten found that Dutch residents migrate from the inner city because it is 'where criminality, vandalism, and general nuisance behaviour is rife, and because of their prejudicial views and racism' (1996: 695). Although clearly not the authors' intention, these findings could be taken to mean that ethnic minority communities do not leave because either they do not object, as strongly as do the Dutch, to crime, vandalism and 'nuisance behaviour' or because, by implication, they are the prime perpetrators of these anti-social activities. The truth of the matter is that the majority cannot move for want of suitable alternatives. The logic of the perception which defines race as the problem means that blame is attached to neither poverty nor poor housing and even less to racism and social injustice but to race. And it is usually the minorities alone who are singled out for blame. In essence, urban problems arise, it is believed, when 'too many' minority group members live 'too closely' together. Having arrived at this diagnosis, it follows that the solutions formulated will necessarily attempt, in various ways, to restrict and control ethnic minority communities, most usually by setting quotas and adopting dispersal policies within house allocation systems. The effect is to limit even further their housing choice. Moreover, dispersal policies, being inherently discriminatory, tend in practice to create the very ethnic minority concentrations that they are designed to avoid. It needs to be clearly understood that both residential quotas and dispersal policies, in aiming to restrict the rights of settlement and freedom of movement of people otherwise legally resident in the country, constitute a serious infringement of basic human rights. More specifically, as Leitner points out, these restrictions violate the fourth protocol of the 1963 European Human Rights Convention (1987: 80).

Power reports that, in Taastrup, the local authority, openly it seems, 'tried to avoid using its nomination rights to house foreigners in social housing areas popular with Danes' (1997: 222). The inevitable consequence was that ethnic minorities were concentrated on the 'very poorest estates like Taastrupgaard' where, in 1990, they constituted 40 per cent of the population. The housing company, having themselves created the situation, claimed that in order 'to avoid ghettoization', it was necessary to disperse minority populations, mainly Turks, by limiting their access to Taastrupagaard and similar estates. Its solution clearly compounded the initial discrimination which, in the first place, led to concentrations being formed. Although clearly in itself discriminatory as it limits housing choice on grounds of ethnic origin, the adoption of dispersal policies was justified, without any apparent sense of irony, as 'a conscious attempt to stop the discriminatory concentration of Turkish families at Taastrupgaard' (Power 1997: 233). In Kolnberg, in 1993, again in the name of fostering integration, 'all new lettings ... [were] reserved for Germans' (p.188). In the Broadwater Farm estate, where the ethnic minority community, mainly of Afro-Caribbean origin, comprised roughly half of the population, the solution to problems of decline and unpopularity devised by Haringey Council, was 'to broaden the social mix on the estate' (Gifford 1986: 21). It was to be achieved by restricting further black entry to the estate. It is worth noting that in none of these situations did the authorities appear to even contemplate the dispersal of whites. It is only ever ethnic minorities who are subjected to dispersal policies.

In Les Minguettes, in reaction to decline, the commune restricted access by immigrant households 'in the hope of stabilising the estate', with flats even left empty rather than let to 'unwanted' applicants, meaning, of course, Arab families (Power 1997: 150). Although prohibited under the 1972 law against racial discrimination, Hargreaves reports that in France there is 'compelling evidence that a general policy of ethnic quotas has been applied on a wide scale'. It is justified on the grounds of a so-called 'threshold of tolerance', usually put at between 10 and 15 per cent of the population. While, as Hargreaves notes, 'there is no reliable evidence to indicate that such a threshold exists', it is widely assumed that if 'crossed in a given locality, the capacity of the native population to absorb minority ethnic groups would be stretched beyond breaking point' (1995: 199). Blanc states that 'in the name of "sociological rebalance"', many public housing organizations break the law by practising the 'one for one' rule which means that properties are only allocated to a foreign or ethnic minority family when the departing tenant is also either foreign or of ethnic minority origin (1992: 19). By responding in this manner to anticipated local racism, real or imagined, the state both legitimizes and panders to it.

The primary motivation behind these policies, Hargreaves suggests, is probably 'anxieties over a possible electoral backlash among native voters' (1995: 199). Attempting to capitalize on fears of a North African 'invasion' in public housing, Le Pen, in his 1988 presidential campaign, proposed reserving public housing only for nationals. But, as Blanc notes, it would have simply created increased vacancies as those who left public housing feeling there were "too many" Arab tenants, 'will certainly not return' (1991: 150). Similarly, in Germany, Faist and Haubermann consider that 'conflicts over housing have occupied a very prominent place in the political debate over immigration' (1996: 91). In these terms, the concentration of ethnic minorities on the worst estates arises, at least in part, because the poor, being both voiceless and powerless, cannot insist on quotas for their own estates. In contrast, housing gate-keepers, within both private and social housing, are often responsive to demands from more powerful groups to limit or even entirely exclude minorities from their areas. In consequence, as no one else will have them, they are shunted on to the poorest estates. It is the solution of least resistance: political expediency combined with prevailing racist and xenophobic attitudes, as much amongst politicians, housing managers and local government officials as within the population at large.

In Belgium in 1984, quotas restricting foreign settlement in particular areas were given legal sanction, allowing communes to refuse foreigners the right to register there. By 1985, six Brussels communes had been granted this legal power (European Parliament 1985: 34). In pre-unification West Berlin, 'underprivileged foreigners, primarily Turks and Yugoslavians' were prohibited from moving into three of the city's twelve boroughs largely because it was thought that 'the concentration of the foreign population in these boroughs would "overload the social infrastructure, isolating them within their subculture, and hindering their integration"' (Arin 1991: 205). However, it is difficult to reconcile this expressed desire for integration with the denial of citizenship rights to even the German-born children of migrant workers who, in reality, are constantly reminded of the temporary nature of their presence in Germany. Thus, during the 1998 state election in Saxony-Anhalt in which the racist and xenophobic DVU polled almost 13 per cent of the vote, Helmut Kohl told a rally in Magdeburg: 'we are friendly to foreigners in our country. But they have to know that they are guests in our country. And if they don't want to be a guest, they can just get out' (*Guardian*, 27 April 1998).

In the Netherlands, in response to rioting in Rotterdam in 1972, sparked off by the eviction of a Dutch family by a Turkish landlord, the city council attempted to restrict ethnic minority settlement to a maximum of 5 per cent per neighbourhood. However, the practice was abandoned in 1974 after it was adjudged to be illegal. By the 1980s, the ethnic minority community in old Rotterdam constituted 25 per cent of the population (Blauw 1991: 43; de Jong and Verkuyten 1996: 689). While the Dutch government claims to firmly reject discrimination within the housing system, it appears to tolerate dispersal even though it is transparently discriminatory and must involve quotas. Thus, Blauw reports that, in the early 1980s, housing authorities 'operated according to rules intended to disperse ethnic minorities over a number of housing blocks in order to prevent concentrations' (1991: 59).

Urban renewal programmes have also been utilized to disperse ethnic minorities from the inner city to outer suburban estates where quotas were often set aimed at avoiding high levels of concentration reforming. In France, for example, Peach observes that 'the effects of clearance policies and also attempts to restrict immigrants, in some cases, to 15 per cent of the subsidised HLM apartments ... has produced some degree of ethnic dispersion' (1987: 39). In Britain, on the other hand, local authorities largely excluded black and Asian families from the massive slum clearance and house-building programmes that lasted roughly from the mid-1950s to the early 1970s. This policy led directly to large-scale black homelessness. As argued elsewhere, the discriminatory avoidance of ethnic minority areas within urban renewal schemes meant that blacks and Asians were virtually absent from the slum clearance rehousing programme. It explains both why so few entered the public sector during this period and why, subsequently, so many were, as homeless applicants, poorly housed. For many the opportunity to acquire new council property, if missed then, never reappeared, as construction levels within social housing in Britain has since been in steady decline (Jacobs 1985: 19–20).

Western Europe's knee-jerk reaction to postwar immigration was, almost universally, to adopt dispersal policies. But, having since been found to be both discriminatory and essentially unworkable, dispersal has, in most places, been formally abandoned although it often tends to reappear in other, less formal guises. Arin notes that, after 13 years, the 1975 ban on entry and settlement of foreigners in three boroughs of West Berlin, 'resulted in no dispersion effects of the migrant labour population'. He suggests that 'it would be naive' to have expected otherwise as the minority concentrations were created by 'the existing mechanisms of the housing market' (1991: 206).

Ethnic minority populations are largely working class and disproportionately suffer poverty and unemployment, the consequence, at least in part, of racism within the labour market. Thus, their housing choices will, in the first instance, be restrained by their weak economic position. In turn, racism, which everywhere permeates both private and public housing, will further restrict their options. In essence, it will largely confine them to those districts, all relatively poor, that already house substantial ethnic minority populations. Thus, for example, in Britain, the percentage of people having incomes less than half the national average ranges from 41 per cent for those of African-Caribbean origin to 45 per cent for Indians, 82 per cent for Pakistanis, and 84 per cent for Bangladeshis, compared to 28 per cent for whites. These levels of poverty are reflected in housing conditions, for instance, 15 per cent of ethnic minority and 40 per cent of Pakistani and Bangladeshi households in Britain live in overcrowded conditions compared to only 2 per cent of white households (Social Exclusion Unit 1998: 30).

In addition to racist housing policies, attempts to disperse ethnic minority families to 'white' areas, particularly to popular estates, are likely to meet with a wall of racist resistance. Racial harassment, ranging from 'insulting behaviour to assault and murder', occurs on such a scale as to seriously limit housing choice and is, in Britain, as Ginsburg comments, 'very significant in perpetuating second class welfare citizenship for black people' (1989: 66). He further observes that 'the fear of possible anti-black racial violence is a factor that often motivates housing managers and black prospective tenants in allocating and choosing tenancies.'

In Northern Ireland, Birrell and Murie show that residential segregation between the Protestant and Catholic communities, created by conflict, intimidation and the application of a 'religious test' by the market, was reinforced by the state in its house-building and slum clearance programmes as it had no option but to reflect the existing sectarian divisions within society (1980: 219). Thus, newly built estates became either all Protestant or all Catholic areas, in a process 'affected by choice, intimidation and the inevitable compliance of housing authorities' (p.220). While no other region within the EU exhibits the extremes of the Northern Ireland situation, 'whites only' areas commonly exist from which ethnic minority groups are effectively excluded by threats of violence. In these circumstances, dispersal is dangerous and is clearly not the solution. It would seem though that the problem is not so much 'black ghettos' as white areas which exclude ethnic minorities.

Dispersal appears to have been tried, at one time or another, wherever ethnic minorities have settled in postwar Europe. Although invariably undertaken in the name of fostering integration and 'good race relations', it is suggested that dispersal simply serves to legitimize racist practices in house allocations. Certainly, ethnic minority communities do not appear to have been successfully dispersed anywhere in Europe. Most are still largely concentrated in areas of poor housing. In these terms alone, dispersal policies have clearly failed. In practice, it seems to involve little more than directing ethnic minorities from one area of poor housing to another and, seemingly, rarely to popular all-white areas. In other words, it appears to have neither dispersed minority communities nor improved their living conditions. But, in addition to a desire for integration, behind dispersal polices there also usually lurks a mixture of base motives: racism, political expediency and fear. In particular, it is the fear of 'black ghettos' forming that is commonly evoked to justify, not only dispersal but also the imposition of ever-tighter restrictions on immigration, the exclusion of refugees and asylum seekers, and the repressive policing of communities already settled. In Britain, for example, Smith writes that 'the notion of stemming immigration to promote integration, usually through spatial dispersal, became the touchstone of national legislation for almost 20 years' (1993: 133).

Ethnicity, class and racism

Racism, it is suggested, permeates the entire housing process, directly and indirectly influencing every aspect of it, whether in owner occupation, the privately rented sector or social housing. It thus becomes virtually impossible to disentangle racism from other factors determining ethnic minority housing patterns. As O'Loughlin writes, 'when we try to understand the level of residential segregation of foreigners, there seems to be general agreement that forcing the explanation into a choice-constraint dichotomy is inappropriate and an intellectual cul-de-sac' (1987: 26). However, this is precisely the path that Peach appears to follow when he argues that 'choice' is of far greater importance than 'constraint'. He derides Marxism for denying the importance of ethnicity and assuming, instead, that the economic position of immigrant groups provides 'the main explanation of ethnic concentrations'. Tellingly, he does not cite references for authors propounding this supposedly Marxist view. In reality, Peach provides little more than a crude parody of Marxism which seemingly entirely neglects racism. But it allows him to dismiss 'class' as relatively unimportant compared to 'the desire to settle or return home, religion, language, family size and structure, the whole complex of what we term ethnic identity' (1987: 49). He identifies ethnicity as 'the positive virtues of association' which he suggests, 'play a major part in the formation of ethnic concentrations' (p.50).

He correctly emphasizes positive aspects in the formation of ethnic minority communities but his attempt to distinguish these from negative factors constraining choice, most particularly class and racism, seems misguided and somewhat superficial. As Gellner put it, 'classes without ethnicity are blind, ethnicity without class is empty' (1998: 61). Historically, Carter argues, 'residential segregation acted as a powerful force against class integration, offering instead the differential incorporation of minority group workers, who were perceived as belonging to separate communities' (1992: 383–4). In these terms, the spatial segregation of minority populations serves to reduce working-class solidarity. Thus, it would seem, both capital and the state have an interest in fostering it.

Peach's emphasis on positive aspects of ethnicity and choice provides a useful antidote to the negative imagery often contained in media presentations of ethnic minority communities. But it also firmly places the onus of blame on ethnic minorities themselves, essentially for being 'clannish' and choosing to create 'ghettos'. By presenting segregation as the choice of migrants, it crucially also ignores the role of racism which, as Smith notes, 'ensured that any choice was exercised in some of the worst segments of the housing system' (1993: 132). In short, it is a perspective which serves to exonerate western Europe from the very serious charge of racism, even though research findings consistently show racism to be deeply embedded within some of its cornerstone institutions, including, of course, those involved in the housing process. 'The phenomenon of ghettoization', as Arin concludes, 'is not a natural event; it has much to do with the housing and urban renewal policies of the state' (1991: 212). It also has much to do with migrant labour systems. The rotation of workers, widespread during the early postwar years, clearly promotes urban decay: temporary residents are likely to have little or no incentive to spend money on repairs and maintenance. Under these circumstances, the priority tends to be cheapness rather than quality, in order to save for the return home.

At its height, the number of returnee migrants was substantial. Thus, for example, in Germany, between 1964 and 1972, the rotation rate among Turks was 30.2 per cent and, for Italians, a massive 85.9 per cent. In France, from 1962 to 1968, the rate of rotation among foreign workers was 41.3 per cent (Carchedi 1979: 45). Where the migrant or 'guestworker' system operated in Europe, two distinct sectors emerged within ethnic minority communities – those who managed to resist rotation and were more or less settled permanently, and those who were temporary workers, 'destined for an extremely short period of residence' (p.46). The existence of a significantly sized temporary population, whether made up of migrant workers or refugees and asylum seekers, is bound to signal to those permanently settled that they and their kind are essentially unwelcome in the country. It is also likely to increase their sense of insecurity and create instability within the community, reinforcing the 'myth of return'. In housing, in so far as it suggests impermanence, its impact is likely to have been entirely negative. For example, in Amsterdam, the Surinamese are prepared to pay a relatively large proportion of their income on housing. Hence, they tend to live in newer and more expensive housing compared to Turks and Moroccans who, preferring cheaper rents, are overrepresented in the older parts of the city. The Surinamese, although suffering high unemployment – 16 per cent in 1993 – were at half or less than half the rate of that suffered by the Turks (32 per cent) and the Moroccans (36 per cent). Moreover, the Surinamese are, as ex-colonials, both Dutch-speaking and citizens. In contrast, the Turks and Moroccans, with relatively poor fluency in Dutch and, even if no longer subject to migrant labour regulations, are, as foreigners, still likely to feel relatively insecure (van Amersfoort and Cortie 1996: 667–9).

It would seem that ethnic minorities who opt for cheap housing, in preference to better and more spacious properties, are all too easily depicted as ill-educated peasants, impervious to the Western virtues of privacy and hygiene, and indifferent and unused to modern conveniences. This view falsely diminishes their experiences of racism and underestimates the extent of their poverty, insecurity and uncertainty about the long-term future, which in reality combine to severely limit their housing choices.

It appears that Peach underestimates the extent to which ethnicity is continually reinforced by and intimately interrelated with racism and class. Take for example, the solidarity that arises from shared experiences of adversity. There can be little doubt that hostility and rejection by the host population often leads minorities to seek refuge in the safety of their own communities, strengthening their identification with the country of origin, its language, religion and culture. The converse seems also to hold: that is, tolerance within an open and pluralist society appears to encourage assimilation. This would seem to mirror the Jewish experience of increasing assimilation within the postwar context of western Europe's growing secularity and declining anti-Semitism, even though 'low-level' anti-Semitism still appears to be almost ubiquitous. Wasserstein, writing the history of the Jews in Europe since 1945, depicts them as a 'vanishing diaspora'. His book, he explains:

> ... is not, taken as a whole, the story of Jews as victims of the hatred of their neighbours but rather as victims of their kindness – of the processes of integration and assimilation that have succeeded, at least in Western Europe, to such a degree as to threaten the collective survival of Jews on the Continent. (1996: xiii).

It needs to be stressed that, in housing terms, the problem is not ethnic minority concentrations *per se* but involuntary concentrations within areas of poor housing. For example, during the nineteenth to the mid-twentieth century, the Jews of London were heavily concentrated in the East End, living in generally overcrowded and often quite appalling housing conditions. Fishman describes houses, near Spitalfields, occupied by Jewish immigrants in 1888, as 'grimy, dilapidated, leprous-walled one- or two-storeyed terraced cottages' (1988: 132). The 'Jewish housing problem' was created by poverty and unemployment within a climate of intense, widespread anti-Semitism, and was reflected in their lack of housing choice, largely confined to East End slums. In the postwar period, Jews increasingly migrated to the more affluent suburbs. Thus, in 1963 in Edgware in north-west London, Jewish households constituted 38 per cent of the population. A massive 95 per cent of them were owner occupiers whereas previously in the East End they had mainly rented their homes (Wasserstein 1996: 76–7). Thus, although Jewish populations in places like Edgware remain highly concentrated, the Jewish housing problem of the past has been resolved. That many still choose to live in close proximity to one another is now of interest to only themselves and, perhaps, a few sociologists.

Thus, in so far as concentrations of Europe's new ethnic minority populations constitute a problem, it is a problem of both poor housing and racism. Nothing demonstrates the existence of that racism better than the fact that it is the ethnic minority presence itself which is still widely defined as the problem, particularly by the city authorities in which these concentrations are located. Discussing Turkish districts in Berlin, Arin stresses that:

> ... the question is not whether the inhabitants of these areas are Turks or not. Nor is it the improvement of the 'social structure' ... or how to distribute Turks equally in West Berlin. The question is how to improve material housing conditions in these areas for their inhabitants. (1991: 213)

Peach suggests that 'if external factors of constraint were dominant ... immigrants would be segregated as a whole from the host community' (1987: 51). But that is to misunderstand the nature of racism as Europe enters the twenty-first century. No European state, outside those of the former Yugoslavia, is avowedly segregationist and, with the exception of minorities in the Balkans, Northern Ireland, and Gypsies everywhere, no ethnic minority is currently being systematically subjected to segregation. Thus, there is every reason to expect racism, in its various forms, to manifest itself extremely unevenly. There is no reason at all to expect total segregation. Goldberg, referring to the process of racial marginalization, argues that it is necessary 'only that some [large] fraction of the racially constituted group be so marginalized, not that all members be dislocated'.

To illustrate, he suggests, as an example, that 'professional blacks may be accepted as neighbours by whites ... while the larger fraction of blacks remains displaced to the periphery' (1993: 48).

Ghettoization?

Ghettoization, is defined by Wacquant to mean: 'involuntary, permanent, and total residential separation premised on caste as the basis for the development of a parallel (and inferior) social structure' (1997: 343). In the major cities of the United States, ghettos are commonly both massive and ethnically homogeneous, often housing populations of tens of thousands or more, virtually all of them of African-American descent. Furthermore, segregation from the rest of the population tends to be almost total. The equivalent simply does not exist in Europe. To illustrate just one of these points, even the most 'immigrant' areas, as Huttman notes, 'such as Kreuzberg in West Berlin or the Bijlmermeer buildings in the Netherlands, no more than half of the population is of one ethnic minority' (1991: 21). 'Ghetto' originally referred to places in which the Jews of Europe were residentially segregated. In its modern usage its meaning has become contextually rooted in urban, black America. In these terms, its increasing use within postwar Europe, to refer to areas of high ethnic minority concentration and/or poverty, renders it meaningless. But, in a European context, as de Rudder argues, the use of the term 'ghetto' seems to have more of an 'ideological than descriptive function'. In particular, she suggests, 'the stigmatization of a residential area as a "ghetto" facilitates removal and dispersal' (1992: 261). It also serves to associate 'race' with social malaise. In the public mind, 'ghetto' powerfully evokes negative stereotypes of the black American ghetto and is commonly used as shorthand for a combination of lawlessness, violence and drug abuse; extreme poverty and urban decay; chronic unemployment and welfare dependency, and social and family dysfunction. 'The ghetto' is depicted as a dangerous, alien and politically subversive place implanted at the heart of European society, and so posing a threat to the very survival of the nation itself. It embodies, in a single word, the whole array of the right wing's traditional anti-urbanism, racism and xenophobia.

Wacquant observes:

> [T]he *cités* of the French urban periphery suffer from a negative public image that instantly associates them with rampant delinquency, immigration and insecurity, so much so that they are almost universally called 'little Chicagos' by both their residents and by outsiders ... [These areas are] widely (mis)represented

> as growing pockets of 'Arab' poverty and disorder symptomatic of the incipient 'ethnicization' of France's urban space. (1993: 369)

Elsewhere, following the disturbances at Broadwater Farm in 1985, Gifford reports that the *Daily Mail* likened parts of the estate to 'Alcatraz', suggesting that 'if you are poor and White, old and ill, its a vicious and frightening prison. White people there … feel they are living in an alien and terrifying land.' The *Daily Express*, attributing the riots to outside agitators, claimed in its headlines that: 'Street fighting experts trained in Moscow and Libya were behind Britain's worst violence.' The story, in fact, originated with the Commissioner of the Metropolitan Police, Sir Kenneth Newman, who alleged that 'groups of trotskyists and anarchists had been identified as orchestrating the disturbances in Tottenham and in Brixton a week earlier' (Gifford 1986: 124). These allegations, apparently without any foundation, were later withdrawn by a police spokesperson.

The notion of the 'ghetto' as a threat to society is constantly voiced within the media and amongst politicians and even academics. For instance, Saunders, concerned about European security, suggests that a nation's defensive capabilities are 'a product of the qualities of the civilian population'. What he appears to mean is that immigration inevitably creates increased cultural heterogeneity and, in western Europe, that might act to reduce the 'sense of shared national purpose which could have negative consequences for national unity in a time of crisis' (1991: 1). In particular, he warns that in Germany there could be 'unanticipated consequences … as guest workers become permanent and the fertility of the immigrant population exceeds that of the native born' (p.2). The German-born children of immigrants are clearly not regarded by him as 'native born'. Saunders also writes that 'of particular concern to France is the growing population of its former North African colonies', likely to promote, he suggests, increased illegal immigration (p.3). But, what apparently disturbs him most is the fear that unemployed immigrant youth, 'their numbers multiplied by high birth rates, may well join radical and terrorist or guerilla groups as an alternative to poverty' (p.3). He does not express similar anxieties about unemployed white youth.

Boyer sees dangers in 'clandestine immigration' leading to the creation of 'vast depressed areas … encouraging violence and marginalisation'. He appears to attribute both the 1980 Brixton riots and those in Les Minguettes, to illegal immigrants. He predicts that control of such areas will involve 'huge investments in security forces and necessitate changes in the ethnic recruitment of police forces' and finally stresses the need 'to avoid the creation of "ghettos", becoming "fish-ponds" in which hostile countries or terrorist groups can recruit agents' (Boyer 1991: 276). Boyer clearly considers the political loyalty of 'immigrants' to be highly suspect. Even their European-born offspring, it appears, are not to be trusted.

The 'ghetto' as scapegoat can, of course, be traced back to deeply embedded European traditions of anti-Semitism. It contains within it an elaborate mythology designed to evoke fear rather than solidarity, loathing and contempt rather than compassion and tolerance, social control and punitive policing rather than pluralism and civil rights, and narrow nationalism rather than a celebration of cultural diversity. It appears to have both survived the postwar creation of welfare states and the translation from anti-Semitism to antipathy towards Europe's new ethnic minority populations, apparently without much need of modification.

While Europe's new ethnic minorities cannot, in any meaningful sense of the word, be said to live in ghettos, Europe's long-established Roma or Gypsy communities, traditionally forcibly segregated, seem to be subjected to renewed pressures towards ghettoization. With their numbers estimated at between 7–8.5 million people, Europe's Gypsies clearly constitute a substantial and rapidly growing population. In numerical terms alone, the housing of Europe's Gypsies is more than a residual problem, demanding serious attention from all European governments. Throughout Europe, the vast majority of Gypsies are firmly located at the very bottom of society; they are economically, socially and politically marginalized within their own countries. As Brearley notes, 'the Roma are the most vilified and harassed minority in Europe today' (1996: 3). Although about 40 per cent are now 'more or less permanently settled', with a further 30 per cent only 'semi-nomadic' (p.13), their housing remains both extremely poor and highly segregated from the rest of society. There appears to be a growing tendency towards Gypsy ghettoization in both eastern and western Europe. For example, Ladanyi finds evidence of growing segregation of Gypsies within the inner slums of Budapest and predicts that 'the spatial concentration of Gypsies will further increase in the near future' (1993: 39). The Spanish Gypsies – *los Gitanos* – Brearley reports, tend to live in 'sprawling slum barrios in large cities' and are 'commonly socially marginalized and poor'. They are also subjected to evictions, not least of all by the authorities, as in Madrid in 1994 when the city council, having demolished their shanty town homes, forced 56 Roma families to live in housing 'near a municipal rubbish tip' and, as a consequence, 'many of the children had diarrhoea.' Madrid's mayor also 'ordered a wall to be constructed so that the Roma could not be seen. Eighty more families soon joined them' (Brearley 1996: 32).

Similarly, the town council of Usti nad Labem, in the Czech Republic, plans 'to ghettoize several hundred Gypsies by building a 115 ft wall around their blocks of flats to segregate them from Czech residents' (*Guardian*, 16

May 1998). The scheme was attacked by the Chief Rabbi of the Czech Republic who, recalling the horrors of the Nazi era, urged Jews 'to mobilise all our strength to ensure that Romanies quickly receive the protection of law that is their inalienable right as citizens of this country and as human beings' (*Jewish Chronicle,* 19 June 1998). As far as is known, humane treatment for Gypsies has not been made a necessary precondition of the Czech Republic's admission to membership of the EU. There appears to be no meaningful programme on offer, by either the EU or any of the member states, to either decently house or integrate Gypsies, where they desire it, within mainstream society. On the contrary, Europe appears at best to be largely indifferent to their plight, seemingly content to leave them on the margins, a deeply despised, impoverished, disadvantaged and isolated minority. The frequent victims of blatant, and often unrecorded discrimination, many Gypsies throughout Europe are forcibly segregated, under appalling housing conditions, from the rest of the population; despite their desperate need, they are also largely excluded from other forms of state welfare provision.

Future prospects

While the 'Gypsy housing question' remains largely neglected, issues surrounding the housing of Europe's new ethnic minorities are now appearing on the European political agenda, albeit still somewhat perfunctorily. For example, the annual meeting of European housing ministers in 1994 was presented with a survey of ethnic minority housing, indicating that at least the European Commission, if not yet all the member states, is beginning to take the issue seriously. Ambitiously titled *Housing Provision of Immigrants and Refugees as a Tool of Social Integration* (Pfeiffer et al. 1994), the survey woefully fails to even begin to address this aspiration, largely, it seems, because of the tardy response and lack of cooperation received from member states. The quality of the information appears extremely variable, making national comparisons virtually impossible. Of the then twelve member states, Ireland, Italy and Portugal did not complete the questionnaire at all, while the United Kingdom, choosing to interpret the remit extremely narrowly, only provided information for the housing of refugees and asylum seekers. Germany's response tended to focus on housing provision for ethnic Germans rather than other ethnic minorities. Similarly, Greece focused on ethnic Greek immigrants. Indeed, the survey would seem to be of interest not so much for the information provided but for its omissions and for the failure of member states to acknowledge the existence, let alone the scale, of the problem. For example, when asked to specify 'problematic aspects', Belgium insisted that their housing problem was 'not specific for immigrants but for all people with low incomes' (p.11). Similarly, Luxembourg sees the problem in terms of a 'general shortage of low price housing' (p.14). Later in the survey it is revealed that in Belgium, 'many private owners and housing offices refuse to rent a house to immigrants' (p.47). In Spain too, it appears that ethnic minorities have difficulties finding accommodation because of 'rejection by some population groups' (p.27). In both these Belgium and Spanish examples, expressions of racism are merely listed as one of many problems faced by immigrants, as if it were a natural phenomenon not worthy of special mention. The German response, after listing the housing problems faced by ethnic Germans, simply states that 'similar difficulties for other immigrants [is] assumed' (p.30). Among the problems listed by the Netherlands, is the 'concentration of ethnic minorities in certain districts of large cities' (p.14). Nowhere in the survey is racism singled out as important.

References

Amersfoort, H. van and Cortie, C. (1996), 'Social Polarisation in a Welfare State? Immigrants in the Amsterdam Region', *New Community*, 22(4).

Arin, C. (1991), 'The Housing Market and Housing Policies for the Migrant Labor Population in West Berlin', in Huttman, E.D. et al. (eds), *Urban Housing Segregation of Minorities in Western Europe and the United States*, London: Duke University Press.

Birrell, D. and Murie, A. (1980), *Policy and Government in Northern Ireland: Lessons of Devolution*, Dublin: Gill and MacMillan.

Blanc, M.(1991), 'Urban Housing Segregation of North African "Immigrants" in France', in Huttman, E.D. et al. (eds), *Urban Housing Segregation of Minorities in Western Europe and the United States*, London: Duke University Press.

Blanc, M. (1992), 'From Substandard Housing to Devalorized Social Housing: Ethnic Minorities in France, Germany and the UK', *European Journal of Intercultural Studies*, 3(1).

Blauw, W. (1991), 'Housing Segregation for Different Population Groups in the Netherlands', in Huttman, E.D. et al. (eds), *Urban Housing Segregation of Minorities in Western Europe and the United States*, London: Duke University Press.

Boyer, Y. (1991), 'Demographic Change, Poitical Priorities and Western Security', in Freedman, L. and Saunders, J. (eds), *Population Change and European Security*, London: Brassey's.

Brearley, M. (1996), *The Persecution of Gypsies in Contemporary Europe*, London: Institute for Jewish Policy Research.

Burrows, D. (1996), *Master Musicians: Handel*, Oxford: Oxford University Press.

Carchedi, G. (1979), 'Authority and Foreign Labour: Some Notes on a Late Capitalist Form of Capital Accumulation and State Intervention', *Studies in Political Economy*, 2.

Carter, F.W. (1992), 'Ethnic Residential Patterns in the Cities', in Engman, M. (ed.), *Ethnic Identity in Urban Europe*, Dartmouth: New York University Press.

Castles, S. and Kosack, G. (1973), 'The Function of Labour Immigration in Western European Capitalism', *New Left Review*, 73.

Collins, S. (1952), 'Social Processes Integrating Coloured People in Britain', *British Journal of Sociology*, 3.

European Parliament (1985), 'Committee of Inquiry into the Rise of Fascism and Racism in Europe', Report on the Findings (Evrigenis Report), Luxembourg: Office for Official Publications of the European Communities.

Faist, T. and Haubermann, H. (1996), 'Immigration, Social Citizenship and Housing in Germany', *International Journal of Urban and Regional Research*, 20(1).

Fanon, F. (1967), *The Wretched of the Earth*, Harmondsworth: Penguin.

Fishman, W.J. (1988), *East End 1888*, London: Duckworth.

Gellner, E. (1998), *Nationalism*, London: Duckworth.

Gifford, Lord (1986), 'The Broadwater Farm Inquiry', Report of the Broadwater Farm Inquiry, London: HMSO.

Ginsburg, N. (1989), 'Racial Harassment Policy and Practice: The Denial of Citizenship', *Critical Social Policy*, 26.

Goldberg, D.T. (1993), 'Polluting the Body Politic', in Cross, M. and Keith, M. (eds), *Racism, the City and the State*, London: Routledge.

Gupta, P.S. (1983), 'Imperialism and the Labour Government of 1945–1951', in Winter, J (ed.), *The Working Class in Modern British History*, Cambridge: Cambridge University Press.

Hargreaves, A.G. (1995), *Immigration, 'Race' and Ethnicity in Contemporary France*, London: Routledge.

Huttman, E.D. (1991), 'Housing Segregation in Western Europe: An Introduction', in Huttman, E.D. et al. (eds), *Urban Housing Segregation of Minorities in Western Europe and the United States*, London: Duke University Press.

Jacobs, S. (1985), 'Race, Empire and the Welfare State: Council Housing and Racism', *Critical Social Policy*, 13.

Jong, W. de and Verkuyten, M. (1996), 'Urban Renewal, Housing Policy and Ethnic Relations in Rotterdam', *New Community*, 22(4).

Kemeny, J. (1987), *Immigrant Housing Conditions in Sweden*, Gavle: The National Swedish Institute for Building Research.

Kemeny, J. and Llewellyn-Wilson, C. (1998), 'Both Rationed and Subsidised: Jersey's Command Economy in Housing', *Housing Studies*, 13(2).

Ladanyi, J. (1993), 'Patterns of Residential Segregation and the Gypsy Minority in Budapest', *International Journal of Urban and Regional Research*, 17(1).

Leitner, H. (1987), 'Regulating Migrants' Lives: The Dialectic of Migrant Labor and the Contradictions of Regulatory and Integration Policies in the Federal Republic of Germany', in Glebe, G. and O'Loughlin, J. (eds), *Foreign Minorities in Continental European Cities*, Stuttgart: Steiner Verlag Wiesbaden GMBH.

O'Loughlin, J. (1987), 'Introduction: Foreign Minorities in Continental Europe', in Glebe, G. and O'Loughlin, J. (eds), *Foreign Minorities in Continental European Cities*, Stuttgart: Steiner Verlag Wiesbaden GMBH.

Peach, C. (1987), 'Immigration and Segregation in Western Europe since 1945', in Glebe, G. and O'Loughlin, J. (eds), *Foreign Minorities in Continental European Cities*, Stuttgart: Steiner Verlag Wiesbaden GMBH.

Pfeiffer, U. et al. (1994), *Housing Provision of Immigrants and Refugees as a Tool of Social*

Integration, Luxembourg: Office for Official Publications of the European Communities.

Power, A. (1997), *Estates on the Edge: The Social Consequences of Mass Housing in Northern Europe*, London: Macmillan

Richmond, A.H. (1955), *The Colour Problem*, Harmondsworth: Penguin.

Rodin, C. (1997), *The Book of Jewish Food*, London: Viking.

Rudder, V. de (1992), 'Immigrant Housing and Integration in French Cities', in Horowitz, D.L. and Noiriel, G. (eds), *Immigrants in Two Democracies: French and American Experiences*, New York: New York University Press.

Saunders, J. (1991), 'Introduction', in Freedman, L. and Saunders, J. (eds), *Population Change and European Security*, London: Brassey's.

Silkin, J. (1946), 'Our Plan for Land and Houses', in Morrison, H. et al. (eds), *Forward from Victory: Labour's Plan*, London: Gollancz.

Smith, S.J. (1993), 'Residential Segregation and the Politics of Racialization', in Cross, M. and Keith, M. (eds), *Racism, the City and the State*, London: Routledge.

Social Exclusion Unit (1998), *Bringing Britain Together: a National Strategy for Neighbourhood Renewal*, CM 4045, London: The Stationery Office.

Wacquant, L.J.D. (1993), 'Urban Outcasts: Stigma and Division in the Black American Ghetto and the French Urban Periphery', *International Journal of Urban and Regional Research*, 17(3).

Wacquant, L.J.D. (1997), 'Three Pernicious Premises in the Study of the American Ghetto', *International Journal of Urban and Regional Research*, 21(2)

Wasserstein, B. (1996), *Vanishing Diaspora: The Jews in Europe since 1945*, London: Hamish Hamilton.

Wistrich, R.S. (1992), *Anti-Semitism: The Longest Hatred*, London: Thames Mandarin.

16 Community, Identity and the State: Minority Struggles within the European Union

Beth Ginsburg and Ranjit Sondhi

It is estimated that there are between 15 and 20 million black and migrant people residing in the member states of the Council of Europe, amounting to between 5–10 per cent of the total population. An estimate of additional undocumented migrant workers amounts to around two million. The new Europe is characterized by racial and cultural diversity: Algerians in France, Turks in Germany and Bulgaria, Kurds in Sweden, Surinamese in the Netherlands, Moroccans in Spain, Roma people in many central European countries, and people of Asian, African and Caribbean origin in Britain. The religious traditions of Europe now must accommodate Islam, Hinduism, Sikhism and Buddhism as well as Judaism and Christianity.

This post-colonial multicultural, multiracial and multi-ethnic Europe presents challenges to societies which imagined themselves as homogeneous. Yet racism, intolerance, anti-Semitism and xenophobia persist, at both personal and institutional levels, in more or less virulent forms in every single country of Europe. Black migrant workers, whether third-country or European nationals, continue to be subjected to control before, after and at the point of entry into a member state. Control before entry is maintained through the passage of increasingly restrictive immigration and asylum legislation and the threat of expulsion or extradition. After entry, it is affected through state and bureaucratic surveillance, identity cards and aggressive policing measures.

Liz Fekete and Frances Webber (1994) indicate how, without exception, in every European state, minorities continue to suffer from extreme forms of prejudice, discrimination and violence. In Germany, an investigation into the events at Rostock revealed police collusion with a racist mob which was left free to set fire to a refugee hostel, almost killing 100 Vietnamese men, women and children. In Spain, attacks on Romanies and African seasonal workers have become commonplace in the last few years, and their homes have been burnt down. In France, several North African youths have died in confrontations with the police, and immigration authorities have been accused of using excessive violence in deporting people. In Poland, Jewish cemeteries have been desecrated and openly anti-Semitic sentiments have been expressed by both politicians and the Church. In Italy, several hundred migrant workers were forced to flee their homes after the locals launched a 'black hunt'. Similar incidents, in which migrant workers have been victimized, have been reported from Austria, the Czech Republic, Belgium, Denmark, Greece, Hungary, Norway, the Netherlands, Sweden and Switzerland.

It is worth noting that even Britain, where race relations legislation has been in force for over twenty years, certainly does not have a clean record. Black and other minority ethnic people are twice as likely to be unemployed compared to white people and, once in employment, are seven times more likely to lose their jobs. African-Caribbean boys are four times more likely than white boys to be excluded from school. Disproportionately large numbers of ethnic minorities continue to live in the poorest housing conditions. Independent research published in 1993 found that one in ten black households in London suffered racial abuse, threats or physical attacks. Incidents ranged from taunts to excrement being thrown at people and violent assaults. This amounts to a total of 48,000 households and even this figure might well be an understatement of the real extent of racial harassment. Young blacks are four times more likely to be stopped and searched than average although their subsequent rate of arrest is no higher than average. According to the government's own surveys, it is estimated that the number of racial attacks and incidents is now 140,000 a year. This is the equivalent of just under 400 such incidents every day. Other research shows that, every other month, a young black person dies in suspicious circumstances in the custody of Britain's prisons, police stations and psychiatric hospitals.

Under these conditions, ethnic minorities in Europe have no alternative but to organize themselves for the preservation of their quality of life, and sometimes for life itself. State instruments of protection, where available, are either not effective enough or themselves not free from prejudice and discrimination. Arguably, the most effective organizations have been perceived to be those who have operated largely outside established institutions, whether they have come together as cultural and social groups or as political movements. Even within existing structures, like trade union and left-wing movements, the tendency for persecuted minorities has been to use ethnicity as a basis for radical grouping to form a Black caucus to further the cause of the ethnic group.

In order to understand the different kinds of survival strategies developed, consideration must be given to a number of specific factors that govern the precise formations of ethnic minority groupings to be found in Europe. Orlando Patterson (1983) has argued that these factors are both 'inner-cultural' and 'outer-structural'. At the inner-cultural level, ethnicity is determined by the manner in which an ethnic minority group shares a crises of alienation and the way in which individuals express their commitment to the group in order to resolve that crisis. At the outer-structural level, their actions are determined by the source, context and timing of the crisis, the relative size and resources of the group, and the policy of its leadership.

Distinctions must also be made between national minorities, regional minorities, immigrant minorities, refugees and asylum seekers. Migrant minorities are the consequences of population flows resulting from economic pressures, natural disasters or brutal force, and the degree to which this movement of peoples is voluntary varies enormously. Their stay in the countries of destination is also subject to varying degrees of control, ranging from permanent settlement to extremely restricted temporary leave. These conditions alone will determine the extent to which members of minority groups are willing and able to participate in public displays of solidarity. For instance, it is common knowledge that some metropolitan companies employ only undocumented migrants, as the low level of organization within this group allows employers to treat them with impunity. On the other hand, settled migrant workers, with permanent leave to remain have been able to fight resolutely, not only for better conditions of work and pay for themselves but also for indigenous workers, for example, Indian Workers' Associations in Britain.

For the purposes of this chapter, we are primarily concerned with community and identity options available to the 'new ethnic minorities'. New ethnic minorities, according to the definition used in the Migration Policy Group's (1996) project on Comparative Approaches to Societal Integration are defined as racial and ethnic minorities who migrated to countries in Europe in the post-colonial period for mostly socioeconomic reasons. As has already been indicated, preconditions for the emergence of these new ethnic minority groups might include the existence of a differential distribution of resources between the minority, a shared historically based cultural experience, and a shared experience, normally of deprivation, in the host country. The extent to which the majority group forms an exclusive ethnic organization rather than joins an existing organization will depend on how much the organizational goals are facilitated by the basis language, shared cultural and religious background and shared symbolic values which provide for communication. Shared language in itself is a rich source for mobilization, but the shared values brought from the homeland and the commonly owned symbolism, in the broader semiotic sense, provide an additional means towards achieving solidarity in order to fight prejudice and discrimination.

There are clearly great advantages in using ethnicity as a basis for radical grouping. For visible minorities, this can mean a strategic withdrawal into a world where they can feel culturally and linguistically at ease before they emerge to operate with more confidence and purpose in wider society. But the best type of ethnicity is one which defines a new place for identity not simply by insisting on difference, but on the fact that it is something constructed, not simply found. This ethnicity is not seen to be tied to fixed unalterable oppositions, and most importantly is not wholly defined by exclusion. Where ethnicity is so deployed, members may draw inwards temporarily in order eventually to move more effectively outward. When constructed in this manner, ethnicity becomes a basis of cohesion and a technique of mobilization, just as nationalism is employed by a subject people to throw off the yoke of imperialism.

The test of any group organized along ethnic lines is the extent to which it is inclusive of other ethnicities or, alternatively, the extent to which it seals itself off from them. Critical questions for such groups are:

- Can the group be intimate with members of another ethnic group, and cherish and celebrate their difference as much as their own?
- Does it have an active policy for building staged alliances and allegiances with other groups across the very boundaries that it seeks to preserve?
- Does it freely grant the freedom to its individual members to move in and out of its ethnic space should they so choose?
- To what extent is it prepared to fight for the rights of others to self-determination and equal participation even before their own are fully realized?

It should be of considerable interest to contrast the development of the Black Peoples' Alliance in Britain in the 1970s, which brought together Asian, African, Caribbean and Irish workers on the same anti-racist platform, with the growth of more ethnicized groupings of the 1980s and 1990s that concerned themselves with preserving particular cultural traditions and values. The first was essentially a political grouping with the aim of improving the general quality of life while the second was a cultural enterprise dedicated to maintaining a specific way of life.

In connection with the last point, careful consideration should be given to the attendant dangers faced by a minority group which deploys a singularly ethnic strategy. For members who feel besieged by an oppressive society, it has a tendency of becoming an end in itself. Ethnic consciousness can be both a way of dealing with and deflecting the issues at the same time. It contains within it the seeds of its own destruction. The history of ethnic groups indicates that although, at times, ethnicity might have been in the best material and social interests of its members, they also pay a heavy price for their commitments. They are periodically subjected by a jealous and prejudiced majority to vicious pogroms that result in the horrors of ethnic cleansing.

Also, an unscrupulous ethnic leader may exploit the ethnic group to sustain some power and influence in wider society to the detriment of the group. In doing so, the life of an ethnic movement might be prolonged beyond the point of usefulness, and this will have been achieved by a descent into ethnic chauvinism. There may also be a tendency for the ethnic strategy of one group to spark imitative or reactive strategies on the part of other groups who might feel that their interests are being forgotten in what they see as a zero-sum world. There are a depressingly large number of examples, in both historical and contemporary times, where pluralist societies have broken up into separate ethnic groups warring against each other for the same scarce resources.

But without doubt, the most frightening danger of an ethnic strategy is when the dominant majority uses its own ethnic strategy in response. Take the question of nation and nationalism. We are aware of the degree to which nations can be constituted, and have been constituted in history, on the basis of an assumed common ancestry, on the concept of a 'hereditary' group of people who feel that through centuries of living together and intermarriage they are tied together by 'ties of blood'. Ethnicity then becomes a constitutive element in the most viciously regressive kind of nationalism or national identity. This kind of ethnicity becomes tied to fixed, permanent, unalterable positions. It becomes wholly defined by exclusion. It becomes armour-plated against other identities.

When this happens, we are well on the road to fascism. Even at this very moment, we are witnessing the resurgence of fascist groups all over the Western world. More alarming is the fact that the moral majority movement, allied with the new right, could easily and spontaneously be transformed into a fascist movement. A severe economic depression combined with a Hitler-type charismatic figure is all that it takes. The recent history of Europe bears witness to that.

In the aftermath of the failure of broad-based movements, ethnicity has at times become the one difference that makes all the difference. Like all such single-issue campaigns, ethnic movements contain within them the power to question the whole politics of the system in the light of the single issue. The legitimacy of any black group is judged at the point when it faces a crisis of direction or of internal policy. In their struggle for equal treatment, blacks may find that they have to align itself with whites, at times against other blacks. There comes a moment when they choose, either to act as a closed group with the ever-present danger of their association becoming a safety valve, or to push the issue to the point when they begin to contradict their own definition and become part of a general campaign for social justice.

But when faced with such a crisis, black groups can abandon the struggle against racism and retreat into culturalism and ethnicism – a struggle for culture and not against racism. The fight is then for, say, blackness, or Asian-ness, or Muslim-ness – not primarily a fight against racism. It represents a retreat from establishing a political culture and into a kind of cultural politics. In virtually all member states, we are in the grip of an ethnic revivalism – in both black and white society. It is therefore incumbent upon us to warn of the irrationalities and inherent dangers of ethnic identification: the recent fate of Sarajevo should make that abundantly clear.

Of late, however, ethnicity is beginning to carry some other meanings, and to define a new space for identity. It insists on location – on the fact that every identity is placed, positioned, in a culture, a language, a history. Every ethnic sentiment comes from somewhere, from somebody in particular. But it is no longer grounded in a set of fixed transcendental categories and which therefore has no guarantees in Nature. It is not to be viewed as having an essentialist, primordial quality. Rather, as has been said, 'ethnicity is a process of invention which incorporates, adapts, and amplifies pre-existing communal solidarities, cultural attributes and historical memories. Ethnicity therefore is an arte-fact not nature-fact' (Green and Grosvenor 1996: 21).

What this brings into play is the instant recognition of the immense diversity and differentiation of the historical and cultural experience of ethnic subjects; that is to say, a recognition that everyone speaks from a particular place, out of a particular history, out of a particular experience, and a particular culture, without being strait-jacketed by the binary oppositions of black and white, male and female, gay and straight. We are all ethnically located, but exist in the knowledge that our boundaries are being constantly crossed and recrossed by the categories of race, gender, sexuality and class.

Generally speaking, it may well be that ethnic groups are 'imaginary communities' with potentially endless variations, fragmentations and displacements. But ethnicity is also, at any given moment, in a particular place, fairly firmly anchored. It must be remembered that the acceptance of the fictional nature of ethnic identity, and of constantly shifting and multiplying identity options, also requires, as a necessity, its opposite: the moment of arbitrary closure. Identity can be likened to discourse; potentially both are endless. But to say anything in particular, one has to stop talking. There must be a full stop at the end of a sentence. So it is with ethnic boundaries. We must acknowledge they are not forever, not totally universally true, not underpinned by an infinite guarantees. But, for the moment, there is always a boundary, no matter how partial, temporary or arbitrary. Otherwise, we would all flow into one another and there would be 'no political action, no cut and thrust of ideology, no positioning, no crossing of lines, no change' (Hall 1987). So there are other identities out there that do matter, that do bear some definite relationship to each other, that must be dealt with somehow. Accepting the necessarily fictional nature of ethnicity does not stop the ethnic subject from engaging in the politics of difference. But it is an altogether gentler politics, a deeply non-violent encounter, in which ethnicity becomes not a brutalizing but a revitalizing force.

And, it also freely admits of the possibility of multiple identities, of which ethnicity is but a part. Nobody identifies with the same group or in opposition to the same set of others all the time. Everybody has more than one answer to the question 'Who am I?'. Individuals have a more or less extensive repertoire of identity options which they call upon or engage with in different contexts and for different purposes. These identities are stored within the individual, and are not always visible to the observer, and it is likely that the individual will not always be conscious of shifting from one identity to another. Also identity is a two-way process, and our observations apply to majority as well as minority populations. But it is not an equal process, as it is usually majority definitions that order the distribution of political and economic resources. It is therefore particularly important for those in power to take account of identity shifts and recognize the positive value of identity options.

Any discussion about the nature of ethnic identity and the extent of ethnic mobilization in Europe must therefore also be firmly placed in a broader socio-political context and take account of the various approaches adopted by member states towards the integration of minorities and to the reduction of inequality. In order to understand and evaluate different government responses towards societal integration, defined here as the mutual and reciprocal coming together of members of the host and immigrant communities, and to mark the changes in these approaches, a project was recently completed by the Migration Policy Group (1996) on Comparative Approaches to Societal Integration.

Two prominent government approaches towards societal integration are: the ethnic minorities approach and the citizens' rights approach. The ethnic minorities approach, as an ideal type, provides targeted programmes to meet the special needs and claims of ethnic minority groups. British government policies present a good example of this approach. However, a critical analysis reveals that the modern state favours certain types of community relations. The politics of equality is likely to be displaced by the politics of diversity, and state funding is much more readily available for groups that are being defined more narrowly along ethnic and cultural lines. The right to be different appears to have superseded the right to equal treatment. Self-determination is bought at the price of equal participation. There is a greater focus on identity than on community. There has been a proliferation of projects in British cities that have been specifically designed – and have attracted generous state funding – for African-Caribbeans and Asians separately, for Hindus, Sikhs or Seventh Day Adventists, or for exclusive cultural, social and linguistic groups, all vying for the same resources.

In contrast, the citizens' rights model is premised on equality of all individuals before law. Individuals will identify themselves as French citizens first and foremost. Ethnic identities are not recognized within the public sphere. In this model, one's cultural, ethnic, religious or racial identities are private matters. The role of the state, in promoting good community relations, is to ensure that every citizen is treated as an equal member of society with the same rights and responsibilities. Consistent with their model, French officials in Council of Europe meetings in this social policy area, refuse to use the terminology of 'ethnic minority' as they perceive it as manufacturing and accentuating societal divisions which, they argue, has been known to create discriminatory and racist attitudes and practices.

Several French government policies provide good examples of the citizens' rights theoretical approach at the practical level. Acquiring French citizenship is central to integration and, in recent years, there has been extra emphasis given to transforming 'l'immigré au citoyen'. According to French civil servants, general policies are implemented to diminish socioeconomic inequalities. For example, socioeconomically deprived areas (which the French officials emphasize are not ethnic minority ghettos, but are inhabited by all races, ethnicities, etc.) are targeted through urban renewal programmes and the French government's *Programme National d'Intégration*, aimed at breathing new life into France's urban neighbourhoods. In addition, deprived youths are targeted for funding through youth work programmes and apprenticeships.

However, the purity of these models is often not retained in practice. In some cases, the rigid belief in models may in fact hinder progress in fighting discrimination. Changing structural and cultural factors have presented challenges to these top-down approaches. High unemployment and public welfare cutbacks within most European states have had a particularly detrimental effect on the already weak societal position of many new ethnic minorities. The responses of governments and minority groups, which may contradict these models, are particularly instructive in understanding the changing nature of societal integration at the practical level.

For example, governments which follow the ethnic minorities approach, have cut back and/or eliminated many of the special programmes for ethnic minorities. Policy makers and politicians now must pick and choose amongst groups, allocating what resources are left to those groups which can exhibit the most need. As a result, minorities must scramble for their piece of the shrinking government funding-pie. This exacerbates insecure relations between groups and forces individuals to narrowly define themselves as belonging to one group or another. This is partly done as a defence mechanism and partly in order to be eligible for special funding and self-help within those groups. The old category of 'black' in Britain, for instance, as political identity no longer captures the government's attention in terms of funding – it is too large and undifferentiated a grouping. In order to delineate who gets what, the British government and ethnic minority group leaders now refer to 'the black and Asian communities'.

Moreover, policy makers have themselves begun to question the foundations of the ethnic minorities approach. They are not convinced that multicultural education and positive action programmes have led to equality. Some believe that it has led to reverse discrimination. Others believe that programmes were never properly funded, and were therefore never given the chance to succeed.

In the case of the citizens' rights approach, what is happening in France reveals the contradictions between this model and practical policy making. The application and extension of social rights in France for non-nationals goes against the logic that French citizenship is needed to shed oneself of other identities. Judgments about the rights of non-nationals issued by the International Court of Justice have made France accountable. Localized resident status also challenges this confined notion of identity through citizenship. (For further explanation of the clash between the French model and world realities, see Favell 1995.) Furthermore, some experts and policy makers, when speaking off the record, question the utility of the French model in meeting the needs of its new ethnic minority populations.

Another general trend, which especially affects new ethnic minorities are governments' increasingly restrictive immigration laws and controls to limit the influx of refugees and asylum seekers. Older generations of immigrants attempt to differentiate themselves from new arrivals in order to legitimate their permanent position in society. Hence, narrowly defined, exclusive group affiliations begin to replace more inclusive forms of identity. For example, in Britain, blacks and Asians see themselves as distanced from the newly arrived communities of refugees and asylum seekers from Africa, the Middle East and eastern Europe. There have been examples of London schools where refugee children have been pejoratively referred to as 'bogus' by other children – white and black alike.

In Germany, the influx of *Aussiedler* (those with German ancestry) has established a class system amongst new arrivals. For example, *Aussiedler* are granted automatic citizenship rights under *jus sanguinis* (citizenship through bloodline), whereas other 'foreigners' are not eligible for automatic citizenship because they lack a German bloodline. Traditionally, 'foreigners' have been provided with extensive socioeconomic rights as legally resident non-citizens. However, a larger budget is now spent on the *Aussiedler* who are entitled to special programmes such as free language training. Foreigners are not eligible for entrance to these programmes.

One response by many new ethnic minority groups to cutbacks in the welfare state has been to seek 'self-help'. In Sweden, for example, with the dismantling of much of the extensive welfare system, individual members of minority groups are being asked what they would like from the government in place of special programmes which it can now ill-afford. In the past, the government encouraged minorities to form groups to enable them to enter into dialogue with the policy makers. Intriguingly, during the discussion of cutbacks in resources, members of these groups requested the Swedish government to 'leave them alone' and to allow them to focus on their small businesses and private lives. In addition, some members of these groups want the opportunity to make a conscious choice as to whether they learn Swedish, if they are new immigrants, or to learn their 'home language' if they are second or third generation. Historically, Swedish-as-a-second-language has been a subject included in the national curriculum.

It is clear that government policies play a major role in shaping the response of ethnic minority groups to differential treatment. Government officials must accept that their actions are as likely to exacerbate racial tension as they are to diffuse it. In particular, they cannot afford to ignore the present climate prevailing across the whole of Europe, in which racial violence requires as much urgent attention as racial discrimination. It has been rightly said that while there is a racism that discriminates, there is also the racism that kills. While the first affects the chances of aspiring black people to improve their socioeconomic status through the use of established anti-discrimination legislation, the latter affects those for whom racial discrimination is compounded by poverty and violence.

This involves examining the position of a whole class of people in the heart of our inner cities that is out of reckoning of mainstream society, out of education, out of training, out of all the statistics, and therefore deschooled, never-employed, criminalized, locked up and sectioned off. It is in that one-third of society, as the black activist and writer Sivanandan suggests, where the poorest sections of our communities – white and black – scrabble over the left-over scraps of work, the rubble of slum housing and the dwindling share of welfare; it is here that racism is at its most murderous (1995). Here there is no discrimination in employment because there is no employment, and no discrimination in services, goods and facilities because these have long since disappeared.

In almost every country in Europe, the growth of extreme right-wing movements is giving cause for concern. And it is in organizing against the racism that kills, that movements have once again been formed across ethnic, class and faith lines. We might note how it is invariably the case that a grassroots community response to the increase in racial violence is stronger, more immediate and carries more conviction than an institutional state response.

But minority groups cannot hold out indefinitely on their own, even with committed support from sympathetic organizations like churches, trade unions and anti-racist alliances. The state can no longer afford to abrogate its responsibility in the elimination of racial discrimination and violence. The improvement of community relations has become part of a public debate in many countries. In terms of policies and practices, some policy makers pick and choose from whatever works regardless of the model, while others are rigidly confined by their model. Simultaneously, groups are constantly forced to respond to government actions and to fill in the gaps which government policies inevitably leave.

On the positive side, states have made some progress in working towards the elimination of racial discrimination. One indication of this progress is how the language used to describe new ethnic minorities is changing, even in Germany where 'foreigners' and 'guestworkers' are now referred to as 'ethnic minorities' by (ironically) the Governmental Office for Foreigners and by some political parties and NGOs. In addition, the German federal government has taken steps to ease the restrictions on naturalization.

However, much more needs to be done in a cohesive manner. To this end, we strongly endorse the following measures in accordance with the recommendations proposed by the Migration Policy Group to the Council of Europe (1996):

- A review of national legislation with a view to removing discriminatory clauses
- In countries of the European Union, the gradual introduction of measures to eliminate the distinction in status between EU nationals living in another member state and long-term third-country nationals residing in the territory

- Extending the right to stand and vote in local elections to legal foreign residents
- Coordinated public and private efforts to encourage voter participation among eligible foreign populations
- Easing access to naturalization, while reassessing the merits of sole-nationality legislation
- Information campaigns targeted at immigrant populations to inform them of naturalization and nationality criteria
- The establishment of supervisory mechanisms to monitor and enforce the implementation of anti-discrimination measures
- The development of measures to inform those responsible for administering criminal justice of their rights and obligations to implement and comply with anti-discrimination laws
- Encouragement of voluntary codes of anti-discriminatory practices in the public and private sector (including the media).

References

Council of Europe (1996), *Review of the Implementation of Community Relations Policies*, Presented at the 6th Conference of European Ministers Responsible for Migration Affairs, Warsaw.

Favell, A. (1995), 'Citizenship and Immigration: Pathologies of a Progressive Idiom', Paper for ECPR Workshop, Bordeaux.

Fekete, L. and Webber, F. (1994), *Inside Racist Europe*, London: Institute of Race Relations.

Green, M. and Grosvenor, I. (1996), 'Making Subjects: Historians, Educations and "Race" Categorisation', Paper presented at CHEA/HES, Toronto.

Hall, S. (1987), 'Minimal Selves', in *Identity*, ICA Document 6.

Migration Policy Group (1996), *Comparative Approaches to Societal Integration*, Brussels: Final Report.

Patterson, O. (1983), 'Implications of Ethnic Identification', in *Minorities: Community and Identity*, Dahlem Konferenzen, Berlin: Springer Verlag.

Sivanandan, A. (1995), 'Racism: Representation and Reality or La Trahison des Clercs', speech delivered at the JCA, London, 18 May.

17 Intercultural Health in Europe

Roy Carr-Hill

I Introduction

The crudest version of interculturality refers to non-nationals of the different member states. The latest estimates of their numbers are given in Table 17.1. A slightly more sophisticated definition would distinguish a variety of different cultural groupings among nationals of any particular country. On this basis, we would distinguish, in the UK for example, between – at least – English, Irish, Scottish and Welsh and possibly also between Cornish, East Enders and Yorkshire women. Moreover, in addition to these sub-national distinctions which exist in all European states, there are also distinctions according to class, religion, sexual orientation, etc. It seems inappropriate however, in a book about social policy, to dwell only on definitions, and we take the pragmatic view that an examination of interculturality of health refers mainly to studies of minority groups within a nation state defined by language, nationality or origin.

The particular issue for this chapter is interculturality's impact on health. Evidence from the UK, which is probably typical of European experience, shows that minority ethnic groups are subject to a worse health experience than whites (Baxter and Baxter 1985; Hopkins and Bahl 1993); and find it harder to gain access to a general practitioner (Rashid and Jagger 1992). In turn, the latter often hold less positive views about their patients (Ahmad et al. 1991). Language barriers are seen as most important (McAvoy and Sayeed 1990; Wright 1983), and cultural differences in health perception and behaviour often inhibit access (Jayaratnam 1993).

However, whilst those working in the field of interculturality or multiculturalism may find the problems of definition daunting, they would

Table 17.1 Number and percentage of foreign citizens in western European countries

Country	Total population ('000s)	Foreign population ('000s)	% of foreigners
Austria	7,861	542	7
Belgium	9,078	901	9
Finland	5,029	37	0.7
France	57,206	3,535	6
Germany	79,750	5,500	7
Greece	10,168	226	2
Iceland	260	5.4	2
Ireland	3,542	88	3
Italy	57,788	710	1
Luxembourg	390	115	29
Netherlands	15,129	728	5
Norway	4,274	148	4
Portugal	9,846	114	1
Spain	39,056	610	2
Sweden	8,644	494	6
Switzerland	6,834	1,191	17
United Kingdom	57,701	1,904	3

Source: Fonteneau (1992: 57).

pale before the impossibility of agreeing on what health is. This goes beyond the simple distinction between health as the absence of disease (the medical model), health as the absence of illness (the sociological model), and health as an ideal (the approach adopted by the World Health Organization). Indeed, there has been a long-standing debate about the different meanings of health among 'indigenous' white populations. Herzlich (1973), in a well-known qualitative study among middle-class respondents in Paris, identified four ways in which 'being healthy' was defined: being able actively to *do* things (functional capability), or alternatively being *restricted* by ill-health, *feeling* healthy, or alternatively *not being ill*. Williams (1983) identified another set of understandings amongst working-class communities in Scotland and Baxter (1990) concluded that there were at least six conceptually distinct meanings.

In this context, at least part of the impact of interculturality could be seen as a consequence of differences in approach to the definitions of health, or differences implicitly imposed by the existing system of health service provision. But postmodern interpretations of early death are in short supply (compare the Red Army Faction (1971ff) who were clear about the relative priority of lives and politics), and there are 'real' differences in rates of death and in morbidity and access to health care. We therefore have to revert (in Section II of this chapter) to a traditional epidemiology of different cultural groupings within Europe and specifically the extent to which intercultural differences can help to account for the observed differences, before examining more measured explanations of differences between and within societies in Section III. The complexity of this exercise is illustrated in Section IV through a discussion of the findings of a comprehensive survey amongst Asian communities in England; and a possible approach to an appropriate policy is discussed in Section V.

II Basic epidemiology

Focusing for the moment on immigrants and their descendants (rather than sub-national groupings or other cultural groupings), there are some clear differences. Rates of perinatal and infant mortality for some European countries are presented in Table 17.2: North African and Turkish people have systematically higher perinatal mortality rates in Belgium, France and Switzerland; those from the Asian subcontinent have higher rates of perinatal mortality but not infant mortality in the UK, and so on. Inequities (and anomalies) of this kind occur when comparing mortality rates for different conditions. For example, within the UK, whilst it is true that those from Africa, India or the Caribbean have raised rates for circulatory diseases, it is the Irish who have the highest rate for all respiratory diseases and deaths from all external causes (see Table 17.3).

It is, however, very risky to pursue the comparison of condition-specific mortality rates across countries in Europe. As Leclerc (1989) showed, what medical professionals claimed are the causes of death depends more on the national medical culture than on the condition; this tendency is exacerbated when considering sub-national groupings because the categorization of cause of death is likely to be imposed by a professional from another (probably the dominant) cultural group. Moreover, there is of course a major problem of treating ethnicity and race as unitary categories (let alone as proxies for 'pure' and fixed gene pools) when no attention is paid to stratification within ethnic minority communities or their medical and social histories.

Equally, one can show differences in data on accidents and injuries. In Tables 17.4a and 17.4b, much higher rates are reported for immigrants in all

Table 17.2 Perinatal and infant mortality in some western European countries (all rates per 1000)

	Still births		Perinatal mortality		Infant mortality	
Belgium			Belgians	10.7		
			Northern EC	6.9		
			Southern EC	9.0		
			North Africans	14.8		
			Turkish	17.7		
France	French	7.1	French	6.0		
	North Africans	13.3	North Africans	15.0		
	Others	10.6	Others	15.5		
Germany			German female	9.5		
			Foreign female	11.5		
			German male	7.3		
			Foreign male	8.5		
Sweden	Swedish	6.6	Swedish	12.5		
	Nordics	6.0	Nordics	12.0		
	Southern Europeans	6.6	Southern Europeans	11.3		
Switzerland			Swiss	9.4	Swiss	8.2
			Italian	11.3	Italians	8.6
			Spanish	9.3	Spanish	7.2
			Turkish	17.5	Turkish	12.3
United Kingdom	UK	5.6	UK		UK	9.7
	Eire	5.9	Eire		Eire	10.1
	Bangladeshi		Bangladeshi		Bangladeshi	9.3
	Indians		Indians		Indians	10.1
	Pakistani		Pakistani		Pakistanis	16.6

Source: Balarajan et al. (1989); Bourdillon et al. (1991); Marmot (1993–94).

four countries; and the more detailed data for France show that this is also true for the different possible consequences of accidents.

Similarly, Arrow (1996), comparing German and other nationals, finds that among foreign female workers, the relative risk of becoming unemployed after a long sick leave is more than four times that of those without such a long absence from work. Obviously, however, these differences need to be understood in terms of the kinds of job that immigrants (compared to the native populations) are actually doing in each of the industries.

Table 17.3 Standardized mortality rates for groups of diseases within the UK

		Ireland	South Asia	Caribbean	African
All circulatory	M	117	133	77	127
	F	118	136	141	136
All respiratory	M	157	88	61	105
	F	140	104	101	106
All external causes	M	190	85	105	99
	F	59	113	100	136

Source: Balarajan and Balsa (1990).
Note: The data is standardized by age, but not by social class (on the assumption that a set of health risk factors may not apply very well to people who have spent half or two-thirds of their lives in the developing world).

Table 17.4a Reported and recorded occupational accidents for natives and immigrants in some western European countries

	Natives	Immigrants	Notes
Netherlands	32.0	92.0	Rates per 1000 insured workers
Germany	79.0	216.0	Rates per 1000 workers, all industries
Switzerland	158.0	230.0	Rates per 1000, building trade
France (metals)	4.7	7.7	Rates per 1000 permanent
(building)	11.4	21.5	disability or death

Table 17.4b Reported and recorded individual injuries in France, 1986

Sector of activity	Foreign workers %	Reported accidents %	Accident leading to an incapacity which is: Permanent %	Temporary %	Rate of permanent invalidity %
Iron & steel	8.8	13.4	17.2	15.6	15.6
Building & public work	20.6	25.9	33.3	31.0	31.0

This raises the issue of whether differences between ethnic or minority groups and the remainder of the population *per se* are the appropriate object of analysis. The next section looks at the complexity of the problems researchers have encountered in accounting for the maintenance and reproduction of inequalities in health between socioeconomic groups in general, and at how those complexities might be taken into account when assessing differences in health between different groups defined by culture; the following section gives a specific illustration of that complexity when attempting to explain intercultural differences.

III Explanation

The existence and persistence of inequalities between groups is indisputable. Indeed, it is a constant surprise to a non-medical epidemiologist that these differences have to be demonstrated: they are the corollary of any form of social differentiation. The first problem is which differences are 'unfair' and whether any change is possible. For some it is fate: Aiach (1989) shows how French commentators interpret mortality differentials between social groups in terms of morality and health behaviour. For others, some inequalities are beneficial: for example, Le Fanu (1993) in order to defend the supposed contribution of income inequality to national economic prosperity, feels obliged to 'prove' that low income does not kill. Against both, writers tend to use claims that inequalities in health have widened or arguments that health and income inequalities are linked, as part of a political statement.

Each of these positions is ideologically informed. It would, of course, be daft to claim that arguments and evidence can be presented totally neutrally. But abusing statistical data in the service of politics – for example, by exaggerating the differences in reaction to the attempts of others to hide them – does not help. A social scientist has an obligation to clarify the assumptions used, ensure that the data used is reliable, and sift evidence carefully: only the truth is revolutionary (Lenin 1905).

A more considered argument would be based on an analysis of how the differences have come about. This is not easy – which is perhaps why many prefer rhetoric. There are five main groups of determinants:

- natural biological variation
- health behaviour
- social conditions at work, at home and in the environment
- access to health and other public services, and
- health-related social selection.

The relative weight of these will vary from country to country and over time.

Health differences due to natural biological variations are usually considered as inevitable rather than inequitable. However, it is important to remember that what is seen as natural (biological) variation has changed over the century so that, for example, the inevitable loss of some children at birth is now seen – at least in the North – as a major tragedy that can nearly always be avoided.

Clearly disparities between groups in deaths which are avoidable – either because there is extreme poverty or because there are well-established treatments – are very important. Indeed, in societies where most die early, where their deaths would usually be avoidable in this sense, it may be the only characteristic worth examining; and Carr-Hill et al. (1987) show how these deaths are especially related to socioeconomic characteristics. But, in our societies, the life expectancy of those who survive perinatal trauma has been 70+ for some time. In general, however, differentials between groups in society – including the differences between men and women – cannot be accounted for on biological grounds and must therefore arise from social and economic causes. Where there are genetic variations between groups, society often exacerbates them: for example, gender differences are imposed on differences between the sexes. The crucial test of whether the health differences between groups in society are unjust is the extent to which the situation causing the ill-health is mainly within the control of those groups. The obvious 'culprit' is poverty or – in the New Europe – social exclusion.

The second problem in searching for explanations of inequalities is identifying accurate data about illnesses or mortality (by cause). This is especially important when making comparisons over time (or between countries) and between sub-groups.

Measuring ill-health

There is no difficulty in counting deaths, but consistent diagnosis of cause of death is much harder to achieve even within a country in the same period. Even the bravest medical epidemiologist tends to concentrate on overall mortality.

Measures of morbidity are more complicated. Unlike mortality, which happens only once, morbidity is repeatable and may last. There are data on incidence relating to numbers of events and prevalence relating to numbers of people who are, at any one time, impaired whether physically or mentally, permanently or temporarily. The difficulty with using any of the data generated by the health care sector is that the registration of conditions depends on the illness behaviours of sufferers and their families (for example, whether people with cancer or sexually transmitted diseases attend for diagnosis).

The extent to which a condition is stigmatized, the level of service provision available, the accuracy and certainty of diagnoses, and social and administrative processes differentially encourage and discourage notification. These all vary in unknown ways over time, between countries and between groups. Moreover, differences are often not so spectacular as with death rates: self-reported data is difficult to interpret and inter-temporal comparison of morbidity is almost impossible (see also Wadsworth 1986).

Some authors focus instead on more long-term and robust indicators such as the rate of low birth weight and achieved adult height. Both are associated with physical and intellectual development both in early and late childhood and in adolescence; and whilst there is genetic variation in height – and possibly in birth weight – between ethnic groups, there is no average genetic difference between sub-groups of the same race. The difficulty is that when making comparisons of differentials over time (or between countries), both the rate of low birth weight and average height are affected by differential survivability.

Debates in health policy: towards explanations

The final and possibly most intractable problem is that, although we can demonstrate several correlates of death rates, it is almost impossible to specify a model linking them together. Without a precise specification of the causal links being proposed and the lag structure of those processes, it is impossible to make any statements more definitive than that we know that certain socioeconomic conditions are associated with early death.

In this context, several issues are important. We consider, very briefly, only two here: associations between levels and inequalities in income and mortality, and the constraints of low income on behaviour.

Levels and inequalities in income

Many have argued that the utility of increasing GNP per capita falls off; indeed it is a trivial statement to those in living and/or working in less developed countries (LDCs) that increasing GNP per capita does not linearly improve living standards (the Human Development Index presumes that increasing income is only effective in improving living standards up to US$7,000 per capita). The contribution of any increment in income after that to living standards is likely to be small and dependent on social organization (thus the same levels of income per capita provided different social support under the previous Soviet system than in present eastern Europe).

Wilkinson (1992) – in a typically parochial analysis – has, however, suggested that, among developed countries, there is a link between inequalities in income and levels of and inequalities in death rates although there is no obvious link between economic and social inequalities and inequalities in health care (Gottschalk et al. 1989). Assuming that one can rely on the data, this is not surprising as, for a given GNP per capita, greater disparities almost certainly mean that more are poor. Whilst *relative* poverty is obviously not irrelevant to one's self-esteem within any specific society or social organization, it is the actual level of material resources which is most important for health and ill-health.

'Life-styles' and low income

The usual approach is to operationalize 'changing life-styles' in terms of measures and indicators of a number of separate behavioural items. However, the concentration on single behavioural patterns or health habits is dangerous in isolation. Complex issues of modifying life-styles are boiled down to the oversimplified view that bad habits can be changed solely by individually oriented health education and stress on personal responsibility, forgetting the socio-cultural, economic and political context of life-style formation.

Consider the well-established link between food and the risk of ill-health. Many people are making efforts to shop for and eat more healthy food. Those working with people on low incomes are aware that it is often these groups who, despite their best efforts, find it most difficult to eat more healthily. This is not because they are less knowledgeable, or because they waste money, or are not interested (Cole-Hamilton and Lang 1987), or because they do not know how to cook (MORI 1993). People on low incomes lack access to good-quality affordable produce as well as experiencing a lack of skills, facilities (DSS 1995) and – perhaps as a result – reduced motivation. Thus, whilst immigrants are more prone to acquire nutritional diseases in part because of dietary change (Wandel 1993), the main reason is 'simply' low income.

Marginality and migration

One possible explanation for the reproduction (or widening) of health inequalities between areas over time is the migration of 'fitter'/healthier people from deprived areas (O'Reilly 1994). This corresponds with the general thesis about the health of emigrant populations that they tend, though not always, to be healthier than the average for society *from* which they have emigrated but less healthy than the average for the society *to* which they migrate. This is not inevitable: Costa et al. (1990), analysing the Turin Longitudinal Study, show how people from the southern regions (of Italy) have lower mortality, whilst those born in the north-east have higher mortality than those always resident; these differences are strongest among men of lower socioeconomic status and weaken with time from immigration.

In particular, ethnic minority communities, in their immigration phase, tend to present with psychosomatic ailments: see, for example, Failde et al. (1992) for France, Priebe et al. (1990) for Germany, Frighi and Mazzetti (1995) for Italy, and Holtedahl (1991) for Norway. In the UK, Greek Cypriots (Mavreas and Bebbington 1990), and the Irish and the Jewish in their earlier periods of settlement (Bowling et al. 1992), have been disproportionately represented amongst the 'mentally ill'.

Note that this is not systematically the case for all immigrant groups: whilst the rates of admission in Table 17.5 are much higher for those born in Northern Ireland or in Eire, they are lower for those born in the Caribbean or the Indian sub-continent. Although the rates of suicide are higher for men born in Ireland, they are lower for women, whilst the reverse is true for those born in the Indian sub-continent.

Table 17.5 Age-standardized rates of admission to mental hospitals 16+ and standardized suicide rates 20–69 by place of birth, 1981 (UK)

	Rates per 100,000	Suicides ages 20–69	
		M	F
England	504	100	100
N. Ireland	838	126	31
Eire	1080		
Caribbean	548	80	84
India	321	71	149
Pakistani/Bangladesh	245		

Source: Soni-Raleigh and Balarajan (1992).

However, it must be recognized that there is often too much focus on the migrant status rather than on poverty. Analysing the pathologies affecting children of Gypsies and Third World immigrants in Spain, Corretger et al. (1992) show that the major pathologies are, in both cases, those associated with poor socioeconomic circumstances as well as hygienic/sanitary deficiencies: imported paediatric pathologies had only a small incidence.

Acculturation, depression and drinking behaviours

The epidemiological perspective on health is imbued with victimology in that little credit is given to the immigrant for taking control or altering her destiny; anti-racism and race equality were subsumed in the technocratic approach to health promotion. Thus, Marmot (1993/4) rather painfully explains how migrants initially bring the pattern of disease with them but slowly adopt – sometimes through generations – the disease pattern of the host community. Indeed, much of the writing on 'socio-cultural' factors and health treats culture as a 'black box': what cannot be explained by demography and socioeconomic status is attributed to 'culture'.

Sometimes there is an attempt to 'unpack' culture in terms of 'acculturative' experiences and sometimes in terms of attitudes and practices.

Difficulties of acculturation – or simply deprivation?

Seitamo, studying the problems of internal cultural migration for adult Skolts, living in the north of Finland, shows how changes in ecology, economies and acculturation have modified roles, affecting the men and women differently. The changes were less confusing for Skolt women than for the men, whose role was radically undermined. The author concludes that 'the developmental process in socialisation has been characterised by a search for balance between the traditional life style and attitudes and the challenges and conflicts that arise from the culture and education of the majority' (1995: 235).

A prime example of the genre is the study by Sam and Berry (1995). They examined the relationship between migration and the incidence of emotional disorders among 568 young (10–17 years) immigrants in Norway, using a questionnaire. Changes in health status as a result of acculturation was found to exist among children, although having to migrate or being born in Norway was not related to mental health status.

A stressful 'acculturative' experience – defined as difficulties in initiating friendship with Norwegian peers – accounted for very little (1 per cent) of self-reported emotional disorders. In contrast, the incidence of depressive tendencies, poor self-image, and psychological and somatic symptoms were found to be related to close and supportive parents, marginality, integration, gender and the number of friends the child had. These accounted for between 12 per cent and 15 per cent of the explained variance. Yet, at another extreme in the UK, ethnic minorities rarely live alone: 4–5 per cent of Asian and 30 per cent of Afro Caribbean elderly live alone compared to 44 per cent of whites (Holland and Leonardo 1987, cited in Jayaratnam

1993). Universal claims about culturally marginal groups are hard to sustain.

Behaviour

Alcohol abuse is a favourite topic for study – see, for example, Hallberg and Mattson (1991) for Sweden, Holder and Edwards (1995) for the UK. Yet, again, there is no consistent picture. Larsen and Negard (1990) compared the drinking patterns and treatment goals of Saami ('Lapp') and Norwegian patient problem drinkers. They differed significantly: Saami clients demonstrated a more periodic drinking pattern and, to a smaller extent, tended to prefer total abstinence or a large reduction in alcohol consumption as compared to Norwegian clients.

Data of this type are often very political: for example, there has been a concerted attempt to introduce ethnic monitoring in the UK but this does not include the Irish who are not seen as ex-colonial subjects (Hechter 1975). Yet the death rates for the Irish in England are high (see Britten 1990). Whilst this may well be due ultimately to the way in which the Irish are treated in England, the immediate cause is, most probably, that they drink more heavily than the English and the Irish in Ireland (see Table 17.6).

Table 17.6 Drinking amongst the Irish in the UK and the Irish in Ireland

	Republic-Irish	Northern-Irish	Republic-British	Northern Irish-British	British-British	Total N (100%)	Irish in Ireland (% distb'n)
% Light	59.0	56.8	55.7	58.3	64.3	10,774	65
% Moderate	28.6	31.5	33.5	25.6	27.3	4,633	30
% High	12.3	11.7	10.9	16.1	8.4	1,448	5
N	227	111	442	168	15,907.0	16,855	2,724

Source: Harrison et al. (1993); OPCS (1990).

Note 1: Republic-Irish: those born in the Irish Republic. Northern-Irish: those born in Northern Ireland. Republic-British: those born in Britain with one or both parents born in the Irish Republic. Northern Irish-British: those born in Britain with one or both parents born in Northern Ireland. British-British: British-born residents whose parents were also born in Britain

Note 2: Light: up to 7 units per week for women, 10 units per week for men. Moderate: 7--25 units for women, 10–35 units for men. Heavy: over 25 units for women, over 35 units for men. Source: OPCS (1990).

IV Health status, risks of 'English' life-style and use of primary care among minority ethnic communities

Attributing differences to immigrant status is therefore complex (see also Uniken Venema et al. 1995). Most of the epidemiological evidence presented is based on doubtful samples and on a presumption that the same processes are applicable to all sub-groups in the population. These problems are illustrated in this section.

The methodology for obtaining a proper sample

The English Health Education Authority commissioned a survey to attempt to assess health status, health-related behaviours and information needs among the black and minority ethnic communities on a national scale.

Own language interviews

In order to reach a representative sample, interviews were conducted where required in national languages (Gujerati, Hindi and Punjabi with Indians; Punjabi and Urdu with Pakistanis, and Bengali with Bangladeshis (for further details, see HEA 1996). In total, interviews were held with 723 African-Caribbeans, 1017 Indians, 923 Pakistanis and 665 Bangladeshis; about half of their interviews were held in their mother tongue. This proportion was considerably higher than expected.

Differences in social demography

Compared to the UK population, fewer were employed whether full- or part-time, with very low rates of participation in the labour force among Bangladeshis and Pakistanis; correspondingly, the rates of long-term unemployment were more than twice as high. The gender pattern was very different: participation rates were higher amongst African-Caribbean and Indian women than amongst the UK population but much lower amongst men from all groups.

Educational qualifications are substantially lower than among the UK population and this is most pronounced among men. These results are at variance with the levels of educational attainment reported in the Labour Force Survey (Office of National Statistics 1997): but it must be remembered that the LFS did not offer any mother-tongue interviewing and also interviewed a slightly younger population (16–64).

The pattern of housing tenure is distinctive, with African-Caribbeans and Bangladeshis having low rates of owner occupancy and very high rates of council renting; whilst Indians and Pakistanis are about 50 per cent more likely than the UK population as a whole to own their houses outright and almost as many are buying on mortgage. However, whilst 70 per cent of the UK population live in detached or semi-detached/end terraces and 20 per cent in mid-terraces, the proportions are almost reversed for Indians and Pakistanis.

Finally, access to a car is much lower amongst ethnic minority groups than among the UK population and between half and two-thirds do not have a licence.

Perceived health status and exposure to risk

Although over four-fifths of each of the minority ethnic groups except the Bangladeshis describe their health as very or fairly good, significantly more of each of the minority groups describe their status as very poor.

There are also important differences in the proportions reporting illness or disability (or limiting long-standing illness or disability) (see Table 17.7). Moreover, responses to the follow-on question, where respondents are asked to itemize the specific illnesses and diseases, suggests that the higher subjective expression of poor health reflects a different underlying epidemiology. For example, there is evidence for ethnic variations in mortality from hypertension (Cruickshank 1993; OPCS 1993); McKeigue and Marmot (1993) and Cruickshank (1991) have found significantly higher rates of non-insulin dependent diabetes amongst South Asians than Europeans. Correspondingly, arthritis/rheumatism/fibrositis are most often mentioned by the UK general population and less frequently by these minority groups, but about 5 per cent of South Asians report diabetes (compared to 1 per cent of the UK

Table 17.7 Prevalence of illness or disability (in brackets, prevalence of limiting long-standing illness or disability): percentages standardized to the age and sex profile of the British population

Group	Afro-Caribbean	Indian	Pakistani	Bangladeshi	UK population
All	29 (20)	26 (16)	30 (20)	36 (26)	27 (15)
Women	28 (18)	27 (16)	30 (20)	35 (26)	28 (16)
50–74	46 (31)	67 (40)	61 (43)	60 (41)	42 (26)
Men	31 (21)	25 (16)	31 (20)	28 (26)	27 (14)
50–74	48 (37)	52 (38)	55 (38)	77 (55)	38 (27)

Source: Health Education Authority (1989); MORI (1993).

population), between 4 per cent and 5 per cent of African-Caribbeans, Indians and Bangladeshis report hypertension or high blood pressure, and Bangladeshis frequently report stomach problems. When asked if they had ever experienced any of a list of problems or diseases, a similar pattern – although less pronounced – emerged; importantly minority ethnic communities less frequently report depression/anxiety/nerves, suggesting that the expression of these conditions requires many generations of acculturation.

The perceived exposure to risk is different as well: factors cited frequently are shown in Table 17.8. Whilst the general UK population – partly as a result of propaganda? – see life-style factors as a major risk, social and environmental factors are mentioned more frequently by the minority ethnic communities. In particular, whilst the African-Caribbean group approximates to the pattern of responses amongst the UK population, the South Asian groups hardly ever mention the amount they smoke, nor stress/worries at work; in contrast, whilst the UK population only rarely cites violent crime and hardly at all the quality of housing, these two are a major concern for each of these minority ethnic communities. When probed further about the quality of housing, the only factor cited frequently by the UK population is the quality of the drinking water: whilst this is also of concern to African-Caribbeans, like the other minority ethnic groups they are also concerned with dampness, noise levels, lack of heating and lack of personal space, presumably for the same reason as for anxiety (see above).

Table 17.8 Perceived exposure to risk

Group	Afro-Caribbean	Indian	Pakistani	Bangladeshi	UK population
My weight	18	16	13	7	24
Amount I smoke	12	3	6	6	18
Stress/worry at work	12	5	3	1	17
Amount of violent crime in area	15	14	13	17	6
Quality of my housing	8	5	11	26	2

Source: Health Education Authority (1989); MORI (1993).

Respondents were also asked whether they were involved in any health-maintaining or health-enhancing activity. Whilst over 60 per cent of the general population report participation, the rates for South Asian groups are substantially lower, especially for women.

Use of primary care services

The rates of consulting last month presented in Table 17.9a are broken down by age, gender and social class for each ethnic group. Rates for females are higher than for males in every sub-group up to age 45, but there is little difference afterwards. For those under 35, the rates do not differ by occupational grouping; however, thereafter the rates among manual groups are higher than among non-manual groups, especially for women. The rates appear to differ between ethnic groups. The actual rates of attendance are much higher than those reported elsewhere. This must be related to the fact that the interviews in this study were conducted in the mother tongue where this was requested. Second, age and gender do not have such a clear-cut relationship to GP attendance as they do among the general public. There appears to be a generation difference in the use of primary care and South Asian males seem to be much more ready to attend surgery than 'white' males.

The 'traditional' demographic variables such as social class and tenure status are only weakly related – if at all – to attendance at GPs' surgeries; employment status is associated but not in the same way (Table 17.9b). Finally, the reported level of worry does not appear to have the same kind of effect that has been noticed in the general population (Table 17.9c).

Multivariate analysis was carried out for whether or not someone attended a GP's surgery in the last month and in the last year separately for each of the ethnic groups and for all the three groups combined with offsets for Pakistanis and Bangladeshis

The results are reasonably consistent across all three ethnic groups. Although the Indian group has the highest attendance rate, there were only small differences between Indian, Pakistani and Bangladeshi groups in the responsiveness to the various influencing variables. Gender and age are not significant, which is substantially different from similar analyses among the general public. Whether or not the individual speaks and reads English seems to affect Pakistani attendance in a complex way, but these variables are not significant for the other two groups.

Employment status and self-reported health status appear with significant coefficients in each of the equations with roughly the same pattern. However, it is noticeable that it is those who are employed (including the base category) who are more likely to have attended than either 'housepersons' or the unemployed; also that the association between self-reported health status and attendance is unclear. With all groups combined, only Pakistanis have a significantly different coefficient. Moreover, in contrast to a similar analysis among the general population, neither the social class variable nor any proxies such as tenure status are ever statistically significant.

Table 17.9a Percent consulting in one month by social class among South Asians, age 35–54

	Male non-manual	Male manual	Male other	Female non-manual	Female manual	Female other
Indian	63	71	63	78	92	91
Pakistani	29	69	84	100	100	93
Bangladeshi	(14)	61	72	71	(0)	28

Source: Health Education Authority (1989); MORI (1999).
Note: Standardized data has been used: 'standardization' means adjusting each observation to take account of household size and of the age–sex breakdown of the general (mostly white) population

Table 17.9b Percent consulting in one month by tenure status, age 55–64

Age group	Male owner occupier	Male renting	Female owner occupier	Female renting
55–64	56	63	61	66
65–74	66	36	61	55

Source: Health Education Authority (1989); MORI (1999).

Table 17.9c Percent consulting in one month by level of anxiety, age 35–54

	Females			Males		
Age group	Absent	Some	High	Absent	Some	High
35–44	37	38	57	34	39	33
45–54	46	61	62	60	39	66

Source: Health Education Authority (1989); MORI (1999).

V Health care policies

The treatment of immigrants by health care services depends both upon their position, role and status within the community at large and upon the knowledge and training of health care workers in particular.

A formalistic approach

Bollini and Siem (1995) frame their review of access of immigrants to health care, accidents and disabilities, and perinatal mortality in terms of the 'entitlement' approach (Sen 1990). In this approach, health is considered as the product of both the individual's private endowments and the social environments she or he faces. Migrants, especially first and second-generation, and ethnic minorities, often have reduced entitlements in receiving societies. Not only are they exposed to poor working and living conditions, which are *per se* determinants of poor health, they also have reduced access to health care for a number of political administrative and cultural reasons (see Table 17.10).

Table 17.10 Social entitlements and legal status

Legal status	Right to reside	Right to work	Right to social security benefits
Resident migrant workers	+++	+++	++
Acknowledged refugees	+++	+++	+++
Temporary migrant workers	+	++	+/–
Asylum seekers	+	+/–	+/–
Illegal migrants	–	–	–

Sources: United States Committee for Refugees (1993); United Nations Department of Economic and Humanitarian Affairs (1986).

For example, the current Italian policy on immigration tends to force immigrants coming from non-EU countries into an illegal position This delays, and in many cases obstructs, their being able to benefit from existing services. Cambieri et al. (1990) and later Bandera (1993) observed the casualty departments of four of the city hospitals, public services and NAGA Care association of volunteers which has been operating in Milan since 1987 offering social and health assistance to immigrants, and nomads who, for legal, economical or cultural reasons, cannot benefit from the Public Health Service. The results confirmed that the Public Health Service tends to favour groups already having a certain privilege and delegates the more 'complex' problems to the voluntary associations. Lacking proper knowledge of the needs and perspective of the users, the system frames the problem in terms of exclusion–inclusion without evaluating the coherence of such a policy.

The dilemmas

One apparently obvious way in which appropriate care can be provided is via professionals of the same culture. But black doctors are ghettoized in unpopular areas of medicine (Smith 1980; Hopkins and Bahl 1993), employment policies are poor (GLARE 1987), and there have been clear cases of racial discrimination (Esmail and Everinton 1993; McKeigue et al. 1990). Similarly, black nurses have been ghettoized in the 'Cinderella' services, on lower grades and excluded from promotion opportunities (Baxter and Baxter 1985).

Mallet et al. (1989) describe the work of GRES 31, a small study group established in 1982 in Toulouse whose aim is to promote health among underprivileged groups such as Gypsies and immigrants from North Africa. Their approach is 'global' meaning that the health problems of an individual cannot be separated from the overall life context of her/his group, so the ethnic culture and collective behaviour of the group is closely related to the demand for care and health outcome.

However the researchers–experimenters cannot avoid certain conflicts among themselves: for example, when an ill child is endangered by the observance of the ethnic or religious (for example, Jehovah's Witnesses) traditions of her or his own group. More generally, efforts to reduce 'clinical imperative', 'state interventionism', 'local bureaucracy' have to be assessed *vis-à-vis* 'macro-problems' such as nuclear risk, AIDS or health care cost containment.

Good practices

In many European countries, there are systematic differences between the treatment of different groups of patients. The intended policies in England suggest a possible code of good practice:

- Programmes should be culturally and socially acceptable and appropriate; they must respect social definitions of privacy frontiers, of the rules for giving and receiving support, and of appropriate channels for action.
- Programmes must build on a community's strengths and insights, and try to reinforce them; they must not contribute to a collective sense of inadequacy or fragility by well-intentioned but culturally inappropriate actions.
- Attempts to modify attitudes and behaviour should be based on an understanding of their cultural origins and significance, their present functions, and their central or peripheral position within the life of the community.

- Outreach programmes should take account of the relative importance, the degrees of tolerance or intolerance, accorded to various problems in a given community. For example, a certain degree of violence might be well accepted, and even valued as a male attribute, in a community based on hazardous and precarious occupations. In a rural community valuing conformity and decency the same events might cause great concern.
- The concept of 'at-risk groups' should be complemented by that of 'target conditions'. Attention should be focused on the way in which specific or general health problems arise from a complex web of social and cultural determinants in a given environment, a web which may extend well beyond the identified 'at-risk group'.

These have, in turn, led to the promotion of a set of 'core' standards (see Appendix).

VI Discussion

Summary of argument

There are clear inescapable inequalities in both achieved health and access to health care, as between the immigrant and the indigenous populations in Europe. There is a mountain of evidence that immigrants and members of minority groups have higher death rates, are more to likely to be exposed to risks and have worse health than the general population. But there are some exceptions and other sub-groups of the population have similarly poor health experience and outcomes. Whilst it is nonsensical to attribute the inequalities to genetic differences, there are several alternatives to discrimination–racism as the explanation, and a coherent account should explore this. To understand how these differences arise however, we had first to explore the difficulties of measuring ill-health, the current debates around health inequalities and the acculturation theses.

A complex epidemiology

When reviewing the findings of the UK HEA Survey – apart from confirming that South Asian groups reported a worse health status – the results presented here are substantially different from those presented by earlier commentators. The rates of consulting are much higher than reported elsewhere, partly due to the interviewees being allowed to respond in their mother tongue; indeed, these results would suggest that evidence not based on mother-tongue interviews should be ignored.

The substantive explanation for the high rates is not clear: obviously a simple assertion of ethnic difference is insufficient. Clearly, these groups have difficulty of access because of their language difficulties; but analysis in terms of self-reported English competence did not show any substantial or systematic differences. 'Obvious' inequalities are not always observed.

Equally, forgetting any crude attempts to explain these differences in terms of race or ethnic identity, the pattern of these results suggest that the classic variables of social differentiation (social class, tenure, etc.) do not operate in the same way with these groups. Exactly how intra-group differentials should be indexed for these groups is unclear; but simple transfer from the native white population is inappropriate, that is, the dominant Western model of the production of 'health' is inappropriate. Whilst it is important to develop practice standards (see Appendix), they must address some of these fundamental conceptual issues.

Epilogue

Many have argued recently that at issue is the hierarchies of dominance between different groups. If so, then the question is how can society be organized so as to reduce those hierarchies? The fundamental contradictions of capitalism lies in the necessity for the capitalist that workers think for themselves and the necessity that they behave as automata. It is only when people are producing what they perceive they need (and not what the nearest advertising agency claims they can be persuaded to want) for themselves (or at least the production process is under their control) that those hierarchies will disappear (cf. Carr-Hill and Lintott 1999). These structures apply within as well as between groups. I suppose one might call that interculturality.

Appendix Core standards

1 **Ethnic monitoring of patients** – Ethnic monitoring of patients should be undertaken for all services.
2 **Religion** – Ensure that cultural and religious beliefs are appropriately observed. Provision of multifaith facilities for in-patients with information for patients about their availability, translated in required languages.
3 **Communication** – Patients should be able to communicate with health workers in the language they feel comfortable with. Services which

patients may need to use should be clearly signposted, enquiry points clearly marked, and essential written information regarding the services made available, in the community languages specified by the purchaser.

4 **Patient choice** – Patients should have the choice of a female clinician and information made readily available regarding this option. Single-sex facilities should be provided wherever feasible.

5 **Diet** – Meals should meet the cultural requirements of service users and be authenticated by the relevant community leaders. Dietary information should be available to suit differing local community cultural requirements, both in hospitals and in the community.

6 **Staffing** – Ethnic monitoring of all staff to be undertaken. All staff involved in providing services should be fully aware of how the health and race standards relate to their areas of work.

7 **Patient complaints** – Ethnic monitoring of complaints should be introduced and maintained.

References

Ahmad, W.I.U., Kernohan, E.E.M. and Baker, M.R. (1991), 'Patients' Choice of General Practitioner: Importance of Patients' and Doctors' Sex and Ethnicity', *British Journal of General Practice*, 41, pp.330–31.

Aiach, P. (1989), 'Political and Scientific Debate on Inequalities in Health in France', in Fox, A.J. (ed.), *Health Inequalities in European Countries*, Aldershot: Gower for the European Science Foundation.

Arrow, J.U. (1996), 'Estimating the Influence of Health as a Risk Factor on Unemployment: A Survival Analysis of Employment Durations for Workers Surveyed in the German Socio-economic Panel (1984–90)', *Social Science and Medicine*, 42(12), pp.1651–9.

Balarajan, R. and Balsa, L. (1990), 'Mortality amongst Immigrants in England and Wales 1979–83', in Britten, M. (ed.), *Mortality and Geography. A Review in the Mid Nineteen Eighties*, OPCS Series, DS8, No. 9, London: HMSO.

Balarajan, R., Yuen, P. and Soni-Raleigh, V. (1989), 'Mortality among Immigrants in England and Wales, 1979–1983', *British Medical Journal*, 59, pp.668–70.

Bandera, L. (1993), [Epidemiology and Health Needs of Immigrants in Milano], *Epidemiologia e Prevenzione*, 17, December, pp.244–58.

Baxter, C. and Baxter, D. (1985), 'Racial Inequalities in Health: a Challenge to the British NHS', *International Journal of Health Services*, 18(4), pp.563–71.

Baxter, C., Henley, A and Mares, P. (1985), *Health Care in Multi-racial Britain*, Cambridge: Health Education Council, National Extension College.

Baxter, M. (1990), *Health and Lifestyles*, London: Routledge.

Bollini, P. and Siem, H. (1995), 'No Real Progress Towards Equity: Health of Migrants and Ethnic Minorities on the Eve of the Year 2000', *Social Science and Medicine*, 41(6), pp.19–28.

Bona, G. and Zaffroni, M. (1994), 'The Health Problems of the Immigrant Child', editorial, *Minerva Pediatrica*, 46(7–8), pp. 311–22.

Bourdillon, F. et al. (1991), 'La sante des immigrés en France', *Social Science and Medicine*, 32(11), pp.1219–27.
Bowling, A., Farquhar, M. and Leaver, J. (1992), 'Jewish People and Ageing: Their Emotional Well-being, Physical Health Status and Use of Services', *Nursing Practice*, 5(4), pp.5–16.
Britten, M. (1990) *Mortality and Geography: A Review in the Mid Nineteen-eighties*, OPCS series DS8, No. 9, London: HMSO.
Cambieri, A. et al. (1990), 'Hospitals and Immigration: Analysis of a Case Series', *Rescente Progressi in Medicina*, 87(7–8), pp.461–73.
Carr-Hill, R.A. (1987), 'The Inequalities in Health Debate: A Critical Review of the Issues', *Journal of Social Policy*, 16, pp.509–42.
Carr-Hill, R.A. (1990), 'The Measurement of Inequalities in Health: Lessons from the British Experience', *Social Science and Medicine*, 31(3), pp.393–404.
Carr-Hill, R., Hardman, G.F. and Russell, I.T. (1987), 'Variations in Avoidable Morality and Variations in Health Care Resources', *Lancet*, 8536, pp.789–91.
Carr-Hill, R. and Lintott, J. (1999), *Consumption, Unemployment and the Quality of Life*, London: Macmillan.
Cole-Hamilton, I. and Lang, T. (1987), *Tightening Belts*, London: London Food Commission.
Corretger, J.M. et al. (1992), 'Marginality, Ethnic Groups and Health', *Annales Espanoles de Pediatria*, 36, Suppl., 48, pp.115–7.
Costa, G. et al. (1990), [Mortality according to Birthplace in a Turin Longitudinal Study], *Epidemiologia e Prevenzione*, 12(44), pp.31–42.
Cruickshank, J.K. (1993), 'The Challenge for the Afro-Caribbean Community in Controlling Stroke and Hypertension' in *The Health of the Nation – The Ethnic Dimension*, North East Thames/North West Thames RHA/Department of Health
Department of Social Security (1995), *Family Resources Survey: Great Britain 1993–94*, London: Government Statistical Service (revised edition February 1995).
Esmail, A. and Everinton, S. (1993), 'Racial Discrimination against Doctors from Ethnic Minorities', *British Medical Journal*, 309, pp. 691–2
Failde, I., Zafra, J.A. and Chavallier, J. (1992), *Hospital Admission Profiles of Spanish Immigrants in Paris*, Assistance Publique: Hopitaux de Paris.
Fonteneau, G. (1992), 'The Rights of Migrants, Refugees or Asylum Seekers under International Law', *International Migration*, 57.
Frighi, L. and Mazzetti, M. (1995), 'Transcultural Mental Health: The Psychopathological Risk Factors for Immigrants and Interventions for Protection', *Annali di Igiene*, 7(3), pp.189–99.
Gillam, S.J. et al. (1989), 'Ethnic Differences in Consultation Rates in Urban General Practice', *British Medical Journal*, 299, pp.953–7.
Gottschalk, P., Wolfe, B. and Hariman, R. (1989), 'Health Care Financing in the UK, US and Netherlands: Distributional Consequences', in *Changes in Revenue Structures*, Cambridge: Cambridge University Press, pp.351–73.
Greater London Association for Race Equality (GLARE) (1987), *No Alibi, No Crisis*.
Halberg, H. and Mattsson, B. (1991), 'Premature Deaths Among Men in a Swedish Municipality – Social Characteristics prior to Death', *Scandinavian Journal of Medicine*, 19(3), pp.181–6.
Harrison, L., Carr-Hill, R. and Sutton, M. (1993), 'Consumption and Harm: Drinking Patterns of the Irish, the English and the Irish in England', *Alcohol and Alcoholism*, 26(6), pp.715–23.

Health Education Authority (1989), *Diet, Nutrition and Healthy Eating in Low Income Groups*, London: HEA.

Health Education Authority (1996), *Blacks and Minority Ethnic Groups Health and Lifestyle*, London: HEA.

Hechter, M. (1975), *Internal Colonisation: The Celtic Fringe in British National Development 1536–1966*, Thesis, Berkeley: University of California.

Herzlich, C. (1979), *Health and Illness*, London and New York: Academic Press.

H.M. Government (1995), *Cooking: Attitudes and Behaviour*, London: HMSO.

Holder, H.D. and Edwards, G. (1995), *Alcohol and Public Policy: Evidence and Issues*, Oxford and New York: Oxford University Press.

Holtedahl, R. (1991), 'Immigrants, Living Conditions and Health', *Tidsskrift for Den Norske Laegeforening*, 111(9), pp.1083–5.

Hopkins, A. and Bhal, V. (eds) (1993), *Access to Health Care for People from Black and Ethnic Minorities 1993*, London: RCP Publications.

Jayaratnam, R. (1993), 'The Need for Cultural Awareness', in Hopkins, A. and Bahl, V. (eds) *Access to Health Care for People from Black and Ethnic Minorities 1993*, pp.11–20.

Karmi, G. (1993), 'Equity and Health Minorities', *Quality in Health Care*, 2, pp.100–103.

Karmi, G. (1995), 'The Ethnic Health Bibliography', *Journal of Public Health Medicine*, 17(1),pp.116.

Larsen, S. and Nergard, R. (1990), 'Cultural Background and Drinking Patterns in Problem Drinkers in Northern Norway', *British Journal of Addiction*, 85(11), pp.1469–73.

Leclerc, A. (1989), 'Differential Mortality by Cause of Death: Comparison between Selected European countries', in Fox, A. (ed.), *Inequalities in Health within Europe*, Farnborough: Gower.

Le Fanu, J. (1993), *A Phantom Carnage. The Myth that Low Income Kills*, London: Social Affairs Unit.

Lenin, V.I. (1905), *What Is to Be Done*, Moscow: Progress Press.

McAvoy, B.R. and Donaldson, L.J. (1990), *Health Care for Asians*, Oxford: Oxford Medical Publications.

McAvoy, B.R. and Sayeed, A. (1990), 'Communication', in McAvoy, B.R. and Donaldson, L.J. (eds), *Health Care for Asians*, Oxford: Oxford Medical Publications.

McKeigue, P.M. and Marmot, M.G. (1991), 'Obesity and Coronary Risk Factors among South Asians', *Lancet*, 337, p.972.

McKeigue, P.M., Richards, J.M. and Richards, P. (1990), 'Effects of Discrimination by Sex and Race on the Early Careers of British Medical Graduates during 1981–87', *British Medical Journal*, 301, pp.961–4.

Mallet, J.O., Letoup, M. and Bare, C. (1989), [Multidisciplinarity in Public Health: The Global Approach and Territorial Dimensions], *Cahiers de Sociologie et de Demographic Medicale*, 29(2), pp.177–91.

Marmot, M. (1993–94), 'Changing Places, Changing Risks: The Study of Migrants', *Public Health Reviews*, 21(3–4), pp.189–95.

Mavreas, V. and Bebbington, P. (1990), 'Acculturation and Psychiatric Disorder: A Study of Greek Cypriot Immigrants', *Psychological Medicine*, 20(4), pp.941–51.

MORI (1993), 'Survey of Skills among 6–17 year old Young People', for Get Cooking Project, London National Food Alliance.

Murphy, J.M. (1976), 'Psychiatric Labelling in Cross-Cultural Perspective', *Science*, 191, pp.1079–28.

Office of National Statistics (1997), *Labour Force Survey Quarterly Bulletin*, London: ONS.

Office of Population Censuses and Surveys (1990), *General Household Survey 1988*, London: HMSO.

O'Reilly, D. (1994), 'Health and Social Inequality in Europe. Migration from Deprived Areas may be a Factor' (letter, comment), *British Medical Journal*, 309, pp.57–8.

Ormel, J. et al. (1994), 'Common Mental Disorders and Disabilities across Cultures. Results from the WHO Collaborative Study on Psychological Problems in General Health Care', *Journal of the American Medical Association*, 272(22),pp.1741–8.

Preibe, S. et al. (1990), 'Psychiatric Disorder in Immigrants', *Psychiatrische Praxis*, 17(5), pp.180–3.

Rashid, A. and Jagger, C. (1992), 'Attitudes to and Perceived Use of Health Care Services amongst Asian and non-Asian Patients in Leicester', *British Journal of General Practice*, 42, pp.197–201.

Sam, D.L. and Berry, J.W. (1995), 'Acculturative Stress among Young Immigrants in Norway', *Scandinavian Journal of Psychology*, 36(1), pp.10–29.

Seitamo, L. (1995), 'Skolt Saami Socialisation with Special Reference to the Traditional Eco-culture and On-going Changes', *Arctic Medical Research*, 54, Suppl. 1, pp.33–41.

Sen, A. (1990), 'Food, Economics and Entitlements', *The Political Economy of Hunger*, Oxford: Oxford University Press, pp.50–68.

Sheldon, T.A. and Parker, H. (1992), 'Race and Ethnicity in Health Research', *Journal of Public Health Medicine*, 14, pp.104–10.

Smith, D. (1980), *Overseas Doctors in the National Health Service*, London: Heinemann.

Soni-Raleigh, V. and Balarajan, R. (1992), 'Suicide and Self-burning among Indians and West Indians in England and Wales', *British Journal of Psychiatry*, 161, pp.365–8.

Uniken Venema, H.P., Garretsen, H.F. and van der Maas, P.J. (1995), 'Health of Migrants and Migrant Health Policy: The Netherlands as an Example', *Social Science and Medicine*, 41(6), pp. 809–18.

United National Department of Economics and Humanitarian Affairs (1986), *The Social Situation of Migrant Workers and Their Families*, Migrant Workers, No. 2, New York.

United States Committee for Refugees (1993), *World Refugee Survey*, Washington, DC: US Committee for Refugees.

Wadsworth, M.E.J. (1985), 'Inter-generational Differences in Child Health', in *Measuring Socio-demographic Change*, OPCS Occasional Paper 34.

Wadsworth, M.E.J. (1986), 'Serious Illness in Childhood and its Association with Later Life Achievement' in R.G. Wilkinson (ed.), *Class and Health: Research and Longitudinal Data*, London: Tavistock.

Wandel, M. (1993), 'Nutrition-related Diseases and Dietary Change among Third World immigrants in northern Europe', *Nutrition and Health*, 9(2), pp.117–33.

WHO (1979), *Schizophrenia: An International Follow-Up Study*, Chichester and NY: John Wiley and Sons.

Wilkinson, R., 'Income Distribution and Life Expectancy', *British Medical Journal*, 304, pp.165–8.

Williams, R.G.A. (1985), 'Concepts of Health: An Analysis of Lay Logic', *Sociology*, 17(2), pp. 185–205.

Wright, C.M. (1983), 'Language and Communication Problems in an Asian Community', *Journal of the Royal College General Practitioners*, 33, pp.101–4.

18 Trade Unions, Migrants and Ethnic Minorities in an Intercultural Europe

John Wrench

The European labour movements have, at best, an ambivalent record on issues of racism, anti-discrimination and the general concerns of migrant workers. Whilst there have been many occasions when the left, together with trade unions, have taken a principled stance against racism, there are other occasions when they have acted less honourably. In the 1960s, unions in Britain actively cooperated with employers in discriminatory treatment of immigrants and ethnic minorities; in the 1980s, the French Communist Party, pandering to racism, led marches against immigrants. It is true that trade unions and their confederations have been the main actors in the application of international and European agreements to protect migrant workers. However, despite the traditional commitment of trade unions to the international solidarity of the working class, they more normally and naturally operate within their own national contexts to pursue the immediate employment and financial interests of their own membership. Issues of countering racism and fostering equal treatment of migrant workers have not been seen as constituting a major priority.

Three dilemmas

It has been argued that trade union policies towards migrant and minority ethnic workers can be categorized by three dilemmas (Penninx and Roosblad, forthcoming). The first is whether to resist state immigration policies, or to cooperate with them in order to influence their operation, so as to minimize negative consequences for union members. The second dilemma arises when immigrants have arrived: should they be included in the union and accorded the full protection given to existing members? Although in theory the extension of membership to migrants, and the principle of equal treatment, are imperative in the fight to defend and improve working conditions, in practice this principle is often contended by workers already in employment (Martens 1999). The third dilemma arises when immigrants are members: should special policies, services and facilities be established for immigrants and ethnic minorities within the workplace or within unions themselves?

There may well be inherent tensions between these stages. As Martens (1999) observes, within the organized labour movement, workers find it hard to understand why they should first be mobilized against imported foreign labour, and then, when that demand has failed, to have to welcome those same workers with open arms and prevent them being singled out for exploitation, segregation and victimization. Castles (1990) also stressed the potential conflict between trade union policies towards immigration, and policies towards migrant workers once they were in the country. Unions may feel that they should oppose immigration, but once migrant workers were within the country it becomes essential to organize them, in order to prevent divisions in the workforce. Yet the fact that they opposed immigration would alienate migrant workers, who would then be less likely to join them (Castles 1990: 6).

Historically, the first two dilemmas have already been transcended for most European union movements. With the inclusion of migrant workers into unions, and the transformation of migrant workers into settled minority ethnic workers, the third dilemma begins to take precedence over the previous two: that of equal versus special treatment. Should a trade union concern itself only with issues common to white and minority ethnic members or should it in addition operate special policies relating to the specific interests of the latter? If minority ethnic workers suffer disadvantages not experienced by white workers, then 'equal treatment' will allow these disadvantages to remain. However, if a union devotes extra resources to issues specifically concerning migrant and minority ethnic members, this may cause resentment and resistance on the part of white workers who see minority ethnic members as getting favourable treatment.

This chapter looks at the policies and practices of different trade union movements in the EU with regard to the existence of migrant workers in the labour market, and to issues of racism and discrimination which affect migrant and minority ethnic workers in Europe. It first looks historically at the reactions of unions in different countries to postwar immigration and the presence of migrant workers and attempts to make some explanations for these differences. It then goes further into issues for unions of the 'third dilemma' on special measures, and suggests a new fourth dilemma related to the illegal labour market.

Different reactions of unions to migrant workers

There is a tremendous variety in the approaches of trade union movements in different countries to migrants and minority ethnic workers. First, these must be seen in relation to a host of complex differences of national context:

> National differences have created unions with distinctive religious political and occupational forms and divisions. This is apparent event within Western Europe, where there was a Southern European model, found in France, Italy and Spain, and characterised by competing Catholic, socialist and communist national confederations; and a Northern European model, evident in Britain, Germany, the Netherlands and Scandinavia, of single centres under Social-Democratic or Labour hegemony. Any such broad categorisation, however, conceals a myriad of local factors, such as linguistic divisions in Belgium or the relative strength of Catholic unionism in Italy. National differences produce variations in union membership, such as the high density in Sweden and low density in France. But equally, the meaning of unionism varies, from the more politicised agencies of community mobilisation of Southern Europe to the more institutionalised and workplace organisation of Northern Europe. (Ackers et al. 1996: 2)

The industrial relations systems vary significantly between countries: 'Systems which in most countries have evolved incrementally over the course of many decades – even centuries – have each acquired a distinctive coloration, adapted to the idiosyncracies of national socio-economic structure, national political regimes, and perhaps also national temperaments' (Ferner and Hyman 1992: xvi).

Amongst other things, the practical significance of trade union policies on ethnic minorities and migrants depends on the importance of trade unions in a member state, as reflected by the level of union density, union power in collective bargaining and union influence in the political system. There is a great deal of variety between EU member states in this. In the Nordic countries, the rate of organization among employees is 80–90 per cent, the highest in the EU, with a correspondingly high degree of influence (Hjarnø 1996). Next comes Belgium, where highly organized trade union institutions are strongly legitimized by their members and solidly established in the workplace, particularly in large enterprises. With a union density of 55–70 per cent (according to different sources), the trade unions occupy a powerful position as regards anything concerning working conditions. In France and countries of southern Europe, in contrast, the rate of unionization is relatively low – around 10–15 per cent – and unions have much less power and political influence.

Unions and immigration policies

In different European countries, trade unions were generally concerned about the negative consequences of labour immigration for their own national bargaining and power structures. Penninx and Roosblad (forthcoming) show that this general concern was expressed differently in different countries. Where countries were characterized by a substantial involvement of trade unions in socioeconomic decision making, the reservations on immigration were transformed into a position that if labour was to be imported, then it should be done in such a way that labour relations and bargaining positions would not be jeopardized (for example, in Austria, Sweden, the Netherlands and the Federal Republic of Germany). However, Penninx and Roosblad argue, the ways of minimizing the perceived dangers of immigrant labour varied. Although all demanded at least equal wages and working conditions for immigrant workers, some required some direct control of recruitment procedures (Austria, Sweden and the Netherlands); some demanded special provisions for housing and language courses, thus adding to the expense of this labour for the employer (Sweden, the Netherlands, Germany), and some worked to ensure that the migrant labour remained with a temporary status, to be deported when necessary (Austria).

In other European countries, where unions are not directly integrated into the processes of decision making in the political system, then they were not directly involved in immigration policy (for example, France). On the other hand, as Penninx and Roosblad argue, not being directly involved in these policies left them free to be able to criticize them. In the UK, things were different: unlike other major European countries such as France and Germany, there was a lack of government planning and involvement in immigration policy once the migration had developed (Layton-Henry 1984: 25). There was therefore no official 'immigration policy' for the trade union movement to be involved in, apart from the immediate postwar years when the unions were involved in agreements over the recruitment of European Voluntary Workers from refugee camps (Kay and Miles 1995).

With the oil crisis, recession and unemployment of the early 1970s, there was a general consensus between western European governments and trade unions on the ending of immigration and the introduction of restrictive immigration policies. However, there did seem to be differences between unions in different countries on the integration of migrants both into society and into the unions themselves. For example, in Germany, trade unions took the initiative in policies to incorporate migrants as equals into society, and were ready to protect their rights, defending them against deportation in the event of unemployment, resisting return migration programmes, and standing up for their rights for reunification with families and spouses (Penninx and Roosblad, forthcoming). In contrast, the Dutch trade unions lagged behind the government in integration policies, and it was policies at a national level which eventually pressured Dutch trade unions to introduce inclusion policies within the unions (Roosblad, forthcoming).

National responses and legal status

When we are trying to understand the widely differing emphases in policies and practices of trade unions on migrants, ethnic minorities, and issues of racism and discrimination, we must look further than the industrial relations systems, the structural location of unions in society and the particular histories of their political ideologies. It is also necessary to include other national contextual differences which are not directly related to characteristics of the unions themselves, but rather reflect differences in national responses to migrant and minority ethnic populations, and the ideologies contained within them. Castles (1995) sets out a typology of such responses. Those relevant to western Europe are 'differential exclusion' – where immigrants are seen as guestworkers, with limited political and social rights (for example, Germany), 'assimilation' – where immigrants are given full rights but are expected to become like everyone else (France), and pluralism or multiculturalism – where immigrants are accepted as members of society with full rights but maintain some cultural differences. This last model is stronger in Australia and Canada, but in Europe elements of it are found in Sweden, the Netherlands and Britain. Such ideologies are directly reflected in the attitudes and practices of trade unions: for example, in Britain, unions are responsive to equal opportunities policies which recognize ethnic difference, whereas in France, unions insist on broader 'equal rights' policies as a means of avoiding discrimination for all citizens and workers.

Related to the above, and also important when looking at trade union responses across Europe, is the differing legal status of different groups of migrant workers in EU countries. The working population of the EU can be divided into five main categories in terms of legal status:

1 Citizens living and working within their own country of citizenship.
2 Citizens of an EU member state who work in another country within the Union (EU denizens).
3 Third-country nationals who have full rights to residency and work in a member state (non-EU denizens).
4 Third-country nationals who have leave to stay on the basis of a revocable work permit for a fixed period of time
5 Undocumented or 'illegal' workers. (Wrench 1996: 3)

The above five categories reflect formal status, and a continuum of rights ranging from full rights and privileges of citizenship in category 1 to relatively few rights in category 5. All the above five categories of legal status can then be further divided into two: white and non-white, or visible minority. In the first two categories, EU citizens living in their own country, and EU citizens working in another EU member state, the non-white groups form a minority. In the next three categories they are more likely to form a majority. In all categories, generally speaking, the non-white workers are likely to suffer disadvantage at least relative to the white members of that legal category. Paradoxically, the relative disadvantage suffered through racial discrimination for citizens in categories 1, 2 and, to a lesser extent, 3, constitutes a more visible and serious social issue precisely because they have more formal rights. They have justifiable expectations of fair and equal treatment and are more likely to be in positions where they are in competition in the labour market with white workers. An increasing proportion of visible minorities within these categories will have been born and educated in an EU country. Further down the hierarchy, it becomes less easy to demonstrate the extent to which the relative disadvantage in employment experience is a result of racial discrimination, partly because the disadvantage on formal and legal grounds is greater and more obvious, and because workers in these categories are less likely to be competing with white nationals in the same labour market. By the time we get to the category 5 workers in the illegal labour market, it is difficult to separate out the effects of 'racism' from the straightforward exploitation of a relatively powerless group of workers. To talk about racial discrimination in the conventional sense is less appropriate as these workers are often in a different labour market to 'normal' citizens (Wrench 1996).

It is clear, then, that the problem of discrimination in the labour market of countries in the EU differs according to which categories most of its migrant and minority ethnic workers fall in to. This will have corresponding implications for the trade union policies and practices on discrimination and equality. In countries of northern Europe, migrants and ethnic minorities are more likely to be skewed towards the top groups of our five legal categories of worker. Here, migrants are longer established and issues of the 'second generation' are important, with trade union activists pressing for policies to tackle the unjustified exclusion of migrants and ethnic minorities from employment opportunities by informal discrimination on 'racial' or ethnic grounds, and the related phenomenon of their over-representation in unemployment. In the UK, for example, most migrants and their descendants are found in group 1; the legal status of migrant workers is generally not a problem, and most of the current issues preoccupying activists concern fighting the informal discrimination which in practice reduces the opportunities of minority ethnic workers, either at the workplace or within the union itself. In other countries of northern Europe, a higher proportion of workers fall into group 3, suffering not only 'informal' racial discrimination but also formal legal discrimination. Here, as these exclusions are related to naturalization and citizenship issues, trade unions are more likely to occupy themselves with these concerns.

There are two main ways in which group 3 workers suffer 'legal discrimination' with regard to employment. First, they are restricted in their freedom to find work in other member states. The inclusion of European citizenship in the Treaty of Maastricht gave the right to citizens of EU countries to move freely within and between member states in search of employment. However, nationals of non-member countries are excluded from these rights, even though they may be established, legally-resident workers of long standing. An example of the negative effect of this restriction can be seen with the closure of old industries which formerly employed large numbers of migrants. After redundancy, EU denizens are able to look for new work in neighbouring countries, whereas non-EU denizens do not have that option (Denolf and Martens 1991).

Secondly, there are not only problems for non-EU denizens who wish to cross borders to look for work. There are also restrictions on the jobs they may apply for within their country of residence. Non-EU denizens who have full rights to work and residency in a member state can nevertheless be denied equal access to some public sector jobs within that country. For example, in France three-and-a-half million national and local government jobs and two-and-a-half million jobs in nationalized or similar undertakings are thus closed to foreigners other than EU nationals. Foreigners are also excluded from a variety of independent professions in France (De Rudder et al. 1995).

In countries of southern Europe, in contrast, immigrants are likely to be over-represented towards the bottom of the five groups. Groups 4 and 5 workers are actively preferred and recruited because they are cheaper, more vulnerable and more pliable – they are less able to resist over-exploitation in terms of work intensity or working hours. Workers in the illegal labour market experience a perverse kind of 'positive discrimination' in the selection process, and then in work suffer the 'negative' discrimination of conditions which indigenous workers would not tolerate. Trade unions in these circumstances are more concerned with measures to empower such workers and reduce their vulnerability to exploitation, with drives to recruit, regularize and train them.

Migrant membership of unions

It is difficult to state accurately the membership levels of migrants in unions in the different EU countries. The density of union membership amongst migrants seem to vary a great deal between different member states; however, the availability of data on this also varies tremendously, and in some countries such data would be impossible to collect. It seems that in some member states migrant workers are under-represented in unions, reflecting the fact that unions have not been seen to be sympathetic to them, or relevant to their issues. Migrants have therefore turned to other organizations to protect their interests. In other countries, unions have positively welcomed migrants, and have set up specialized departments within the unions to deal with them, and in some cases they are even over-represented in unions. Over-representation might be the result of quite different factors: for example, the fact that migrant workers are simply concentrated in those industrial sectors or occupations which exhibit a high union membership rate, regardless of the ethnic background of the workers. It might reflect an ideological sympathy by groups of migrants to unions, rooted in anti-colonial struggles prior to migration (as has been suggested in the UK). Or it may reflect legal or administrative imperatives, such as Denmark, where a high general union membership rate reflects the fact that the unions are important providers of services and administrators of unemployment funds (Scheuer 1992; Lind 1995), and where foreign workers were obliged to join an unemployment insurance scheme during their first two, vulnerable, years of employment. Whereas in some European countries the above-average unemployment rates of migrant workers is used to explain their decline in union membership, in Denmark high unemployment rates actually strengthen trade union membership rates, just the opposite relation between business cycles and unionization that is usually observed (Lind 1995: 18). A study by the ILO (1976) suggested that where unions have the character of a popular mass movement, the union density for immigrant workers is generally higher than in those countries where unions are organizations of militant activists (quoted in Knocke, forthcoming).

The nature of special policies

In the main migrant-receiving countries of the EU, unions are now generally happy to see migrants extended full rights of citizenship and to regard them in principle as workers to be organized. The exceptions here seem to be Austria, where the trade unions have cooperated at a national level to keep foreign workers in an inferior status (Gächter 1995), and Greece, where migrant workers seem to have been generally ignored by unions (Fakiolas 1995). The resistance – or at least ambivalence – of unions to the postwar inflow of labour migrants has now changed to an acceptance of immigration and a recognition of the need to organize them within the unions. In other words, the first two dilemmas set out at the beginning of this article are generally no longer issues, and the main concern is the exact nature of the special policies relating to migrants and minority ethnic workers. The minimalist position could be characterized by the stage known in the UK as 'incorporation' (Wrench and Virdee 1996: 265). This is where union membership is extended to minority ethnic workers, but where the basis of inclusion goes no further than that consistent with a traditional trade union class analysis. Membership unity is seen as central; thus any special measures which distinguish between types of workers are to be discouraged. The natural preference is to be 'colour blind'. The 'hard' position within this was to extend no special measures at all to migrant workers, as was the position of many British unions in the 1960s. A later, more flexible, position is to encourage the adoption of some measures which take account of the different circumstances of minority ethnic members, such as producing literature in different languages.

In the UK, and increasingly in other countries, there are now arguments as to what 'special policies' are allowable in principle, and what exact form they should take in practice. Special policies can be roughly categorized as follows:

- Policies concerned to better the integration of migrants into society
- 'Multicultural' activities at the workplace and within the union
- Activities at the workplace and within the union to counter racism and discrimination
- Activities internal to the union itself which are designed to increase the participation of immigrants and ethnic minorities in union structures.

Policies concerned to better the integration of migrants into society

In Spain and Italy, for example, unions have assisted with the setting up of special offices or worked with voluntary groups to help migrants with the regularization of their status, or with finding housing or employment; they have also helped with initiatives to counter false information about migrants put out by the national media, or participated in anti-racist demonstrations. In France, Germany, and Sweden, unions pressed politicians for improvements in the social and employment rights of migrants, where necessary getting involved in fighting rules which allowed deportations. After time they began to lobby for new laws against discrimination. Generally speaking, activities at this level have aroused relatively little controversy among the membership.

'Multicultural' activities at the workplace and within the union

This might include the provision of literature in foreign languages, or multicultural training and information provision for members. Many unions provide recruitment material and broader information such as health and safety regulations in languages appropriate to the major migrant/ minority ethnic groups in the labour market. In Sweden and the UK, for example, unions produced a range of literature in minority languages; the French CGT produces a bi-monthly journal directed at immigrant workers, and in Germany, unions run courses for their members on 'intercultural awareness'. Unions in many countries have supported minority ethnic members in calls for working arrangements which allow for cultural and religious differences, such as flexibility in holiday arrangements, work times which allow for regular prayers, and a prayer room. However, some critics have argued that, though such multicultural and linguistic initiatives are valuable, they do nothing to address issues of discrimination, justice and equality.

Specific activities at the workplace and within the union to counter racism and discrimination

These are often slower to be implemented than the other two, perhaps because of a 'denial of racism' common within organizations and societies with democratic ideologies (van Dijk 1993), and because they are more likely to provoke resistance from some existing members. The Federation of Dutch Trade Unions (FNV) produced a manual on fighting racism, and introduced a policy allowing for the expulsion of active racists; a number of British unions have introduced similar measures and are actively trying to improve their record on assisting members who have been victims of harassment or discrimination. However, a general criticism by commentators on European trade unions is the persistence of an attitude which locates problems of racism and discrimination as a general social problem 'out there' rather than something close to home at the workplace or within the union itself. It seems that unions have been ready to involve themselves in anti-racism at a national level (for example, countering racist propaganda, involvement in national demonstrations and campaigns to raise public awareness) whilst being far more reluctant to institute equal treatment measures within their own union. Examples of such activities within the union might be the adoption of an equal opportunities policy with regard to the union's role as an employer itself, or union disciplinary procedures against racism by union members (see TUC 1996). The potential difficulties which can arise between unions and their membership here are exemplified by the 1996 dispute at Ford at Dagenham, in the UK, when it was revealed that the practice of allowing lorry drivers to prioritize the recruitment of their own families and relations had led to the virtual exclusion of ethnic minority workers from that section. Three hundred lorry drivers resigned from the Transport and General Workers Union and joined another union in protest at the TGWU's drive to eliminate what the union called 'entrenched institutional discrimination' in the recruitment of drivers (*The Times*, 5 December 1996).

Activities internal to the union itself which are designed to increase the participation of immigrants and ethnic minorities in union structures

These measures are often the last to be adopted, and more frequently encounter resistance from within the union. They might include positive action measures which encourage migrants not only to join unions, but also to share union responsibilities, and work to remove barriers which prevent migrant and minority ethnic workers from reaching union office.

The rationale and nature of special organizational forms within the union for migrant and minority ethnic members is a subject of great debate. White indigenous workers can see structures such as separate committees as divisive and promoting class disunity, whilst migrant and minority ethnic activists can see them as tokenistic and symbolic devices which deflect criticism away from the leadership and provide an 'alibi' that the union is doing something. In Germany, for example, foreign workers are often free to establish themselves as groups within unions, but sometimes the unions are happy to leave these groups simply to deal with all the problems relating to foreigners. There are exceptions – I.G.Metall tries to make its union structures flexible enough to involve its 'foreigners' committees' directly in mainstream activities. One of the specified aims of these committees is to 'strengthen the representation of foreign officials in the trade union decision-making bodies' (Kühne, forthcoming).

In the UK, the current arguments for self-organization within unions are rooted in the conviction of black trade unionists that the movement still drags its feet in fighting the racism they experience. However, there is division within the migrant/minority ethnic membership on the nature of such forms (see Virdee and Grint 1994). Some black union activists feel that because black members are a numerical minority within unions, then this prevents their voices being heard by the democratic majority. The only way to get their voices heard is by self-organization within the unions, in their own separate structures. Other black activists argue that radical black members should be working to galvanize unions into a more radical, less reformist stance, and should not be diverted into separate structures where they can be more easily contained by the white reformist leadership.

Conclusion

In EU countries where migrants and their descendants have full citizenship rights, union activists are more concerned with tackling the inequality resulting from informal 'racial' discrimination. In countries where citizenship is more difficult to obtain, the migrant workers are more commonly found in group 3 – non-EU denizens – and here unions are more likely to be concerned about the removal of legal discrimination. However, one problem in these countries is that unions have often been slower to take up those issues of discrimination which affect their citizens and denizens from visible minority backgrounds, and in particular, those problems of unequal treatment and exclusion which operate at an informal level, in the workplace or within the union itself.

The activities of unions in the South of Europe show how the issue of discrimination is seen differently to those of the North. Discrimination in northern countries of Europe tends to be seen as a problem of the exclusion of ethnic minorities from the best jobs, and the resulting higher unemployment for such groups, particularly of young people. In Spain, Portugal and Italy, however, there is more concern about the deliberate inclusion of migrants in highly exploitative or illegal work. The unions regard their actions to pursue the equal treatment of foreign and national workers as alleviating discrimination and the social dumping which results from this. Similarly they see their campaigns for the regularization of illegal workers as a step to end the discrimination suffered by these workers. Furthermore, this type of action comes more naturally to these unions. In France and countries of southern Europe, unions are traditionally more political, and are more likely to adopt a role of 'community mobilization'. This affects the type of 'anti-racism' they operate, so that measures to fight racism and discrimination include combating the legal discrimination experienced by migrants, and attempting to empower them in various ways so as to reduce their vulnerability to exploitation. In countries of northern Europe, where unions are more institutionalized and organized around the workplace, then they more easily embrace anti-discrimination measures located within the organization, such as equal opportunity policies.

Of course, the generalizations made in this paper are not watertight, and there are no simple categorizations of a straight North–South divide. Whilst one of the factors defining trade union action in the South has been the more insecure status of workers historically found in illegal employment, this illegal employment also exists, and is growing, in some countries of the North, too. Similarly, over time and with family reunions, the problems in the North which are specific to second- and third-generation descendants of migrants will also increase in the South. Furthermore, all the specifically national generalizations are to a degree over-simplifications, and can be in danger of being overstated. For example, the argument that French unions don't engage in actions which are 'ethnically specific' is modified by the fact that there are occasions when French unions have supported their Muslim members in their demands for timetables which allow for prayer times, and rooms where prayers can take place (Lloyd, forthcoming).

Social movements

One indication of a potential 'convergence' of issues between unions in different member states is the question of the employment of migrant/minority ethnic workers in highly degraded sectors of work in some northern European countries, in the direction of some of that experienced in the high-exploitation sectors of the South. In the UK, for example, there is an expanding cohort of workers in part-time work, contract work, low-paid sweatshop and service-sector work, illegal and unregulated work, and homework. Although seemingly a relic of a previous industrial era, the old-fashioned traditional sweatshop represents an important component of the 'new workplace' (Ackers et al. 1996). Through the growth of subcontracting from core, assembly and manufacturing customers, such factories are an increasingly central element in the new two-tier manufacturing world. The introduction in manufacturing of Japanese-style management practices, contracting out, and so on, has increased the numbers of small- to medium-sized employers who are under intense pressure from their customers, the major assemblers, and who become even more opposed to trade unions than they would normally be. In the service sector, competitive tendering and contracting out has the same effect. The over-representation of women, minority ethnic workers and migrants in these sectors provides extra opportunities for employers to divide, segment and individualize their workforce.

Unions feel they need to target these particular groups of workers. However, there are new problems facing unions over the need to recruit and organize the expanding cohorts of more severely exploited migrant and minority ethnic workers, in the context of an unfriendly economic (and in the case of the UK – political –) climate (Wrench and Virdee 1996). There are many who believe that unions which are primarily 'workplace centred' will need to change their approaches, become more flexible and move away still further from traditional ideas and practices of trade unionism before they will be able to attract and retain the new generations of migrant and minority ethnic workers. It is also argued that unions will need to become more responsive to the issues concerning migrant women workers. Recent decades have witnessed the increased participation of women in the labour force, and within this a greater proportion of married women. By the year 2006, almost 90 per cent of the increase in the labour force in the UK will be accounted for by women; in a broader context, women have been entirely responsible for the growth in employment in Europe in the last two decades (*Guardian*, 9 April 1994). As men in their forties and fifties are being steadily ejected from the labour force, they are being replaced by women in much inferior sectors of employment – the 'poor work' sectors. Even unions with good records of organizing migrant workers have been guilty of neglecting the issues of migrant women. For example, in Sweden, where there is a strong egalitarian ethic, male and female immigrant workers are unionized to the same degree. However, case studies of Swedish industry show that union representatives and foremen can be carriers of 'gender prejudice' in ignoring immigrant women for advancement to better jobs, leaving them trapped in monotonous line jobs (Schierup and Paulson 1994; Knocke 1994). Immigrant women also feel marginalized when all their elected representatives are male (Knocke, forthcoming). It is perhaps significant that in a year-long union-backed strike to organize sweatshop workers in Britain, which failed in 1993 despite widespread public support, the strikers were mainly minority ethnic women (Wrench and Virdee 1996).

Many labour movement activists now argue that the trade union movement has no hope of bringing unionization to new groups of unorganized migrant workers unless it works in cooperation with communities and links unionization to broader issues such as illegal work, women's rights, sexual and racial harassment at the workplace, health and safety, harassment by the police and immigration authorities, cultural, linguistic and religious rights, and so on. This suggests that pressures exist for some Northern union movements to become less narrowly based around the workplace, and move in the direction of 'social movements' such as those found in the South. Many people have argued that working-class action via organized trade unions is no longer the important social movement to produce necessary social change. 'New Social movement' theorists see change as being initiated by more varied groups – feminist groups, environmental movements, young people's groups, and other movements related to particular issues (Castells 1983). Black people's groups could be added to this list and, within this scenario, the trade union movement becomes just one of a number of social movements. In this new context, unions should not simply restrict their activities to the workplace, but should also concern themselves with the broader issues of migrant workers in society.

There will probably be differences in the responsiveness of European unions to new pressures. Penninx and Roosblad venture the hypothesis that trade unions that are not structurally involved in decision making (France) or those which are increasingly marginalized in this respect in the course of time (UK) will eventually be more inclined to reform their traditional trade union structures into those bearing more resemblance to social movements. On the other hand, those trade unions that are strongly involved in socioeconomic decision making (possibly backed by 'parented' political parties in power) are possibly more inclined to stick to traditional structures, involving themselves less clearly in other aspects than those that are directly relevant for their worker members (Penninx and Roosblad, forthcoming).

A fourth dilemma – illegal labour

In Denmark, interviews with 3,340 members affiliated to the Danish Confederation of Trade Unions (LO) found strong feelings that unions should adopt a broader mandate, including environmental issues and the promotion of personal values (Bild et al. 1995). However, one aspect of a 'broader' union approach which will not have been in the minds of these Danish trade unionists is the willingness in recent years of previously workplace-centred unions in Europe to take up the cause of undocumented migrants in illegal employment. Increasingly, European unions are seeing it as important to secure rights and protection for all workers, including undocumented migrants, and not to limit the right to join a trade union to those who are legally resident in a country. This presents something of a 'fourth dilemma' for unions, a dilemma which will be experienced differently by, for example, unions in Scandinavia compared to unions in southern Europe. In Denmark, employers' use of immigrant illegal labour is virtually unknown. This does not signify a difference in moral attitude, but is simply a reflection of the importance of collective agreements between unions and employers' organizations in Danish society. Thus both unions and employers effectively 'police' the use of such labour. In countries where collective agreements play a minor role, enforcement is left to the state, and as this process is expensive and time-consuming, it is frequently neglected (Hjarnø 1996).

The dilemma for unions is that organizing migrant workers in the illegal labour market implies an acceptance, or even an encouragement, of a group of workers whose presence undermines the conditions that unions have long fought for. Unions in some southern European countries are working to get undocumented migrants organized and legitimized, and this means that until they have achieved work permits for the undocumented workers, the unions are implicitly accepting the law-breaking committed by the employers. Undocumented immigrants are only present in a national labour market because there are employers who are willing to break the law which prohibits the employment of foreign nationals without work permits. Logically, unions which want to operate lawfully and maintain the standards fought for in collective agreements should work to expose these 'criminal' employers – and by implication, the undocumented immigrants – to the police. This, in the long run, would be a more effective strategy in the preservation of standards of employment for all workers. However, in the short run, this strategy may well lead to many undocumented workers losing their jobs, or even suffering deportation, and this could seriously alienate the union's own migrant membership, especially those who are from the same ethnic minority origin as the undocumented workers. Furthermore, a campaign to expose employers for hiring undocumented workers may further erode the employment chances of ethnic minorities in general by encouraging employers to employ only people who don't look 'foreign' (*The Times*, 4 December 1996).

In conclusion, we can see that there are still many questions being raised within European trade union movements regarding the specific forms of their relationship with migrant and minority ethnic workers. With some exceptions, there is now a broad acceptance of the need to incorporate migrant workers within unions and take some account of the special issues relating to them. However, as this chapter has shown, there are clear differences in national emphasis in union activities in this area, related to the particular national histories of the union movements' structural forms, their relationship with the state, the different national responses to immigration and ethnic diversity, the predominant legal status of migrant or minority ethnic workers in the country, and other factors of national and historical context.

Despite these differences, and the correspondingly different ways that, for example, anti-discrimination activities find practical expression, there are grounds for thinking that future pressures may lead to some convergence. Unions which are ideologically driven to anti-racism at a national level and to fight politically for the social and employment rights of migrants may feel the pressure from new migrant members to look more critically at what is happening in their own workplaces, on works councils, within the union hierarchy, and amongst the ranks of its own membership. Unions which have been primarily concerned with protecting the immediate interests of their own members may feel pressures to broaden their activities and take on board wider issues of concern to migrant workers, their families and descendants, outside the workplace.

Within all this there seem to be a number of recurring themes relevant to all union movements in the major migrant-receiving countries of the EU. One is that a colour-blind and gender-blind incorporation of migrants and ethnic minorities into unions in the name of class unity, without any concession to different interests, special measures or new organizational forms, is increasingly untenable. Major questions of debate here are what 'special measures' are acceptable and appropriate, and what are the precise organizational forms that unions should adopt in accommodating migrant members. What mechanisms will encourage the participation of migrant workers actively in union hierarchies in decision-making functions: positive action training, changes in internal union committee structures, or measures to remove internal barriers to participation? What is the nature of the relationship of unions to external migrant organizations? How far should the recognition of cultural and religious difference go in practical terms, within the workplace and the union itself? To carry this too far may be divisive and counter-productive to achieving union ends; however, to make no concession to such genuine differences may be a form of racism in itself, and equally divisive. Whatever the compromise, it is to be stressed that the recognition of a degree of multiculturalism in practice does not go far enough if there is no corresponding recognition of the forces of racism and discrimination, not just out there in the wider society, but close to home in the workplace and within the unions themselves.

References

Ackers, P., Smith, C. and Smith. P. (1996), 'Against all Odds? British Trade Unions in the New Workplace', in Ackers, P., Smith, C. and Smith, P. (eds), *The New Workplace and Trade Unionism*, London: Routledge.

Bild, T. et al. (1995), *The Employee Perspective on Working Life and Politics: A Study of Members Affiliated to the Danish LO Department of Economics*, Åalborg University.

Castells, M. (1983), *The City and the Grassroots*, London: Edward Arnold.

Castles, S. (1990), *Labour Migration and the Trade Unions in Western Europe*, Occasional Paper No. 18, Centre for Multicultural Studies, University of Wollongong.

Castles, S. (1995), 'How Nation-states Respond to Immigration and Ethnic Diversity', *New Community*, 21(3).

Denolf, L. and Martens, A. (1991), *Van 'mijn' werk naar ander werk: Onderzoeksrapport over de arbeidsmarkpositle van ex-mijnwerkers*, Brussels: Permanente Werkgroep Limburg.

De Rudder, V., Tripier, M. and Vourc'h, F. (1995), *Prevention of Racism at the Workplace in France*, Dublin: European Foundation for the Improvement of Living and Working Conditions.

Dijk, van, T. (1993), 'Denying Racism: Elite Discourse and Racism', in Wrench, J. and Solomos, J. (eds), *Racism and Migration in Western Europe*, Oxford: Berg.

Fakiolas, R. (1995), 'Preventing Racism at the Workplace in Greece', Dublin: European Foundation for the Improvement of Living and Working Conditions.

Ferner, A. and Hyman, R. (eds) (1992), *Industrial Relations in the New Europe*, Oxford: Blackwell.

Gächter, A. (1995), 'Forced Complementarity: The Attempt to Protect Native Austrian Workers from Immigrants', *New Community*, 21(3)

Hjarnø, J. (1996), *Illegals on the European Labour Markets*, Migration Papers No. 1, Danish Centre for Migration and Ethnic Studies, Esbjerg: South Jutland University Press.

ILO (1976), *Trade Union Activities of Foreign and Migrant Workers in the Member States of the Council of Europe*, Geneva: International Labour Office.

Kay, D. and Miles, R. (1995), 'Migration, Racism and the Labour Market in Britain 1946–1951', in van den Linden, M. and Lucassen, J. (eds), *Racism and the Labour Market: Historical Studies*, Bern: Peter Lang.

Knocke, W. (1994), 'Gender, Ethnicity and Technological Change', *Economic and Industrial Democracy*, 15(1).

Knocke, W. (forthcoming), 'The Case of Sweden', in Penninx, R. and Roosblad, J. (eds), *Trade Unions, Immigration, and Immigrants in Europe, 1960–1993*, Oxford: Berghahn.

Kühne, P. (forthcoming), 'The Case of Germany', in Penninx, R. and Roosblad, J. (eds), *Trade Unions, Immigration and Immigrants in Europe 1960–1993*, Oxford: Berghahn.

Layton-Henry, Z. (1984), *The Politics of Race in Britain*, London: Allen and Unwin.

Lind, J. (1995), *Trade Unions in a Changing Society*, CID Studies No. 14, Copenhagen: Copenhagen Business School.

Lloyd, C. (forthcoming), 'The Case of France', in Penninx, R. and Roosblad, J. (eds), *Trade Unions, Immigration, and Immigrants in Europe, 1960–1993*, Oxford: Berghahn.

Martens, A. (1999), 'Migratory Movements, the Position, the Outlook: Charting Theory and Practice for Trade Unions', in Wrench, J., Rea, A. and Ouali, N. (eds),

Migrants, Ethnic Minorities and the Labour Market: Integration and Exclusion in Europe, Basingstoke: Macmillan.

Penninx, R. and Roosblad, J. (eds) (forthcoming), *Trade Unions, Immigration and Immigrants in Europe 1960–1993*, Oxford: Berghahn.

Roosblad, J. (forthcoming), 'Dutch Trade Unions, Immigrants and Immigration: Myopic Politics of Equality', in Penninx, R. and Roosblad, J. (eds), *Trade Unions, Immigration and Immigrants in Europe 1960–1993*, Oxford: Berghahn.

Scheuer, S. (1992), 'Denmark: Return to Decentralisation', in Ferner, A. and Hyman, R. (eds), *Industrial Relations in the New Europe*, Oxford: Blackwell.

Schierup, C-U and Paulson, S. (eds) (1994), *Arbetets etniska delning*, Stockholm: Carlssons.

TUC (1996), *United against Racism in Europe*, London: Trades Union Congress.

Virdee S. and Grint, K. (1994), 'Black Self Organisation in Trade Unions', *Sociological Review*, 42(2).

Wrench, J. (1987), 'Unequal Comrades: Trade Unions, Equal Opportunity and Racism', in Jenkins, R. and Solomos, J. (eds), *Racism and Equal Opportunity Policies in the 1980s*, Cambridge: Cambridge University Press.

Wrench, J. (1996), *Preventing Racism at the Workplace: A Report on 16 European Countries*, Luxembourg: Office for Official Publications of the European Communities.

Wrench, J. and Virdee, S. (1996), 'Organising the Unorganised: 'Race', Poor Work and Trade Unions', in Ackers, P., Smith, C. and Smith, P. (eds), *The New Workplace and Trade Unionism*, London: Routledge.

19 Intercultural Relations in British Cinema Since 1960

Phillip Drummond

Cinema and the intercultural

1991. On a visit to Moscow, I walk into my first class in Film Studies in the new Russia. In my bag is a collection of films on video, intended as a present for the school – amongst them, David Lean's famous film version of *Doctor Zhivago*, which I saw as a schoolboy myself at around the time of my first visit to the former Soviet Union in the mid-1960s. By a remarkable coincidence the teenage pupils are studying their own rare and precious copy of this very film. As a result, I am drafted in to continue teaching the class. We talk about their understandings of the film, and one boy ventures to comment that he doesn't find it 'realistic'. When I ask why, he explains that, contrary to the film, there are no daffodils in Russia ... I explain that it is a British film, made with American money and shot in Spain because the Soviet Union was then still a difficult place to represent, both for insiders and outsiders, as the author of the novel on which the film was based found to his cost. Although we started talking about a film, in no time at all we are in fact discussing national flora, history, politics, the way the film industry works, ideas about realism, spectatorship and social change. Meanwhile, at a cinema in central Moscow, *Gone with the Wind*, a film recollecting the end of an era in another country, is opening for the first time in fifty years and, in another strange synchronicity, in my bag there is a copy of it as another gift ...

Many issues are bound up in this anecdote. We are talking here, for instance, about a variety of nations – Russia, Britain, the United States, Spain. In this story those countries come together as reference points and as experiences. We are talking about the 'national' as mediated by the cinema, and about the abilities and inabilities of this powerful medium to convey both the generalities and the specifics of peoples and of habitats and lifestyles. We are talking about the politics of representation, about the permitted extents and boundaries of showing and of telling in the public sphere, talking about the ways in which spectators see, and in the process make good and also imperfect sense of sounds and images of people and of places. We are talking, finally, about the history of these factors across a quarter of a century (between *Zhivago* and the classroom meeting) or a century and a quarter (from the represented US Civil War of *Gone with the Wind* to the film's own production on the eve of the Second World War to its arrival in Moscow in a later massive moment of social change).

This reference to the United States should remind us of the obvious, namely, the domination of the world cinematic order by the sheer power, volume and internationalizing experience of Hollywood cinema. Any discussion of interculturalism in the cinema must start from this fundamental fact. This means, to quote the title of Jeremy Tunstall's standard history, that in a profound sense *the media are American* (Tunstall 1994). Tunstall identifies five stages in the process. First, although the original global media corporations of the later nineteenth century were English and French, it was Pulitzer and Hearst who established the modern newspaper as 'the daily entertainment sheet', to be promptly copied by European innovators (for example, the *Daily Mail* from 1896 onwards). The second stage was the development of the motion picture from its primitive origins in 1895 as it became the modern entertainment feature film between 1915 and 1920, a form which was then exported around the world during the subsequent decade. The third period is marked by the arrival of the synchronized sound feature film in the later 1920s, and the rise of powerful corporations in recorded music and commercial network radio.

The fourth period involved the consolidation of American commercial television between 1955 and 1965, and, specifically, the development of the Hollywood TV entertainment series, all predicated on the new telefilm recording technology. The US's powerful production base also allowed it to become a key supplier for other national television services springing up around the world, both in Europe and the developing countries. The fifth stage was the channel multiplication revolution of the 1980s, supported by the technology of the space satellite and computerized information technology. A sixth epoch, heralded by Tunstall but accelerating most substantially in the few years since his second edition, is furnished by the development of the Internet from its origins in military communications to become the widespread, domesticated multimedia delivery system of the millennial period.

Hollywood was, of course, partly a European invention, thanks initially to the arrival of eastern European migrants at the turn of the century, and the successive waves of immigration in the dark years of the 1930s (see Gabler 1988). But as trade wars have repeatedly sharpened national boundaries, Europe's hold on the market for cinema has been tenuous in recent years, resulting in a marked economic and cultural imbalance. In most European countries, Hollywood films account for around 70 per cent of box-office takings, whilst in the UK and Germany the figure rises to around 80 per cent. Between 1984 and 1992, US sales of programming in Europe rose from £330 million to £3.6 billion. In the last twelve years, European films have lost half their theatrical market – down from 30 per cent to 15 per cent – and two-thirds of the cinema-going audience. Only 10 per cent of European films are shown in a territory beyond their point of origin, and very few indeed are distributed throughout Europe as a whole. A low and declining number of European films are shown in the United States, where only 1 per cent of the country's cinemas regularly play foreign-language material (Finney 1996; see also Nowell-Smith and Ricci 1998).

Over and above these large-scale economic patterns, films themselves regularly dramatize some of the features of this major intercultural tension between Europe and the United States. In the case of the British cinema, 'Britishness' is thus challenged, in the passive sense, by the arrival of other nationalities upon its shores, most notably migrants from North America who present the financial power and dynamism of the New World and rock the protocols of the Old. Encounters between British and Americans are at the heart of crime dramas such as *The Long Good Friday*, *Stormy Monday* (in which US gangsters extend their empires to London and to Newcastle) and *Brannigan* (in which John Wayne brings Chicago-style policing to London). The social and romantic comedies *A Fish Called Wanda*, *Four Weddings and a Funeral* and *A Touch of Class*, and the intimate elegies *Remains of the Day* and *Shadowlands*, are based on this principle of difference. *Local Hero* creates a whimsically archetypal contrast between the big-city wealth of Dallas (represented by Burt Lancaster) and the small-town values of the north-east coast of Scotland.

Only occasionally do US visitors face a more vigorous challenge, and then it comes from the hidden depths of archaic rural life in the English and Scottish regions (*An American Werewolf in London*, *Straw Dogs*, *Loch Ness*), or from their own troubled past in America (as in the Blacklist drama *Fellow Traveller*). Only infrequently is the trajectory reversed so that the United States has to cope with European visitors (*The Europeans*, *Dreamchild*, occasionally that cool English cipher James Bond), although British actors become villainous fixtures in a number of American films of the later period (for example, Anthony Hopkins as Hannibal Lecter in *The Silence of the Lambs*, Alan Rickman in *Die Hard*).

Key intercultural cycles

Where Britain's own relationship to the intercultural circulation of the cinema is concerned, a number of key cycles provide the framework in the postwar period – the war film, the horror film, the comedy and the postcolonial films that deal with Africa and India. The first and most deep-seated category is the war film, recycling through the 1950s and the 1960s particular re-enactments of the events of 1939–45, offering images based on a wide variety of European theatres of war and constructing in the process influential representations of the key antagonist, Germany (see Hurd 1984 and Chapman 1998). These films are predictably concerned with expedition, adventure and resistance – *Battle of Britain, The Victors, Mosquito Squadron, Murphy's War, Operation Crossbow, Where Eagles Dare* – but in certain striking cases the trope is reversed so that fantasies of invasion are the prism through which the encounter with another culture is imagined (*The Riddle of the Sands, The Eagle Has Landed, It Happened Here*).

The genre also contains films pursuing the issue of lurking war criminals (*The Odessa File*), fantasies of a secret war continued in 1945 (*The Holcroft Convention*) and the postwar search for Nazi gold (*Inside Out*). Largely Anglocentric in attitude, the cycle none the less expands to embrace films examining the plot to overthrow Hitler (*Night of the Generals*) and the POW breakout plot seen from the German side (*The Mackenzie Break*). It includes films which attempt to question the morality of war, either in serious form (*The Guns of Navarone, The Long Day's Dying*) or via satires such as *How I Won the War, Adolf Hitler: My Part in His Downfall*, and the film based on the long-running Home Guard comedy, *Dad's Army*. Set in postwar Germany, *The Bofors Gun* would take a jaundiced view of British military life. The Great War, too, could now be seen in a more critical way – *Oh What A Lovely War!* and *King and Country* – although an old- fashioned hero could make a postmodern comeback in the time-shift adventure *Biggles*.

War came to be seen as the crucible in which complex interpersonal and intercultural relationships would be proposed and would need to be worked out, psychological and sometimes sexual in character. These would sometimes continue to centre on the soldiery (*Yanks, Memphis Belle, The Return of the Soldier*) but frequently soldiers in their personal relationships with civilians, often across national and gender boundaries, would be the primary focus in a long series of films: *Another Time, Another Place, Chicago Joe and the Showgirl, The Dressmaker, Elenya, Hanover Street, Hope and Glory, Letters to an Unknown Lover, A Month in the Country, Secret Places, Souvenir, That Summer of White Roses, The Triple Echo.* As memories of war gave way to new forms of intercultural understanding, Germany could now be represented as the terrain on which new dramas of identity and mission would henceforth be played out: *Chinese Boxes, England Made Me, Fatherland, Flight to Berlin, Loose Connections, Melancholia, Parker, The Romantic Englishwoman*.

The Europe of the period, as it recovered from a second world war, was embroiled in the pressures of the less immediately violent but still threatening pressures of a different collision. The key Cold War film is the black comedy, *Dr Strangelove ... Or How I Learned to Stop Worrying and to Love the Bomb*, hysterically fantasizing military paranoia in the stand-off between the United States and the USSR. Two years later, using the alarming realism of drama documentary, *The War Game* coolly catalogued the impact of a Soviet nuclear attack on Britain in the context of an imaginary East–West conflict in Korea. The film's grim catalogue of images of the successive stages in the breakdown of the social fabric, and of the nation's unpreparedness, was powerful enough for the film to be refused a television airing by its producers, the BBC, for some twenty years, but guaranteed it an effective campaigning role in the anti-nuclear movement of the period.

The Berlin of the Second World War film thus re-emerged as the focus for the Cold War spy film, the symbolic venue for sometimes mortal combat over national identity and secret information. Established in the 1960s with *Funeral in Berlin* and *The Spy Who Came in from the Cold*, this theme could still figure in the 1990s in a film like *The Innocent*. The former Soviet bloc more generally could be drawn into this tradition, with Frank Sinatra drawn into intrigue in East Germany in *The Naked Runner*, and Prague the explicit backdrop for *Hot Enough for June*. But twenty years later, in the period of *glasnost*, Russian sailors can visit Liverpool and become the love-objects of an intercultural romantic comedy, *Letter to Brezhnev*, whilst Liverpool's favourite sons, the Beatles, can be followed through their formative period on the music scene in Hamburg (*Backbeat*). The Czech capital can thus remain the forbidding setting for a further version of *The Trial*, but it can also become the site for the gentler interpersonal and intercultural issues in the eponymous *Prague*.

A second area of intercultural conflict was dramatized in the horror films of the 1950s and beyond, most frequently associated with the output of Hammer Films. Here, the key sub-genres were those associated with the substantial *Dracula* and *Frankenstein* cycles. Based on nineteenth-century myths by British writers, and most fully exploited by British studios in the 1950s and 1960s, both cycles locate their chosen monsters in central and eastern Europe. The Frankenstein cycle exploits increasing concern with the ability of modern science to control and even create the conditions of human existence, whilst the Dracula films draw on older myths for their depictions of the boundary states between the human and the undead. The films pit the geography of Britain against a broader, wilder Europe. The

Frankenstein films take elements of Shelley's complex intercultural journey structure – from Ingolstadt in Germany to the polar ice-cap, taking in Switzerland, England, Ireland and the Orkneys along the way – whilst the Dracula films alternate between Stoker's interest in the vampire's Transylvanian origins and his invasion and infection of the English landscape.

If Frankenstein gets lost in scientific fantasy whilst at university in Germany, then Dracula emerges from the hidden depths of Transylvania fully formed. Where the Frankenstein cycle is concerned with the ethics of scientific knowledge and experiment, Count Dracula represents a deformed aristocracy feeding on the other reaches of the social order and in frequent contestation with the world of science represented by Dr Van Helsing. The monster in the Dracula cycle is not an artefact associated with modernity, but an atavistic relic of a bygone era, who perpetuates himself through time by drinking the blood of others. Whereas for Frankenstein's monster human company can be dramatized as a tragic impossibility, for Dracula it is an essential consumable, and the act of consumption itself creates companions and replicants, fresh vampires.

This stress on corporeal interchange provides the opportunity for sexual and erotic motifs which made these films controversial in the early stages of the cycle, their scandalous identities later reinforced by a contamination scenario which offered scope for metaphorical links with the contemporary iconography of AIDS. Whilst typically defending the status quo against the horrors of the unknown and the unnatural, in the more subtle versions the films' interest in otherness and monstrosity thus offers the spectator more complex fantasies. Space could be created for imaginative curiosity and even sympathy with the monster as outsider, spawning additional myths about the monster as lost child along the way, most recently and most flamboyantly in Kenneth Branagh's *Mary Shelley's Frankenstein* with its emphatically tragic elaboration of the the scientific monster as an abandoned child who seeks revenge for the humanity he can never fully inhabit upon the family he can never fully join or replicate himself. (For studies of British horror, see Pirie 1973 and Hutchings 1993.)

A further key miscellany, playing with the identity of the human body in a very different vein, was collected under the *Carry On* ... banner. The punning title prepared the viewer for a world of British farce in which, in spite of social mayhem among the institutions of daily life – the 'carry on' – the essential thing was to continue, to 'carry on'. In these highly popular films, directed by Gerald Thomas over the quarter-of-a-century between 1958 and 1982, a virtual repertory company of *farceurs* engage in a riotous play of breakneck action, visual humour, and relentlessly innuendo-laden dialogue. The films are apt both to rely on stereotype in the areas of race and gender, and yet to play self-consciously with these. Whilst comfortably apolitical, they could also satirize the absurdities of social institutions and the associated hierarchies of social authority. Tellingly, getting on for half the thirty titles in the series are based on references to Englishness and its others (see Jordan 1983).

In *Carry On Cruising* and *Carry on Abroad,* the British are uprooted from their domestic routine and confronted by the different practices of continental holidays. The French, for their part, could be viewed through two dominant frames – sexuality, and revolutionary history – in a parody of the contemporary sex film, in *Carry On Emmanuelle,* or by returning to the period of the French Revolution, in *Carry On – Don't Lose Your Head.* The extension of the Roman Empire to Britain would be captured through the even more distant prism of *Carry On Cleo,* whilst the more recent colonial experience of the British Empire was robustly mocked in *Carry On Up the Khyber,* a tale of the Raj involving Sir Sidney Ruff-Diamond (James), the Khasi of Kalahar (Williams) and the Third Foot and Mouth Regiment. Central Africa would be the backdrop for *Carry On Up the Jungle,* featuring Prof. Inigo Tinkle (Frankie Howerd), Bill Boosey (James), and, in blackface, Bernard Bresslaw as Upsidasi, whilst in the northern part of the continent the Foreign Legion spoof *Carry On – Follow that Camel,* based at Fort Zuassantneuf, would irreverently introduce the prophet Mustapha Leke.

The tropics would provide the magic potion which would be the making of Dr Nookey (Jim Dale) and Gladstone Screwer (James) in *Carry On Again, Doctor,* but other regions did not escape the zany if increasingly threadbare disrespect of the *Carry On* series as it made intertextual nonsense of some of the cinematic trends of the period. The Americas would be targeted in the western spoof, *Carry On Cowboy,* and in the comic addendum to the 1992 celebrations, *Carry On Columbus. Carry On Spying* would go to Vienna and the Casbah for its satire on the Bond films. In a Cold War reflex, a glamorous Russian archaeologist, Prof. Anna Vooshka (in fact the German starlet Elke Sommer) would provide the focus for Anglo-Saxon sexual tension in *Carry On Behind.*

A further, more serious framework was provided by the legacy of Empire as Britain adjusted its memories of hegemony in India and Africa (see Richards 1973). One strand in this tradition, with its roots in the imperialist cinema of the 1930s, saw Africa as the territory for historic military conflict and engagement. Films like *Khartoum, East of Sudan, Young Winston* and *Zulu* went back to an earlier cinema, to the high period of expeditionary colonialism, for re-endorsements of the British mission, or for anticipations of subsequent conflicts with other European powers (the main antagonist is German in the pre-First World War drama *Shout at the Devil*). This tendency would be updated in a more contemporary account of British military adventures in Africa such as *Guns at Batasi*. The Second World War would provide an overlapping frame through which the territory could be remembered (*Foxhole in Cairo, The Hill, Play Dirty*).

In the post-colonial period, the military scenario would relentlessly accommodate plotlines hinging on mercenary conflicts which would involve British participants in an equally brutal if less clear-cut world of political and national purpose and allegiance (*The Mercenaries, The Wild Geese, Dogs of War, A Game for Vultures, The Wilby Conspiracy*). Egypt and Morocco would also provide the focus for more ancient concerns. Their distant mysteries would provide the seedbed for motifs in the horror genre, imagining the threat of distant civilizations (the *Mummy* cycle and the *Dr Phibes* films). The predominant metaphor would be that of the unfathomable and irreducible desert (*Sands of the Desert, Sands of the Kalahari*), challenging the cool understandings of urban society and sometimes seen as the crucible for erotic and romantic encounters and the resulting struggle to maintain a sense of rational identity (*Station Six Sahara, The English Patient*).

Less violent adventure was provided by the more direct vision of Africa as the site of precious but elusive natural objects. Its mineral wealth would provide the pretext for dramas based on mining (*Gold*) and smuggling (*Death Drums Along the River*), while quests for diamonds and lost spacecraft could offer other grounds for the cultural encounter (*Call Me Bwana, No Secrets, Jane and the Lost City*). Animals became convenient metonyms for the dangerous natural riches of Africa. This could be seen conservatively, as in *The Last Safari*, or with a progressive sense of the ecological relationship, as in *Born Free* and *Living Free*. *The Lion* would make pointed links between childhood and the local fauna in a drama about the reconstitution of family relationships across cultural and geographical divides. This theme would receive its most troubled articulation in *Greystoke: Tarzan, Lord of the Apes*, in which the Tarzan myth is updated once again to elaborate, in a stark contrast between African and English life-styles, and between the animal and human kingdoms, an anguished story of childhood separation.

A different brand of cinema, however, examined the human dimensions of the continent in greater detail. It would focus on the plight of disoriented children (*Sammy Going South, The Kitchen Toto*) and satirize the decadent expatriate community in Kenya (*White Mischief*) or attempts to Americanize its farming system (*Africa Texas Style*). In the more recent period it would come closer to the realities of apartheid by getting inside the tortured mind of a member of the South African Defence Force (*On the Wire*) or, through a new engagement with the potential of documentary drama, by opening up the histories of anti-apartheid heroes in films such as *A Private Life*, dramatizing the experiences of Jack and Stella Dupont, or *A Dry White Season*, the life-story of the murdered journalist Ruth First. The most important British film about Africa in the period would be *Cry Freedom*, a drama based on newspaper editor Donald Woods' involvement in the case of the murdered activist Steve Biko, his subsequent politicization and his eventual flight from the country.

Director Richard Attenborough also contributed the most politically explicit account of India in the period, in his biopic *Gandhi*. Most of the India films look back to the period of the Raj without a direct sense of politics, and are ambiguously fascinated by the values of a lost Empire. Other cinematic representations of India could concern themselves with such standard preoccupations as the fearful thuggees (*The Deceivers, The Stranglers of Bombay*), or could offer a parody of imperialist adventures in the region (*The Man Who Would Be King*). India would become the displaced arena for analysis of social and sexual relationships amongst the military, in *Conduct Unbecoming*, whilst an ambivalent account of the period, seen from the Indian side, characterizes *The Brigand of Kandahar*.

Founded on miscegenation fantasies, *Passage to India* predicated the encounter between India and Britain on the case of an alleged sexual assault ambiguously set against the mysteries of the Indian landscape, but other films were content to recast the colonial relationship in gentler and more meditative terms as they recall the past in terms of the present, notably the films emerging from the intercultural identities of the Merchant/Ivory team (*Heat and Dust, Autobiography of a Princess, The Assam Garden, Hullabaloo over Bonnie and George's Pictures*). Modern India breaks through in *Electric Moon* and *In Custody* and in the encounter between American disillusionment and Indian stamina in *City of Joy*.

Our collection of templates concludes with a single figure, and yet an entire genre, summing up many of the tendencies and tropes we have been outlining here: James Bond and the Bond films. Uplifted from the literary fiction of the 1930s, Bond is a British agent who stands in for Britain in many of the various international contexts alluded to already. This long cycle (18 films since 1960, and still in production) plays exaggerated and spectacular games with national identity and international encounters. Bond, defending the interests of the Free World against a variety of challenges and threats, sees his mission through with a cool 'international' set of competences which marks him off from a range of 'nationally' demarcated adversaries.

Bond is 'controlled' from Whitehall as he makes his neo-colonial journeys around the globe. His main venues are North America and the Caribbean, and the Orient and Asia, but European venues are sometimes important in the films. *From Russia with Love* plays out its final drama on the Orient Express from Istanbul to Venice and in the Venetian lagoon; *On Her Majesty's Secret Service* is set in Switzerland; *For Your Eyes Only* is set in Greece.

Sometimes, European venues act as the pretext for further international travel: *A View to a Kill* starts in France before moving to the United States, whilst the plot of *Octopussy* links intrigue in India to the familiar melting-pot of postwar Berlin.

The films work to distinguish Bond from his opponents along a line of contrasts. Bond represents the Free World against that of Communism, or, in the later films, against international dominance of various political and national persuasions. He is individualistic against not only the massed might of his opponents, but against the bureaucratic dead hand of Whitehall; he is honourable and self-sacrificing against the corruption and self-interest of his enemies, and he is intuitive and innovatory in approach to combat against the enemy. He has a strong sexual persona which weds him to the pleasure principle against the death-wish of his enemies, with their perverse relationship to sexual identity and experience, and the historic repression of the English.

The Bond film cycle moves us on a stage from the 1930s values of Fleming's literary template, emphasizing comedy, spectacle and technology, although Bond's sense of difference from the official values of the nation state marks one important difficulty in asserting that he is the most important cinematic Englishman of his generation. Though he was rendered more fully 'English' later in his career through the actors George Lazenby, Roger Moore and Timothy Dalton, it is the *Scottishness* of the most famous and still most popular Bond, Sean Connery, which marks his difference from national norms and confirms the ironic nationalism of the Bond project (see Woolacott and Bennett 1987).

Imagining the Nation 1: *Chariots of Fire*

Looking at the cinema's repertory of national iconography leads back, inevitably, to its representation of the 'national' itself, in this case its accounts of Britain and of Britishness. I want to illustrate the case by taking two of the most powerful examples of 1980s British cinema, Hugh Hudson's *Chariots of Fire* (1981) and Martin Stellman's *For Queen and Country* (1988). In *Chariots,* we follow the careers of the real-life British athletes Harold Abrahams and Eric Liddell in the post-First World War years leading up to the 1924 Olympic Games in Paris, where a famous victory is recorded against the United States. In *For Queen and Country,* we follow the odyssey of a young black British soldier – modelled on the experiences of an acquaintance of the director – as he leaves the Parachute Regiment after service in Northern Ireland to pick up life as a civilian in the uncertain world of the late 1980s. At either end of this climactic decade, these films stand as paradigm cases for analysis of intercultural representation and the cinema.

Films belong to social moments and to social processes, and these offer one important framework for understanding their meanings and effects. A liberal and subtle text, *Chariots of Fire*, is none the less a product of the early Thatcher years, when a new jingoism and new triumphalism were emerging, cohering most dramatically around the Falklands campaign of 1982, the year in which *Chariots* was winning Oscars and its scriptwriter Colin Welland told the Academy of Motion Pictures 'The British are coming!'. Powerfully attractive at the British box office, the film went on to be the biggest British money spinner until eclipsed by that other intercultural confection, *Four Weddings and a Funeral*, a decade later. *For Queen and Country*, by contrast, appeared towards the fag-end of the Thatcher years, drawing on the disillusion of the period. An offspring of the increasing synergy between television and independent cinema, its darker vision of Britain and Britishness did not meet with the same critical acclaim or public enthusiasm, and has it been little seen since its original short-lived release.

Both these very different films have biographical intentions – explicit in the case of *Chariots*, implicit in the case of *For Queen and Country*. They aim to describe key passages in the lives of British subjects – figures who achieved national fame and were inscribed into the official histories before passing on (*Chariots*), an unknown figure who was still alive and able to critique the film's representation of his life and times (*For Queen and Country*). *Chariots* looks back from the recent (1978) past to dramatize a distant history (1919–24); *For Queen and Country* moves quickly onwards from the recent past to set its story in the moment of the film's own production (1988). Each film mixes generic templates. *Chariots* mixes the tradition of the text in which human beings overcome difficult obstacles to triumph in a climactic finale – a structure found not only in films dealing with sporting achievement but also the courtroom drama – with the story of characters at odds with the moves of unfamiliar (here academic) institutions, from *A Yank at Oxford to Bachelor of Hearts*. *For Queen and Country* replays the scenario of disorientation and attempted reconstruction which is a staple of the war film genre from *The Best Years of Their Lives* to *Born on the Fourth of July*.

The plotline of *Chariots* works out a number of convergences which reach their multiple climax in the concluding sequences at the Olympic Games in Paris in 1924. Its first mission of convergence is to collect together the differences represented by its two principal protagonists, Harold Abrahams and Eric Liddell. The former is a Cambridge undergraduate who overcomes the anti-Semitism of the postwar years to become an Olympic runner, helped by another talented outsider, his coach the half-Italian, half-Arab Sam Mussabini.

The latter is a Scottish rugby star, born in China, who is still tightly bound in to the Christian scruples of his missionary family, and who, at the Games, refuses to betray his religious conscience by running on the Sabbath. The differences posed by Liddell and by Abraham are ranged against the world of Cambridge – the gentlemanly ethos of which cannot come to terms with Abrahams' adoption of a professional coach – and of the British Olympic committee, chaired by the Prince of Wales, whose members are eventually obliged to understand the genuine force of Liddell's religious sensibilities.

Liddell's is the humbler trajectory, south from Scotland, switching sports and sinking his Scottishness into the wider British interest. Abrahams is an insider – Repton, the army, Caius College, the Olympic squad – who still feels excluded, and hence spurred on, by his sense of Jewishness. The first narrative convergence brings together the parallel worlds of the two athletes. The film opens with them preparing for the Olympics at Broadstairs in 1924, before taking us into flashback to Abrahams' arrival at Cambridge in 1919, which is in turn contrasted with Liddell's participation – first as prize-giver and then as participant – in a Highland Games gathering in 1920. An early stage in the drama will therefore be the delineation of the contrasting worlds of the two figures, and their gradual drawing together in their own internal competition, with Liddell emerging as victor but with both men going on to join the same overall British squad.

The second narrative convergence pits Britishness against a wider world symbolized by the international rivalry of the Olympic Games. Here the key competition is provided by the United States, and it is victory against the US which completes the film's interest in juxtaposing and resolving differences between national representatives and types. The American challenge has its own symbolism: in a fast-moving montage, the US contingent are seen preparing themselves via regimented training methods, under the control of a ferocious coach. British athletes win, the film appears to suggest, by a different, less technical method which springs from inner conviction and personal motivation.

A third narrative convergence confirms the film's own allegiance to Abrahams by offering, in a crucial postscript, a sense of his true personal destination following his Olympic triumph. In a scene which further inflects the ideological momentum I have been describing, he hangs back on the train at Victoria until the jingoistic razzmatazz has died away. This final convergence is with his lover, Sybil, whom he embraces on the platform in a reunion without official witnesses. The resolution of character via athletic victory, establishing both his Britishness and, in turn, British superiority to North America, turns back to a more individual form of resolution via heterosexual romance and the confirmation of the romantic couple as the routine destination for the ideological completion of personal identity.

The film has other intensities as it adjusts its journey through national types and relationships. Its interest in images of nationhood, as we have noted, is bound up with a variable series of concerns around religion. Liddell is committed to a 'muscular Christianity' whilst a more secular Judaism is the case with Abrahams. Its narrative of nation and religion may culminate in the heterosexual union of Abrahams and Sybil, but the film has a strong homoerotic undertow. This is expressed through its choreography of the male body in repeated action, harmonious and also agonized, endlessly threaded through with looks exchanged by men, focusing on the nature of the other male's imaginative and physical potency.

Generically, the film is not just a sporting drama and a biopic but also a form of melodrama, its powerful musical accompaniment provided by Vangelis' sometimes triumphal but often yearning and wistful score. This contemporary sonority is counterpointed by the narrative quotations from Gilbert and Sullivan, creating, in an internal throwback from the post-First World War years to the closing decades of the nineteenth century, tolling invocations of British popular culture's continuing concern with themes of personal and social identity. The musical intensity serves to bind the spectator into the drama at a more profound level than mere observation or mere identification with characters and plots. Its emotional qualities also conjure, in their subtler cadences, the final convergence, that between past and present, reminding us that *Chariots of Fire* is also a film working and playing to bridge the distance between the period of the film's release (1981) and the period within which its drama is played out (1919–24).

Its intercultural drama thus has a further series of dimensions, strongly linked to processes of maturation and decay, remembering and forgetting. We start in 1978 at the memorial service for Abrahams; we move back to the Olympic training camp of 1924; further still to Cambridge, and Abrahams' arrival there in 1919; forward by a year to the introduction of Liddell and his arrival in the Highlands from his birthplace in the Orient, and then down through the next four years back to 1924, where we end the film but are brought back into the present by a title telling us of the eventual fates of Liddell and of Abrahams. The nature of personal and social change is thus high on the film's imaginative agenda, leaving us to wonder about the other differences that the interval of some fifty years might represent in terms of the way questions of personal and national identity can be framed and dramatized (see Higson 1995; 1996).

Imagining the Nation 2: *For Queen and Country*

The contradictory discourse of triumphal yearning which is one of the hallmarks of *Chariots of Fire* produces effects for the spectator very different from those offered by a film drawn from the other end of the 1980s, *For Queen and Country*, a drama of race, identity and nation set on the streets of London in the here and now. Like *Chariots, For Queen and Country* starts by establishing the past, the world before the film began which conditions and determines the possibilities of the present. We move from Northern Ireland in 1979, where two British soldiers escape a terrorist ambush, to the Falklands conflict of 1982, where the same men are seen going into action, in the dark, against unseen opponents. The past in this film is harsher than in *Chariots*, and, unlike *Chariots*, it moves quickly into the present to tease out the meanings it has set in train. If *Chariots* was a film of convergence and harmonization, *For Queen and Country* attempts convergence but achieves instead disintegration; the optimism of *Chariots* is replaced by the tragic sensibility of the later film.

The plot has two stories, the story of an individual and of a city, or a part of it. Reuben James (played by Denzel Washington, in a daring and successful excursion into British cinema for the black American star) is a Caribbean-born black Briton who has entered the army to escape the negativity of the inner city. He returns to civvy street to build a new life, only to discover the new conditions of Thatcher's Britain, and to learn that membership of 'Two Para' cuts no ice in the gloomy job market of the 1980s. Instead, a range of uncertain relationships beckon him in a forbidding urban jungle which features none of the familiar and reassuring iconography of either real or cinematic London. It is a warren of walkways and underpasses in which human life is dwarfed and hemmed in by the bleak materials and shadows of a world of shabby, brutal concrete. It becomes an increasingly abstract and symbolic space, most patently in the later stages of the film, when Reuben tracks down Lynford's band of rioters to their Dickensian lair in the dark bowels of the estate.

Male solidarity is offered by Reuben's army friend Fish, already invalided out after losing a leg in a Falklands firefight. Fish's drinking and womanizing eventually destroy his relationship with his wife Babs, who returns to Ireland leaving Fish adrift in a London spiralling into violence and social chaos. Reuben is offered a partnership in a health club run by his old acquaintance Colin, now a suavely pragmatic yuppie. In his quest for money to solve Fish's domestic problems, an initially suspicious Reuben eventually has no option but to become Colin's minder in his real business, drugs. Lynford is still a petty thief who tries to lure Reuben back into their former life-style on the streets. Stacey, the mother of a girl who burgles Reuben's flat, looks set to bring Reuben back to normality but is repelled by her discovery that, like her husband before him, Reuben is still not averse to using a gun; she promptly leaves him.

Two events bring Reuben's crisis to a head. When he applies for a new passport, he learns that while he has been away, the provisions of the 1981 Nationality Act mean that, following the independence of his home island of St Lucia, he is no longer automatically a British citizen, although this is a status which he can now purchase. Outraged by the fact that he has fought for Queen and country whilst no longer automatically a full citizen, he prefers to opt for a St Lucian passport, and buys an air ticket home to go back to his roots. But his departure is caught up in the aftermath of the killing of a local police officer, and his involvement with Colin is used against him to force him to identify the culprits – Lynford and his friends, who, as victims of police harassment, are now hell-bent on taking the law into their own hands and who engage the police in a full-blooded battle which engulfs the estate in fire and mayhem.

In a complex and hectic finale, Reuben is rescued from a vengeful Lynford by Fish, who is then shot dead by the impulsive and racist police officer Challoner. Although the riot appears to have died down, the now-isolated Reuben takes on a new, deadly mission. Equipping himself with the rifle he earlier took away from the increasingly deranged Fish, and returning to the military identity which was his at the beginning of the film, he shoots Challoner. In an eerie finale which echoes the ambush at the start of the film, he is observed walking alone through the estate by police marksmen, one of them his former army buddy Bob, now also a local police officer. An unseen superior asks 'What are you waiting for, Harper?', and, as we watch Reuben through the gun sights, we hear a shot. The film ends.

As this account of its narrative complexity suggests, *For Queen and Country* is a more ambitious – and much bleaker – film than *Chariots*. In *Chariots*, the parallelism between Abrahams and Liddell gave way to a series of ideological convergences which erased difference; here a narrative built on repeated processes of relationship and separation concludes on the emphasis of difference, with no fewer than three of its principal protagonists eventually dead at each other's hands. Whereas the characters in *Chariots* are liberated into new, broader roles and identities, finally endorsed by Olympic success and romantic union, the central character of *For Queen and Country* is repeatedly pushed into isolation and separation.

The films' intercultural trajectories fall into different registers. In *Chariots*, the journey undertaken by the protagonists extends from the genteel environs of London, Cambridge and the Scottish Highlands as far as the Olympic stadium in Paris. In *For Queen and Country*, Reuben brings back home with him the memories of near-death in Northern Ireland and, from the Falklands, the mutilation of a close friend. Whereas the journey in *Chariots* is outwards, to win victory overseas and to return triumphant, the journey in *For Queen and Country* begins elsewhere, and the trophies that come home are ambivalent and even ominous. Whereas a jubilant nation embraces the victors in *Chariots*, in *For Queen and Country*, London – or, as the film simply calls it, 'England' – is a new and threatening territory which Reuben must negotiate anew, almost as though for the first time.

The journey Reuben makes back into the heart of the city is, in one sense, the journey undertaken by a number of returning soldiers in the cinema. The tradition in these films is often psychological and physical, suggesting that war has driven a wedge between the soldier and the society which must be psychically unravelled and physically annealed. *For Queen and Country* reverses this tendency. The figure who fits this mould is a subsidiary character, Fish, who goes from being Reuben's saviour in Northern Ireland to the plucky but increasingly wayward cripple whom Reuben rescues from financial ruin in London. Reuben himself is seen as highly capable of re-entering the society on equal terms, but it is depicted as a world with little interest in the reintegration of its old soldiers.

The opening title of the film reminds us that Reuben's experience is not new or unique to him, and that it is as much material as spiritual. It is founded on the longer-term experience of having and not having, and of the ambivalence of 'birthright' entitlement in a society predicated on the difference between personal fantasies of belonging and the real privilege embodied in material possessions. As the opening caption tells us in the words of an earlier English soldier,

> There are many thousands of us soldiers that have ventured our lives; we have had little propriety in the kingdom as to our estates, yet we have had a birthright. But it seems now, except a man hath a fixed estate in this kingdom, he hath no right ... I wonder we were so much deceived.
>
> *Sexby, Soldier in Cromwell's New Model Army, 1647* (Thompson 1980: 25)

This voice from an earlier instance of civil disturbance in England, echoing down from the pages of E.P. Thompson's *The Making of the English Working Class*, announces the political intentions of a film intent on critiquing the confused politics of wealth, opportunity and personal identity in Thatcher's Britain. It prepares us for a vision of war not as an external mission against an enemy out there, but as an internal conflict over the politics of power and social class within.

Reuben's dilemma – his quest for social identity and rights – is compounded by the passport drama, when Reuben's 'Britishness' is called into question in a still more profound sense. This blockage prevents his escape to Paris for a weekend with Stacey, and it is a more radical fantasy of cultural renewal – the return to a more basic existence in St Lucia – which dominates Reuben's vision in the later stages of the film but will, likewise, prove unrealizable. So too will Fish's intention to go to Ireland to bring back Babs, Ireland being a country repeatedly invoked by a chain of minor signifiers in the text: Babs jokingly welcomes Reuben back to London as her 'Irish lover', Fish wins the money for the Paris trip on a horse called 'Irish eyes', Reuben drinks Guinness with a Jamesons in the bar scene where Lynford uses him as an alibi, a drunk sings 'I'll take you home again, Kathleen'. Between them, Reuben and Fish do not succeed in starting a new life in the fantasy geographies of Paris, St Lucia or Ireland, but lose their lives in the anonymous, urban hell from which the Parachute Regiment provided only dark and violent excursions.

The development of narrative in *For Queen and Country*, unlike that of *Chariots*, is thus concerned with singular rather than comparative individuation, and with the representation of a world which cannot finally be reconciled to itself. In *Chariots*, the scene with the Olympic Committee and the Prince of Wales allows full rein to Hudson's and Welland's satiric vision of reactionary elements amongst the English upper class, but it is eventually an aristocrat, Lord Lindsay, who defuses the drama of conscience by offering his own place to Liddell. It is a liberal vision of the workings of the English class system which, earlier, saw Lindsay appear in the Trinity quad for the challenge race, complete with cigarette holder and bottle of champagne, to casually join Abrahams in the college dash to 'help push him along'. By stern contrast, the social classes enjoy little solidarity in *For Queen and Country*.

If representational issues have changed, then so too have representational processes. Allowing for the changes in the time-frame discussed earlier, the narrative progression in *Chariots* is linear and developmental, preoccupied with the evolution of the athletic prowess of the main characters and predicated upon the simple question: will they win in Paris? The process of the narrative can offer occasional delays and challenges, but it will not throw the quest off course. The ending of the text comes as a logical, positive culmination of the simplified form of narrative suspense which has been created for the spectator.

In *For Queen and Country*, a more complex attitude to narration prevails, signalled by a very different musical accompaniment – the music of alarm and dread and threat, very unlike the empathetic and celebratory main score of *Chariots*. Narrative relationships are not developmental and hence predictable, and action takes unexpected detours. The movement is not onwards to triumph, but downwards to defeat; the conclusion is resolutely tragic, returning the film to some of the conditions of the war film as which it started, littering the cinematic stage with bodies. Amongst them is its ostensible hero, who becomes a murderer who is in turn murdered by the forces of law and order in the person of his former army friend, Bob. *For Queen and Country* thus offered the most clear-cut explanation of the critical concerns of a new black sensibility in British cinema in the 1980s (see Mercer 1988).

Considerations

The many films I have invoked in this discussion do not represent a scientific sample, but a personal selection from which I have drawn patterns which other analysts might scan in different ways. At the heart of such an enterprise is a more complex debate about the national identity of cultural fictions such as feature films. I have drawn exclusively on what I have regarded as 'British' films, and yet national boundaries of a conventional kind are not always clear-cut in relation to an industry so complexly marked by the movements of international capital and by the fundamental need to address the North American market in terms of distribution/exhibition deals. Although produced from a British base, for instance, the Bond films I was discussing earlier were overseen for many years by an American producer and made their most substantial profits in the United States. *Chariots of Fire* itself, although ostensibly a 'British' film, benefited from 'Egyptian' money, whilst *For Queen and Country* was built around the emerging star persona of a North American lead actor.

I have suggested two ways of working – the kind of rapid generalization which draws on key features of the text and takes these as key aspects of a tendency or type, and a more detailed textual immersion which allows the text to suggest broader currents of meaning and significance. Comparisons such as these begin to illustrate the complexity – semiotic and ideological – with which cultural texts such as the fictional feature film treat the stuff of everyday life, recent or remote. In their quest for realism, *Chariots* and *For Queen and Country* produce a world which is recognizable and understandable, and as they do so they negotiate a series of suggestions and propositions to the spectator through the illusionistic effects of cinematic textuality and the free-but-controlled play of the spectator, both emotional and cognitive. These strategies involve the spectator's 'real-life' experience mixed in with the experience of viewing itself, in an equation which guarantees a certain 'realism'.

During viewing, a range of emotional as well as cognitive effects are in process, comprising the relationships of cinematic character, sound and image, narrative. The process is complex and ultimately unknowable, but the components that interest me most, in this essay, are to do with representation and textual form, notions of the textual subject, and the judicial role of the spectator. A concern with textual form and representation, for example, begins to offer a more specific way of reading some of the general issues raised by our analysis of *Chariots* and *For Queen and Country*. Here, the twin axes of 'showing' and of 'telling' are of paramount importance. That is to say, the film can on the one hand 'show' something – in an image, perhaps with an accompanying sound – but this does not in itself establish very much. The sign must be mobilized and contextualized by being 'told' – that is, by being woven into a flow of images and sounds, a narration from whose pressures and with whose support its meaning may emerge as a specific semiotic function or effect.

In *Chariots*, for example, some of the references to anti-Semitism are textured in this way. When Abrahams and Montagu arrive at Caius College, Cambridge, in 1919, there is a frosty exchange with the college porter, whom Abrahams reproves before leaving for his room. The porter turns to Montagu and says 'Well, one thing's for sure. With a name like "Abrahams", he won't be singing in the chapel choir, will he?'. As Montagu looks away in distaste, the scene dissolves to the freshmen's dinner, heralded, on the soundtrack, by the sound of the college choir singing. The remark made by the porter has not been crudely negated by this musical transition, but it implicitly suggests that his notion of cultural separation is out of place. It is the nature of the suggestion that marks the off-stage voice of the narration, creating contrast, nuance and modality. This tactic pushes the text in the direction of irony and demands a more 'knowing' spectator.

A different way of understanding this issue is to think of textual form in terms of overall narrative shape and direction. Both films, quite clearly, pursue traditional narrative patterns of quests for missing objects – personal fulfilment, social and national identity. The narrative of *Chariots* is based on a model of convergence, building to a resolution where individuals were translated beyond themselves into larger personal and national identities. A successful final resolution marked the film as a kind of social comedy, in perhaps the deeper, Shakespearean sense. The opposite is true of *For Queen and Country*. Here structures of divergence were in play, repeatedly separating the hero from potential social links and pushing him into a downward spiral of separation and escape which became a tragedy, with death his only form of resolution.

Both films also have another kind of ideological shape, different in each case. The successful resolution of *Chariots* is of course the Olympic success of 1924, the success of the distant world within the film which the film is calling back to life to speak within the present. But the film is more intelligent than to imply that the past and present can be so simply elided, which is why the funeral and the concluding captions also remind us that these things are over and that these supremely strong and powerful young men are now dead or ageing. The film thus oscillates between exultation in former prowess and a recognition that things are not now what they were then, and it is this oscillation which provides the poignancy of the film's specific vision of nostalgia and of 'heritage'.

The closure of *For Queen and Country* works a very different series of effects, more directly ideological in character. In dramatizing the unlawful execution of Reuben by a police marksman, it provocatively plays on cultural memories of the alleged 'shoot-to-kill' policy in Northern Ireland – where the film began, the concluding ambush (by police) echoing the first (by terrorists). The ending of *For Queen and Country* thus poses the spectator with a considerable challenge: not, 'yes, these men really existed and now I know a little more about their lives and the world in which they moved' (*Chariots*) but 'even if this character is fictional, can unlawful acts like these really occur with the approval of the State?' (*For Queen and Country*).

A concern with the textual subject, on the other hand, looks at things in a rather different way. Since both films, for example, are so heavily populated by men, and since the relationships between men are so powerfully important and troubled (whereas the role of women is less significant), it would be equally productive to read these films as dramas about masculinity in crisis in the modern period. All the men in *Chariots* and *For Queen and Country* are struggling for self-definition, which can only be achieved in competition with each other. In both cases this culminates in intense physical struggle, which in the later film proves to be fatal both for the hero and for other key characters. It is not too great a step to then see these texts of masculinity as powered by strong homoerotic drives in terms of their representations of the interactions of the male body and the male look, setting up in at least the case of *Chariots* a strong tension between the male connectedness throughout the text and the separation of the hero into heterosexuality at the close.

These characters are gendered structures, both 'real' persons and agents/functions of the story. They occupy various positions – central and subordinate – in the text, and have differing degrees of narrative power bestowed upon them. They range from rounded social 'types' to flatter 'stereotypes'. These structural issues affect both major and minor characters. *Chariots*, for example, is based upon a series of comparisons and contrasts between two central characters, surrounded by subordinates; in *For Queen and Country*, Reuben is alone at the centre of a complex circuit of partial relationships. In *Chariots*, for instance, Abrahams' trainer Sam Mussabini introduces a crucial image of national/racial difference, and he is in any case an important character where narrative development is concerned, but his 'personal' role is limited. The task here is thus both to understand not only the values which are invested in various character portrayals, but how these are distributed in structural and narrative terms.

What are then the benefits of this way of thinking intercultural issues in the cinema, and how can we develop it? To begin with, this is a partial account, both in terms of the limitations of this author and the circumscriptions which I have chosen for this initial essay in the field. A fuller account, for example, would go deeper and go wider and would undoubtedly find ways of drawing in those major examples from this recent period of British cinema as it imagines its way into other cultures and other nations beyond the European fold. It would want to go back to the 1960s to revisit *Lawrence of Arabia*, that key text in the evolution of British representations of the Middle East, and its contemporary, *The Bridge on the River Kwai*, for its continuation of the war film genre in Orientalist terms.

Such a discussion would come forward to the 1980s to discuss British director Alan Parker's twin dramas about the history of race relations in America, *Mississippi Burning* and *Come See the Paradise*, the latter with a very different understanding of Japaneseness than that in *Kwai*. North America would also be the reference point for analysis of *The Killing Fields*, the major British film on the war in Cambodia. It would take on the explosion of independent black British production following the arrival of Channel Four, an important context in the case of *For Queen and Country*. It would celebrate the liberalization of the treatment of race, nationality and personal identity in British cinema and television in the last twenty years whilst critiquing a solid counter-current of repetition and regression. These considerations would suggest, as I hope the present essay has begun to do, that intercultural relations are not a special and occasional topic for the cinematic imaginary, but a pervasive and routine component of the cinema's everyday reworking of the social world.

References

Bordwell, D. (1994), *Making Meaning: Inference and Rhetoric in the Interpretation of Cinema*, Cambridge, MA: Harvard University Press.

Chapman, J. (1998), 'Our Finest Hour Revisited: The Second World War in British Feature Films since 1945', *Journal of Popular British Cinema*, 1 (1), pp. 63–75.

Drummond, P. (1997), *High Noon*, London: British Film Institute.

Finney, A. (1996), *The State of European Cinema: A New Dose of Reality*, London Cassell.

Gabler, N. (1988), *An Empire of Their Own: How the Jews Invented Hollywood*, New York: Crown.

Higson, A. (1995), *Waving the Flag: Constructing a National Cinema in Britain*, Oxford: Oxford University Press.

Higson, A. (ed.) (1996), *Dissolving Views: Key Writings on British Cinema*, London: Cassell.

Hill, J. and Gibson, P.C. (eds) (1998), *The Oxford Guide to Film Studies*, Oxford: Oxford University Press.

Hurd, G. (ed.) (1984), *National Fictions: World War II in British Films and Television*, London: British Film Institute.

Hutchings, P. (1993), *Hammer and Beyond: The British Horror Film*, Manchester: Manchester University Press.

Jordan, M. (1983), 'Carry on ... Follow That Stereotype', in Curran, J. and Porter, V. (eds), *British Cinema History*, London: Weidenfeld and Nicolson.

Mercer, K. (ed.) (1988), *Black Film, Black Cinema*, London: ICA.

Nowell-Smith, G. and Ricci, S. (eds) (1998), *Hollywood and Europe: Economics, Culture, National Identity 1945–1995*, London: British Film Institute.

Pirie, D. (1973), *A Heritage of Horror: The English Gothic Cinema 1946–1972*, London: Gordon Fraser.

Richards, J. (1973), *Visions of Empire*, London: Routledge and Kegan Paul.

Shohat, E. and Stam, R. (1994), *Unthinking Eurocentrism: Multiculturalism and the Media*, London: Routledge.

Thompson, E.P. (1980), *The Making of the English Working Class*, rev. edn, Harmondsworth: Penguin.

Tunstall, J. (1994), *The Media Are American*, 2nd edn, London: Constable.

Woolacott, J. and Bennett, T. (1987), *Bond and Beyond: The Political Career of a Popular Superhero*, London: Macmillan.

Index